T0213793

Lecture Notes in Computer Science 10136

Commenced Publication in 1973
Founding and Former Series Editors:
Gerhard Goos, Juris Hartmanis, and Jan van Leeuwen

Editorial Board

David Hutchison
  Lancaster University, Lancaster, UK
Takeo Kanade
  Carnegie Mellon University, Pittsburgh, PA, USA
Josef Kittler
  University of Surrey, Guildford, UK
Jon M. Kleinberg
  Cornell University, Ithaca, NY, USA
Friedemann Mattern
  ETH Zurich, Zurich, Switzerland
John C. Mitchell
  Stanford University, Stanford, CA, USA
Moni Naor
  Weizmann Institute of Science, Rehovot, Israel
C. Pandu Rangan
  Indian Institute of Technology, Madras, India
Bernhard Steffen
  TU Dortmund University, Dortmund, Germany
Demetri Terzopoulos
  University of California, Los Angeles, CA, USA
Doug Tygar
  University of California, Berkeley, CA, USA
Gerhard Weikum
  Max Planck Institute for Informatics, Saarbrücken, Germany

More information about this series at http://www.springer.com/series/7407

Chen Ding · John Criswell · Peng Wu (Eds.)

Languages and Compilers for Parallel Computing

29th International Workshop, LCPC 2016
Rochester, NY, USA, September 28–30, 2016
Revised Papers

 Springer

Editors
Chen Ding
University of Rochester
Rochester, NY
USA

John Criswell
University of Rochester
Rochester, NY
USA

Peng Wu
Huawei Inc.
Santa Clara, CA
USA

ISSN 0302-9743 ISSN 1611-3349 (electronic)
Lecture Notes in Computer Science
ISBN 978-3-319-52708-6 ISBN 978-3-319-52709-3 (eBook)
DOI 10.1007/978-3-319-52709-3

Library of Congress Control Number: 2017930201

LNCS Sublibrary: SL1 – Theoretical Computer Science and General Issues

© Springer International Publishing AG 2017
This work is subject to copyright. All rights are reserved by the Publisher, whether the whole or part of the material is concerned, specifically the rights of translation, reprinting, reuse of illustrations, recitation, broadcasting, reproduction on microfilms or in any other physical way, and transmission or information storage and retrieval, electronic adaptation, computer software, or by similar or dissimilar methodology now known or hereafter developed.
The use of general descriptive names, registered names, trademarks, service marks, etc. in this publication does not imply, even in the absence of a specific statement, that such names are exempt from the relevant protective laws and regulations and therefore free for general use.
The publisher, the authors and the editors are safe to assume that the advice and information in this book are believed to be true and accurate at the date of publication. Neither the publisher nor the authors or the editors give a warranty, express or implied, with respect to the material contained herein or for any errors or omissions that may have been made. The publisher remains neutral with regard to jurisdictional claims in published maps and institutional affiliations.

Printed on acid-free paper

This Springer imprint is published by Springer Nature
The registered company is Springer International Publishing AG
The registered company address is: Gewerbestrasse 11, 6330 Cham, Switzerland

Preface

This volume contains the papers presented at LCPC 2016: the 29th International Workshop on Languages and Compilers for Parallel Computing held during September 27–29, 2016, in Rochester, New York.

Since its founding in 1988, the LCPC workshop has been a leading venue for research on parallelizing compilers and related topics in concurrency, parallel languages, parallel programming models, runtime systems, and tools. The workshop spans the spectrum from foundational principles to practical experience, and from early ideas to polished results. LCPC encourages submissions that go outside the scope of scientific computing and enable parallel programming in new areas, such as mobile computing and data centers. The value of LCPC stems largely from its focused topics and personal interaction. This year's location, in Rochester, NY, was both scenic and convenient. September weather is beautiful, as is the university campus, located at the confluence of the Genesee River and the historic Erie Canal.

Specific topics of LCPC 2016 included:

- Compiling for parallelism and parallel compilers
- Static, dynamic, and adaptive optimization of parallel programs
- Parallel programming models and languages
- Formal analysis and verification of parallel programs
- Parallel runtime systems and libraries
- Performance analysis and debugging tools for concurrency and parallelism
- Parallel algorithms and concurrent data structures
- Parallel applications
- Synchronization and concurrency control
- Software engineering for parallel programs
- Fault tolerance for parallel systems
- Parallel programming and compiling for heterogeneous systems

There were 26 submissions. Each submission was reviewed by at least three, and on average 3.5, Program Committee members. The committee decided to accept 23 papers, of which 20 are regular papers (up to 15 pages) and three are short papers (up to five pages).

The workshop program includes three keynotes:

- "Parallel Computation Models and Systems, Dataflow, Coelets, and Beyond" by Guang R. Gao of University of Delaware
- "Towards High-Level High-Performance Software Development" by P. (Saday) Sadayappan of Ohio State University
- "The Multi-core Problem as an Algorithmic Problem" by Leslie Valiant of Harvard University

There was also one invited talk on "Tapir: Embedding Fork-Join Parallelism into LLVM's Intermediate Representation" by Tao Schardl of MIT.

We would like to thank Pengcheng Li for creating the workshop website at http://www.cs.rochester.edu/u/cding/lcpc2016/ and compiling the final publication package, and the computer science staff for the help in organizing the workshop and the financial support from Huawei, IBM, as well as the Goergen Institute of Data Science and Department of Computer Science at University of Rochester. The generation of the proceedings was assisted by the EasyChair conference system.

December 2016   Chen Ding
                                                              John Criswell
                                                                 Peng Wu

Organization

Program Committee

Ayon Basumallik	MathWorks Inc., USA
James Brodman	Intel, USA
Arun Chauhan	Indiana University, USA
John Criswell	University of Rochester, USA
Chen Ding	University of Rochester, USA
Matthew Fluet	Rochester Institute of Technology, USA
Jeff Huang	Texas A&M University, USA
Hironori Kasahara	Waseda University, Japan
Frank Mueller	North Carolina State University, USA
P. Sadayapan	Ohio State University, USA
Xipeng Shen	North Carolina State University, USA
Michelle Strout	University of Arizona, USA
Peng Tu	Intel, USA
James Tuck	North Carolina State University, USA
Peng Wu	Huawei US Research Lab, USA

Contents

Run-time and Performance Analysis

Large Scale Parallelism

QUARC: An Array Programming Approach to High Performance Computing

Diptorup Deb$^{(\boxtimes)}$, Robert J. Fowler, and Allan Porterfield

Department of Computer Science, University of North Carolina at Chapel Hill,
Chapel Hill, USA
diptorup@cs.unc.edu, {rjf,akp}@renci.org
http://cs.unc.edu/

Abstract. We present QUARC, a framework for the optimized compilation of domain-specific extensions to C++. Driven by needs for programmer productivity and portable performance for lattice QCD, the framework focuses on stencil-like computations on arrays with an arbitrary number of dimensions. QUARC uses a template meta-programming front end to define a high-level array language. Unlike approaches that generate scalarized loop nests in the front end, the instantiation of QUARC templates retains high-level abstraction suitable for optimization at the object (array) level. The back end compiler (CLANG/LLVM) is extended to implement array transformations such as transposition, reshaping, and partitioning for parallelism and for memory locality prior to scalarization. We present the design and implementation.

Keywords: Array-programming · Domain-specific languages

1 Introduction

QUARC is an embedded C++14 domain-specific compilation framework for optimizing expressive high-level C++ template code. It addresses performance and productivity challenges in lattice quantum chromodynamics (LQCD) in exploration of new physics and new algorithms. QUARC provides a compact, high-level notation with support for aggressive optimization and performance portability across architectures and machine implementations. QUARC provides notation and mechanisms to solve partial differential equations over complex vector fields discretized on structured lattices. While the design choices for QUARC are driven by the needs of LQCD, we plan to generalize QUARC to other domains.

It is increasingly difficult to extract high levels of portable performance from today's high-end systems. A single node of a current-generation HPC system has features such as deeply nested cache hierarchies, multi-core parallelism, and short-vector SIMD units. Domain-specific and architecture-specific knowledge and labor are required to design efficient concrete data layouts and code. The resulting hand-optimized codes bear little resemblance to the original abstract concepts and they are difficult to debug and to maintain.

© Springer International Publishing AG 2017
C. Ding et al. (Eds.): LPC 2016, LNCS 10136, pp. 3–17, 2017.
DOI: 10.1007/978-3-319-52709-3_1

These issues spring from weaknesses in architecture-neutral abstract parallel programming frameworks. Libraries such as Intel TBB [7] and Kokkos [2] address some of the challenges. Increasingly, languages such as C/C++ are the choice for HPC programming, but they lack support for abstract arrays as *first-class* objects. Various libraries and domain specific-languages (DSLs) [20], [6] extend the expressiveness of C++ using template meta-programming techniques like expression templates (ETs). These suffer performance problems because the concrete implementation of the array expressions, particularly *scalarization* of loops, occurs at the time of template instantiation. This makes it difficult or impossible for the compiler to retain enough context to infer the programmer's intent or to infer properties such as lack of aliasing or side effects. Subsequent compiler-driven analysis and optimization are thwarted.

1.1   The LQCD Problem Domain

QCD is the theory of the *strong* force, one of the four fundamental forces in nature. LQCD discretizes space and time on a four-dimensional lattice. Each lattice site is represented by at least one 12-dimensional complex vector (*spinors*) and eight (3×3) $SU(3)$ matrices (*gauge links*). The lattice usually is represented using a nest of array and structure types using as much as 2 kilobytes per site. In production, the lattice sizes can be as large as $128^3 \times 256$.

LQCD programs typically involve stencil computations. Often, a stencils is applied once per iteration of an implicit solver. Every stencil computation involves multiple short matrix-vector products, like the one shown in Listing 1.2, that can touch up to 3 K bytes per lattice site, leading to poor memory locality and a low computational intensity. These characteristics constrains stencil optimization strategies like *time-tiling* LQCD thus requires strategies for optimization that have proven hard to automate. Recent performance studies [9] have highlighted this increasing *software gap* by comparing hand optimized LQCD kernels to QDP++ [20], an existing C++ ETs-based LQCD DSL. Reported numbers show an 8× performance difference on Intel's Xeon Phi accelerators and a 2.6× gap on regular Intel Xeon processors.

1.2   The QUARC Approach

QUARC optimizes kernels like that shown in Listing 1.1. It supports dynamic arrays of arbitrary rank as first-class objects. The intermediate representation preserves array semantics, allowing QUARC to use existing analysis and optimization passes in LLVM, as well as to add domain-specific transformations. The main innovations are:

– It provides a loop-less declarative syntax that makes arrays first-class objects, and provides a framework for defining array operators.

```
//===------ Basic lattice QCD data types  ----===//
typedef std::complex<double> c;
// 3-D complex vector
typedef std::array<c, 3> su3Vec;
// 3x3 complex matrix
typedef std::array<su3Vec, 3> su3Mat;
// Packed array of 8 SU3Matrices
typedef std::array<su3Mat, 8> wG;
// 12-D complex vector
typedef std::array<su3Vec, 4> wS;
// 4-D lattice of 12-D complex vectors
typedef quarc::mdarray<wS, 4, PERIODIC> wSLattice;
// 4-D lattice of packed 3x3 complex matrices
typedef quarc::mdarray<wG, 4, PERIODIC> wGLattice; int
  main () {
    wSLattice s_in(16,16,16,16), s_out(16,16,16,16);
    wGLattice g(16,16,16,16);
    //  ... intializations


    //===------ An abridged QCD stencil  ----===//
    // operator* : su3_mult_op mkernel (Listing 1.2)
    // operator+ : complex vector addition
    // gshift    : described in Sect.\,2.2
    // adj()     : complex adjunct
    s_out = g.get<0>() * s_in.gshift<1,0,0,0>()
          + g.get<1>() * s_in.gshift<0,1,0,0>()
          + g.get<2>() * s_in.gshift<0,0,1,0>()
          + g.get<3>() * s_in.gshift<0,0,0,1>()
          + adj(g.get<4>()) * s_in.gshift<-1,0,0,0>()
          + adj(g.get<5>()) * s_in.gshift<0,-1,0,0>()
          + adj(g.get<6>()) * s_in.gshift<0,0,-1,0>()
          + adj(g.get<7>()) * s_in.gshift<0,0,0,-1>();
    return 0;
}
```

Listing 1.1. A lattice QCD stencil written in QUARC syntax

- To define stencils, QUARC uses a *generalized shift* (gshift) operation providing a multi-dimensional view of the array accesses to the compiler. Enabling exact dependence and reuse-distances analyses, and avoiding issues such as *delinearization* [13]. The gshift operator cleanly separates stencil-related accesses from those occurring inside the pointwise operations.
- QUARC defers loop generation (*late scalarization*) of array expressions to the compiler. Late scalarization facilitates optimizations such as common subexpression elimination or expression fusion to array expressions. This opens the possibility of generating domain- and architecture-specific loop constructs after incorporating other optimizations.

– It provides uniform support for data transformations including tiling for shared-memory parallelism, partitioning for distributed parallelism, improving memory locality, and aligning data for vectorization. QUARC includes classical array transformations like *reshape, transpose* and *catenate* [14,15]. These enable the modification of array properties such as *rank* (number of dimensions) and *shape* (extent of each dimension). Combining such transformations with dependence- and reuse-distance analyses makes it possible to derive data layout transformations such as *structure of arrays* (SoA) to *arrays of structure of arrays* (ASoA) required for vectorizing LQCD kernels on short-vector SIMD machines.

```
template<typename T1, typename T2>
auto su3_mult_op(T1 m,T2 v){
  T2 r;
  for(int i=0;i<3;i++) {
    r[i][0]=0.0;r[i][1]=0.0;
    for(int j=0;j<3;j++) {
      r[i][0] += m[i][j][0] * v[j][0];
      r[i][0] -= m[i][j][1] * v[j][1];
      r[i][1] += m[i][j][0] * v[j][1];
      r[i][1] += m[i][j][1] * v[j][0];
    }
  }
  return r;
}
```

Listing 1.2. Mkernel defining a pointwise SU3 matrix-vector product

2   An Array Programming Approach to Parallelism

Compilers for data-parallel programming languages like HPF [16] have focused on loop-centric transformations that alter the execution schedule of loop iterations to remove true dependence, improve cache-locality, and introduce parallelism. Without a data-centric view of the array expressions data-layout transformations become very challenging.

As a domain-specific compilation framework, QUARC can exploit inherent guarantees that allow us to take a radically different approach. QUARC statements are guaranteed to be data-independent, with all arrays having the same rank and shape (refer Sects. 3.3 and 3.4). This allows QUARC to be fully data-centric and to make loop generation a final step in the optimization process. In addition to traditional *loop-tiling* optimizations, QUARC can do data-layout transformations to support short-vector SIMD units.

2.1   QUARC Array Transformations

Array operations have been defined formally [14,15] for APL [8] and similar array-programming frameworks. Such operations can alter the structural properties of arrays, and offer the necessary semantics for defining data-reordering within arrays. Mainstream procedural languages, like C/C++, have offered very limited support for such array operations.

Notations for Defining Array Properties. We use Λ to denote an n-dimensional LQCD lattice defined using QUARC arrays. Upper-case Roman characters used in a postfix notation denote array properties. Lower-case Greek letters denote array operations. Operations are written using C-like function call notation.

The dimensionality of the arrays is denoted by N and the extent of each dimension by B_i. The shape vector, made up of the dimensional extents, is represented as S and an index coefficient vector holding the cumulative sizes for each dimension is referred to as I_c. We initialize S and I_c as

$$S_{initial} = \{B_i | N < i <= 0\}, \tag{1}$$

$$I_{c\_initial} = \{ \prod_{i=N-2}^{0} B_i, \prod_{i=N-3}^{0} B_i, \ldots, 1 \}. \tag{2}$$

A set of abstract array operations are used to model the data transformations. Selecting an element from a list is done using the (ι) operator. Reshaping array dimensions is done via the (ρ) operator. Reshaping is defined as

$$S_{new} = (\rho(\Lambda S, R_f)), \tag{3}$$

where R_f denotes a vector containing the reshape factors for all of the dimensions. Reshaping introduces padding only if $\iota R_f i$, for a given dimension does not divide the original B_i evenly. The new extents are

$$B_{i\_new} = \frac{\iota(\Lambda S, i)}{\iota(R_f, i)} = \begin{cases} B_i, & \text{if } \iota(R_f, i) == 1 \\ \{\iota(R_f, i), \lceil \frac{\iota(\Lambda S, i)}{\iota(R_f, i)} \rceil\} & \text{otherwise} \end{cases},$$
$$\text{where } 0 < \iota(R_f, i) < B_i. \tag{4}$$

Transpose (Φ) generalizes two-dimensional matrix transpose to transpose an array about any diagonal, and catenation (κ) is used to merge or to linearize two adjacent dimensions into one. For both operation the required dimensions are specified as a two-tuple argument.

QUARC Representation of Array Expressions. We introduce additional terminology for explaining the QUARC program structure. A QUARC kernel (Q_k) is a single array statement inside a QUARC program. Conceptually, it is an abstract countable loop over all values of the index set of the arrays referenced in the statement. Mini-kernel (`mkernel`) is a pointwise array operator or second-order array function. The iteration domain of a Q_k is denoted as AI_s. It the set of all the execution instances that need to be completed when processing the Q_k. In QUARC, the AI_s geometrically represents an n-orthotope or *hyperrectangle*, with origin as the lower bound and upper bounds equal to the corresponding B_i.

Each point in AI_s is termed an iteration point and is identified by an $\boldsymbol{n}$-tuple coordinate. Finally, the index space or the data domain is represented as D_s. It is the set of all array elements accessed by the Q_k. Although arrays are stored in a one-dimensional linearized address space, D_s is an $\boldsymbol{n}$-dimensional space. We only consider monolithic addressing (Sect. 3.2) of QUARC arrays, therefore AI_s and D_s are always equivalent for every Q_k.

2.2   An Array-Transformation Mechanism

The present array-transformations in QUARC are driven by a reuse-distance based algorithm to derive SIMD friendly data-layouts for LQCD stencils. Reuse-distance is defined as the measure of non-unique data referenced between two successive uses of a given array reference. Various well-known canonical cache-blocking optimizations are based on reuse-distance, such as those provided by Wolf and Lam [24]. Henretty *et al.* [5] introduced a novel data-layout transformation for short-vector SIMD also using reuse-distance analysis to identify SIMD vector-stream alignment conflicts (SACs). Their algorithm uses the SAC metric to define $\Phi\rho$ transforms on the innermost dimension of multi-dimensional arrays to enhance vectorizability.

The QUARC array-transformation algorithm expands on Henretty *et al.*'s algorithm. We incorporate κ along with $\Phi\rho$ and apply the transformation to any dimension of the array. The technique derives the *gather-scatter* data-layout transformation and the required data mappings. Extending the transformation to outer dimensions can lead to an exhaustive search for the best layout. To reduce the search space, we use a LQCD-specific transformation. Most LQCD configurations use three equal-sized spatial dimensions and a time dimension twice the extent of the others. Thus, QUARC usually can ensure that the longest dimension is always innermost before starting layout transformations.

Step 1: Analyze Outer Accesses. The first step evaluates the accesses at the outermost nesting level and identifies SACs. We then apply $\kappa\Phi\rho$ to the innermost dimension, and proceed outwards until SACs are removed. Algorithm 1 provides an outline of the QUARC array-transformation algorithm using the kernel in Listing 1.1 as the input. The transformations are applied to both S and I_c. The final state of S provides the new shape with an innermost vector dimension, and the final state of the I_c gives the mapping to the old index space.

Step 2: Analyze mkernels. Along with analysis on the outer array accesses the mkernels are also analyzed for vectorizibility. For example, the mkernel in Listing 1.2 has no vectorizable loops, but has interleaved data accesses.

Step 3: Finalizing Data-Layout. In the final step the analyses from the earlier steps are combined to derive the data-layout for the complete Q_k. For Listings 1.1 and 1.2 after creating a vector dimension from the outermost dimensions the inner nested dimensions are permuted out.

Algorithm 1. QUARC array transformation outline

Input : $\Lambda\sigma$, where $\Lambda N = 4$
Input : Dimensional Reuse Distance Vector
Input : Linearized Reuse Distance Vector
Input : Vector Length (V_l)
Output: Index set transformation map

1   *permute dimensions to ensure* $B_0 \geq B_1 \geq B_2 \geq B_3$
2   **if** *More than one dimension has a SAC* **then**
3 | abort ;   `// Λ too small to benefit from layout transforms`
4   **else**
5 | **if** $B_0 > V_l$ **then**
6 | | $R_f =\ <1, 1, 1, V_l>$;
7 | | $S_1 = \rho(\Lambda S, R_f)$;   `//` $< B_3, B_2, B_1, V_l, \frac{B_0}{V_l} >$
8 | | $S_2 = \Phi(S_1, (1, 0))$;   `//` $< B_3, B_2, B_1, \frac{B_0}{V_l}, V_l >$
9 | **else**
10 | | *factorize* V_l *to* $(\frac{V_l}{2}, 2)$;
11 | | $R_f =\ <1, 1, \frac{V_l}{2}, 2>$;
12 | | $S_1 = \rho(\Lambda S, R_f)$;   `//` $< B_3, B_2, \frac{V_l}{2}, \frac{B_1}{\frac{V_l}{2}}, 2, \frac{B_0}{2} >$
13 | | $S_2 = \Phi(S_1, (1, 0))$;   `//` $< B_3, B_2, \frac{B_1}{\frac{V_l}{2}}, \frac{V_l}{2}, \frac{B_0}{2}, 2 >$
14 | | $S_3 = \Phi(S_2, (2, 1))$;   `//` $< B_3, B_2, \frac{B_1}{\frac{V_l}{2}}, \frac{B_0}{2}, 2, \frac{V_l}{2} >$
15 | | $S_4 = \kappa(S_3, 1, 0))$;   `//` $< B_3, B_2, \frac{B_1}{\frac{V_l}{2}}, \frac{B_0}{2}, V_l >$
16 | **end**
17   **end**
18   *create a mapping function from* D_s *to* D'_s

2.3 Parallel Code Generation

The output of the array-transformation phase of the QUARC analysis is a mapping from D_s to the new data space, D'_s. These spaces can be of different dimensionality, as the transforms can change the rank of the arrays. D'_s gets broken into multiple split index sets to handle different boundary regions, and each set is materialized into actual loop nests. For the set operations and the loop generation, we use the integer set operations and a polyhedral code generator from the Integer Set Library (*isl*) [22]. (See Sect. 5.3.) After transforming the arrays, we annotate different dimensions with the parallelization strategy to be used. Typically, the innermost dimension is designated as a vector dimension, and the outermost is parallelized using threads or MPI. We propagate this metadata into the *isl*-generated loops using existing LLVM infrastructure.

3 QUARC Language Design

QUARC uses C++14 template meta-programming to implement a DSL interface that generates annotations recognized by the compiler. Figure 1 presents

$$\begin{array}{ll}
\langle quarc\_kernel \rangle & ::= \langle mdarray\_terminal \rangle = \{ \\
& \quad | \ \langle bin\_expr \rangle \ | \ \langle gshift\_expr \rangle \ | \ \langle unary\_expr \rangle \ | \\
& \quad \langle terminal\_expr \rangle \ \} \ \{...\} \\
\langle gshift\_expr \rangle & ::= \langle mdarray\_terminal \rangle \ , \langle integers \rangle \{...\} \\
\langle bin\_expr \rangle & ::= \{ \ \langle terminal\_expr \rangle \ | \ \langle binary\_expr \rangle \ | \ \langle shift\_expr \rangle \ | \\
& \quad \langle unary\_expr \rangle \ \} \ \{2\}, \langle bin\_op \rangle \\
\langle unary\_expr \rangle & ::= \langle terminal\_expr \rangle \ | \ \langle bin\_expr \rangle \ | \\
& \quad | \ \langle shift\_expr \rangle \ | \ \langle unary\_expr \rangle, \langle unary\_op \rangle \\
\langle terminal\_expr \rangle & ::= \langle mdarray\_terminal \rangle \ | \ \langle scalar\_terminal \rangle \\
\langle bin\_op \rangle & ::= \langle is\_arithmetic \rangle \{2\}, \langle bin\_mkernel \rangle \\
\langle unary\_op \rangle & ::= \langle is\_arithmetic \rangle, \langle unary\_mkernel \rangle \\
\langle bin\_mkernel \rangle & ::= \langle is\_arithmetic \rangle \ \langle id \rangle \\
& \quad | \ (\ \langle is\_arithmetic \rangle \ \langle id \rangle, \langle is\_arithmetic \rangle \ \langle id \rangle \ ) \\
\langle unary\_mkernel \rangle & ::= \langle is\_arithmetic \rangle \ \langle id \rangle \ (\ \langle is\_arithmetic \rangle \ \langle id \rangle \ ) \\
\langle mdarray\_terminal \rangle & ::= \langle mdarray \rangle \\
\langle scalar\_terminal \rangle & ::= \langle is\_arithmetic \rangle \\
\langle mdarray \rangle & ::= \langle is\_arithmetic, rank, boundary\_fn, shape \rangle
\end{array}$$

Fig. 1. QUARC array syntax pseudo-BNF

an abridged BNF grammar for the QUARC DSL. By definition, QUARC programs are valid C++14 code compilable by any C++14 compiler. The language semantics are close to the C++ ETs idiom [21]. The ETs idiom uses overloaded operators and proxy expression objects to build array expressions without intermediate containers. ETs have been used widely, in various scientific computing DSLs and BLAS libraries DSLs [6,17,20] to embed array semantics in C++. QUARC differs from conventional ETs. First, with the aforementioned system of annotations, we embed extended type information in the syntax to extend the type system abstractly and to make QUARC arrays first-class objects. The annotations are transparent to the end user and need no manual intervention while programming in the QUARC DSL. Second, the late-scalarization technique pushes loop generation from the template-instantiation phase into the compiler back end. These design choices enable the QUARC optimizer (QOPT) to derive non-trivial low-level optimizations. In the next section, we describe the QUARC DSL syntax and API semantics.

3.1   QUARC Arrays

QUARC's mdarray data type is an abstract composite type that is represented using a four-tuple: <type, rank, boundary-function, shape>. The type specifies the C++ data type of the array elements. The current implementation limits the types to those matching the C++14 type trait is_arithmetic. The rank property is the number of dimensions of the array. Boundary-function is a user-definable index function to handle boundary conditions, and shape defines the extent of each dimension. Of these properties, element-type, rank and boundary-function are compile-time constants, specified as template arguments.

The **shape** property is specified using C++14's variadic template feature. A combination of static and run-time checks is used for full type inference.

3.2 Array Addressing Modes

QUARC provides two addressing modes for the **mdarray** instances. Monolithic addressing operates on entire arrays and is used in array expressions. Elemental addressing is similar to C++ subscript operation. In this paper, we focus on the monolithic addressing mode. Monolithic addressing eschews explicit subscripts. Allowing only an n-tuple address offsets or "shifts", where n is the rank of the array. By default the shifts are all generated as "0s". Non-zero shifts are specified using the **gshift** operator.

There are two significant benefits of this approach. By design, the programmer uses whole-array subscripts, and the address linearization happens after performing optimizations. Thus, we do not have to deal with the *delinearization problem* of recovering a multi-dimensional view of the array accesses [13]. All references except the boundary values use the same index function, differing only in the constant term. Such references are termed *uniformly generated references* [24]. Moreover, every subscript implicitly describes an affine function, with a single index variable (SIV). This practice makes it possible to compute exact dependence distance vectors as well as reuse-distances. Together, these features support optimizations that otherwise have been hard to implement in C++ ETs-based array programs.

3.3 Array Operators

QUARC array operators are higher-order functions that take a callback function (**mkernel**) in a template argument to do the actual elemental array operations. The design cleanly differentiates the stencil operations, defined using **gshifts**, from the **mkernels**. Allowing us to derive data-layouts after analyzing both operations. The **mkernels** are required to be "pure" or "side-effect free", such that every QUARC expression induces a completely statically determinable control flow. The language semantics allow **mkernels** to operate on different types. For example, as shown in Listing 1.1 in QUARC it is possible to define arrays of matrices and arrays of vectors, and then to create a multiplication operator to operate on them, producing another array of vectors.

3.4 Array Statements

QUARC array-statement semantics are similar to those of other high-level languages supporting array objects, such as Fortran 90 and HPF. The right-hand side (RHS) is evaluated completely without side effects and only then is the result written into the left-hand side (LHS). We disallow the use of the same array on both sides. In the future, we intend to remove this restriction by using data-dependence analysis to identify the intersecting hyperplane in the index space between the left- and right-hand sides, and to introduce a temporary minimal-size variable. All arrays in an expression are assumed to be non-aliasing. We enforce the restriction that they have the same rank and shape.

4   The QOPT Architecture

QOPT, QUARC's underlying optimization framework, is built on top of the LLVM compiler infrastructure. It uses *isl* for set operations and loop generation. The optimization workflow is a five-step process, as depicted in Fig. 2. First, a preprocessing step detects all Q_ks in a procedure. After, preprocessing an abstract binary expression tree (Q_k-BET) representation is generated for each Q_k. The possibility of early transformations is explored using the Q_k-BET representation, and involves potentially combining the trees of multiple Q_ks.

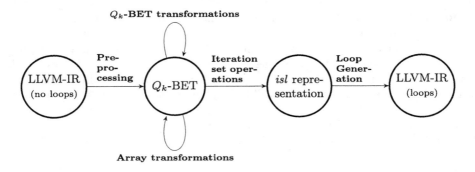

Fig. 2. The QOPT architecture

After early transformations on the Q_k-BET, QOPT evaluates the applicability of array transformations for memory locality and SIMD-friendly data-layouts. The array transformations may lead to data layout changes. If so, an abstract map from the old to the new layout is generated to build the required *gather-scatter* code during the code-generation phase.

Following the array transformations, QOPT converts the Q_k-BETs into multiple iteration sets using *isl*. The iteration sets separate the iterations that require boundary-value computations from iterations that process only inner (non-boundary) elements of the arrays. The iteration sets and the corresponding loop-bounds are determined by the shape of the arrays and by the shifts specified in the array accesses. In the final step, QOPT scalarizes the iteration sets into actual loops in the LLVM IR language.

5   Array Expressions to Optimized Code

5.1   Preprocessing

The preprocessor recognizes QUARC annotations and applies program transformations that reduce code complexity while maintaining the semantic structure for further analysis and transformation passes. For example, it inlines all functions generated by QUARC templates other than the `mkernel` calls. This step significantly prunes the call graph, yet retains the separation of high-order stencil operators and the pointwise `mkernel` operations.

The preprocessor also annotates the LLVM IR to enable the construction of the Q_k-BETs. Listing 1.3 shows an abridged state of the IR after preprocessing a binary array expression that has a single `gshift` access. Each `quarcc_build_*_expr` call represents the creation of the proxy expression objects. The `quarcc_kernel_dispatch` is the call to the actual Q_k function. In the code-generation phase, the proxy objects are removed completely, while the Q_k call is transformed into inline loop nests.

```
/* Original code : a1 = a2.gshift<1,0>() + a2; */
%1 = call __quarcc_build_gshift_expr__(%a2)
%2 = call __quarcc_build_bin_expr__(%1, %a2)
call __quarcc_kernel_dispatch__(%a1, %2)
```

Listing 1.3. State of IR after preprocessing

5.2 Q_k Expression Tree Generation and Early Optimizations

The Q_k-BET is the intermediate representation that QOPT uses for all analysis and transformations. Generation of the Q_k-BET is also a two-step process. In the first step, QOPT analyzes the `quarcc_kernel_dispatch` function to build an abstract expression tree that does not contain the actual array references used in a particular instance of the Q_k. The `quarcc_kernel_dispatch` takes two parameters: the LHS subexpression that is always a single `mdarray` reference, and the RHS subexpression. To build the tree, QOPT recursively uses *def-use* chain analysis of the RHS subexpression parameter. Specifically, it looks for two specially annotated functions: `mkernel` and `access`. These two are the nodes of the tree, with the `accesses` forming the leaves and the `mkernels` forming the internal nodes. The access function, as described in Sect. 3.2, contains only the shift values. These are then extracted using LLVM's ScalarEvolution analysis.

After building the expression tree, QOPT *materializes* the actual Q_k-BET by building a second tree, a data structure that we call the "expression-builder-tree". The expression-builder-tree is constructed using successive *def-use* analyses of the arguments passed to the `quarcc_build_*_expr` calls, immediately preceding the `quarcc_kernel_dispatch`. The leaves of the expression-builder-tree store the actual array references to be used in the Q_k. QOPT builds a complete binary expression tree for every Q_k by matching these two trees.

Q_k-BET Merging. QOPT looks for opportunities to *fuse* adjacent Q_ks to enhance memory locality in the body of a potentially fused loop nest. It limits fusion to adjacent Q_ks that share at least one array reference. Because all arrays in a Q_k have the same shape, the fused loop iteration space is the same as the original abstract iteration space of each Q_k. This strategy was used to simplify code generation in the current implementation.

We currently restrict fusion to kernels that are completely data-independent. QOPT does not try to fuse two kernels where the LHS of one kernel is accessed using a non-zero shift on the RHS of the other kernel. The fusion of the Q_ks is done using the Q_k-BET representation, thus merging the expression trees into a single tree. Scalarization then builds a single loop body for the fused tree.

```
/* Original a1 = a2.gshift<1,0>() + a2; */
   // No boundary operations needed
   for (int c0 = 0; c0 < D0 - 1; c0 += 1)
     for (int c1 = 0; c1 < D1; c1 += 1)
       a1[c0][c1] = a2[c0+1][c1] + a2[c0][c1];
   // Requires boundary function(PERIODIC) call
   if (D0 >= 1)
     for (int c1 = 0; c1 < D1; c1 += 1)
       a1[D0][c1] = a2[PERIODIC(D0+1)][c1] + a2[c0][c1];
```

Listing 1.4. Code generated after late scalarization

5.3   Late Scalarization

Late scalarization is the phase in which QOPT concretizes the abstract Q_k-BET representation. To help explain the process, we formally define an **out-of-bound set** (OB_s) as the subset of D_s for which a shifted array access in the Q_k leads to an out-of-bound access. Every dimension can have two OB_s, each corresponding to the lower and upper bounds of that dimension. Thus, there can be a maximum of $2n$ OB_ss for a given Q_k. Geometrically, the out-of-bound sets represent faces or boundaries of the n-orthotope.

To compute the OB_s for a given Q_k, QOPT first calculates the maximal positive and negative shifts for every dimension. The OB_s for a given dimension, i, are computed by subtracting the maximal negative shift from the lower bound, then subtracting the positive shifts from the B_i. Thus, no OB_s are generated if the maximal shift in a given direction is 0.

Index-Set Splitting. Once QOPT generates the OB_s it proceeds to split D_s into disjoint subsets to separate all of the iterations for which a boundary function call is required. To build these split sets, QOPT successively finds all possible combinations of adjacent facets of the n-orthotope. For every combination, the OB_s corresponding to each facet in the combination is intersected with D_s, and all other OB_s not in that particular combination are subtracted from D_s.

In the worst case, where each dimension has a non-zero shift in both directions, the process is equivalent to computing each lower dimensional *facet* or k-orthotope of the original n-orthotope, where $k = (0..n]$. Since each k-orthotope in turn has $2k$ facets, the total number of split sets generated is S, where

$$S = \sum_{k=0}^{n-1} {}_nC_k 2^{n-k} + 1. \qquad (5)$$

It can be shown that S equals 3^n. This is because each facet must have its center as a valid I_p, and the set of all the centers is the set of points each of whose coordinates can have only three possible values $\{0, \lfloor B_i/2 \rfloor, B_i\}$. Thus, the total number of centers, and by corollary the number of hyperrectanges, has to be 3^n. Hence, in the worst case the number of split sets is exponential in the number of dimensions. Listing 1.4 shows the generated loop nests for the example introduced in Listing 1.3. We show the equivalent C++ code for what QOPT generates in the LLVM IR language.

6   Related Work

C++ ETs Optimizations. Various approaches to array semantics in C++ using the C++ ETs idiom have been explored. Iglberger *et al.* [6] and Härdtlein *et al.* [4] presented techniques to improve the sequential performance of ETs. The Boost.SIMD package [3] provides an abstract interface built using ETs that automate generation of SIMD intrinsics to enable vectorized code generation. These designs do not have a compiler-based component. Winter *et al.* [23] designed a just-in-time compilation framework for ETs to optimize GPU kernels. None of these approaches addresses the optimization of multiple statement. There are no provisions for data layout transformations or for cache-blocking.

DSL Compilation Strategies. Compiler-driven techniques with goals similar to ours have also been attempted. The ROSE [26] compiler framework was originally designed as a preprocessor generator that could do automatic property discovery and optimizations from C++ ETs. The telescoping languages [11] design was also an influential proposal addressing many of these issues.

Stencil Compilers. Special-purpose stencil compilers have been the target of many research efforts. The Rice dHPF compiler allowed compilation of stencil codes for distributed memory systems [16]. More recently, Datta *et al.* [1], Kamil *et al.* [10] and Tang *et al.* [19] offered solutions for shared memory multi-core platforms. Henretty *et al.* [5] built a stencil compiler incorporating data-layout transformations for short-vector SIMD machines.

Compiler Driven Data-Layout Optimizations. Automating data-layouts selection for vectorization has been addressed by number of recent works. Majeti *et al.* [12] offered an automated solution for SoA to AoS transformations targetting heterogeneous platforms. Sung *et al.* [18] provided a transformation technique for structured grid applications on GPUs. Xu and Gregg [25] designed a pragma based semi-automatic technique that also transforms SoA to AoS.

7   Status and Work in Progress

Currently, QUARC can process simple examples end-to-end to generate single-threaded X86_64 executables. We currently support multi-dimensional arrays, but do not yet support arrays nested at each lattice site to support the SU(3) algebra used in LQCD. Ongoing work is addressing the extension of the semantics to nested arrays with the objective of generating optimized code for non-trivial

LQCD applications. This work will relax the current type restriction (Sect. 3.1) on the `mdarrays`.

We are in the process of integrating the late scalarization module with LLVM's parallel code generation framework to support OpenMP outlining and vector code generation. We are also extending the array transformation framework to support data partitioning at the level of MPI nodes.

Acknowledgement. This work was supported in part by the DOE Office of Science SciDAC program on grants DE-FG02-11ER26050/DE-SC0006925 and DE-SC0008706.

References

1. Datta, K., Murphy, M., Volkov, V., Williams, S., Carter, J., Oliker, L., Patterson, D., Shalf, J., Yelick, K.: Stencil computation optimization and auto-tuning on state-of-the-art multicore architectures. In: Proceedings of the 2008 ACM/IEEE Conference on Supercomputing, SC 2008, pp. 4:1–4:12. IEEE Press, Piscataway (2008). http://dl.acm.org/citation.cfm?id=1413370.1413375
2. Edwards, H.C., Trott, C.R.: Kokkos: enabling performance portability across many-core architectures. In: Proceedings of the 2013 Extreme Scaling Workshop (XSW 2013), XSW 2013, pp. 18–24 (2013). http://dx.doi.org/10.1109/XSW.2013.7
3. Estérie, P., Gaunard, M., Falcou, J., Lapresté, J.T., Rozoy, B.: Boost.SIMD: generic programming for portable SIMDization. In: Proceedings of the 21st International Conference on Parallel Architectures and Compilation Techniques, PACT 2012, pp. 431–432. ACM, New York (2012). http://doi.acm.org/10.1145/2370816.2370881
4. Härdtlein, J., Pflaum, C., Linke, A., Wolters, C.H.: Advanced expression templates programming. Comput. Vis. Sci. **13**(2), 59–68 (2009). http://dx.doi.org/10.1007/s00791-009-0128-2
5. Henretty, T., Veras, R., Franchetti, F., Pouchet, L.N., Ramanujam, J., Sadayappan, P.: A stencil compiler for short-vector SIMD architectures. In: Proceedings of the 27th International ACM Conference on International Conference on Supercomputing - ICS 2013, p. 13 (2013). http://dl.acm.org/citation.cfm?doid=2464996.2467268
6. Iglberger, K., Hager, G., Treibig, J., Rüde, U.: Expression templates revisited: a performance analysis of current methodologies. SIAM J. Sci. Comput. **34**(2), C42–C69 (2012). http://dx.doi.org/10.1137/110830125
7. Intel Corporation: Intel Threading Building Blocks (2016)
8. Iverson, K.E.: Notation as a tool of thought. Commun. ACM **23**(8), 444–465 (1980). http://doi.acm.org/10.1145/358896.358899
9. Joo, B., Smelyanskiy, M., Kalamkar, D.D., Vaidyanathan, K.: Wilson Dslash kernel from lattice QCD optimization, July 2015. http://www.osti.gov/scitech/servlets/purl/1223094
10. Kamil, S., Husbands, P., Oliker, L., Shalf, J., Yelick, K.: Impact of modern memory subsystems on cache optimizations for stencil computations. In: Proceedings of the 2005 Workshop on Memory System Performance, MSP 2005, pp. 36–43. ACM, New York (2005). http://doi.acm.org/10.1145/1111583.1111589
11. Kennedy, K., Broom, B., Chauhan, A., Fowler, R.J., Garvin, J., Koelbel, C., Mccosh, C., Mellor-Crummey, J.: Telescoping languages: a system for automatic generation of domain languages. Proc. IEEE **93**(2), 387–408 (2005)

12. Majeti, D., Barik, R., Zhao, J., Grossman, M., Sarkar, V.: Compiler-driven data layout transformation for heterogeneous platforms. In: Mey, D., et al. (eds.) Euro-Par 2013. LNCS, vol. 8374, pp. 188–197. Springer, Heidelberg (2014). doi:10.1007/978-3-642-54420-0_19

13. Maslov, V.: Delinearization: an efficient way to break multiloop dependence equations. In: Proceedings of the SIGPLAN 1992 Conference on Programming Language Design and Implementation, pp. 152–161 (1992)

14. More, T.: Axioms and theorems for a theory of arrays. IBM J. Res. Dev. **17**(2), 135–175 (1973). http://dx.doi.org/10.1147/rd.172.0135

15. Mullin, L.: A mathematics of arrays. Ph.D. thesis, Syracuse University, December 1988

16. Roth, G., Mellor-Crummey, J., Kennedy, K., Brickner, R.G.: Compiling stencils in high performance fortran. In: Proceedings of the 1997 ACM/IEEE Conference on Supercomputing, SC 1997. pp. 1–20. ACM, New York (1997). http://doi.acm.org/10.1145/509593.509605

17. Haney, S., Crotinger, J., Karmesin, S., Smith, S.: Easy expression templates using PETE, the Portable Expression Template Engine. Technical report LA-UR-99-777 (1999)

18. Sung, I.J., Stratton, J.A., Hwu, W.M.W.: Data layout transformation exploiting memory-level parallelism in structured grid many-core applications. In: Proceedings of the 19th International Conference on Parallel Architectures and Compilation Techniques, PACT 2010, pp. 513–522. ACM, New York (2010). http://doi.acm.org/10.1145/1854273.1854336

19. Tang, Y., Chowdhury, R.A., Kuszmaul, B.C., Luk, C.K., Leiserson, C.E.: The pochoir stencil compiler. In: Proceedings of the Twenty-Third Annual ACM Symposium on Parallelism in Algorithms and Architectures, SPAA 2011, pp. 117–128. ACM, New York (2011). http://doi.acm.org/10.1145/1989493.1989508

20. USQCD: QDP++ (2002). http://usqcd-software.github.io/qdpxx/

21. Veldhuizen, T.: Expression templates. C++ Report **7**, 26–31 (1995)

22. Verdoolaege, S.: *isl*: an integer set library for the polyhedral model. In: Fukuda, K., Hoeven, J., Joswig, M., Takayama, N. (eds.) ICMS 2010. LNCS, vol. 6327, pp. 299–302. Springer, Heidelberg (2010). doi:10.1007/978-3-642-15582-6_49

23. Winter, F.T., Clark, M.A., Edwards, R.G., Joo, B.: A framework for lattice QCD calculations on GPUs. In: 2014 IEEE 28th International Parallel and Distributed Processing Symposium. IEEE, May 2014. http://dx.doi.org/10.1109/IPDPS.2014.112

24. Wolf, M.E., Lam, M.S.: A data locality optimizing algorithm. In: Proceedings of the ACM SIGPLAN 1991 Conference on Programming Language Design and Implementation, PLDI 1991, pp. 30–44. ACM, New York (1991). http://doi.acm.org/10.1145/113445.113449

25. Xu, S., Gregg, D.: Semi-automatic composition of data layout transformations for loop vectorization. In: Hsu, C.-H., Shi, X., Salapura, V. (eds.) NPC 2014. LNCS, vol. 8707, pp. 485–496. Springer, Heidelberg (2014). doi:10.1007/978-3-662-44917-2_40

26. Yan, Y., Lin, P.H., Liao, C., de Supinski, B.R., Quinlan, D.J.: Supporting multiple accelerators in high-level programming models. In: Proceedings of the Sixth International Workshop on Programming Models and Applications for Multicores and Manycores, PMAM 2015, pp. 170–180, ACM, New York (2015). http://doi.acm.org/10.1145/2712386.2712405

Utilizing Concurrency: A New Theory for Memory Wall

Xian-He Sun$^{(\boxtimes)}$ and Yu-Hang Liu

Illinois Institute of Technology, Chicago, USA
{sun,yuhang.liu}@iit.edu

Abstract. In addition to locality, data access concurrency has emerged as a pillar factor of memory performance. In this research, we introduce a concurrency-aware solution, the memory Sluice Gate Theory, for solving the outstanding memory wall problem. Sluice gates are designed to control data transfer at each memory layer dynamically, and a global control algorithm, named layered performance matching, is developed to match the data transfer request/supply at each memory layer thus matching the overall performance between the CPU and memory system. Formal theoretical analyses are given to show, with sufficient data access concurrency and hardware support, the memory wall impact can be reduced to the minimum. Experimental testing is conducted which confirm the theoretical findings.

1 Introduction and Highlight

Memory wall problem refers to the relatively slow memory performance forming a wall between CPU and memory [1]. This wall causes CPUs to stall while waiting for data and slows down the speed of computing. The widely accepted solution for memory wall problem is the memory hierarchy approach. During the last thirty years, the design of the memory hierarchy has been enhanced to have more layers, larger caches, and built-in on-chip caches to match the increasingly large performance gap between computing and memory access. Besides the traditionally-focused locality, data access concurrency has become increasingly important, and can determine the performance of a memory system [2, 3].

Concurrency has been built into each layer of a memory hierarchy to support concurrent data access. However, a system is hard to reach the optimal locality and concurrency at the same time. Even it does, that does not mean it has reached the optimal system performance. Similarly, adding the optimizations of each memory layer of a memory hierarchy does not necessarily lead to the best system optimization. Locality and concurrency influence each other, within their layer and beyond their layer, and the influences are application dependent. These complicate the concurrency-aware data access optimization process.

In this study, we propose a new theory, Sluice Gate Theory, to fully utilize memory hierarchy systems. Sluice Gate Theory claims that memory hierarchy is a designed sluice to transfer data to computing units, and through multi-level sluice gate control we can match data flow demand with supply. Therefore, we can reduce memory stall

© Springer International Publishing AG 2017
C. Ding et al. (Eds.): LCPC 2016, LNCS 10136, pp. 18–23, 2017.
DOI: 10.1007/978-3-319-52709-3_2

time to the minimum under existing technologies, and provide a practical solution for the long-standing memory wall problem. Two techniques, the C-AMAT (Concurrent AMAT) model and the LPM (Layered Performance Matching) method, are developed to provide a constructive proof for Sluice Gate Theory.

C-AMAT serves as a gate calculator which finds a locality-concurrency balanced optimal configuration to match the data access requests and supplies at each layer of a memory hierarchy [2]. LPM controls the global memory system optimization and provides global control parameters to each memory layer [4]. Sluice Gate Theory provides a formal proof of the correctness of the LPM approach. That is, with sufficient data access and hardware concurrency, the LPM method can find a system configuration to match the demand with supply, whereas the matching will reduce the memory stall time to the minimum. Sluice Gate Theory utilizes the substantial memory concurrency that already exists at each layer of current memory systems to explore the combined effort of capacity, locality, and concurrency; and provides a constructive method for software and hardware co-design of memory systems. Only major theoretical results are presented in this paper. All the proofs can be found in [5], and the paper of C-AMAT [2] and LPM [4] are available online.

Sluice Gate Theory proves that through "matching" at each memory layer, the memory stall time can be reduced to the minimum. The terms "sluice" and "gate" are carefully chosen, implying data moves toward the computing unit in a specially designed, gate controlled data channel. Figure 1 illustrates data movement and the "sluice" and "gate". The channel has stages with different devices (the registers, multi-level on-chip or off-chip caches, main memory, disk, and so on), has width in different forms (concurrency), and has speed in different measurements (bandwidth, frequency, latency). It is multi-staged to mask the performance difference between computing units and memory devices. At each stage, a "sluice gate" is placed to control the data movement. C-AMAT measures the supply rate and controls the "width" of the channel by increasing data access concurrency to meet the data access demand at each memory layer. This concurrency is not only for improving the data movement speed, but equally important for overlapping computing and data transfer. Data locality will increase the cache hits at the "gate" and, therefore, reduce the request at the next level of the memory hierarchy. The number of stages can be increased to improve concurrency, locality, and to adapt a new hardware device.

The LPM algorithm controls the matching process. It determines the data demand/supply matching threshold at each memory layer, and makes sure the thresholds can be reached through locality and concurrency optimizations. Due to the request and device differences at each stage, the sluice gates need to be locally controlled and adjusted to best fit the local demand. Since the performance at one memory layer will influence the performance of other memory layers, the performance matching of a memory system needs to be globally coordinated. Performance matching of a memory system is an uneasy task. Fortunately, the C-AMAT model and LPM algorithm have been developed for local calculation and global coordination, respectively. Jointly, C-AMAT and LPM provide a constructive proof of the Sluice Gate Theory.

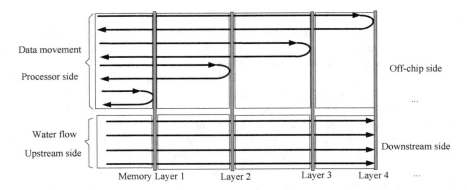

Fig. 1. Compare between data access movement and water flow

2   The Theoretical Treatment of Memory Sluice Gate Theory

Theorem 1 (*Layered Performance Matching (LPM)*): *If a matching can be achieved at each memory layer for a given application for any matching threshold $T > 0$ through optimization, then the LPM algorithm can find a performance matching for the application.*

With the LPM theorem, we now analyze the assumptions of the LPM theorem.

Theorem 2 (*Data Concurrency*): *If an application has sufficient hit concurrency and has sufficient pure miss concurrency or sufficiently low pure miss rate or pure miss penalty at layer L_i, then at memory layer L_i, we can find a performance matching for any matching threshold $T_i > 0$.*

All the optimization parameters used in Data Concurrency Theorem, hit concurrency, pure miss concurrency, pure miss rate, and pure miss penalty are data access concurrency parameters introduced by C-AMAT [2]. They can be optimized through increasing software and hardware concurrency. They do not depend on the memory device hardware peak performance. In other words, the concurrency theorem says through concurrency improvement we can find a match at memory layer L_i. The theorem shows the great potential of data access concurrency.

Based on the Data Concurrency and the LPM Theorem, the following result shows that we can remove the memory wall effect through increasing data concurrency.

Theorem 3 (*Concurrency Match*): *If an application has sufficient hit concurrency and has sufficient pure miss concurrency or sufficiently low pure miss rate or pure miss penalty at each memory layer, then the LPM algorithm can find a performance matching for the application for any matching threshold $T_1 > 0$.*

The proof of the Concurrency Match Theorem has only used the concurrency parameters. The following theorem shows the contribution of data locality in performance matching.

Theorem 4 (Data Locality): *Increasing data locality at memory layer j ($1 \leq j \leq i$), will decrease the data access request rate at the memory layer L_{i+1}.*

From Data Concurrency Theorem and Data Locality Theorem, we can see data concurrency and data locality playing different roles in the performance matching process. Data concurrency improves the supply in a memory performance matching, and data locality reduces the request in memory performance matching. They are both vital in memory performance matching.

Recall the impact of the memory wall problem is the large ratio of memory stall time compared to the total application runtime. Therefore, we can claim that the memory wall effect is negligible small if memory stall time is less than 1% of the application's pure execution time (we think 1% is small enough, but it can be x% for any x > 0). With this one percent definition, we have the final result.

Theorem 5 (Sluice Gate): *If a memory system can match an application's data access requirement for any matching threshold $T_1 > 0$, then this memory system has removed the memory wall effect for this application.*

The Sluice Gate Theorem is of great significance. It claims that the memory wall impact can be reduced to the minimum and to be practically eliminated through data access concurrency, on conventional memory hierarchy architectures. For a long time, the memory wall problem has been the wall standing on the road of improving computing system performance. It has been believed that the memory wall problem only can be solved through technology advancements of memory devices. The Sluice Gate Theorem gives an alternative approach via data concurrency.

The performance match can be found as stated in Data Concurrency Theorem is in a theoretical sense. Theoretically achievable does not mean we can achieve it in today's engineering practice, but through engineering effort we may achieve it someday. While we may not have sufficient data access and dynamic hardware concurrency in practice, Sluice Gate Theory gives a direction of software/hardware co-design and optimization to reduce memory stall time to the minimum.

3   Experimental Results and Conclusion

A detailed CPU model and the DRAMSim2 module in the GEM5 simulator were adopted to achieve accurate simulation results. We have conducted several case studies, and only show one, the Multiple Dimension Exploration case study, here in.

Under the five configurations A to E, Table 1 shows the corresponding average LPMRs (LPM Ratios) of the 410.bwaves benchmark in the SPEC CPU 2006 benchmark suit. We use the LPM algorithm [4] to find an optimal architecture match for the given software implementation. The goal of the optimization is to keep the memory stall time per instruction within 1% of CPI_{exe}, where the CPI_{exe} is 0.261 cycles per instruction on average. The calculated matching thresholds, T_1 and T_2, for L1 and L2 cache of the 410.bwaves benchmark are 1.52 and 2.14, respectively. Table 1 shows under Configuration A, the LPMRs are higher than the threshold values of T_1 and T_2, so that the optimizations are carried in both layers at the same time. To increase concurrency, we doubled the IW and ROB size, transformed the architecture from configuration A to configuration B in Table 1. However, the mismatches are still higher than their thresholds. Then we continue the optimization process and transform the configuration B to configuration C, and then to D. Configuration D meet the "1%" requirement. As an optional step, we continue to check if hardware is overprovided. We do a fine tune to reduce possible hardware overprovision to achieve cost efficiency, which leads to the final configuration E.

Table 1. LPMRs under five machine configurations

Configuration		A	B	C	D	E
Sluice width	Pipeline issue width	4	4	6	8	8
	IW size	32	64	64	128	96
	ROB size	32	64	64	128	96
	L_1 cache port number	1	1	2	4	4
	MSHR numbers	4	8	16	16	16
	L_2 cache interleaving	4	8	8	8	8
Mismatching degree	$LPMR_1$	8.1	6.2	2.1	1.2	1.4
	$LPMR_2$	9.6	9.3	3.1	1.6	1.9

Please notice with the original configuration A, the memory stall time is 0.396 cycles per instruction, which contributes more than 60% of the total execution time (0.653 cycles per instruction). With the configuration E, the final memory stall time is less than 1% of the pure execution time (which is less than 0.4% of the original total execution time). Therefore, the memory system performance speedup is greater than 150. The performance improvement is huge.

Sluice Gate Theory provides a system approach to solve the long-standing memory wall problem. Its correctness is verified with rigorous mathematical proofs, and its practical applicability is supported with its associated C-AMAT model and LPM method for performance measurement and optimization. Sluice Gate Theory utilizes existing data concurrency and optimizes the combined performance of data locality and concurrency to reduce the overall memory stall time. It is powerful and imperative for the advancement of modern memory systems. Sluice Gate Theory is based on data concurrency. It calls for the rethinking from a data centric view. It calls for the development of compiler technologies to utilize data access concurrency and to develop concurrency-aware locality optimizations, and provides a guideline for such optimization and utilization.

References

1. Wulf, W.A., McKee, S.A.: Hitting the memory wall: implications of the obvious. ACM SIGARCH Comput. Archit. News **23**, 20–24 (1995)
2. Sun, X.H., Wang, D.: Concurrent average memory access time. IEEE Comput. **47**(5), 74–80 (2014)

3. Chou, Y., Fahs, B., Abraham, S.: Microarchitecture optimizations for memory-level parallelism. In: Proceedings of 31st International Symposium on Computer Architecture, June 2004
4. Liu, Y.H., Sun, X.H.: LPM: concurrency-driven layered performance matching. In: 44th International Conference on Parallel Processing (ICPP). IEEE (2015)
5. Sun, X.-H., Liu, Y.-H.: Sluice gate theory: have we found a solution for memory wall?. Illinois Institute of Technology Technical report (IIT/CS-SCS-2016-01) (2016). Full paper is available upon request

ParFuse: Parallel and Compositional Analysis of Message Passing Programs

Sriram Aananthakrishnan[1]([✉]), Greg Bronevetsky[2], Mark Baranowski[1], and Ganesh Gopalakrishnan[1]

[1] University of Utah, Salt Lake City, USA
{sriram,baranows,ganesh}@cs.utah.edu
[2] Google Inc., Mountain View, USA
bronevet@google.com

Abstract. Static analysis discovers provable true properties about behaviors of programs that are useful in optimization, debugging and verification. Sequential static analysis techniques fail to interpret the message passing semantics of the MPI and lack the ability to optimize or check the message passing behaviors of MPI programs. In this paper, we introduce an abstraction for approximating the message passing behaviors of MPI programs that is more precise than prior work and is applicable to a wide variety of applications. Our approach builds on the compositional paradigm where we transparently extend MPI support to sequential analyses through composition with our MPI analyses. This is the first framework where the data flow analysis is carried out in parallel on a cluster, with the message-carried data flow facts for refining inter-process data flow analysis states. We detail ParFuse – a framework that supports such parallel and compositional analysis of MPI programs, report its scalability and detail the prospects of extending our work for more powerful analyses.

1 Introduction

HPC systems have become increasingly complex as we step into the exascale computing era. In parallel, MPI has also evolved, introducing sophisticated communication primitives for interprocess communication. Debugging and performance tuning of message passing programs have become notoriously difficult. With the growing complexity of writing message passing programs, tools to assist developers are crucially needed. While many dynamic and runtime tools exist to assist MPI programmers, only a handful of static analysis based tools exist in comparison. Static analysis of MPI programs can discover provably true properties about the communication behaviors of the MPI programs which are useful in optimization, error detection and verification. For instance, compilers can replace point-to-point operations in a neighborhood communication pattern with their optimized collective counterparts [11] if the MPI program's communication topology can be determined.

© Springer International Publishing AG 2017
C. Ding et al. (Eds.): LCPC 2016, LNCS 10136, pp. 24–39, 2017.
DOI: 10.1007/978-3-319-52709-3_3

Many standard dataflow analyses such as constant propagation are MPI agnostic i.e., they do not model the effects of dataflow due to MPI communication, losing precision at the call sites of MPI operations and thereby missing the opportunity to apply program optimizations. Static analysis of MPI programs require abstractions for modeling the communication behaviors where the abstraction must provide an interpretation for MPI operations and compute the possible message matches. This task is challenging requiring composition of multiple static analyses.

Prior work on analyzing MPI programs have focused on a non-compositional approach. The message passing semantics are modeled by constructing a communication graph [2,19,20] and the analysis associates special transfer functions for each MPI operation to interpret the dataflow information along the communication edges. Adopting a new dataflow analysis for MPI programs under this setting requires implementing the special transfer functions corresponding to each MPI operation. In this paper, we build on the compositional principles of the Fuse [3] framework where we implement a suite of analyses for modeling the MPI message passing semantics. Our approach allows any dataflow analyses to be composed with MPI analyses which transparently adds MPI support for the MPI-agnostic analyses.

In this paper, we offer the first static analysis method with the following features:

- We introduce specific abstractions for MPI operations which enables us to reach a useful level of accuracy that covers many real applications.
- Our abstractions for MPI operations are built on top of the Fuse framework where MPI-agnostic static analyses are leveraged with MPI support through composition with our MPI analyses.
- Our analysis is carried out in parallel on a cluster to ameliorate the cost when analyzing an MPI program with N processes. We provide an evaluation of the scalability of our approach.
- Visualization of possible communication matches as an automatically generated "dot graph" built using our compositional infrastructure for analyzing MPI programs.

The rest of the paper provides background on compositional analysis and prior work in Sect. 2, our abstractions for MPI semantics in Sect. 3, MPI analyses that realizes our abstraction in Sect. 4, our parallel and compositional ParFuse framework in Sect. 5 and the results in Sect. 6. Related work and concluding remarks follow.

2 Background

2.1 Compositional Analysis

In a prior project [3], we introduced the Fuse compositional framework that simplifies composition of static analyses through a data structure called Abstract

Transition System (ATS). ATSs are graphs where the nodes correspond to different possible code execution paths and edges represent transitions from one program state to another. Static analyses can be executed on ATSs and compute constraints (e.g. dataflow facts) on reachable program executions, which are stored as annotations on each ATS node. The ATS organizes the constraints on reachable executions using sets of program state components (memory locations, values or operations). This allows analyses to portably communicate the constraints on reachable executions as set constraints on state components to other analyses, which we denote as "abstract objects". While the abstract objects are opaque (their individual values may be infinitely many), its implementations must include standard set operations such as overlaps, must-equals, equal-sets, subset etc. This enables other analyses to compare two abstract objects and make complex inferences based on them without knowing how they were computed. The graph representation for the ATS makes it easier to transparently introduce path pruning (by eliminating nodes that correspond to impossible execution paths), path-sensitivity or context-sensitivity (e.g. multiple copies of a function's body for each code location from which the function may be called). The structure of the graph is made available via a standard graph interface and Fuse uses it to execute additional analyses with the added precision by associating constraints on the modified graph.

Fuse enables analysis interactions through a novel query interface which allows analyses to prove new constraints. The interactions between the analyses are organized as a client-server architecture where clients are static analyses asking questions and servers are static analyses providing answers to client's questions. Client queries are either a graph query or a set query where the graph queries (GetATSInit, GetATSFin) are used for traversing the graph and set queries (GetMemLoc, GetValue, GetCodeLoc) are used accessing the constraints at an ATS node. To access the set constraints at an ATS node, the clients provide a program segment and ask for the set of memory locations, values, or operations denoted by the program segment. The server provides an approximate interpretation of the program segment and returns abstract objects for the set query. The interactions are orchestrated by a composer entity which forwards the queries from clients to the servers and returns the abstract objects from the servers back to the clients.

Illustration. Consider the source code in Fig. 1 requiring composition of multiple static analyses. The analyses constant propagation Fig. 1(b), unreachable code elimination Fig. 1(c), points-to analysis Fig. 1(d) and constant propagation Fig. 1(e) interacts using the Fuse query interface to determine the value of the expression $*p + 5$. Constant propagation Fig. 1(b) determines the outcome of the branch condition as true. Unreachable code elimination Fig. 1(c) queries constant propagation for GetValue($arr[1] == 3$). Constant propagation responds with an abstract value object $\{True\}$ which allows unreachable code analysis to eliminate the infeasible path. Points-to traverses the modified graph and computes the constraint $p \rightarrow arr[0]$. Constant propagation Fig. 1(e) queries points-to for GetMemLoc($*p$) using which it computes the value of $*p + 5$.

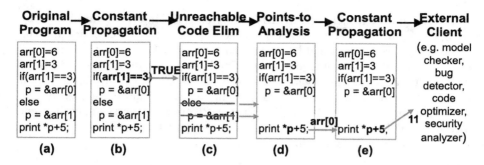

Fig. 1. Compositional analysis by fuse

Key Advantages. Fuse allows for a configurable program analyses where the developer picks the static analyses to be applied on a given program. The analysis composition is described as a composition command. The Fuse query interface allows analyses to communicate constraints in an API-agnostic way i.e., without being aware of analysis specific API such as LLVM's Alias Analysis interface [13]. Fuse simplifies analysis composition and allows modular abstractions to be introduced and flexibly composed with other analyses. We will leverage this capability in this paper to create a set of new analyses that model MPI semantics and compose our MPI analyses with traditional analyses that model non-MPI aspects of a program's behavior. This enables traditional static analyses to accurately analyze a wide range of properties (e.g. optimization potential or memory safety) of MPI applications.

2.2 Prior Work: Dataflow Analysis of MPI Programs

The fundamental challenge in reasoning about MPI programs is identifying the communication topology of the MPI program i.e., statically matching the send-receive operations. While this problem is undecidable in general, analyses compute approximations for it. The computed approximation must be sound (i.e., it must connect each pair of send and receive operations that may possibly match) but does not need to be complete (i.e., some of the matched operations may not actually match in a real execution). Abstracting the communication topology requires: (1) an abstraction for the MPI operations and (2) a matching of the send abstractions with the receive abstractions. One simple abstraction for the communication topology is to group all the send operations into one equivalence class and all the receive operations into another equivalence class and match the two equivalence classes. While sound, this simple abstraction is imprecise for practical purposes.

MPI operations can be grouped into equivalence classes based on the static code location. Strout et al. [20] use this abstraction to construct the MPI-ICFG where the matchings are computed by (i) grouping all the send operations from a send statement into an equivalence class (ii) grouping all the receive operations from a receive statement into an equivalence class (iii) connecting the send and receive equivalence classes. MPI-ICFG extends the interprocedural CFG by adding communication edges between the send and receive CFG nodes and the dataflow analysis is performed by propagating dataflow facts over the communication edges. The matchings are further refined using tags, datatypes and simple path constraints. This approach has two drawbacks. First, this approach uses a single CFG for modeling the message passing behaviors and consequently, the abstraction for MPI operations groups the MPI operations issued by different processes executing the same path into a single equivalence class. For instance, consider the following code snippet

```
while(true) {
if(rank
else MPI_Recv(buf ,.. rank-1);
}
```

MPI-ICFG for the code snippet groups the send operations of all even processes into one equivalence class and the receive operations of all odd processes into another and connects the two equivalence classes. While sound, this abstraction allows communication between process 0 and process 3 which never happens in the original program. Furthermore, when the target expressions of MPI operations and path constraints are complex (left-neighbor, right-neighbor expressions), refinement of the send-receive matchings is cumbersome. Second, this approach ignores the matches-before ordering of MPI matching semantics, thereby losing opportunities for potential refinement.

Bronevetsky [2] constructed a parallel control-flow graph (pCFG) which improves the matching precision by grouping processes into equivalence classes and the equivalence classes were split at communication points or branch conditions and merged whenever they were identical. Message passing semantics are simulated by performing the analysis on the pCFG. To precisely match MPI operations in pCFG, the analysis would first block on corresponding MPI operations and the symbolic constraints on the target expression of a send must isomorphically match the symbolic constraints on the target expression of a receive operation. While scalable, this approach makes matching difficult when complex abstractions are used to describe the equivalence classes and target expressions evaluating to multiple values.

3   Approximating MPI Semantics

Our key insight is that computing an approximation of the communication topology with a reasonable precision on an unbounded number of processes is expensive and cumbersome. In our approach, we relax the unbounded constraint and fix the number of processes and compute an approximation for a fixed number of processes. This means that the program must be analyzed separately for each number of processes the user wants to run with; this can be done as a final compilation pass at job load-time.

Abstracting MPI Operations. Our approach analyzes a concurrent MPI program with N processes using a cross-product of the ATSs given by $A_{T_1} \times A_{T_2} \times \cdots \times A_{T_N}$ where we associate an analysis instance for each process. For abstracting the MPI operations, we group MPI operations issued from an ATS node of a process into an equivalence class. Our abstraction differentiates the MPI operations issued by different processes, in different locations in the code, which allows ParFuse to compute more precise matchings than previous approaches. Furthermore, our abstraction allows ParFuse to compute process-sensitive value approximations (i.e., specific to each process) for the buffers of the MPI operations.

MPI Matching. The challenge in matching the abstractions for MPI operations i.e., their equivalence classes, is that they must be matched following the out-of-order matching semantics of the MPI. Blocking operations are matched in the program order i.e., the order in which they are issued by the program. However, non-blocking operations are matched out of order i.e., two non-blocking operations to two different process are matched in any order. But two non-blocking operations to the same process are matched in the program order. MPI enforces this by the non-overtaking rule. One way to formalize the out-of-order matching of MPI is through matches-before relations. Vakkalanka et al. [21] introduce intra matches-before relations (within a process) between the MPI operations issued by a process where the matches-before relations are due to the MPI matching semantics. The intra matches-before ordering between the operations is summarized as follows.

- Two blocking or non-blocking MPI point-to-point operations are matches-before ordered if they are send/receive to the same process and two operations are unordered if they are send/receive to different processes (non-overtaking rule).
- The non-blocking point-to-point operations are ordered before their respective `MPI_Wait` operations.
- MPI-specific strong-ordering points such as Barrier and Wait are matches-before ordered with any MPI operations that follow in program order.

Explicitly matching the equivalence classes of MPI operations following the matches-before ordering is cumbersome in practice. *We simplify matching by delegating the task to the MPI runtime.* In our approach, when a dataflow analysis reaches the ATS node of a send or a receive equivalence class it issues the operation to the MPI runtime where they are matched and exchange dataflow facts as the message payload.

While our approach simplifies MPI matching, it imposes three restrictions: First, we require that the matches-before ordering must be exactly determinable at compile time. Second, we require that the MPI operations are deterministic as the non-deterministic MPI operations have many possible matching choices that are not explored by the MPI runtime. Third, we require the divergent paths of the MPI processes where MPI send/receive operations are potentially issued to be loop-free. While these restrictions may seem onerous, we believe that composable static analysis of many MPI programs can be achieved under these restrictions, and that the data flow facts obtained under these restrictions can prove to be useful, while guaranteeing soundness. In particular, all of our MPI benchmarks yielded useful data flow facts under these restrictions. Furthermore, by introducing new MPI analyses (i.e., improving the MPI abstractions), our framework allows MPI-agnostic analyses to be MPI-aware on a larger set of applications. By fixing the number of processes and using the MPI runtime for matching provides ParFuse an unique opportunity towards building a parallel dataflow analysis framework for MPI programs where the framework is deployed as an MPI application.

Novelty. Our approach improves upon the prior work where our abstraction for MPI operations allows ParFuse to compute more precise matchings. We differ from other approaches in matching the MPI abstractions where we delegate the matching to the MPI runtime. By performing the matching on the fly we do not require a priori construction of a communication graph for dataflow analysis. We realize our abstractions by implementing MPI specific analyses in the Par-Fuse framework. Our method allows analysis of each process to be carried out independently in parallel allowing ParFuse to scale better. Lastly, by building on the compositional principles of Fuse framework our work enables compositional reasoning of MPI programs.

4 MPI Analyses in ParFuse

Our approach for approximating MPI semantics is based on the following key ideas. First, we relax the unbounded process constraint by fixing the number of processes for the analysis. Second, we associate the MPI operations issued from an ATS node into a group. Third, we match the send-receive groups using the MPI runtime and exchange dataflow facts as message payload in-lieu of actual messages. We realize these novel ideas by modularly introducing MPI specific analyses into analysis composition using Fuse's compositional principles and transparently extending MPI support to existing MPI-agnostic analyses.

MPI Context Sensitivity (MCC). The role of MCC is to implement our abstraction for MPI operations by replacing the context-insensitive single copy of the ATS node for an MPI function body (empty stub) with multiple copies creating one copy for each call site. MCC operates on an input ATS and emits a MPI context sensitive ATS as its output. Observe that the ATS node is specific to each process and context of MPI operations at two different processes are not equal. The successors of MCC operate on the MPI context sensitive ATS allowing them to interpret the message passing semantics due to MPI operations issued from the same ATS node.

MPI Value (MV). MPI value provides semantic interpretation of MPI specific variables `rank` (the pid of the MPI process) and `size` (the total number of MPI processes). The values of `rank` and `size` are assigned by the MPI runtime when the program executes the functions MPI_Comm_rank and MPI_Comm_size respectively. The transfer function of MV semantically interprets the two MPI operations MPI_Comm_rank and MPI_Comm_size using MPI_COMM_WORLD as the argument and assigns positive integer constants to the variables rank and size as assigned by the MPI runtime. Analyses such as constant propagation when composed with MV, can infer new information based on the values computed by MV.

MPI Communication (MCO). MPI communication analysis provides semantic interpretations for the MPI communication operations such as MPI_Send, MPI_Recv by executing the operations. The message payload is the dataflow facts corresponding to the buffer of the MPI operations. MCO traverses the ATS of a previously completed analysis and at ATS nodes of MPI communication operations queries a prior analysis for the set of values denoted by the buffer using the Fuse query interface function GetValue. The abstract value object obtained from a prior analysis is serialized using the boost serialization API [1]. The MCO executes the MPI_Send operation to transmit a serialized representation of the abstract value object as the message payload.

The envelope information of the MPI operations such as target and tag must be known to execute the MPI operations. As such, the execution of MCO must be preceded by a value analysis, such as constant propagation, which can compute this information. Then MCO can obtain the values for target and tag by the value analysis by calling GetValue on these variables. The MCO analysis requires that the values of the expressions target and tag evaluate to integer constants and aborts if the values are unknown. The restriction that the matches-before ordering of the MPI operations be exactly determinable at static time ensures that the values of the expressions exactly target and tag evaluate to integer constants. With the values for target, tag and *buf obtained from a prior analysis, MCO transmits the analysis information to the MPI runtime by executing the MPI operations.

MCO of the receiveing process deserializes the received information and caches the abstract value object at the call site of the MPI_Recv operation. The value approximation computed by a dataflow analysis is moved from the MCO of a sending process to the MCO of the receiving process. The portable query interface makes it possible for ParFuse to transparently add a dataflow analysis into the analysis composition and MCO propagates the dataflow facts from one process to another through the MPI runtime.

5   ParFuse Framework

We realize our methods for analyzing MPI programs in the ParFuse framework. ParFuse creates N instances of the Fuse compositional analysis framework, one for each ATS graph of a process. Each Fuse instance F_i executes an identical composition command containing a list of analyses that are composed using sequential composition where the analyses are executed one after the other. The ParFuse framework with N Fuse instances is deployed itself as an MPI program where each MPI process is a Fuse instance.

5.1   Analysis Composition Recipe

The standard dataflow analyses such as constant propagation (CP), points-to analysis (PT), unreachable code elimination (UC), calling context sensitivity (CCS), array analysis (ARR) have been observed to be useful to compose with our MPI analyses and will be the focus of our experiments, although any standard dataflow analyses can be composed in the ParFuse framework. First, these analyses benefit from MPI semantics provided by the MPI analyses. Second, these analyses are also instrumental in static determination of the matches-before ordering required by the MPI analyses. We illustrate this using a simple example shown in Fig. 2a. Let CC denote the composition command and we will add analyses to CC based on the demands of the MPI program. For notational convenience, we differentiate two instances of an analysis appearing in CC using subscripts. For instance, CP_1 is the first instance of constant propagation and CP_2 is the second instance. Figure 2a shows the base ATS graph computed by the syntactic analysis (SYN) that transforms the source code to an ATS and provides syntactic constraints for memory, values and code locations. MPI analysis begins with the abstraction of MPI operations and we introduce MPI Context Sensitivity (MCC) into analysis composition which assigns a unique context to MPI operations based on the ATS node.

$$CC = SEQ(SYN, MCC)$$

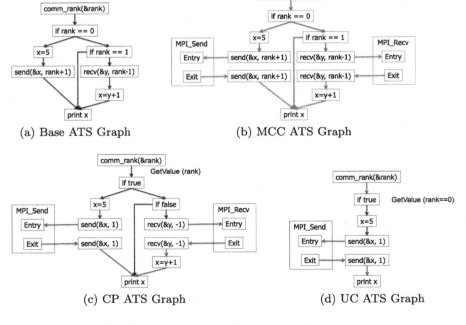

(a) Base ATS Graph   (b) MCC ATS Graph

(c) CP ATS Graph   (d) UC ATS Graph

Fig. 2. Analysis composition recipe: illustration

The ATS graph extended by MCC calling-site context for each MPI operation is shown in Fig. 2b. The ATS graph constructed by MCC is identical for both process 0 and process 1. For matching the send-receive groupings using the MPI runtime, determining the value of the target expressions $rank + 1$ and $rank - 1$ of the send and receive operations is critical. We will extend the composition command CC with points-to (rank is passed using pointers to MPI_Comm_rank), constant propagation (to propagate initial constants from MPI headers to MPI operations), MPI value (which interprets MPI_Comm_rank) and another constant propagation (propagate the rank value to target expressions) to determine the value of the target expressions of the send and the receive operation. Unreachable code elimination (UC) is then added to prune infeasible paths.

$$CC = SEQ(SYN, MCC, PT, CP_1, MV, CP_2, UC)$$

The ATS graph for process 0 after CP_2 is shown in Fig. 2c and the ATS graph after UC is shown in Fig. 2d.

With the value of target expressions known, we can now introduce MPI communication analysis for matching the send-receive groupings using the MPI runtime and propagating the dataflow fact $\{x\} \rightarrow 5$ from the send call site of process 0 to the receive call site of process 1. This is illustrated in Fig. 3 The points-to composed earlier disambiguates the points-to relations at MPI call sites. MCO of process 0 queries CP_2 of process 0 for the values of x and propagates the value from the sender (rank=0) to the receiver (rank=1). The received value object is cached by the MCO of process 1. By adding another instance of constant propagation after MCO, the received value is propagated to the rest of the program.

$$CC = SEQ(SYN, MCC, PT, CP_1, MV, CP_2, UC, MCO, CP_3) \tag{1}$$

The analysis composition CC described above is the basic recipe for analyzing MPI programs with message passing behaviors. The Fuse query interface allows for transparent exchange of dataflow facts between the analyses and the MPI communication analysis (MCO) communicates the dataflow facts through MPI message passing operations.

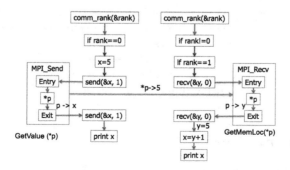

Fig. 3. MPI runtime matching using MCO

5.2 Illustration: Configurable Analysis of MPI Programs

We demonstrate the flexibility of our approach by proving a message passing dependent property shown in Fig. 4 that requires a non-trivial composition of standard dataflow and MPI analyses. ParFuse proves the property with two Fuse instances using the following analysis composition.

$$CC = SEQ(SYN, MCC, PT, CP_1, MV, CP_2, UC_1, MCO_1, CP_3, UC_2, CP_4, MCO_2, CP_5)$$

```
if(rank == 0) {
    x = 2;
    MPI_Send(&x, 1, MPI_INT, rank+1, 0, MPI_COMM_WORLD);
    MPI_Recv(&z, 1, MPI_INT, rank+1, 0, MPI_COMM_WORLD,
        MPI_STATUS_IGNORE);
}
else if(rank == 1) {
    MPI_Recv(&y, 1, MPI_INT, rank-1, 0, MPI_COMM_WORLD,
        MPI_STATUS_IGNORE);
    if(y==2) z = 3;
    else z = 4;
    z = z+2;
    MPI_Send(&z, 1, MPI_INT, rank-1, 0, MPI_COMM_WORLD);
}
assert(z == 5);
```

Fig. 4. Configurable program analysis example

The analysis composition consists of 13 instances of dataflow analyses which are composed sequentially one after the other. The two Fuse instances are executed independently of each other where MCO_1 propagates the value of x from the sender to the receiver. CP_3 propagates the received value to the branch condition, using which UC_2 eliminates the infeasible path. CP_4 on the receiver side computes precise value for z which is propagated back to the sender using MCO_2. Finally, the newly received value is propagated to the assert statement by CP_5. The compositional reasoning of ParFuse simplifies the task of proving the message passing dependent property which is otherwise cumbersome when using the existing non-compositional static analysis techniques for MPI programs. ParFuse makes it possible to configure program analyses to target the complexity of the program and the property to be proven. ParFuse also makes it easy to add new MPI analyses implementing different abstractions for MPI operations with varying cost/accuracy tradeoffs.

6 Experimental Results

We implemented the ParFuse framework in the ROSE [18] compiler infrastructure where our current implementation provides semantic interpretations for the following MPI operations: `MPI_Comm_rank`, `MPI_Comm_size`, `MPI_Barrier`, `MPI_Bcast`, `MPI_Send`, `MPI_Recv` and `MPI_Reduce`. Our goal is to evaluate the performance of realistic compositions of analyses that include our MPI analyses. Instead of timing the executions of MPI analyses, we will pick a concrete analysis task, compose a variety of standard dataflow analyses with MPI analyses to accomplish this task and measure the performance of the analysis execution for varying process counts. Two factors determine the choice of our analysis composition: (i) analysis composition required to accomplish the concrete analysis task (ii) analysis composition required to resolve the send-receive matching unambiguously. The communication topology of an MPI program is a useful property to be known statically with many applications such as debugging, overlapping the computation with communication, optimal process placement etc. For the concrete analysis task, we will synthesize the communication topology of the MPI program as a DOT [10] graph. For this, we will compose MPI Dot Value (MDV) (a visualization tool) with our MPI analyses. MDV assigns unique id to the call sites of MPI send operations. The MPI Communication analysis (MCO) employs the Fuse API GetValue to obtain the unique id as a value object from MDV and transmits the value object to the matching receive call sites. The MDV at a receiving process employs the Fuse API GetValue and queries MCO to update the receive call sites with the received information. The communication graph in the DOT language is then synthesized by adding edges between send and receive ATS nodes using the received information. MDV also exemplifies the versatility of the ParFuse framework where non-dataflow facts such as unique ids are exchanged through our compositional principles.

Table 1. Analysis composition summary

Benchmark	Analysis composition
Jacobi	$SEQ(SYN, MCC, PT_1, CP_1, MV, CP_2, UC, ARR, PT_2, MDV_1, MCO, MDV_2)$
Heat	$SEQ(SYN, CCS, MCC, CP_1, ARR_1, CP_2, PT_1, MV, CP_3, UC, CP_4, ARR_2,$ $PT_2, MDV_1, MCO, MDV_2)$
2D diffusion	$SEQ(SYN, CCS, MCC, CP_1, ARR_1, CP_2, PT_1, MV, CP_3, UC, CP_4, ARR_2,$ $PT_2, MDV_1, MCO, MDV_2)$
Prime	$SEQ(SYN, CCS, MCC, CP_1, PT, MV, CP_2, UC, MDV_1, MCO, MDV_2)$
Quadrature	$SEQ(SYN, CCS, MCC, CP_1, PT, MV, CP_2, UC, MDV_1, MCO, MDV_2)$

We chose the following MPI programs: (i) Jacobi [16] iteration solving the Laplacian equation in two dimensions (ii) Heat [6] equation solver solving the time dependent heat equation in one dimension (iii) 2D Diffusion [9] solver solving the diffusion equation (iv) Prime [5] counting parallelized using MPI (v) Quadrature [4] approximating an integral using the quadrature rule for our study. The programs are of varying complexity in their source code requiring different analysis composition to unambiguously resolve the send-receive matching. Table 1 summarizes the analysis composition required for each benchmark to synthesize the communication topology as the DOT graph. The analyses are repeatedly applied as the reapplication discovers new information. For instance, to determine the memory locations denoted by the expression `arr[maxn/size]`, where `size` is assigned by `MPI_Comm_size`, constant propagation (CP) must be reapplied after MPI value (MV). The array analysis (ARR) composed after the CP queries CP for the value of the index expressions and consequently, determines the set of memory locations denoted by the the expression `arr[maxn/size]`. We evaluated the performance of our analysis composition with varying process counts up to 1024. The experiments were performed on a cluster with over 290 nodes (5104 cores, 32 GB memory per node). The nodes are Intel Xeon (Sandy-bridge/Ivybridge E5-2670 and Haswell) processors and are connected through the Mellanox FDR Infiniband interconnect. Figure 5 shows the plots comparing the average execution time (wall time) of the application and the analysis com-

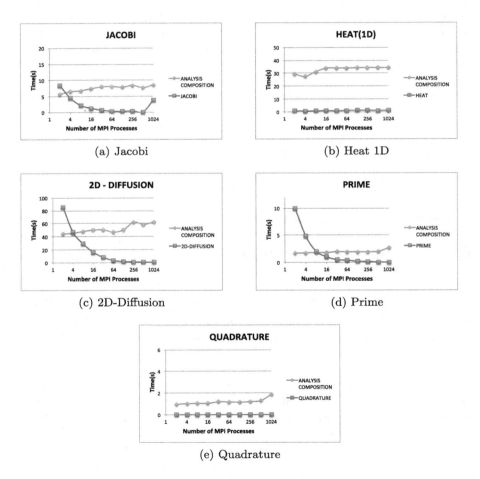

(a) Jacobi

(b) Heat 1D

(c) 2D-Diffusion

(d) Prime

(e) Quadrature

Fig. 5. Scalability evaluation

position for each benchmark. The input problem size for the applications Jacobi, Prime and 2D Diffusion was not changed and with increasing process count they exhibit strong scaling whereas the input problem size for applications Heat and Quadrature was increased proportionally to the number of processes and they exhibit weak scaling. Figures 5a to e show a weak scaling for our analysis composition. Our results show that our approach scales linearly with increasing process counts. The challenge lies in picking the suite of analyses for disambiguating the communication and carrying out the analysis task for proving properties. Our current method is partial where the analyses are manually picked based on the complexity in the source code (arrays, pointers, mpi variables etc.). We repeatedly apply the analyses until the necessary information for disambiguating the communication is determined. We can overcome this challenge i.e., the phase ordering problem [7] by performing a tight composition which is computationally expensive and learning based approaches [12] that learns the characteristics of the code being optimized and decides the best ordering of the analyses. Tight composition [14] evades the phase ordering problem by discovering all the information in one phase. Our preliminary implementation of tight composition reveals that this effort merits further investigation.

7   Related Work

In Sect. 2.2, we summarized prior work on dataflow analysis of MPI programs. In this section, we will summarize non-dataflow static techniques for analyzing MPI programs and dataflow analysis techniques for non-MPI message passing programs. McPherson et al. [15] employed a tree based data structure for understanding the call sites of the MPI operations. The tree based structure allowed them to compute the value of target expressions when they involve rank and size on demand. They used a bit vector for a process sensitive computation of the target expressions of the MPI operations. Similar to our approach, they bound the number of processes and determine the values of target expressions and the message payload size at the call sites of the MPI operations. Their approach did not however match the send receive operations and simulate the message passing behaviors. Droste et al. [8] implemented static checks purely based on the AST of the program. While the tool implements many useful checks based on the ATS, it was able to match MPI operations only when the target expression is trivial (constants) and the other arguments are exactly the same. Their technique solely relied on the AST producing sub-optimal results when matching point-to-point MPI operations. Reif [17] introduced a monotone lattice theoretic dataflow framework for communicating concurrent processes. Similar to our approach, Reif bounded the number of processes. The matching however was computed explicitly considering the semantics of the message passing operations. The framework was monolithic and was applied on a simpler message passing model than MPI.

8   Concluding Remarks

This paper presents a compositional approach towards building a dataflow analysis framework for analyzing MPI programs. Our approach builds on the compositional principles of the Fuse framework where abstractions for message passing operations are modularly introduced, by adding MPI specific analyses into analysis composition. We implemented a specific abstraction for MPI operations that allowed us to compute a more precise matching of the MPI operations than previous approaches. We adopted a simple solution for matching MPI abstractions by delegating it to the MPI runtime where our analysis is not burdened with simulating the complex matching semantics of MPI. Our compositional approach provides a mechanism to extend sequential dataflow analyses to work with MPI programs. Standard dataflow analyses can be transparently added into the analysis composition with the MPI analyses where the MPI analyses handles the task of abstracting message passing semantics. Our design choice of fixing the number of processes provided us a unique opportunity for carrying out the analysis of each process independently of each other, allowing the analyses to be executed in parallel on a cluster and help our techniques scale for a large number of processes. The framework is also first in its kind where the dataflow facts are exchanged as message payload in lieu of actual messages.

Acknowledgments. This research was supported in part by NSF ACI 1148127, CCF 1439002, CCF 1346756 and DOE grant "Static Analysis using ROSE".

References

1. BOOST Team. Boost Serialization API (2004)
2. Bronevetsky, G.: Communication-sensitive static dataflow for parallel message passing applications. In: CGO (2009)
3. Bronevetsky, G., Burke, M., Aananthakrishnan, S., Zhao, J., Sarkar, V.: Compositional dataflow via abstract transition systems. Technical report, LLNL (2013)
4. Burkardt, J.: Quadrature using MPI (2010). http://people.sc.fsu.edu/jburkardt/c_src/quad_mpi/quad_mpi.html
5. Burkardt, J.: Couting Primes using MPI (2011). https://people.sc.fsu.edu/jburkardt/c_src/prime_mpi/prime_mpi.html
6. Burkardt, J.: Heat Equation solver in MPI-C (2011). http://people.sc.fsu.edu/jburkardt/c_src/heat_mpi/heat_mpi.html
7. Cooper, K.D., Subramanian, D., Torczon, L.: Adaptive optimizing compilers for the 21st century. SC **23**, 7–22 (2002)
8. Droste, A., Kuhn, M., Ludwig, T.: MPI-Checker: Static Analysis for MPI. In: LLVM-HPC (2015)
9. Formal Verification Group at University of Utah. 2D Diffusion Equation Solver in MPI-C (2009). http://formalverification.cs.utah.edu/MPI_Tests/general_tests/small_tests/2ddiff.c
10. Gansner, E., Koutsofios, E., North, S.: Drawing Graphs with DOT (2006)
11. Hoefler, T., Schneider, T.: Runtime detection and optimization of collective communication patterns. In: PACT (2012)

12. Kulkarni, S., Cavazos, J.: Mitigating the compiler optimization phase-ordering problem using machine learning. In: OOPSLA (2012)

13. Lattner, C.: LLVM Alias Analysis Infrastructure. http://llvm.org/docs/AliasAnalysis.html

14. Lerner, S., Grove, D., Chambers, C.: Composing dataflow analyses and transformations. In: POPL (2002)

15. McPherson, A.J., Nagarajan, V., Cintra, M.: Static approximation of MPI communication graphs for optimized process placement. In: Brodman, J., Tu, P. (eds.) LCPC 2014. LNCS, vol. 8967, pp. 268–283. Springer, Heidelberg (2015). doi:10.1007/978-3-319-17473-0_18

16. MCS, Argonne National Laboratory. Simple Jacobi Iteration in C (2000). http://www.mcs.anl.gov/research/projects/mpi/tutorial/mpiexmpl/src/jacobi/C/main.html

17. Reif, J.H.: Data flow analysis of communicating processes. In: POPL (1979)

18. ROSE Compiler Team. ROSE User Manual: A Tool for Building Source-to-Source Translators

19. Shires, D., Pollock, L., Sprenkle, S.: Program flow graph construction for static analysis of MPI programs. In: PDPTA (1999)

20. Strout, M.M., Kreaseck, B., Hovland, P.D.: Data-flow analysis for MPI programs. In: ICPP (2006)

21. Vakkalanka, S., Vo, A., Gopalakrishnan, G., Kirby, R.M.: Reduced execution semantics of MPI: from theory to practice. In: Cavalcanti, A., Dams, D.R. (eds.) FM 2009. LNCS, vol. 5850, pp. 724–740. Springer, Heidelberg (2009). doi:10.1007/978-3-642-05089-3_46

Fast Approximate Distance Queries in Unweighted Graphs Using Bounded Asynchrony

Adam Fidel$^{(\boxtimes)}$, Francisco Coral Sabido, Colton Riedel, Nancy M. Amato, and Lawrence Rauchwerger

Parasol Lab, Department of Computer Science and Engineering,
Texas A&M University, College Station, USA
fidel@cse.tamu.edu

Abstract. We introduce a new parallel algorithm for approximate breadth-first ordering of an unweighted graph by using bounded asynchrony to parametrically control both the performance and error of the algorithm. This work is based on the k-level asynchronous (KLA) paradigm that trades expensive global synchronizations in the level-synchronous model for local synchronizations in the asynchronous model, which may result in redundant work. Instead of correcting errors introduced by asynchrony and redoing work as in KLA, in this work we control the amount of work that is redone and thus the amount of error allowed, leading to higher performance at the expense of a loss of precision. Results of an implementation of this algorithm are presented on up to 32,768 cores, showing 2.27x improvement over the exact KLA algorithm and 3.8x improvement over the level-synchronous version with minimal error on several graph inputs.

Keywords: Parallel graph algorithms · Breadth-first search · Distance query · Approximate algorithms · Asynchronous · Distributed memory

1 Introduction

Processing large-scale graphs has increasingly become a critical component in a variety of fields, from scientific computing to social analytics. Due to the ever growing size of graphs of interest, distributed and parallel algorithms are typically employed to process graphs on a large scale.

Computing shortest paths in networks is a fundamental operation that is useful for multiple reasons and many graph algorithms are built on top of shortest paths. For example, computing centrality metrics and network diameter relies on distance queries. In addition to being a building block for other algorithms, shortest path queries can be used on their own to determine connectivity and distances between particular vertices of interest. For many large real-world graphs, computing exact shortest paths is prohibitively expensive and recent work [22,27,28,30] explores efficient approximate algorithms for this problem. In unweighted graphs, an online distance query can be answered through the use of breadth-first search (BFS).

© Springer International Publishing AG 2017
C. Ding et al. (Eds.): LCPC 2016, LNCS 10136, pp. 40–54, 2017.
DOI: 10.1007/978-3-319-52709-3_4

In this work, we introduce a novel approximate parallel breadth-first search algorithm based on the k-level asynchronous [15] (KLA) paradigm. The KLA paradigm bridges level-synchronous processing [20] (based on the bulk-synchronous parallel model [34]) and asynchronous processing [26], allowing for parametric control of the amount of asynchrony from full (asynchronous) to none (level-synchronous). In a level-synchronous execution of breadth-first search, distances are correct at the end of a level, at the cost of expensive global synchronizations. On the other hand, a high amount of asynchrony in breadth-first search may lead to redundant work, as the lack of a global ordering could cause a vertex to receive many updates with smaller distances until the true breadth-first distance is discovered. Each update to the vertex's state will trigger a propagation of its new distance to its neighbors, potentially leading to all reachable vertices being reprocessed many times and negating the benefit of asynchronous processing.

Our novel algorithm controls the amount of redundant work performed by controlling how updates trigger propagation and allowing for vertices to contain some amount of error. In short, by only sending the improved values to neighbors if the change is large enough, we limit the amount of redundant work that occurs during execution. We modify the KLA breadth-first search algorithm by conditionally propagating improved values received from a neighbor update.

The contributions of this work include:

- **Approximate k-level asynchronous breadth-first search algorithm.**
  We present a new algorithm for approximate breadth-first search that trades accuracy for performance in a KLA BFS. We prove an upper bound on the error as a function of degree of approximation.
- **Implementation that achieves scalable performance.** Our implementation in the STAPL Graph Library shows an improvement of up to 2.27x over the exact KLA algorithm and 3.8x improvement over the level-synchronous version with minimal error. Results show that our technique is able to scale up to 32,768 cores.

2   Approximate Breadth-First Search

Our algorithm is implemented in the k-level asynchronous paradigm. In KLA, algorithms are expressed using two operators. The vertex operator is a fine-grained function executed on a single vertex that updates the vertex's state and issues visitations to neighboring vertices. It may spawn visitations through the use of `Visit(u, op)` or `VisitAllNeighbors(v, op)`, where u is the ID of a single neighbor and v is the ID of the vertex being processed. These visitations are encapsulated in the neighbor operator, which updates a vertex based on values received from a single neighbor.

In the exact KLA breadth-first search, skipping the application of the neighbor operator could lead to an incorrect result, but reduces the performance overhead of redundant work that is often seen in highly asynchronous algorithms. We show that the amount of error can be bounded, while improving the performance of the distance query.

2.1   Algorithmic Description

In this section, we show how to express approximate breadth-first search using the KLA paradigm. The goal is to compute, for each vertex, the distance from the vertex and the root in the breadth-first search tree. We denote this distance as $d(v)$.

> **Function** *VertexOperator(v)*
>   **if** *v.color = GREY* **then**
>   v.color = BLACK
>   VisitAllNeighbors(v, NeighborOp, v.dist+1, v.id)
>   return true
>   **else**
>   return false
>   **end**

Algorithm 1: k-level asynchronous BFS vertex operator.

Initially, all vertices except the source have distance $d_k(v) = \infty$, no parent, and color set to black. The source vertex sets its distance to 0, itself as its parent and marks itself active by setting its color to grey. Algorithm 1 shows the vertex operator that is executed on all vertices in parallel. Each vertex determines if it is active by checking if its color is set to grey. If so, it issues visitations to all of its neighbors, sending its distance plus one. The traversal is completed if all invocations of the vertex operator return false in a superstep (i.e., none of the vertices are active).

Algorithm 2 presents the neighbor operator for the exact breadth-first search algorithm. The distance and parent are updated if the incoming distance is less than the vertex's current distance. In addition, the vertex sets its color to grey, marking it as active, and returns a flag indicating that it should be revisited. In the k-level async model, if the invocation of the neighbor operator returns true, the vertex operator will be reinvoked on that vertex only if its hop-count is still in bounds of the KLA superstep. That is, if $d(v) \bmod k = 0$, then the visitation is at the edge of the superstep and thus the vertex operator will not be invoked until the start of the next superstep.

In this work, we introduce a new neighbor operator in Algorithm 3 that allows for the correction of an error and repropagation of the corrected distance under certain conditions. We use tolerance $0 \leq \tau < 1$ to denote the amount of error a vertex will allow until it propagates a smaller distance. For a visit with current distance d and better distance d_{new}, we will propagate the new distance if $(d - d_{new})/d \geq \tau$. We now need to store two distances: one that represents the current smallest distance seen and the distance of the last propagation. The last propagated distance is required as a vertex may continually improve its own distance, but it will only repropagate if a neighbor visitation contains a distance that is τ-better than its last propagated distance. By following a vertex's parent property, the algorithm also provides a path from every reachable vertex to the source, similar to the traditional version of breadth-first search. However,

Function *NeighborOperator(u, dist, parent)*

> **if** $u.dist > dist$ **then**
>> u.dist ← dist
>> u.parent ← parent
>> u.color ← GREY
>> return true
>
> **else**
>> return false
>
> **end**

Algorithm 2: Original k-level asynchronous BFS neighbor operator.

Function *ApproximateNeighborOperatorTolerance(u, dist, parent)*

> **if** $u.dist > dist$ **then**
>> u.dist = dist
>> first_time ← u.parent = none
>> better ← (u.prop - dist)/u.prop $\geq \tau$
>> **if** $first\_time \lor better$ **then**
>>> u.parent ← parent
>>> u.prop ← dist
>>> u.color ← GREY
>>> return true
>>
>> **end**
>
> **else**
>> return false
>
> **end**

Algorithm 3: Approximate k-level asynchronous BFS with tolerance neighbor operator.

these vertices may report a larger distance than the length of the discovered path, due to updates that were not propagated.

The parameter τ controls the amount of tolerated error. Note that if $\tau < 1/|V|$, then there is no error in the result and the neighbor operator is equivalent to the exact version in Algorithm 2.

2.2   Error Bounds

As the approximate breadth-first search may introduce error, we quantify the error that may be caused due to asynchronous visitations. We denote the breadth-first distance of a vertex v at the end of a KLA traversal using $d_k(v)$, where k is the level of asynchrony. Similarly, $d_0(v)$ is the true breadth-first distance for vertex v. In this section, we will show that the error of the breadth-first distance is bounded by $d_k(v) \leq d_0(v)k$.

Lemma 1. *At the end of the first KLA superstep, all reached vertices have distance $d_k(v) \leq k$.*

Proof. Assume at the end of the first superstep, there exists a vertex v with distance $d_k(v) > k$. This means that v was reached on a path from the source that has $h > k$ hops. This is not possible, as the traversal will not allow a visitation that is more than k hops away. Therefore $d_k(v) \leq k$. □

Theorem 1. *At the end of the algorithm, all reachable vertices will have distance $d_k(v) \leq ks_v$, where s_v is the superstep in which v was discovered.*

Proof. Assume that after superstep s all reached vertices will have distance $d_k(v) \leq sk$. Lemma 1 shows this holds for $s = 1$. All active vertices will issue visitations to their neighbors, traveling up to at most k hops in superstep $s + 1$. Consider a previously unreached vertex u that will be discovered in superstep $s+1$ from some vertex w that was discovered in superstep s. Vertex w was on the boundary of superstep s and has distance at most sk from the source. Therefore, $d_k(u) \leq d_k(w) + k$ because u will be discovered from a path that is up to k hops from w.

$$
\begin{aligned}
d_k(u) &\leq d_k(w) + k \\
&\leq sk + k \qquad \text{(inductive hypothesis)} \\
&\leq (s + 1)k \qquad \text{(simplification)}
\end{aligned}
$$

Through induction, $d_k(u) \leq sk$ for a vertex u discovered in superstep s. □

Lemma 2. *If there exists a path π from the source to a vertex v, then v must be discovered no later than superstep $|\pi|$.*

Proof. We will show the lemma holds by induction. If the length of path π is 1, vertex v shares an edge with the source. Then in the first superstep, the source will visit all edges and discover v.

Suppose the lemma holds for any path with length i. Let π be a path with length $|\pi| = i+1$. Then the ith vertex along the path, v_i, will have been discovered in or before the ith superstep. Now, by Algorithm 1, the vertex v_i will traverse all of its outgoing edges in or before the $(i + 1)^{th}$ superstep and discover the $(i + 1)^{th}$ vertex along the path π. This proves the lemma holds for any path π of length $i + 1$. Therefore, the lemma holds for any path π by induction. □

Lemma 3. *If there exists a path from the source to a vertex v, then v will be discovered at the latest in superstep $d_0(v)$.*

Proof. If a vertex has distance $d_0(v)$, then the shortest path π^* to v has length $|\pi^*| = d_0(v)$. By Lemma 2, this path must be discovered at the latest in superstep $d_0(v)$. □

Theorem 2. *At the end of the algorithm, all reachable vertices will have distance $d_k(v) \leq d_0(v)k$.*

Proof. By Theorem 1, $d_k(v) \leq s_v k$. We know through Lemma 3 that v will be visited by superstep $d_0(v)k$. Combining these, the approximation of the true breadth-first distance is off by at most a multiplicative factor of k: $d_0(v)k$. □

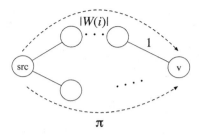

Fig. 1. Example graph showing two different paths from the source to a vertex v.

2.3   Bounds with Tolerance

When using the tolerance heuristic, a vertex with distance d will only propagate a new distance d_{new} if the following is true:

$$\frac{d - d_{new}}{d} \geq \tau \tag{1}$$

In the exact k-level asynchronous algorithm, all vertices that are distance $d_0(v)$ away from the source will be visited in superstep $\frac{d_0(v)}{k}$. However, since we allow some bounded error, it is possible for a vertex to be visited in the $\frac{d_k(v)}{k}$ superstep, which may be later than its original visitation. In addition, all edges that are traversed through visitations will be visited in the same superstep in which the visit was issued. However, not all visitations trigger a propagation of a better distance to the vertex's neighbors.

We will denote the discovered distance of a vertex using the tolerance heuristic as $d^\tau(v)$. In this section, we will prove that by using this heuristic, if a vertex v is reached at the end of the first superstep, then $d^\tau(v) \leq \frac{\sum_{j=0}^{d_0(v)-1}(1-\tau)^j}{(1-\tau)^{d_0(v)}}$.

Lemma 4. *All vertices with a true distance of 1 will propagate a distance that is at most $\frac{1}{1-\tau}$.*

Proof. Because the distance from the source to v is 1, the shortest path $\pi^* =<(src, v) >$ will be processed eventually in the traversal. Consider that vertex v is discovered along a path π from the source and marks itself as distance $|\pi|$. Once the path π^* is processed, v will not propagate its distance if $\frac{|\pi|-1}{|\pi|} < \tau$. Simplifying, the length of the path is $|\pi| < \frac{1}{1-\tau}$. Therefore, v will propagate a distance that is at most $\frac{1}{1-\tau}$, otherwise a repropagation will be triggered. $\square$

Theorem 3. *At the end of the first superstep, all reachable vertices will propagate a distance at most $\frac{\sum_{j=0}^{d_0(v)-1}(1-\tau)^j}{(1-\tau)^{d_0(v)}}$.*

Proof. Let $W(i) = \frac{\sum_{j=0}^{i-1}(1-\tau)^j}{(1-\tau)^i}$ denote the length of the longest path that will be tolerated by a vertex of true distance i without triggering a propagation.

Lemma 4 shows that this holds for vertices with true distance 1. Assume that this property holds for vertices of distance i.

Let v be a vertex with true distance $i + 1$ discovered along some path π. By definition, v will not repropagate upon seeing a path π_{new} if the following holds:

$$\frac{|\pi| - |\pi_{new}|}{|\pi|} < \tau \tag{2}$$

The shortest path π_{new} that could be discovered without repropagating could have length $|\pi_{new}| = W(i) + 1$. Any path longer than π_{new} would have triggered a repropagation along the path, by definition of $W(i)$. See Fig. 1 for an example. The vertex will not propagate the better distance if the threshold is not met:

$$\frac{|\pi| - \left(\frac{\sum_{j=0}^{i-1}(1-\tau)^j}{(1-\tau)^i} + 1\right)}{|\pi|} < \tau \tag{3}$$

Written in terms of $|\pi|$, this can be simplified:

$$
\begin{aligned}
|\pi| &< \frac{\frac{\sum_{j=0}^{i-1}(1-\tau)^j}{(1-\tau)^i} + 1}{1-\tau} \\
&= \frac{\sum_{j=0}^{i-1}(1-\tau)^j}{(1-\tau)^{i+1}} + \frac{(1-\tau)^i}{(1-\tau)^{i+1}} \\
&= \frac{\sum_{j=0}^{i}(1-\tau)^j}{(1-\tau)^{i+1}} \\
&= W(i+1) \qquad\qquad\qquad\qquad \text{(definition of } W(i))
\end{aligned}
$$

The bound therefore holds for vertices with true distance $i + 1$ and thus all vertices by induction.   □

As shown in Algorithm 3, a vertex always updates its distance upon seeing a better distance, without necessarily propagating it. This means that a vertex's discovered distance is at most its propagated distance. That is, all vertices discovered in the first superstep will have distance at most $d^\tau(v) \le \frac{\sum_{j=0}^{d_0(v)-1}(1-\tau)^j}{(1-\tau)^{d_0(v)}}$.

Note that in the case of $\tau = 0$, $d^\tau(v) = \sum_{j=0}^{d_0(v)-1} 1/1 = d_0(v)$. Therefore, $\tau = 0$ is equivalent to the exact algorithm.

2.4   Combined Bounds

By the definition of KLA, the maximum distance that any vertex can be assigned in the first superstep is k. Therefore, for a vertex of true distance i, its discovered distance can be at most k. $W(i)$ is the length of the longest path that can be tolerated by a vertex of true distance i without propagation. However, if this path is longer than k, then it will not be visited and thus the worst case distance will be less than $W(i)$. Now, solving $W(i) = k$ for i only considering $\tau > 0$ because, as shown above, there is no error for $\tau = 0$, we find:

$$k = W(i) = \frac{\sum_{j=0}^{i-1}(1-\tau)^{j}}{(1-\tau)^{i}}$$

$$= \frac{\frac{1-(1-\tau)^{i}}{1-(1-\tau)}}{(1-\tau)^{i}} \qquad \text{(Partial geometric sum, where } 1 - \tau > 0)$$

$$k\tau = \frac{1-(1-\tau)^{i}}{(1-\tau)^{i}}$$

$$k\tau + 1 = \frac{1}{(1-\tau)^{i}}$$

$$i = \log(\frac{1}{k\tau+1})/\log(1-\tau)$$

If a vertex v has at most true distance i, then its discovered distance is bounded by $W(i)$. However, if the true distance is greater than $\log(\frac{1}{k\tau+1})/\log(1-\tau)$, then the vertex's discovered distance can be no more than k, because the path that causes the bound of $W(i)$ is no longer reachable in k hops.

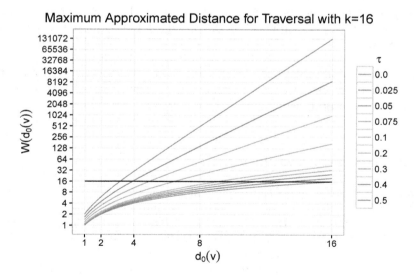

Fig. 2. Computed distance $d_{k}^{\tau}(v)$ vs actual distance $d_{0}(v)$ for multiple τ and fixed k.

Therefore, if a vertex v is reached in the first superstep, the maximum distance $d_k^\tau(v)$ that v can have is:

$$d_k^\tau(v) \leq \begin{cases} d_0(v) & \tau = 0 \\ \frac{\sum_{j=0}^{d_0(v)-1}(1-\tau)^j}{(1-\tau)^{d_0(v)}} & d_0(v) \leq \log(\frac{1}{k\tau+1})/\log(1-\tau) \\ k & otherwise \end{cases}$$

Figure 2 presents the trend of this function for various values of τ and a fixed value $k = 16$. We see that $W(i)$ can grow very rapidly, but is bounded by at most k. For $\tau = 0$, the approximated distance is the same as the exact distance.

Using the same technique as Theorem 2, we can show that error will accumulate across supersteps in an additive way. Therefore, the total distance that a vertex at the end of the algorithm will have is $d_k^\tau(v) \leq d_0(v)k$.

3   Implementation

We implemented the approximate breadth-first traversal in the STAPL Graph Library (SGL) [14–16]. SGL is a generic parallel graph library that provides a high-level framework that abstracts the details of the underlying distributed environment. It consists of a parallel graph container (`pGraph`), a collection of parallel graph algorithms, and a graph paradigm that supports level-synchronous and asynchronous execution of algorithms.

The `pGraph` container is a distributed data store built using the `pContainer` framework (PCF) [31] provided by the Standard Template Adaptive Parallel Library (STAPL) [10]. It provides a shared-object view of graph elements across a distributed-memory machine. The STAPL Runtime System (STAPL-RTS) and its communication library ARMI (Adaptive Remote Method Invocation) use the remote method invocation (RMI) abstraction to allow asynchronous communication on shared objects while hiding the underlying communication layer (e.g. MPI, OpenMP).

4   Experimental Evaluation

We evaluated our technique on two different systems.

CRAY-XK7. This is a Cray XK7m-200 system which consists of twenty-four compute nodes with AMD Opteron 6272 Interlagos 16-core processors at 2.1 GHz. Twelve of the nodes are single socket with 32 GB of memory, and the remaining twelve are dual socket nodes with 64 GB of memory.

IBM-BG/Q. This is an IBM BG/Q system available at Lawrence Livermore National Laboratory. IBM-BG/Q has 24,576 nodes, each node with a 16-core IBM PowerPC A2 processor clocked at 1.6 GHz and 16 GB of memory. The compiler used was `gcc` 4.8.4.

The code was compiled with maximum optimization levels (`-DNDEBUG -O3`). Each experiment has been repeated 32 times and we present the mean execution time along with a 95 % confidence interval using the t-distribution. We also measure the relative error of a vertex's distance, where error is defined as $(d_k^\tau(v) - d_0(v))/d_0(v)$. We show the mean relative error across all vertices.

4.1 Breadth-First Search

In this section, we evaluate our algorithm on various graphs in terms of execution time and relative error.

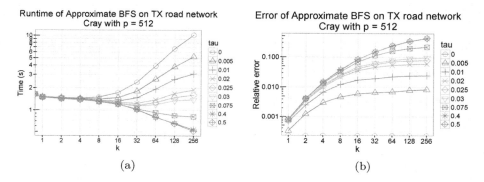

Fig. 3. Approximate BFS with tolerance heuristic on TX road network with 512 cores on Cray evaluating (a) runtime and (b) error.

In Fig. 3, we evaluate both the execution time and error on the Texas road network from the SNAP [2] collection on 512 cores on the CRAY-XK7 platform. This graph has 1.3 million vertices and 1.9 million edges. As expected, a lower value of τ results in slower execution time as more repropagations occur with lower tolerance. In the extreme case of $\tau = 0$, every message that contains a better distance is propagated and thus it is the same as the exact version of the algorithm. Figure 4(a) shows the number of repropagations that occur as we vary the level of asynchrony and τ. As expected, higher values of k result in many more visitations, while higher τ triggers relatively less visitations. This behavior results in the corresponding time and error tradeoffs we observe in Fig. 3.

Figure 4(b) shows speedup vs error on the Texas road network. Speedup is defined as the ratio of the exact algorithm's execution time with the fastest k and the approximate algorithm's execution time. If an application is willing to tolerate error in the result, we see that we are able to achieve 2.6x speedup for an execution with 42 % error.

Figure 5 shows that we see similar benefit using the road network graph on the IBM-BG/Q platform for a fixed value of k. We see that the exact version of the KLA breadth-first search ($\tau = 0$) is slower than the level synchronous version, and the approximate version is faster than both. At 32,768 cores, the approximate version is 2.27x faster with around 17 % mean error.

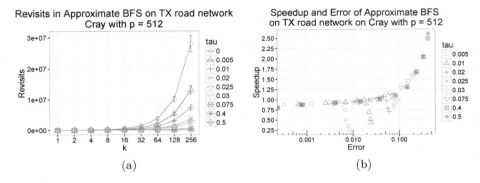

Fig. 4. Approximate BFS with tolerance heuristic on TX road network with 512 cores on CRAY-XK7 evaluating (a) number of repropagations that occur during traversal and (b) speedup over the fastest k.

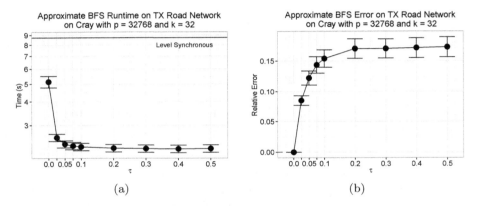

Fig. 5. Strong scaling of approximate BFS on IBM-BG/Q platform evaluating sensitivity of (a) runtime and (b) error.

Random Neighborhood. We next evaluate the algorithm on a deformable graph that allows us to vary the diameter from very large (circular chain) to very small (random graph). This results in graphs with different diameters by allowing any given vertex to randomly select and connect only to its $\pm m$-closest neighboring vertices. This is similar to the approach described by Watts and Strogatz [35] where the rewiring mechanism is limited in terms of distance.

Figure 6 shows the performance and error of an execution of this algorithm on a random neighborhood graph on 512 cores on the CRAY-XK7 platform. As shown, we see a benefit for using the approximate version for higher values of k. At a k of 512, the approximate algorithm has a 1.12x speedup over the fastest exact version but only has an error of 0.3 %. Because this graph does not have as much opportunity for wasted work as the road network, the benefits

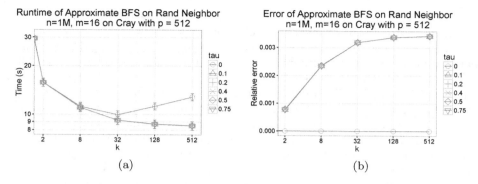

Fig. 6. Approximate BFS with tolerance heuristic on random neighborhood network ($n = 1,000,000$ and $m = 16$) with 512 cores on CRAY-XK7.

of approximation are not as pronounced, but we still see an improvement in performance with negligible error.

5 Related Work

Graph Processing and Breadth-First Search. The vertex-centric programming model, popularized by Pregel [20] and its open-source equivalent Giraph [3], has become a standard in parallel graph processing. The so-called *think like a vertex* paradigm allows algorithm writers to express their computation in terms of vertex programs, which describe the operations to be executed on a single vertex and its incident edges. Whereas Pregel's model is push-based, GraphLab [19] offers a pull-based model based on the three operators gather-apply-scatter.

Many general purpose frameworks and runtimes [12,21,23] for graph processing have been proposed and are used in practice. Galois is an amorphous data parallel processing framework with support for many vertex-centric paradigms [24]. Grappa [23] is a distributed shared memory framework designed specifically for data-intensive applications. Graph-based domain-specific libraries [17] exist and have been shown to perform well in practice.

Many techniques have been proposed specifically to improve breadth-first search. Most notably, the Graph 500 benchmark [1] has sparked much research into improving [8,9] breadth-first search on scale-free networks for distributed-memory architectures. A hybrid top-down bottom-up breadth-first search was presented in [6] that shows large improvement on scale-free networks.

Approximation. Decades of research exist for efficiently approximating graph features, including diameter [11], neighborhoods [25] and triangles [7]. In this work, we focus on single-source distance queries for unweighted graphs.

In [29], the authors propose automatic synthesis of approximate graph programs through several auto-approximation techniques. Our work is similar to the task skipping approach where inputs from neighbors are ignored under certain conditions. However, the authors primarily focus on single-core processing while we consider distributed-memory parallel algorithms.

There has been a large body of work to approximate the all-pairs shortest path problem for weighted graphs through the use of distance oracles [4,13,32] ([30] provides a comprehensive survey). An $O(\min{(n^2, kmn^{1/k})})$-time algorithm for computing a $2k - 1$ approximation has been presented in [5]. In [27], a distributed-memory algorithm using local betweenness is presented. We focus our work on online queries of unweighted shortest paths from a single source.

Ullman and Yannakakis [33] show a high-probability PRAM algorithm for approximating a breadth-first search tree by performing multiple traversals from landmark vertices. This was extended to weighted graphs [18] on a concurrent-write PRAM using a hop-limited traversal, similar to the k-level async model. A recent work [22] introduces a $(1 + o(1))$-approximation for weighted graphs using multiple rounds of an exact BFS.

To the best of our knowledge, our approach is the first to incorporate asynchrony into the approximation and leverage the benefit of asynchronous processing for performance.

6   Conclusion

In this paper, we presented a novel parallel algorithm for approximating breadth-first distances in a graph. We provide bounds for the error of such an approach and show that experimentally, the observed errors are much lower than the theoretical bounds. Our implementation shows substantial benefit in some cases with only minor losses in precision of the exact answer.

Acknowledgments. We would like to thank Daniel Latypov for help with aspects of the proof. We would also like to thank our anonymous reviewers.

This research supported in part by NSF awards CNS-0551685, CCF 0702765, CCF-0833199, CCF-1439145, CCF-1423111, CCF-0830753, IIS-0916053, IIS-0917266, EFRI-1240483, RI-1217991, by NIH NCI R25 CA090301-11, and by DOE awards DE-AC02-06CH11357, DE-NA0002376, B575363. This research used resources of the National Energy Research Scientific Computing Center, which is supported by the Office of Science of the U.S. Department of Energy under Contract No. DE-AC02-05CH11231.

References

1. The graph 500 list (2011). http://www.graph500.org
2. Stanford large network dataset collection (2013). http://snap.stanford.edu/data/index.html
3. Avery, C.: Giraph: large-scale graph processing infrastructure on hadoop. In: Hadoop Summit (2011)
4. Baswana, S., Kavitha, T.: Faster algorithms for all-pairs approximate shortest paths in undirected graphs. SIAM J. Comput. **39**(7), 2865–2896 (2010)
5. Baswana, S., Sen, S.: Approximate distance oracles for unweighted graphs in expected O(n2) time. ACM Trans. Algorithms **2**(4), 557–577 (2006)

6. Beamer, S., Asanović, K., Patterson, D.: Direction-optimizing breadth-first search. In: Proceedings of the International Conference on High Performance Computing, Networking, Storage and Analysis, SC 2012, pp. 12:1–12:10. IEEE Computer Society Press, Los Alamitos (2012)

7. Becchetti, L., Boldi, P., Castillo, C., Gionis, A.: Efficient algorithms for large-scale local triangle counting. ACM Trans. Knowl. Discov. Data **4**(3), 13:1–13:28 (2010)

8. Buluç, A., Beamer, S., Madduri, K., Asanović, K., Patterson, D.: Distributed-memory breadth-first search on massive graphs. In: Bader, D. (ed.) Parallel Graph Algorithms. CRC Press (2015)

9. Buluç, A., Madduri, K.: Parallel breadth-first search on distributed memory systems. In: Proceedings of 2011 International Conference for High Performance Computing, Networking, Storage and Analysis, SC 2011, pp. 65:1–65:12. ACM, New York (2011)

10. Buss, A.A., Harshvardhan, Papadopoulos, I., Pearce, O., Smith, T.G., Tanase, G., Thomas, N., Xu, X., Bianco, M., Amato, N.M., Rauchwerger, L.: STAPL: standard template adaptive parallel library. In: Proceedings of SYSTOR 2010: The 3rd Annual Haifa Experimental Systems Conference, Haifa, Israel, 24–26 May 2010, pp. 1–10. ACM, New York (2010)

11. Ceccarello, M., Pietracaprina, A., Pucci, G., Upfal, E.: Space and time efficient parallel graph decomposition, clustering, and diameter approximation. In: Proceedings of the 27th ACM Symposium on Parallelism in Algorithms and Architectures, SPAA 2015, pp. 182–191. ACM, New York (2015)

12. Gregor, D., Lumsdaine, A.: The parallel BGL: a generic library for distributed graph computations. In: Parallel Object-Oriented Scientific Computing (POOSC), July 2005

13. Gubichev, A., Bedathur, S., Seufert, S., Weikum, G.: Fast and accurate estimation of shortest paths in large graphs. In: Proceedings of the 19th ACM International Conference on Information and Knowledge Management, CIKM 2010, pp. 499–508. ACM, New York (2010)

14. Harshvardhan, Fidel, A., Amato, N.M., Rauchwerger, L.: The STAPL parallel graph library. In: Kasahara, H., Kimura, K. (eds.) LCPC 2012. LNCS, vol. 7760, pp. 46–60. Springer, Berlin Heidelberg (2012)

15. Harshvardhan, Fidel, A., Amato, N.M., Rauchwerger, L.: KLA: a new algorithmic paradigm for parallel graph computations. In: Proceedings of the International Conference on Parallel Architecture and Compilation Techniques (PACT), PACT 2014, pp. 27–38. ACM, New York (2014). Conference Best Paper Award

16. Harshvardhan, Fidel, A., Amato, N.M., Rauchwerger, L.: An algorithmic approach to communication reduction in parallel graph algorithms. In: Proceedings of the International Conference Parallel Architecture and Compilation Techniques (PACT), PACT 2015, pp. 201–212. IEEE, San Francisco (2015). Finalist for Conference Best Paper Award

17. Hong, S., Chafi, H., Sedlar, E., Olukotun, K.: Green-Marl: a DSL for easy and efficient graph analysis. In: Proceedings of the Seventeenth International Conference on Architectural Support for Programming Languages and Operating Systems, ASPLOS 2012, pp. 349–362. ACM, New York (2012)

18. Klein, P.N., Subramanian, S.: A randomized parallel algorithm for single-source shortest paths. J. Algorithms **25**(2), 205–220 (1997)

19. Low, Y., Bickson, D., Gonzalez, J., Guestrin, C., Kyrola, A., Hellerstein, J.M.: Distributed graphlab: a framework for machine learning and data mining in the cloud. Proc. VLDB Endow. **5**(8), 716–727 (2012)

20. Malewicz, G., Austern, M.H., Bik, A.J., Dehnert, J.C., Horn, I., Leiser, N., Czajkowski, G.: Pregel: a system for large-scale graph processing. In: Proceedings of the 2010 International Conference on Management of Data, SIGMOD 2010, pp. 135–146. ACM, New York (2010)
21. Méndez-Lojo, M., Nguyen, D., Prountzos, D., Sui, X., Hassaan, M.A., Kulkarni, M., Burtscher, M., Pingali, K.: Structure-driven optimizations for amorphous data-parallel programs. In: Proceedings of the 15th ACM SIGPLAN Symposium on Principles and Practice of Parallel Programming, PPoPP 2010, pp. 3–14. ACM, New York (2010)
22. Nanongkai, D.: Distributed approximation algorithms for weighted shortest paths. In: Proceedings of the 46th Annual ACM Symposium on Theory of Computing, STOC 2014, pp. 565–573. ACM, New York (2014)
23. Nelson, J., Holt, B., Myers, B., Briggs, P., Kahan, S., Ceze, L., Oskin, M.: Grappa: a latency-tolerant runtime for large-scale irregular application. In: WRSC 2014, April 2014
24. Nguyen, D., Lenharth, A., Pingali, K.: A lightweight infrastructure for graph analytics. In: Proceedings of the Twenty-Fourth ACM Symposium on Operating Systems Principles, SOSP 2013, pp. 456–471. ACM, New York (2013)
25. Palmer, C.R., Gibbons, P.B., Faloutsos, C.: ANF: afast and scalable tool for data mining in massive graphs. In: Proceedings of the Eighth ACM SIGKDD International Conference on Knowledge Discovery and Data Mining, KDD 2002, pp. 81–90. ACM, New York (2002)
26. Pearce, R.A., Gokhale, M., Amato, N.M.: Multithreaded asynchronous graph traversal for in-memory and semi-external memory. In: Conference on High Performance Computing Networking, Storage and Analysis, SC 2010, New Orleans, LA, USA, 13–19 November 2010, pp. 1–11 (2010)
27. Qi, Z., Xiao, Y., Shao, B., Wang, H.: Toward a distance oracle for billion-node graphs. Proc. VLDB Endow. **7**(1), 61–72 (2013)
28. Qiao, M., Cheng, H., Chang, L., Yu, J.X.: Approximate shortest distance computing: a query-dependent local landmark scheme. IEEE Trans. Knowl. Data Eng. **26**(1), 55–68 (2014)
29. Shang, Z., Yu, J.X.: Auto-approximation of graph computing. Proc. VLDB Endow. **7**(14), 1833–1844 (2014)
30. Sommer, C.: Shortest-path queries in static networks. ACM Comput. Surv. **46**(4), 45:1–45:31 (2014)
31. Tanase, G., Buss, A.A., Fidel, A., Harshvardhan, Papadopoulos, I., Pearce, O., Smith, T.G., Thomas, N., Xu, X., Mourad, N., Vu, J., Bianco, M., Amato, N.M., Rauchwerger, L.: The STAPL parallel container framework. In: Proceedings of the 16th ACM SIGPLAN Symposium on Principles and Practice of Parallel Programming, PPOPP 2011, San Antonio, TX, USA, 12–16 February 2011, pp. 235–246 (2011)
32. Thorup, M., Zwick, U.: Approximate distance oracles. In: Proceedings of the Thirty-Third Annual ACM Symposium on Theory of Computing, STOC 2001, pp. 183–192. ACM, New York (2001)
33. Ullman, J., Yannakakis, M.: High-probability parallel transitive closure algorithms. In: Proceedings of the Second Annual ACM Symposium on Parallel Algorithms and Architectures, SPAA 1990, pp. 200–209. ACM, New York (1990)
34. Valiant, L.: Bridging model for parallel computation. Comm. ACM **33**(8), 103–111 (1990)
35. Watts, D.J., Strogatz, S.H.: Collective dynamics of 'small-world' networks. In: Nature, pp. 440–442 (1998)

Energy Avoiding Matrix Multiply

Kelly Livingston[1(✉)], Aaron Landwehr[1], José Monsalve[1],
Stéphane Zuckerman[1], Benoît Meister[2], and Guang R. Gao[1]

[1] Computer Architecture and Parallel Systems Laboratory,
Electrical and Computer Engineering Department,
University of Delaware, Newark, DE, USA
{kelly,aron,josem,szuckerm}@udel.edu, ggao.capsl@gmail.com
[2] Reservoir Labs, 632 Broadway, New York,
NY 10012, USA
meister@reservoir.com

Abstract. As multi and many core chips steadily increase their core count, we observe a phenomenon we call memory hierarchy capacity per capita inversion. To overcome this inversion while remaining energy-efficient, we present a dynamic tiling scheme which we apply to solve the classic Matrix Multiply algorithm. The tiling scheme follows a Hilbert-Inspired Curve strategy to minimize data movement energy, while still allowing for slack and variance within the computation and memory usage of a chip. Our algorithm is energy-conscious: it uses a machine model which does not require symmetric memory (in size or addressing) anywhere in the hierarchy. It only concerns itself with the energy consumption of all memories. This property makes it very robust to chip variance and allows all possible resources to be utilized, which is necessary for future near-threshold voltage designs. Initial results, obtained on a future many-core simulator targeting the Traleika Glacier architecture, give initial estimates of memory reads and writes to all parts of the chip as well as relative energy consumption.

1 Beyond Traditional Tiling: Targeting Exascale

Matrix Multiply (MM) has been studied for decades. Early works presented algorithmic improvements for asymptotic reduction of operations of MM to $O(N^{log_2(7)})$ by trading multiplications for simpler addition and applying recursively [21]. More recent work has looked at communication avoidance by seeking to minimize bytes read per floating point operation and attempting to reach the known lower bound which can provide more locality and less communication [2,11,17]. Other previous works have taken the traditional algorithm and looked within the context of architecture and memory subsystems.

© Springer International Publishing AG 2017
C. Ding et al. (Eds.): LCPC 2016, LNCS 10136, pp. 55–70, 2017.
DOI: 10.1007/978-3-319-52709-3_5

Projects like ATLAS [23] looked to apply auto-tuning techniques so that optimal tiling is created for each memory level, which produced excellent results. As multicore solutions evolved, these solutions and others [1, 10] evolved to better leverage parallelism and solve problems that arise from shared cache structures. Traditionally, lower level data in a cache required replication to higher levels of caches. While we see efforts to advance the efficiency of complex cache hierarchies to loosen this constraint [18] the principle of having larger cache capacity at levels farther from the processor is still true today. However, we see a shift for future architectures starting with GPUs.

We are targeting the Traleika Glacier (TG) architecture, a prototype design chip for exploring Near Threshold Voltage (NTV) computing and an extension of the Runnemede many-core processor architecture [6]. TG is highly hierarchical: execution engines are grouped into blocks; blocks are grouped into units; and units are grouped under a single chip as shown

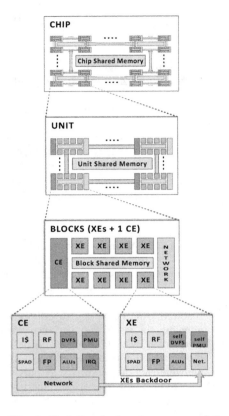

Fig. 1. Traleika glacier strawman architecture

in Fig. 1. The sizes of memory are very unconventional as well. Figure 2 compares the memory hierarchy of a CPU, the 10 core Intel Xeon Processor E5-2470 v2 with a GPU, the NVidia Tesla K80, and TG [6]. As the figure illustrates, for

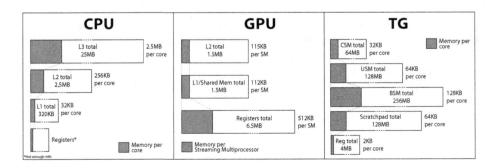

Fig. 2. Graphic representation of capacity per capita inversion

chip designs with dense amounts of compute, the higher level memory would occupy far too much area on die and thus is reduced. This reduction creates a *memory capacity per capita inversion* (CPCI) for the levels of the memory hierarchy. Unfortunately, this inversion violates many of the assumptions made in classical cache analysis algorithms. And it is difficult to analyze the chip as a distributed memory machine since there is still significant locality associated with every memory in the hierarchy. Thus, TG supports configuring all levels of memory as scratchpad or potentially as incoherent cache [16] in order to research the best way to utilize the hierarchy. Our solution for TG similarly follows how GPUs, leveraging the shared memory, permanently store results in the lower levels of memory, leaving the higher level cache for read-only accesses of A and B [19,20,22]. Further, this trend can extend every level of programmer controlled shared memory in a CPCI hierarchy. This opens many possibilities for unique and interesting techniques for utilizing this space including tiling which this paper will leverage.

Section 2 extends tiling, specifically looking at tiling for energy efficiency. Section 3 introduces a novel method for dynamically generating tile shapes using a hilbert inspired ordering. Section 4 combines these two techniques to provide a methodology for creating a tiling scheme for any memory layout and explain how to use asynchronous tasks to build a robust MM algorithm. Section 5 provides specific details about our experimental testbed using the FSIM simulator and the results.

2   Energy Efficient Tiling

2.1   Tiling Principles—The Matrix Multiplication Example

At the core of numerous numerical packages such as LU factorization, MM is an ideal candidate for tiling. In fact, it is a common benchmark or the core routine of benchmarks used to test hardware due to its large reuse of data which can test memory and caching subsystems. It can be computed with a triple nested loop, making the asymptotic computational complexity $O(N^3)$. In this paper, MM is defined as $C_{M,N} = A_{M,K} \times B_{K,N}$, $A, B, C \in \mathbb{R}^2$, $M, N, K \in \mathbb{N}^*$.

There are three traditional ways to tile MM: inner product (*i.e.*, dot product), outer product (*i.e.*, cross product), and a combination of the former two. Inner product ordering reduces accesses to C; outer product ordering reduces accesses to A and B, but requires additional local memory and synchronization. A hybrid combination will perform a trade-off to reuse A, B, and C. Traditionally, a new tile, static in both size and shape, will be used for each level of memory since more temporary space is available at farther memory levels and thus can provide more reuse of A, B, and C. The remainder of this section introduces a novel hybrid method of distributing a tile amongst multiple levels of a CPCI hiearchy with a dynamic shape that can better utilize memory and reduce data movement.

2.2 Energy Efficient Tiling

As previously mentioned, outer product tiling is the only way to provide reuse of the A and B matrix at the expense of more temporary storage and strict synchronization. The resulting energy consumption during computing can be divided up into energy to do compute and energy to move data. As we shrink lithography processes more, data movement and leakage will begin to dominate energy consumption [5]. Since leakage occurs regardless of executing tasks, an algorithm must keep all processors busy with little scheduling downtime. Thus, we also rely on asynchronous fine-grained scheduling in order to keep processors busy where synchronization is occuring, and double buffering to create slack in the synchronization, in way similar to Garcia et al. [14]. For reducing data movement, we propose a method to model the energy consumed by a tiling scheme to quickly determine a near-optimal tile size for a given amount of memory. This method creates a machine model using a few assumptions:

1. Accessing data (read or write) from any kind of memory can be approximated as a particular static cost composed of dynamic access, leakage, and communication energy for both a farther memory and a closer memory.
2. The static cost is the average for all the values of that memory level regardless of variances in location, temperature, or circuit performance.
3. The shared memory structure is physically near all neighbors and the distance travelled dominates the static energy cost function.

The total energy consumed for a subtiling according to these assumptions is modelled in Eq. 1. E is the static energy cost per access to either a memory higher (HM) in both capacity and access energy or a lower memory (LM) in which we are tiling. Matrices are $A_{M,K}$ and $B_{K,N}$ in HM with sub-tiles in LM with dimensions $m \times n$ for outer product and k for inner product.

$$HM_{Total} = 2MN \cdot E_{HM} + \left(\frac{NMK}{n} + \frac{NMK}{m} \right) \cdot E_{HM}$$
$$LM_{Total} = \frac{MN}{mn} \cdot \frac{K}{k}(2 + 2k) \cdot mn \cdot E_{LM} \qquad (1)$$
$$E_{Total} = HM_{Total} + LM_{Total}$$

In the HM energy consumption, every C result is read and written once because of the inner product ordering of the tile. m and n accesses for the A and B tiles are reduced by using outer product ordering of the smaller subtile. These reductions require increases in access to the lower memory (LM). First, a subtile must read in a partial sum from the LM subtile, then read k values from the A input buffer and k values from the B input buffer, perform k computes, and finally write back the partial sum to the result subtile. This operation is performed for the $m \cdot n$ values for each result tile every $\frac{K}{k}$ synchronization points at the energy cost of LM. Then the final results are written back out to HM, and the procedure will be repeated for the $\frac{MN}{mn}$ number of result tiles needed to complete the matrix in HM. To optimize the energy consumed by data movement, we make several changes of variables and a memory constraint. Let $R = \frac{E_{HM}}{E_{LM}}$ define the ratio of energy consumption from higher to lower memory, and let $S = \frac{m}{n}$ define the ratio of the longest side to the shortest side of the subtile (for this derivation, we assume m is longer). When $S = 1$, the tile is square, and as the tile becomes more rectangular, the squareness factor increases. Equation 1 can then be simplified to Eq. 2.

$$E_{Total} = E_{LM} \cdot \left(MNK \cdot \left(\frac{2}{k} + 2 \right) + \frac{(1+S) \cdot MNK}{Sn} \cdot R + 2MNR \right) \quad (2)$$

Next, we make a memory constraint and thus define Q as the quantity of memory available for tiling in LM. We also will constrain our equation to a tiling scheme which will double buffer the A and B input vectors in order to loosen synchronization requirements which results in a memory constraint definition in Eq. 3.

$$Q = Sn^2 + (1+S) \cdot 2kn \qquad \rightarrow \qquad k = \frac{Q - Sn^2}{(1+S) \cdot 2n} \quad (3)$$

Substituting k in our original expression and simplifying, we derive the total energy consumed as a function of higher tile dimensions, ratios, quantity of memory, and a single variable n to define the subtiling in Eq. 4.

$$E_{Total} = (1+S) \cdot \frac{4Sn^2 + (Q - Sn^2) \cdot R}{(Q - Sn^2) \cdot Sn} \cdot MNK \cdot E_{LM} + (2MNK + 2MNR) \cdot E_{LM} \quad (4)$$

And lastly to find the minimum energy, we differentiate and set to 0 in Eq. 5. Solving the quadratic for n^2 we obtain the final equation, Eq. 6.

$$\frac{dE_{Total}}{dn} = 0 = -1 \cdot \frac{((1+S) \cdot (Q^2 R - 2QS \cdot (R+2)n^2 + n^4 \cdot (R-4) \cdot S^2)}{Sn^2 \cdot (Q - Sn^2)^2} \cdot MNK \cdot E_{LM} \quad (5)$$

The proper amount of memory that should be dedicated to the outer product result tile is a function of the energy access ratio between HM and LM regardless of the shape of the tile. We denote this function as the *fill factor*: it is designated as FF in Eq. 6. It is important to understand that this model is based on the three assumptions where the energy is static, which is not necessarily true. Where the inner product length is extremely short, there will be potential startup overheads that are not amortized such that the energy factor does not properly relate to the real energy cost. Similarly, in the case where the inner product is very long due to a low fill factor, the bandwidth requirements will increase to the HM which typically requires more energy per operation when accessed at higher bandwidths. Thus, this model should only be utilized as a first order approximation strategy for an overall tiling scheme.

$$Sn^2 = Q \left(\frac{(R+2) - \sqrt{8R+4}}{R-4} \right)$$

$$FF = \begin{cases} \frac{(R+2) - \sqrt{8R+4}}{R-4} & R \neq 4 \\ \frac{1}{3} & R = 4 \end{cases} \quad (6)$$

Other limits and checks should be imposed as well to ensure this is the optimal tiling. One such requirement is that $k \geq 1$ and $n \geq 1$ can be violated by the non-discrete fill factor calculation and by using Eqs. 3 and 6, additional constraints to the tiling shown in Eq. 7 can be added to make sure enough memory is available.

$$1 \leq \frac{Q - Sn^2}{(1 + S) \cdot 2n} \qquad \rightarrow \qquad Q \geq \frac{4(S + 1)^2 FF}{S(FF - 1)^2} \qquad (7)$$

Lastly, we previously defined S as $\frac{m}{n}$, where m and n are sides of a full rectangle tile. S' is defined as an imperfectly filled tile which contains work equivalent to S. To do this, the outer product work of the partial tile and the A and B input buffer width requirements of the partial tile are matched to determine what the full tile equivalent would be. After simplification and derivation, it yields Eq. 8.

$$S' = \frac{Inputs^2 - 2Work + Inputs\sqrt{Inputs^2 - 4Work}}{2Work} \qquad (8)$$

...with $Work = Sn^2$, and $Inputs = (1 + S)n$. We will see in future sections how these constraints and S' can be applied to coarsen tiles and lower runtime overhead, and still ensure that sufficient memory is left for input buffers.

3   Hilbert Inspired Global Layout

Beyond the mathematical modelling used to obtain basic rectangular tiling to assign the proper amounts of A, B, and C tiles in memory level (in the abstract sense), we need an automatic method for explicitly aggregating tiles which creates a tile shape that has the least projected surface area for both dimensions (thus a low S'). Explicit aggregation is important since recursive implicit aggregation like in cache-oblivious algorithms

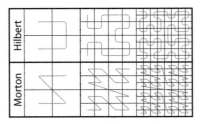

Fig. 3. Order 1 through 3 Hilbert and Morton curves

would fail to expand memory consumption in the lower memories. Our method must also be able to adapt to any memory layout, and be robust for any problem dimension. This makes a space filling curve an excellent candidate since these curves map a higher order space into a one dimensional space perfect for linearly enumerating as asynchronous tasks while also ensuring a good amount of locality. Some space-filling curves like Morton curves are computationally very inexpensive, but they have unbounded Hölder continuity and thus if used recursively could lead to large jumps within the matrix. Better candidates are Peano or Hilbert curves. Figure 3 provides examples of Hilbert and Morton curves.

Once the requirement to replicate data down a cache-like hierarchy is removed, the freedom to pin tiles anywhere in the hierarchy is possible. However, there is no obvious strategy to get the best layout. We present a data layout and an asynchronous scheduling technique which maximizes memory utilization, adapts to different memory sizes, preserves locality even during dynamic throughput changes in processors, and is based on energy optimal tiling principles. This produces tiles in certain memory locations in the method shown in Fig. 8. In order to achieve the properties described, the aggregations are not perfectly square or perfectly filled, which will incur some performance penalty that must be quantified before describing our curve technique.

3.1 Measuring S' Empirically

Hungershöfer and Wierum [15] show that for all sections of a Morton and a Hilbert curve, Hilbert curves have slightly lower average surface area to volume but also contain a higher worst case surface area to volume ratio.

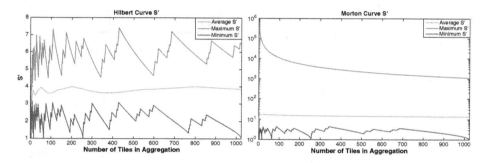

Fig. 4. S': Equivalent full tile aspect ratio matching work: inputs of a partial tile

Figure 4 shows our calculations for worst case, average, and minimum S' values for every possible aggregation that follows the curve order for each curve length using a 1024×1024 Morton and Hilbert curves. For S', the Hilbert curve outperforms Morton by a factor of four on average and has a bounded maximum below 8 whereas the Morton curve produces large maximum aspect ratios. This is because S' is more related to projected surface areas than standard surface areas, giving an even larger penalty to Morton curves and making the choice of Hilbert inspired curves as the most reasonable choice.

3.2 Decomposition Rules for Layout

Figure 5a gives an example curve for any arbitrarily dimensioned problem which provides good locality for tiling, which we call *Hilbert Inspired Curve* (HIC). To this end, we implement a pseudo-Hilbert curve algorithm influenced by the works of Zhang *et al.* [24] and Chung *et al.* [9], which will be close to a Hilbert curve in S' performance. Unlike Zhang *et al.* where divisions create splits with sections having power of 2 dimensions on the outer portions of the matrix, our algorithm makes simple divisions by 2, split in both dimensions until we reach a base case. While Zhang's technique generates more regular patterns at the expense of different aspect ratios throughout the matrix, our technique ensures a Hilbert order with as close to the overall aspect ratio of the matrix at the expense of a more complex base case ordering.

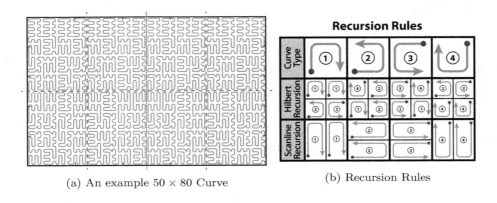

(a) An example 50 × 80 Curve   (b) Recursion Rules

Fig. 5. HIC: Hilbert Inspired Curve. (Color figure online)

In order to lower the aspect ratio of the tiles and reduce the expected S', HIC will make scanlines of tiles following Chung *et al.*'s work, rather than using Hilbert recursion.

This is because dividing a rectangular tile into a more square tile occurs only until the longer length switches axes and is no longer smaller than the current S value. This creates the condition shown in Eq. 9.

$$S > \frac{1}{\frac{S}{2}} \quad \rightarrow \quad S > \sqrt{2} \tag{9}$$

This is equivalent to always dividing the longest dimension of the tile, similarly to many cache oblivious algorithms, except the single dimension split is only performed when the curve types allow a scanline recursion. This results in the recursion rules laid out in Fig. 5b.

In the base case where either tile dimension goes below 7, HIC terminates recursion and specifies every possible scanline order in a look-up table similar to Zhang. We ensure that a split in the base case cannot result in two odd tiles by shifting the split as necessary. This reduces our look-up table to 4 cases for each curve type, resulting in 64 total scanline orders. Figure 6 illustrates the scanline order for all cases of base tiles for a curve traversing from lower left to lower right. The other three curve orientations are not presented. Dots indicate start points for each scanline and the highlighted case does not have a contiguous end/start connection between the two upper subtiles as previously mentioned.

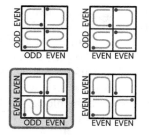

This is exactly what we see in our example tile from Fig. 5a, with the ratio $8 : 5 > \sqrt{2}$, and so a single dimension cut on the X axis is made

Fig. 6. Portion of scanline look up table

in the middle (shown in blue dashes). This produces two tiles with $S = 5 : 4$. Hence Hilbert recursion begins with the first 2 cuts (shown in red dashes). Several aspect ratios were tested to ensure S' values were still reasonable to evaluate the impact of these changes and allow arbitrary matrix dimensions, instead of the traditional Hilbert curve. Results are presented in Fig. 7.

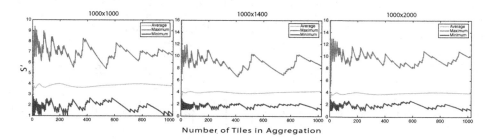

Fig. 7. S' for 3 different aspect ratios

While the maximum value has reached as high as 16 for smaller tile sizes, the overall S' values remain nearly the same as the original Hilbert curve, which will bode well in Sect. 4 when utilizing this curve to aggregate tiles in a CPCI hierarchy.

4   Tiling Up and Down a Hierarchy Efficiently

4.1   Aggregating Tiles

The first step to implement our algorithm is to query the runtime for all program available memory in the chip memory hierarchy. Then a tree is built where the smallest memory closest to the processor is a leaf and the memory shared between different groups of processors are inner nodes. Next the base tile size and inner product length n and k are determined, (see Sect. 2). Of course, a tile size of 1 could work but the overhead of runtime queues, curve pointer calculations, and synchronization would be cost prohibitive. If the base tile size is made too coarse, then smaller regions of memory will be unusable: fragment pieces of memory during tiling create excessive work stealing, and (for small problem sizes) expose too little concurrency. Hence the importance of determining the proper base tile size. For the purposes of our experiments, we picked our base tile sizes empirically, but this process is autotunable.

Bottom-up tile formation starts by attempting to aggregate base blocks together into larger tiles that can form outer products while still having enough memory available for the input buffers. All aggregations must follow a global layout dictated by the HIC. Thus, the task is simply to divide what portions of memory will be A input buffers, B input buffers, and C result tiles for that memory block using the FF equation from Fig. 6 and the HIC curve function to project what inputs will be needed. Once the children of a subtree have finished, the subtree attempts to partition the shared memory using the FF equation with one exception: it regards the value Q in the equation as not only the size of its memory but also the result tiles from all its children in the calculation. This exception is made due to assumption 3 of our machine model from Sect. 2. It is intuitive: any child could steal work from another child at the cost of the shared memory access when gross imbalance occurs. The rest of the memory in the subtree is divided

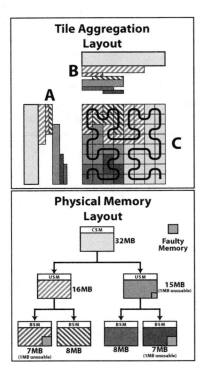

Fig. 8. Example tiling and memory layout (These memory capacities are for illustrative purposes only)

and utilized for the A and B tiles according to the dimensions created by the HIC. Additionally, we insure that an upper level input buffer can hold a large enough buffer (product length of k) to support lower level input buffer reads. This assignment continues sequentially all the way through the memory tree until the root finishes by initiating the first data movement of matrices from DRAM. After all nodes of the memory tree are initialized, data layout is finished and the spawning of tasks for computation can begin.

4.2 Creating Tasks

As mentioned earlier, outer product operations have synchronization requirements if multiple operations are occuring in parallel. In order to perform these operations, yet still maintain high performance, we implement a hierarchically double-buffered and load-balanced asynchronous computation. This is similar in style to Garcia et al. [14].

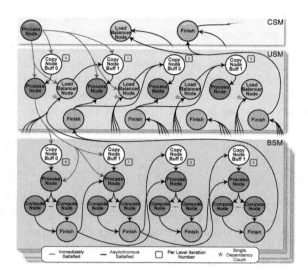

As shown in Fig. 9, there are 4 kinds of nodes that we give to the runtime. Each node has a set of dependencies that must be satisfied before it can placed in the running queue. Similarly, once a node finishes, it will satisfy its future dependencies by making calls to the runtime with a globally unique identifier for each dependency.

Once higher memory level work is available, each execution engine performs direct DMA transfers, bypassing all other memory structures. While we could have provided

Fig. 9. Data dependency graph

additional data reuse by recruiting groups of XEs in the same block or unit to perform a similar input broadcast into the lower level buffer just as the lower level tiles did, this would add more synchronization and potentially affect performance.

5   Experimental Results

5.1   Testbed

We experiment using FSim, which is a heavily multithreaded and multi-process functional simulator created by Intel. It models the TG architecture: execution and control engines, load-store queues, memory controllers and memory banks at each level of the TG hierarchy, are all implemented as individual threads. The runtime we used on FSim only allows up to $\frac{1}{8}$ of the targeted 2048-core TG chip to be simulated: up to 4 units of 8 blocks each, with 8 execution engines and one control engine in each block ($\approx$256 cores). Because we are only simulating part of the chip, we reduce the chip area to 64 mm^2 for performing on-chip network energy calculations, and modify the amount of memory in the Unit and Chip shared memories in order to maintain a hierarchy inversion ratio of 2:1 as seen in Table 1.

Table 1. Simulation parameters

Chip shared memory	16 MB
Units/chip	4
Unit shared memory	8 MB
Blocks/unit	8
Block shared memory	2 MB
Base tile size → n	30
Base tile size → k	30

We trace and count all matrix data movements from any memory module in the hierarchy using our runtime; in addition we report relative energy consumption provided by FSim that includes dynamic tiling computations and runtime overheads. However, FSim is not cycle accurate: we are unable to estimate static power consumption or the actual performance of the MM, but all dynamic energy consumption is measured using approximations developed from architectural designs. For this paper, since we are more interested in data movement, we fix the voltage to be in superthreshold operation so all dynamic energy consumption is on that order.

5.2   Tiling Related Results

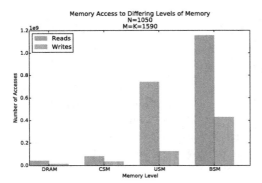

Fig. 10. Memory accesses

Figure 10 shows the number of memory accesses to all shared memories on the chip. Our energy-aware algorithm gives a clear preference for the closer memory operations, preferring to access BSM 20 times more than DRAM. In fact, the algorithm favors the local operations so strongly that *the number of DRAM operations is exactly the lower bound on the number of accesses to do the MM operation*. This is in spite of the C matrix being 83% of the size of the CSM showing that our algorithm can easily operate on working sets larger than the highest capacity of memory in the hierarchy.

It is not necessary to compare this method to other standard cache-oblivious algorithms, since they follow the inclusion property.

This is because any algorithm that only uses the CSM would certainly be unable to fit all 3 matrices in memory, necessitating that at least one of them be accessed a second time. Since all our energy consumption in the on-chip memories is less than 25%, it is already clear that we would consume less energy than any competitor that does not have some kind of explicit outer product layout. This is why we specifically chose this single case to illustrate our point.

5.3   Machine Related Results

The preference for on-chip memory operations over DRAM accesses is very helpful for off-chip bandwidth utilization as well. Given that a 1050 × 1590 × 1590 requires a total of 5.3 GFLOP and our tiling scheme is able to only require 60 MB of loads or stores to DRAM, with throughput levels of 1.75 TFLOP/S which we would expect that $\frac{1}{8}$ of a chip could perform, it would still only require a DRAM bandwidth of 20 GB/s.

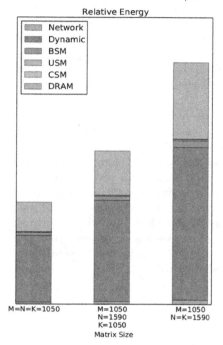

Fig. 11. Relative energy consumption

This could potentially be an even larger reduction in off-chip bandwidth requirements if the full memory capacity were simulated. This comes at a cost with large increases in on-chip accesses which we would expect an on-chip network could handle the added requirements.

Figure 11 shows the relative energy consumption (without static energy) to the 4 different shared memory regions of the chip as well as the dynamic energy consumption of the processors for three different MM sizes. Here we notice that even though the BSM, USM, and CSM are read and written orders of magnitude more than the DRAM, the energy consumed by the DRAM is still much more than the more local memory operations.

6 Related Work

Space-Filling Curves. Chatterjee *et al.* [7] studied recursive data layouts for multiple kinds of Morton curves as well as Hilbert curves in the context of Matrix Multiply, while Bader and Zenger [3] created an algorithm using Peano curves. More recently, Ballard *et al.* [4] used a Morton inspired ordering in which they divide by the largest dimension which in a square matrix resolves to Morton order. These works solely looked at the locality properties of space filling curves in order to provide cache friendly ordering. In addition, our work incorporates a hierarchy of scratchpad memories and ensures the tiling scheme provides energy optimal data movement. Furthermore, this technique also leverages the curve in a scheduler for more choreographed data movement to increase locality.

Cache Oblivious and Communication Avoiding Algorithms. Frigo *et al.* [13] define an algorithm as being cache-oblivious when the algorithm is cache optimal without requiring any parameters defining the cache. They do this by using the inclusion property of caches to simplify the problem into a 2 memory space problem: fast cache memory and slow system memory, similar to our formulation. They then can infer cache optimality for any algorithm that provably minimizes communication between these two memories so long as the algorithm is not a function of the sizes. However, this means exclusive caches or noncoherent caches or scratchpads like the CPCI hierarchies we target can not apply to a cache-oblivious algorithm or if so a complex analysis of the coherence algorithm is necessary to determine what the maximum working set the cache can hold and under what conditions of memory operations that maximum working set can exist. We only require the energy cost to be inclusive and let the capacity be a variable we define in our model. The downside to our algorithm is that it naturally operates using a machine model where all data movement is explicit and formulating an algorithm within a traditional cache hierarchy would be difficult if not impossible for some caches.

More recent work includes communication avoiding (CA) classes [2,11,17]. They extend the cache oblivious concept to networks. CARMA [12] utilizes a breadth-first\depth-first hybrid algorithm that leverages additional available memory to reduce communication across distributed-memory and NUMA machines. It is not obvious how CARMA would handle an inverted memory hierarchy such as TG since it is usually applied to distributed memory systems. Additionally, we assume that energy consumption will be a dominating and limiting factor within a chip in future architectures rather than bandwidth. Because CA algorithms are cache-oblivious, they place equal weight on memory accesses regardless of the energy liabilities they generate which could limit overall performance when thermal constraints are considered.

7   Conclusion

This paper has presented a novel energy-aware algorithm targeting future many-core architectures. It relies on the memory capacity inversion property and applies a custom space-filling curve to implement our tiling method and achieve energy efficient matrix multiplication execution. We provide a demonstrative simulation experiment to show the advantages of our techniques and predict an energy-optimal bandwidth to flop ratio absent of other bottlenecks in the TG design. While this work provides a precise account of dynamic energy expenditure and makes every effort to amoritize overheads properly, a not-yet implemented cycle-accurate simulator would quantify the scheduling overheads of our algorithm, which would allow for the computation of the total estimate of energy per operation. This would inform computer architects in how inverted memory hierarchies could be utilized. Likewise, our machine model is extensible: bandwidth consumption can be modelled, following Chen et al.'s work [8]. From a compiler perspective, our proposed algorithm can be integrated in a more general framework, taking advantage of polyhedral models to extend our dynamic space filling curves and energy model. From a runtime standpoint, there is the potential for using runtime information to guide custom schedulers for optimal locality using our framework. Lastly, initial confirmation of the energy model can be empirically made on systems like KNL which have scratchpad modes for the in-package memory.

Acknowledgments. Authors would like to thank Shekhar Borkar, Joshua Fryman, Romain Cledat, Ivan Ganev, Bala Seshasayee and others on the Intel XStack team for information on memory energy ratios, use of FSim, and computing resources. This material is based upon work supported by the Department of Energy [Office of Science] under Award Number DE-SC0008717. This research is also based upon work supported by the National Science Foundation, under award XPS-1439097.

References

1. Agullo, E., Demmel, J., Dongarra, J., Hadri, B., Kurzak, J., Langou, J., Ltaief, H., Luszczek, P., Tomov, S.: Numerical linear algebra on emerging architectures: the plasma and magma projects. J. Phys.: Conf. Ser. **180**(1), 012037 (2009)
2. Baboulin, M., Donfack, S., Dongarra, J., Grigori, L., Rémy, A., Tomov, S.: A class of communication-avoiding algorithms for solving general dense linear systems on CPU/GPU parallel machines. Procedia Comput. Sci. **9**, 17–26 (2012). Proceedings of the International Conference on Computational Science, ICCS 2012
3. Bader, M., Zenger, C.: Cache oblivious matrix multiplication using an element ordering based on a Peano curve. Linear Algebra Appl. **417**(23), 301–313 (2006). Special Issue in Honor of Friedrich Ludwig Bauer
4. Ballard, G., Demmel, J., Lipshitz, B., Schwartz, O., Toledo, S.: Communication efficient Gaussian elimination with partial pivoting using a shape morphing data layout. In: SPAA 2013, Montréal, Québec, Canada. ACM (2013)
5. Borkar, S.: Role of interconnects in the future of computing. J. Lightwave Technol. **31**(24) (2013). ISSN: 0733-8724
6. Carter, N.P., Agrawal, A., Borkar, S., Cledat, R., David, H., Dunning, D., Fryman, J.B., Ganev, I., Golliver, R.A., Knauerhase, R.C., et al.: Runnemede: an architecture for ubiquitous high-performance computing. In: HPCA (2013)
7. Chatterjee, S., Lebeck, A.R., Patnala, P.K., Thottethodi, M.: Recursive array layouts and fast parallel matrix multiplication. In: SPAA, Saint Malo, France. ACM (1999)
8. Chen, G., Anders, M., Kaul, H., Satpathy, S., Mathew, S., Hsu, S., Agarwal, A., Krishnamurthy, R., Borkar, S., De, V.: 16.1 a 340mv-to-0.9v 20.2tb/s source-synchronous hybrid packet/circuit-switched 16 × 16 network-on-chip in 22nm tri-gate CMOS. In: 2014 IEEE International Solid-State Circuits Conference Digest of Technical Papers (ISSCC) (2014)
9. Chung, K.-L., Huang, Y.-L., Liu, Y.-W.: Efficient algorithms for coding Hilbert curve of arbitrary-sized image and application to window query. Inf. Sci. **177**(10), 2130–2151 (2007). Including Special Issue on Hybrid Intelligent Systems
10. D'alberto, P., Bodrato, M., Nicolau, A.: Exploiting parallelism in matrix-computation kernels for symmetric multiprocessor systems: matrix-multiplication and matrix-addition algorithm optimizations by software pipelining and threads allocation. ACM Trans. Math. Softw. **38**(1) (2011)
11. Demmel, J.: Communication-avoiding algorithms for linear algebra and beyond. In: IPDPS 2013 (2013)
12. Demmel, J., Eliahu, D., Fox, A., Kamil, S., Lipshitz, B., Schwartz, O., Spillinger, O.: Communication-optimal parallel recursive rectangular matrix multiplication. In: IPDPS (2013)
13. Frigo, M., Leiserson, C.E., Prokop, H., Ramachandran, S.: Cache-oblivious algorithms. In: Proceedings of the 40th Annual Symposium on Foundations of Computer Science, FOCS 1999, Washington, DC, USA. IEEE Computer Society (1999)

14. Garcia, E., Orozco, D., Khan, R., Venetis, I., Livingston, K., G. Gao.: A dynamic schema to increase performance in many-core architectures through Percolation operations. In: HiPC 2013, Bangalore, India. IEEE Computer Society (2013)
15. Hungershöfer, J., Wierum, J.-M.: On the quality of partitions based on space-filling curves. In: Sloot, P.M.A., Hoekstra, A.G., Tan, C.J.K., Dongarra, J.J. (eds.) ICCS 2002. LNCS, vol. 2331, pp. 36–45. Springer, Heidelberg (2002). doi:10.1007/3-540-47789-6_4
16. Intel: Strawman system architecture and evaluation (2004). http://tinyurl.com/j6xxg22. Accessed 10 July 2016
17. Irony, D., Toledo, S., Tiskin, A.: Communication lower bounds for distributed-memory matrix multiplication. J. Parallel Distrib. Comput. **64**(9), 1017–1026 (2004)
18. Jaleel, A., Borch, E., Bhandaru, M., Steely Jr., S.C., Emer, J.: Achieving non-inclusive cache performance with inclusive caches: temporal locality aware (TLA) cache management policies. In: MICRO 2010, MICRO '43, Washington, DC, USA. IEEE Computer Society (2010)
19. Juega, J., G'omez, J., Tenllado, C., Verdoolaege, S., Cohen, A., Catthoor, F.: Evaluation of state-of-the-art polyhedral tools for automatic code generation on GPUs (2012)
20. Leung, A., Vasilache, N., Meister, B., Baskaran, M., Wohlford, D., Bastoul, C., Lethin, R.: A mapping path for multi-GPGPU accelerated computers from a portable high level programming abstraction. In: GPGPU-3, March 2010
21. Strassen, V.: Gaussian elimination is not optimal. Numer. Math. **13**(4), 354–356 (1969)
22. Verdoolaege, S., Carlos Juega, J., Cohen, A., Ignacio Gómez, J., Tenllado, C., Catthoor, F.: Polyhedral parallel code generation for CUDA. ACM Trans. Archit. Code Optim. **9**(4) (2013)
23. Whaley, R.C., Dongarra, J.J.: Automatically tuned linear algebra software. In: SuperComputing 1998, San Jose, CA. IEEE Computer Society (1998)
24. Zhang, J., Kamata, S., Ueshige, Y.: A pseudo-Hilbert scan algorithm for arbitrarily-sized rectangle region. In: Zheng, N., Jiang, X., Lan, X. (eds.) IWICPAS 2006. LNCS, vol. 4153, pp. 290–299. Springer, Heidelberg (2006). doi:10.1007/11821045_31

Resilience and Persistence

Language Support for Reliable Memory Regions

Saurabh Hukerikar[✉] and Christian Engelmann

Computer Science and Mathematics Division,
Oak Ridge National Laboratory, Oak Ridge, TN, USA
{hukerikarsr,engelmann}@ornl.gov

Abstract. The path to exascale computational capabilities in high-performance computing (HPC) systems is challenged by the inadequacy of present software technologies to adapt to the rapid evolution of architectures of supercomputing systems. The constraints of power have driven system designs to include increasingly heterogeneous architectures and diverse memory technologies and interfaces. Future systems are also expected to experience an increased rate of errors, such that the applications will no longer be able to assume correct behavior of the underlying machine. To enable the scientific community to succeed in scaling their applications, and to harness the capabilities of exascale systems, we need software strategies that enable explicit management of resilience to errors in the system, in addition to locality of reference in the complex memory hierarchies of future HPC systems.

In prior work, we introduced the concept of explicitly reliable memory regions, called *havens*. Memory management using havens supports reliability management through a region-based approach to memory allocations. Havens enable the creation of robust memory regions, whose resilient behavior is guaranteed by software-based protection schemes. In this paper, we propose language support for havens through type annotations that make the structure of a program's havens more explicit and convenient for HPC programmers to use. We describe how the extended haven-based memory management model is implemented, and demonstrate the use of the language-based annotations to affect the resiliency of a conjugate gradient solver application.

1 Introduction

The high-performance computing (HPC) community has their sights set on exascale-class computers, but there remain several challenges in designing

---

This work was sponsored by the U.S. Department of Energy's Office of Advanced Scientific Computing Research. This manuscript has been authored by UT-Battelle, LLC under Contract No. DE-AC05-00OR22725 with the U.S. Department of Energy. The United States Government retains and the publisher, by accepting the article for publication, acknowledges that the United States Government retains a non-exclusive, paid-up, irrevocable, world-wide license to publish or reproduce the published form of this manuscript, or allow others to do so, for United States Government purposes. The Department of Energy will provide public access to these results of federally sponsored research in accordance with the DOE Public Access Plan (http://energy.gov/downloads/doe-public-access-plan).

© Springer International Publishing AG 2017
C. Ding et al. (Eds.): LCPC 2016, LNCS 10136, pp. 73–87, 2017.
DOI: 10.1007/978-3-319-52709-3_6

these systems and preparing application software to harness the extreme-scale parallelism. Due to constraints of power, emerging HPC system architectures will employ radically different node and system architectures. Future architectures will emphasize increasing on-chip and node-level parallelism, in addition to scaling the number of nodes in the system, in order to drive performance while meeting the constraints of power [1]. Technology trends suggest that present memory technologies and architectures will yield much lower memory capacity and bandwidth per flop of compute performance. Therefore, emerging memory architectures will be more complex, with denser memory hierarchies and utilize more diverse memory technologies [2]. The management of resilience to the occurrence of frequent faults and errors in the system has also been identified as a critical challenge [3]. HPC applications and their algorithms will need to adapt to these evolving architectures, which will also be increasingly unreliable. These challenges have led to suggestions that our existing approaches to programming models must change to complement existing system-level approaches [4]. The demands for massive concurrency and the emergence of high fault rates require that programming model features also support the management of resilience and data locality in order to achieve high performance.

Recent efforts in the HPC community have focused on improvements in the scalability of numerical libraries and implementations of Message Passing Interface (MPI) libraries for these to be useful on future extreme-scale machines. However, there is also a need to develop new abstractions and methods to support fault resilience. In prior work, we proposed a resilience-driven approach to memory management using havens [5]. Havens offer an explicit method for affecting resilience in the context of memory management decisions. In haven-based memory management, each allocated object is placed in a program-specified haven. The havens guarantee a specified level of robustness for all the program objects contained in a memory region. The objects contained in havens may not be freed individually; instead the entire haven is deallocated, leading to the deletion of all the contained objects. Each haven is protected by a detection/correction mechanism, and different havens in a program may be protected using different resilience schemes. The use of havens provides structure to resiliency management of the program memory by grouping related objects based on the objects' individual need for robustness and the performance overhead of the resilience mechanism. This approach to memory management enables HPC applications to write their own disciplines to enhance the resilience features of arbitrary types of memory.

Traditional region-based systems were designed to statically assign program objects to memory regions, based on compiler analysis, in order to eliminate the need for runtime garbage collection [6]. In contrast, the primary goal of havens is to provide a scheme for creating regions within heap-allocated memory with various resilience features. In our initial design, we defined interfaces for the creation and use of havens that were implemented by a library interface [5]. In this paper, we develop language support in order to make havens clearer and more convenient to use in HPC application programs by supporting as many C/C++ language constructs as possible.

This paper makes the following contributions:

- We make a realistic proposal for adding language support for havens to mainstream HPC languages.
- We develop type annotations, which enable static encoding of the decisions for a program object's allocation and deallocation into the robust regions. They also provide opportunities to optimize the trade-off between the robustness and performance overhead for protecting program objects.
- We investigate how affecting the resilience of individual program objects using these static annotations affects their fault coverage and performance during application execution.

2   Havens: Reliable Memory Regions

Havens are designed to support resilience-driven memory management. The runtime memory is partitioned into robust regions, called havens, into which program objects are allocated. Various object deallocation policies may be defined for each haven, but the default is to free all the objects in a haven at once by deleting the entire pool of memory. Therefore, havens enable the association of lifetime to the reliable memory regions. Each memory region is protected by a predefined robustness scheme that provides error detection and/or correction for all objects in the haven. Any robustness scheme used by a haven is intended to be agnostic to the algorithm features, and to the structure of the data objects placed in havens. The concept of havens maintains a clear separation between the memory management policies and the mechanism that provides error resilience. Different havens used by an application may be protected using different detection/correction schemes, such as software-based parity, hashing, replication, etc., each of which may carry a different level of performance overhead. Therefore, havens enable the program memory to be logically partitioned into distinct regions each of which possess a specific level of error resilience and performance overhead.

From the perspective of an HPC application program, havens enable applications to exert fine-grained control on the resilience properties of individual program objects. Since different havens may have varying guarantees of resilience and performance overhead, object placement in havens may be driven by the trade-off between criticality of the object to program correctness and the associated overhead. Havens are used to create a logical grouping of objects that require similar resilience characteristics. Havens also enable improvements to the locality of dynamically allocated objects by placement and aggregation of various objects based on an application's pattern of use. Furthermore, havens permit HPC applications to balance the locality of program objects with their resilience needs. For example, a runtime system may dynamically map a haven onto specific hardware units in the memory hierarchy in an effort to improve the locality of its program objects; such mapping may also be guided by the availability of hardware-based error detection/correction in the memory unit that cooperates with the software-based protection scheme of the haven.

3 Using Havens for Resilience-Driven Memory Management

3.1 Basic Operations

While developing the concept of havens, we defined an interface for HPC programs to effectively use the reliable memory regions in their application codes [5]. The abstract interface is based on the notion of a haven manager, which provides a set of basic operations that must be implemented to fully support the use of havens. The operations are summarized below:

1. `_haven_create_`: The request for the creation of a haven by an application returns a handle to the memory region, but no memory is allocated. The choice of the error protection scheme is specified during the haven creation operation.
2. `_haven_alloc_`: An application requests a specified block of memory within a haven using this interface. This operation results in the allocation of the memory and the initialization of state related to the protection scheme.
3. `_haven_delete_`: The interface indicates intent to delete an object within the haven, but the memory is not released until the haven is destroyed.
4. `_haven_read_` and `_haven_write_`: These interfaces read and update the program objects contained in the haven; the operations are performed through these interfaces, rather than directly on the objects, to enable the haven manager to maintain updated state about the robustness mechanism.
5. `_haven_destroy_`: The interface requests that the haven be destroyed, which results in all memory blocks allocated in the region to be deallocated. Upon completion of this operation, no further operation on the haven are permitted, and the memory is available for reuse. The state related to the robustness scheme maintained by the haven manager is also destroyed.
6. `_haven_relax_` and `_haven_robust_`: These interfaces enable the error protection scheme applied to a haven to be turned on and off based on the needs of the application during program execution.

3.2 Haven Library Interface

The implementation of the havens library is similar to the one in [5], in which the heap is divided into fixed-size pages, and each new haven creation is aligned to a page boundary. The library maintains a linked list of these pages. We provide the library API functions for each of the primitives that enable basic haven operations: the `haven_alloc()` and `haven_new()` implement the abstraction for the allocation of objects into the associated region. With the library-based implementation of the haven interfaces, we require no changes to the representation of pointers. Pointers may reference havens or access individual objects in the havens. Since the library implementation does not differentiate between the pointer types, any conversions between these two kinds of pointers are potentially unsafe, and may lead to incorrect behavior. We only support per-region allocation and deallocation, and therefore per-object deallocation is an illegal operation. The `haven_release()` enables the expression of the end of object life. However, the `haven_destroy()` operation must be invoked to release the memory, which is achieved by concatenating the haven's page list to the global list of free pages.

3.3   Protection Schemes for Havens

In our initial implementation of havens, the memory regions are guaranteed highly-reliable behavior through comprehensive protection based on a light-weight software-based parity scheme. This scheme requires the haven manager to maintain a pair of signatures for each memory region, which are of word length for error correction, and an additional word length signature for error detection. The detection signature contains one parity bit per word in the memory region. As memory is allocated for the region and initialized, the correction signature S1 retains the XOR of all words that are written to the memory region. We apply an XOR operation on every word that is updated in the memory region and the correction signature S2.

Silent data corruptions or multi-bit errors are detected by checking the detection signature for parity violations. The detection signature also enables the location of the corrupted memory word to be identified. The value at the corrupted memory location may be recovered using the signatures S1 and S2. The XOR of these two signatures S1 and S2 equals the XOR of all the uncorrupted locations in the haven. Therefore, the corrupted value in the memory region is recovered by performing an XOR operation on the remaining words in the haven with the XOR of the signatures S1 and S2. The recovered value overwrites the corrupted value, and the detection signature is recomputed. This parity-based protection is an adaptation of an erasure code. Using this scheme, multibit corruptions may be recovered from unlike hardware-based ECC, which offers only single bit error correction and double bit error detection. The scheme maintains limited state for the detection and correction capabilities and therefore carries very little space overhead in comparison to other software-based schemes such as software-based ECC and checksums. Additionally, the detection/recovery operations are transparent to the application. The detection is a constant time operation while the recovery is a $O(n)$ operation based on the size of the haven.

4   A Haven Type System

4.1   Goals

Havens express the intended relationships between locality and resilience requirements of various program objects. The use of havens brings structure to memory management by grouping related program objects based on their resiliency and locality needs. The initial prototype implementation of havens contains library interfaces for each of the primitive haven operations [5]. The language support for havens aims to make programming HPC applications with havens straightforward and productive by making the programs using havens clearer and easier to write and to understand. Our design of the haven language support seeks to address the following seemingly conflicting goals:

- **Explicit:** HPC programmers control where their program objects are allocated and explicitly define their robustness characteristic and lifetime.
- **Convenience:** A minimal set of explicit language annotations that support as many C/C++ idioms as possible in order to facilitate the use of havens-based memory management in existing HPC application codes, as well as in the development of new algorithms.
- **Safety:** The language annotations must prevent dangling-pointer dereferences and space leaks.
- **Scalability:** The havens must support various object types and the performance overhead of any resilience scheme scales well even with large number of objects.

The language support enables HPC programmers to statically encode memory management decisions for various program objects. By making the structure of the havens and their resilience features explicit, the number of runtime checks and modifications to the haven structure and the resilience scheme are reduced.

4.2 Type Annotations for Havens

In the haven-based model for memory management, the heap is divided into regions, each containing a number of program objects. Therefore, havens are abstract entities that represent an aggregation of program objects. Pointers to havens refer to these abstract entities in the heap, whose resilience scheme is defined upon creation and provides protection to all program objects that are contained within the haven. The definition of a haven pointer type provides a statically enforceable way of specifying the resilience scheme, type and size information for the encapsulated objects inside the haven. A haven type statically ensures that programs using this region-based model of memory management are memory-safe, i.e., they don't permit dangling references. The `haven_ptr` is a new type for handles to havens. The declaration of a `haven_ptr` typed pointer leads to the creation of a haven, but the declaration of a haven does not allocate any memory. The haven-typed pointer object is declared and the haven is subsequently deleted as shown in Listing 1.1.

```
haven_ptr h1;
. . .
deletehaven h1;
```

Listing 1.1. Type Annotations for Havens

The `haven_ptr` is *smart* pointer object that contains the pointer reference to a haven and also maintains bookkeeping information about the objects resident to the haven, including their sizes and a reference count. This information enables the library to optimize the resilience scheme that protects the haven. For example, in the parity-based protection scheme, the haven is protected using a pair of parity signatures. The availability of the count and sizes of the objects inside the haven enables statically creating sub-havens that are each protected by pair of signatures. We define the `deletehaven` operator that provides a static mechanism to reclaim the memory allocated for objects inside a haven, and also discards the bookkeeping information and any state maintained by the resilience scheme (for e.g., the signatures that provide parity protection for the haven).

The library implementation of havens permits unsafe operations, since a haven h may be deleted even if the program contains accessible pointers to objects in h. With the introduction of the `haven_ptr` type, we also address the issue of safety. When the `deletehaven` operator is encountered, the safety of the delete operation is guaranteed by checking the reference counts included in the `haven_ptr` typed pointer object. The delete operation succeeds when the `haven_ptr` contains all null object pointers, and the operation results in releasing the storage space for the haven, along with the program objects contained in the haven. When the `haven_ptr` typed pointer object contains a non-zero count of active object references, the delete operation fails.

4.3 Subtyping Annotations

A subtype annotation is used to constrain the membership of an object to a specific haven. Each object type is annotated with a region expression, which explicitly specifies the haven to which values of that type belong. The region expression is always bound to the type declaration of an object.

```
//Declare new haven pointer h1
haven_ptr h1;

//Declare variable x as member of the haven h1
int<h1> x;
x = 4;

//Delete haven releases memory for haven and the contained variable x
deletehaven h1;
```

Listing 1.2. Subtype Annotations for Havens

The `type<haven_ptr>` defines a subtype for non-pointer variables that guarantees the allocation of the qualified object within a haven. The type annotation enables local variables and global variables in C/C++ programs to be associated with a haven. The haven membership of the annotated variable also guarantees the variable with the protection offered by the haven's specified resilience scheme. The declaration of a single integer variable inside a haven is written as shown in Listing 1.2.

The `type*<haven_ptr>` annotation defines a subtype for pointer objects. The inclusion of the `haven_ptr` specifies membership of the object referenced by the annotated variable to the haven. The declaration of an array inside a haven and the allocation of memory for the array is written as shown in Listing 1.3.

```
//Declare new haven pointer h2
haven_ptr h2;

//Declare vector pointer as member of the haven h2
double*<h2> vector;

//Allocate memory for vector of size N
vector = haven_alloc(N * sizeof(double));
. . .

//Set vector pointer to be null; without this deletehaven fails
vector = null;

//Delete haven release memory for haven and the contained vector
deletehaven h2;
```

Listing 1.3. Declaration of an array object within a haven

The membership relationship between variables and havens expressed by the subtyping annotations also enables programmers to imply locality of reference for all program objects that are associated with a haven.

Restrictions: With the use of the type annotations for object pointers, programmers need to differentiate between traditional C/C++ pointers and pointers that specify haven membership. Any conversion between these two kinds of pointers is potentially unsafe and may lead to incorrect program behavior. Therefore, we define a **null** haven, which enables traditional C/C++ pointers to be viewed as pointers to objects inside this **null** region. The compiler guarantees safe assignments of pointer variables through static analysis or runtime checks.

4.4   Defining Lifetimes

Through language support, we also define the notion of lifetimes for havens. The basic idea is to define the scope of computation for which a haven is valid. We define the reference lifetime for a haven as shown in Listing 1.4. This syntax enables the creation of dynamic havens, whose lifetime is the execution of the statement s; the statement s may be a compound statement. The program objects that are allocated within the haven **hx** are guaranteed error protection through the haven's default resilience scheme. The explicit definition of lifetimes for the havens enables programs to scope specific regions of computation that must be executed with high reliability.

```
haven hx
{
   //statement s
}
```

Listing 1.4. Defining lifetime scope for havens

4.5   Example: Vector Addition

The example in Listing 1.5 shows the skeleton of the vector addition code, in
which the objective is to protect the operand vectors **a** and **b**. The example omits
the details of the vector initialization and the addition routines. The declaration
of the **haven_ptr** pointer variable with identifier **h3** creates the haven. Upon
creation of the haven, the parity signatures are initialized, but no memory is
allocated.

```
//Create a haven for vectors
haven_ptr h3;

//Declare vectors as members of the haven h1
double*<h3>    a = haven_alloc(N * sizeof(double));
double*<h3>    b = haven_alloc(N * sizeof(double));

//Declare traditional vector pointer as member of null haven
double*<null> c = malloc(N * sizeof(double));

//Vector addition c = a + b
vector_addition(c, a, b);

//Set vector pointers to null; without this deletehaven fails
a = null; b = null;
free(c);

deletehaven h3;
```

Listing 1.5. Example: Resilient Vector Addition using Havens Language Support

The sub-type declaration of the array pointers makes the relationship
between the operand vectors and the haven **h3** explicit and ensures the allocation of the vectors inside the haven. When the **haven_alloc** allocation requests
are made, the library initializes the resilience scheme for the haven and allocates
the vectors **a** and **b** of size N elements. The array pointer to the result vector **c**
is a traditional pointer that is declared as a sub-type to a **double*** that estab-
lishes membership of the null haven. When the vector addition function returns,
the operand vector pointers are set to null so that the **deletehaven** operator is
able to release the memory associated with the haven **h3** that includes vectors
a and **b**.

5   Application-Level Resilience Models Using Havens

A variety of algorithm-based fault tolerance (ABFT) strategies have been extensively studied over the past decades. Many of these techniques are designed to
take advantage of the unique features of an application's algorithm or data structures. These techniques are also able to leverage the fact that different aspects of
the application state have different resilience requirements, and that these needs
vary during the execution of an application. However, the key barrier to the
broader adoption of algorithm-based resilience techniques in the development of

HPC applications is the lack of sufficient programming model support since the use of these features requires significant programming effort.

We explore three generalized application-level resilience models that may be developed using havens, and whose construction is facilitated by the language-based annotations. These models are intended to serve as guidelines for HPC application programmers to develop new algorithms as well as adapt the existing application codes to incorporate algorithm-based resilience capabilities:

- **Selective Reliability:** Based on the insight that different variables in an HPC program exhibit different vulnerabilities to errors, havens provide specific regions of program memory with comprehensive error protection. With this model, HPC programmers use havens as mechanisms to explicitly declare specific data and compute regions to be more reliable than the default reliability of the underlying system.
- **Specialized Reliability:** Various protection schemes that provide error/detection and correction capabilities for havens guarantee different levels of resiliency. Also, based on the placement of havens in physical memory, the software-based schemes may complement any hardware-based capabilities. Havens provide simplified abstractions to design resilience strategies that seek to complement the requirements of different program objects with the various hardware and software-based protection schemes available.
- **Phased Reliability:** The vulnerability of various program objects and computations to errors varies during program execution. Havens may also be used to partition applications into distinct phases of computations. Since the various resilience schemes incur overheads to the application performance, the protection features of specific data regions and compute phases may be enabled or disabled in order to trade-off performance overhead and resilience.

6   Experimental Results

To apply the static annotations in an HPC application, we must identify program objects that must be allocated in havens, and annotate their declarations with the type qualifiers. These experiments evaluate the use of haven-based memory management using the type qualifiers for a conjugate gradient code by including the type and subtype qualifiers on its various application objects. We use a pre-conditioned iterative CG algorithm and we validate the correctness of the outcome of the solver with a solution produced using a direct solver. We compare the evaluation with the results from our previous implementation that required insertion of raw library interfaces. One of the important advantages of using the static annotations is that the number of lines of code changed is reduced significantly when compared to the changes required for insertion of library calls in the same application code, which improves code readability.

In the CG algorithm, which solves a system of linear equations $A.x = b$, the algorithm allocates the matrix A, the vector b and the solution vector x. Additionally, the conjugate vectors p and the residual vector r are referenced during each iteration of the algorithm. The program objects in the CG application demonstrate different sensitivities to errors. Errors in the operand matrix A or vector b fundamentally changes the linear system being solved. For errors in these structures even if the CG solver converges to a solution, it may be significantly different from a correct solution. The preconditioner matrix M demonstrates lower sensitivity to the errors, as do the vectors x, p, r. These features of the CG algorithm form the basis for the strategic placement of the objects into havens, since the allocation of only sensitive data structures into havens provides a substantially higher resilient behavior in terms of completion rates of the CG algorithm for reasonable overheads to performance than a naive placement strategy. We present a detailed sensitivity analysis in [5].

Here, we evaluate the performance benefits gained from the use of static annotations for the various objects in the CG code. We perform two sets of experiments: (i) we allocate only one structure using the haven static annotations, while the remaining structures are allocated using the standard memory allocation interfaces; (ii) we strategically annotate the data structures of the CG to allocate structures to havens in specific combinations. We evaluate the following combinations: (i) allocation of only the static state, i.e., the matrix A and vector B, the preconditioner M into havens, while the dynamic state, i.e., all the solution vectors, are allocated using standard memory allocation functions; (ii) allocation of only matrix A and vector B into havens; (iii) only the dynamic state is provided fault coverage using havens. We compare these strategies with allocations in which havens provide complete coverage and with experimental runs which do not allocate any structure using havens.

The performance overhead of using havens in terms of the time to solution of the CG solver for the above selection of program objects for allocation into havens is shown in Fig. 1. The annotation of all the program variables to be allocated into havens provides higher fault coverage, but it results in higher overhead to the time to solution for the CG application. When the variables are allocated using raw library interfaces, each program object is protected by a pair of signatures, which provides monolithic protection for the entire haven. When these objects are qualified with the static annotations in the application code, the compiler and library have a better understanding of the size and structure of the program objects. Therefore, the larger program objects, notably the operand matrix A and the preconditioner matrix M, are split and protected by multiple pairs of parity signatures. This split protection is transparent to the application programmer and the application still accesses the matrix elements as a single data structure. The use of multiple signatures improves the read/write overhead for the objects and the observed overhead with static annotations for all program objects is 11% lower than the library-based allocation for the same set of objects. The operand matrix A occupies a dominant part of the solver's memory, occupying over 50% of the active address space, whereas the solution vector x, the conjugate vectors p and the residual vector r and the preconditioner matrix M account for the remaining space. Therefore, the annotation of matrix A individually results in 9% lower overhead than with monolithic parity protection using library interfaces. The improvement in performance when smaller data objects are statically annotated is only within 2% of the version using library interfaces for the same objects.

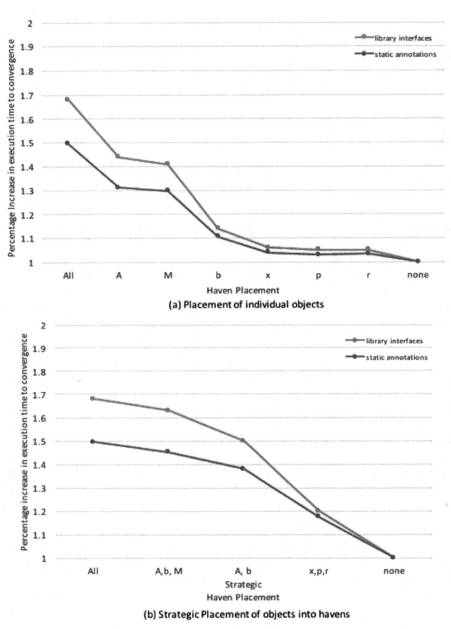

(a) Placement of individual objects

(b) Strategic Placement of objects into havens

Fig. 1. Performance overheads of havens with static annotations

7 Related Work

Much research has been devoted to studies of algorithms for memory management, which are based on either automatic garbage collection or explicit allocation/deallocation schemes. The concept of regions was implemented in storage systems, which allowed objects to be allocated in specific *zones* [7]. While each zone permits a different allocation policy, the deallocation is performed on a per-object basis. The vmalloc library [8] provides programmers with an interface to allocate memory and to define policies for each allocation. Region-based systems, such as arenas [9], enable writing special-purpose memory allocators that achieve performance by creating heap memory allocation disciplines that are suited to the application's needs. Implementations such as vmalloc place the burden of determining policy of allocation of objects to regions on the programmer [8]. Other schemes have used profiling to identify allocations that are short-lived and place such allocations in fixed-size regions [10]. Several early implementations of region-based systems were unsafe; the deletion of regions often left dangling pointers that were subsequently accessible. Such safety concerns were addressed through reference counting schemes for the regions [11].

For dynamic heap memory management through static analysis, regions provide [6] an alternative to garbage collection methods. In this approach, the assignment of program objects to regions is statically directed by the compiler in an effort to provide more predictable and lower memory space. The approach was refined by relaxing the restriction that region lifetimes must be lexical [12]. Language support for regions is available in many declarative programming languages such as ML [13], Prolog [14]. Cyclone is a language designed to be syntactically very close to C, but which provides support for regions through an explicit typing system [15]. The Rust programming language [16] also provides support for regions.

Recent efforts seek provide programming model support for reliability, such as containment domains [17], which offer programming constructs that impose transactional semantics for specific computations. Our previous work on *havens* [5] provided a reliability-driven method for memory allocations. Rolex [18] offers language-based extensions that support various resilience semantics on application data and computations. Global View Resilience (GVR) supports reliability of application data by providing an interface for applications to maintain version-based snapshots of the application data [19]. In support of fault tolerance of in explicit memory allocation/deallocation, the `malloc_failable` interface is used by the application to allocate memory on the heap; callback functions are used to handle error recovery for the memory block [20].

8 Conclusion

Resilience is among the major concerns for the next generation of extreme-scale HPC systems. With the rapid evolution of HPC architectures and the emergence of increasingly complex memory hierarchies, applications running on future HPC systems must manage the locality and maintain reliability of their data. Havens provide an explicit software-based approach for HPC applications to manage the resilience and locality of their programs. In this paper, we focused on developing language support for havens with emphasis on providing structure to the haven-based memory management. Through type annotations, a programmer expresses the intended relationships between locality and resilience requirements of various objects in the application program. The type annotations enable the resilience requirements of program objects to be encoded within the heap memory-management idioms. The static typing discipline for application codes written in C/C++ also guarantees the safety of memory operations by preventing dangling-pointer dereferences and space leaks. The structured haven-based management facilitated by the language support provides the mechanisms for the development of effective application-based resilience models for HPC applications.

References

1. Shalf, J., Dosanjh, S., Morrison, J.: Exascale computing technology challenges. In: Palma, J.M.L.M., Daydé, M., Marques, O., Lopes, J.C. (eds.) VECPAR 2010. LNCS, vol. 6449, pp. 1–25. Springer, Heidelberg (2011). doi:10.1007/978-3-642-19328-6_1
2. Kogge, P., Bergman, K., Borkar, S., Campbell, D., Carlson, W., Dallya, W., Denneau, M., Franzon, P., Harrod, W., Hill, K., Hiller, J., Karp, S., Keckler, S., Klein, D., Lucas, R., Richards, M., Scarpelli, A., Scott, S., Snavely, A., Sterling, T., Williams, R.S., Yelick, K.: Exascale computing study: technology challenges in achieving exascale systems. Technical report, DARPA, September 2008
3. DeBardeleben, N., Laros, J., Daly, J., Scott, S., Engelmann, C., Harrod, B.: High-end computing resilience: analysis of issues facing the HEC community and path-forward for research and development. Whitepaper, December 2009
4. Amarasinghe, S., Hall, M., Lethin, R., Pingali, K., Quinlan, D., Sarkar, V., Shalf, J., Lucas, R., Yelick, K., Balaji, P., Diniz, P.C., Koniges, A., Snir, M., Sachs, S.R., Yelick, K.: Exascale programming challenges: report of the 2011 workshop on exascale programming challenges. Technical report, U.S. Department of Energy, Office of Science, Office of Advanced Scientific Computing Research (ASCR), July 2011
5. Hukerikar, S., Engelmann, C.: Havens: explicit reliable memory regions for HPC applications. In: IEEE High Performance Extreme Computing Conference (HPEC), pp. 1–6, September 2016
6. Tofte, M., Talpin, J.P.: Implementation of the typed call-by-value λ-calculus using a stack of regions. In: Proceedings of the 21st ACM SIGPLAN-SIGACT Symposium on Principles of Programming Languages, POPL 1994, pp. 188–201. ACM, New York (1994)
7. Ross, D.T.: The AED free storage package. Commun. ACM **10**(8), 481–492 (1967)
8. Vo, K.P.: Vmalloc: a general and efficient memory allocator. Softw. Pract. Exp. **26**(3), 357–374 (1996)
9. Hanson, D.R.: Fast allocation and deallocation of memory based on object lifetimes. Softw. Pract. Exp. **20**(1), 5–12 (1990)

10. Barrett, D.A., Zorn, B.G.: Using lifetime predictors to improve memory allocation performance. In: Proceedings of the ACM SIGPLAN 1993 Conference on Programming Language Design and Implementation, PLDI 1993, New York, NY, USA, pp. 187–196 (1993)

11. Gay, D., Aiken, A.: Memory management with explicit regions. In: Proceedings of the ACM SIGPLAN 1998 Conference on Programming Language Design and Implementation, PLDI 1998, pp. 313–323. ACM, New York (1998)

12. Aiken, A., Fähndrich, M., Levien, R.: Better static memory management: improving region-based analysis of higher-order languages. In: Proceedings of the ACM SIGPLAN 1995 Conference on Programming Language Design and Implementation, PLDI 1995, pp. 174–18 (1995)

13. Tofte, M., Birkedal, L., Elsman, M., Hallenberg, N., Olesen, T.H., Sestoft, P., Bertelsen, P.: Programming with regions in the ML kit. Technical report (diku-tr-97/12), University of Copenhagen, Denmark, April 1997

14. Makholm, H.: A region-based memory manager for prolog. In: Proceedings of the 2nd International Symposium on Memory Management, ISMM 2000, pp. 25–34. ACM, New York (2000)

15. Grossman, D., Morrisett, G., Jim, T., Hicks, M., Wang, Y., Cheney, J.: Region-based memory management in Cyclone. In: Proceedings of the ACM SIGPLAN 2002 Conference on Programming Language Design and Implementation, PLDI 2002, pp. 282–293. ACM, New York (2002)

16. Rust: the rust programming language. http://www.rust-lang.org

17. Chung, J., Lee, I., Sullivan, M., Ryoo, J.H., Kim, D.W., Yoon, D.H., Kaplan, L., Erez, M.: Containment domains: a scalable, efficient, and flexible resilience scheme for exascale systems. In: Proceedings of the International Conference on High Performance Computing, Networking, Storage and Analysis, pp. 58:1–58:11 (2012)

18. Hukerikar, S., Lucas, R.F.: Rolex: resilience-oriented language extensions for extreme-scale systems. J. Supercomput. **72**, 1–33 (2016)

19. Chien, A., Balaji, P., Beckman, P., Dun, N., Fang, A., Fujita, H., Iskra, K., Rubenstein, Z., Zheng, Z., Schreiber, R., Hammond, J., Dinan, J., Laguna, I., Richards, D., Dubey, A., van Straalen, B., Hoemmen, M., Heroux, M., Teranishi, K., Siegel, A.: Versioned distributed arrays for resilience in scientific applications: global view resilience. Procedia Comput. Sci. **51**, 29–38 (2015)

20. Bridges, P.G., Hoemmen, M., Ferreira, K.B., Heroux, M.A., Soltero, P., Brightwell, R.: Cooperative application/OS DRAM fault recovery. In: Alexander, M., et al. (eds.) Euro-Par 2011, Part II. LNCS, vol. 7156, pp. 241–250. Springer, Heidelberg (2012). doi:10.1007/978-3-642-29740-3_28

Harnessing Parallelism in Multicore Systems to Expedite and Improve Function Approximation

Aurangzeb[✉] and Rudolf Eigenmann

Purdue University, West Lafayette, USA
orangzeb@purdue.edu

Abstract. Approximating functions in applications that can tolerate some inaccuracy in their results can deliver substantial performance gains. This paper makes a case for harnessing available parallelism in multicore systems to improve performance as well as the quality of function approximation. To that end, we discuss a number of tasks that the function approximation schemes can offload to available parallel cores. We also discuss how leveraging parallelism can help provide guarantees about results and dynamically improve approximations. Finally, we present experimental results of a function approximation scheme.

1   Introduction

Many applications from different domains such as audio, video, machine learning, computer vision, gaming, data analytics, and simulations can tolerate a certain degree of inaccuracy in their results. Approximate computing aims to increase performance of these applications and/or reduce their power requirement in exchange for some tolerable loss in accuracy. Applications amenable to approximation can be concerned with performance, power, or both. In this paper, our focus is on performance only. The literature mentions a number of software, hardware, and hybrid techniques that work at different granularities. Application functions/procedures that have pure function behavior (i.e. they consistently produce the same output for a given input and have no side effects) lend themselves to approximation. Software function approximation schemes have been shown to offer significant performance benefits and we focus on black-box techniques [1,3].

Software black-box function approximation schemes are oblivious to the internals of the original function and seek to approximate a candidate function based on its input-output behavior. This behavior is captured during *training*, which is a process of obtaining outputs from the original function. The schemes typically store the training inputs and corresponding outputs in some data-structure as training history. The schemes draw inferences from the raw history and prepare approximations by further processing the history and performing scheme-specific tasks. During *production*, the schemes choose and execute the approximations. Some schemes also have the capability to monitor the quality

© Springer International Publishing AG 2017
C. Ding et al. (Eds.): LCPC 2016, LNCS 10136, pp. 88–92, 2017.
DOI: 10.1007/978-3-319-52709-3_7

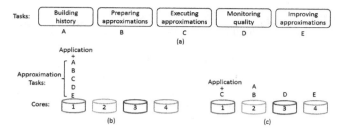

Fig. 1. (a) Tasks that black-box function approximation schemes perform. (b) Sequential execution of the application - all tasks assigned to one core. (c) Most of these tasks can be executed in parallel on multiple cores, as outlined in the subsequent sections.

of approximation results at runtime. If needed, they can update the history and modify approximations dynamically. Figure 1(a) depicts these tasks. Section 2 describes how the schemes can harness available parallel cores in multicore systems by offloading some of these tasks to improve their performance and quality of results. By exploiting parallelism, they can also provide better monitoring of results and be equipped with the capability of dynamically improving the quality of results. Section 3 describes our experiments with a black-box function approximation scheme, called *history-based piecewise approximation* [1]. It divides the input range of a function into uniform and non-uniform regions and applies low-order polynomial approximation in each region.

2   Function Approximation and Available Parallelism

This section describes the tasks that software black-box function approximation schemes can offload to available parallel cores. In case of sequential applications, the schemes can freely use the parallel cores, whereas for parallel applications the cores are employed when idle, using low priority threads. Figure 1(b) and (c) compare a scheme that does not exploit parallelism to one that does.

2.1   Building History

Function input-output history provides the basis for approximation to black-box function approximation schemes. Building a relevant history is important for accuracy of the approximation. Some schemes build the history offline. Where inputs during production may be significantly different than those seen during offline training, online training can improve the results. However, there may be overheads in such schemes, as the expensive original functions need to be called. Online training schemes can benefit from available parallel cores to build the history. In the simplest case, for every seen input, the scheme can invoke the original function in one of the available parallel cores and insert the results into the history. One drawback is that "cold start" may result in poor approximation until the history is rich enough. To overcome this problem, the schemes can speculatively build history. Below we describe some ways a scheme can do speculative training to build history online, harnessing available parallelism.

Around Most Recent Input: For speculative training, a scheme can use arbitrary inputs that are around the most recent actual input.

In Most Frequent Region: A scheme can divide the seen inputs in different regions and use arbitrary inputs in the most frequent region for speculative training.

In Most Frequent Region of Higher Output Variation: In addition to forming regions of seen inputs, a scheme can also track the output variation in those regions and can use arbitrary inputs in the most frequent region of the highest output variation.

2.2   Preparing Approximations

The schemes process the raw history, draw inferences, and perform scheme-specific tasks to prepare approximations for execution during production. For instance, the history-based piecewise approximation scheme [1] creates regions of input and computes polynomials for each region. It also considers the output variation in the regions and decides to use constants for some regions. During production, the scheme finds the region of the input and evaluates the corresponding polynomial. Offloading the inference and approximation preparation tasks to idle cores can improve the performance of a scheme.

2.3   Monitoring Quality

Monitoring the quality of approximation requires invoking the original function during production and comparing the exact result with the output obtained from executing approximation. Since it is an expensive process, a scheme can only monitor the output occasionally, which makes it difficult to provide guarantees for the quality of results. However, offloading the monitoring to available parallel cores can enable a scheme to potentially monitor the results of every input. It can also enable a scheme to provide guarantees for the approximations. For instance, a scheme may guarantee that a certain percentage of function invocation will result in an output that is within the specified tolerable error. At runtime, for each input, the scheme will decide whether to invoke the original function or the approximation, based on the monitoring information. Similarly, a scheme may offer statistical guarantees within a confidence interval.

2.4   Improving Approximations

The accuracy of approximation depends on many factors, including, the quality and quantity of training data, ability of drawing inferences, and sophistication of the approximation scheme. Harnessing idle cores can allow a scheme to dynamically improve its capabilities during runtime. It can help a scheme update its history by doing dynamic online training, draw new inferences, and improve its approximation strategies, without having any adverse effects on the performance. For example, it can allow the history-based piecewise scheme [1] to update history dynamically, adjust regions, compute new polynomials, and change approximation strategies for regions.

3   Experimental Results

This section describes results of our experiments with the history-based piecewise approximation scheme [1]. Currently, this scheme does not monitor results, offer guarantees, or dynamically improve results. However, it can be extended to reap the benefits of harnessing parallelism described in this paper. As for building history, it performs online training. We present results of testing three variants of the history-based non-uniform piecewise scheme on top++ application [2]. These variants are: BSA (binary search over sorted array), BST (binary search tree) and RBT (red-black tree). We chose the top++ application because the candidate function for approximation in this application is quite compute-intensive, which leads to higher overheads. The overheads of building history and preparing approximations by the variants of the non-uniform scheme for a training length of 125 are 60%, 54%, and 54%, respectively. We have extended the scheme to harness parallelism and used the *Around Most Recent Input (AMRI)* speculation described in Sect. 2.1. For each input, we use six speculative training inputs that are ± 0.04 apart. Table 1 compares the application speedup and percentage error in results by the current versions of all variants of the non-uniform scheme that uses single core with ones by the new versions of the extended scheme that uses available parallel cores, for top++ application. The results show that employing three idle cores reduces the overhead of the scheme on a 4-core machine, substantially improving the average application speedup from 1.5x to 2.2x.

Table 1. Effect of harnessing parallelism for building history using AMRI speculation on application speedup and percentage error of non-uniform piecewise schemes.

	BSA		BST		RBT	
	Speedup	%Error	Speedup	%Error	Speedup	%Error
Current version	1.62x	0.09%	1.52x	0.012%	1.5x	0.012%
AMRI speculation	2.3x	0.06%	2.14x	0.006%	2.08x	0.006%

4   Conclusion

Software black-box function approximation schemes that aim to increase performance of applications amenable to approximation can harness available parallel cores in multicore systems to improve and expedite function approximation. They can leverage the idle cores in building history, preparing and improving approximations, and monitoring quality and offering result guarantees.

References

1. Aurangzeb, Eigenmann, R.: History-based piecewise approximation scheme for procedures. In: 2nd Workshop on Approximate Computing (WAPCO), January 2016
2. Czakon, M., Mitov, A.: Top++. http://www.alexandermitov.com/software/115-top-versions-and-downloads
3. Samadi, M., Jamshidi, D.A., Lee, J., Mahlke, S.: Paraprox: pattern-based approximation for data parallel applications. ACM SIGARCH Comput. Archit. News **42**, 35–50 (2014)

Adaptive Software Caching for Efficient NVRAM Data Persistence

Pengcheng Li[1](✉) and Dhruva R. Chakrabarti[2]

[1] University of Rochester & Hewlett Packard Labs, Rochester, USA
pli@cs.rochester.edu
[2] Hewlett Packard Labs, Palo Alto, USA
dhruvac@gmail.com

Abstract. Persistent memory is getting increasingly popular. However, the existence of transient CPU caches brings a serious performance issue for utilization of persistence. In particular, cache lines have to be flushed frequently to guarantee consistent, persistent program states. In this paper, we optimize data persistence by proposing a software cache. The software cache first buffers lines that need to be flushed, and then flushes them out at an appropriate later time. The software cache supports adaptive selection of the best cache size at run-time.

1 Introduction

Persistent memory or non-volatile memory (NVRAM) technologies, such as memristors and phase change memory (PCM), are increasingly popular. Persistent memory is byte-addressable and directly accessible (i.e., without DRAM buffers) with CPU loads and stores. Data in NVRAM will not be erased if the creator process does not clean it. It enables data reuse across system restarts and of course process restarts. This in-memory durability model can greatly change the programming paradigm for many applications [1].

A problem of NVRAM data persistence is the transient memories in current computer architectures, such as CPU caches. At any point of program execution, some of the updates to persistent memory may only reside in CPU caches and have not yet propagated to NVRAM. If there is a failure at this point of execution, the program state in NVRAM may not be consistent thus preventing full recovery.

Consistent persistent states are guaranteed by forcing all data out of caches to persistent memory in the event of any tolerated failure. In `Atlas` [1] programming model, a *failure-atomic section (FASE)* foresees a failure. A FASE is a code segment that changes program invariants. Either all or none of the updates in a FASE are visible in NVRAM. Therefore, persistent data is guaranteed to be consistent at the end of a FASE.

In this paper, we propose a software cache to reduce the number of cache line flushes. Its purpose is to cache the data writes and combine multiple writes into a single cache flush at the time of eviction. We flush all cache lines in the software cache at the end of a FASE. In addition, we develop a reuse-based locality theory that allows us to optimize it by choosing the best cache size.

© Springer International Publishing AG 2017
C. Ding et al. (Eds.): LCPC 2016, LNCS 10136, pp. 93–97, 2017.
DOI: 10.1007/978-3-319-52709-3_8

For the purpose of disambiguity, if without explicit clarification of hardware cache, "cache" in this paper refers to the software cache.

2   Software Cache

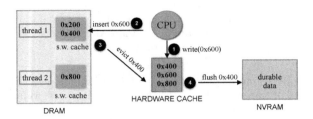

Fig. 1. Illustration of the software cache. The software cache has two cache lines and is full. Thread 1 writes a new cache line 0x600. 0x400 is evicted from the software cache and flushed out of the hardware cache.

The software cache is a per-thread in-memory local store. It is in control of determining when to flush a cache line to persistent memory. Figure 1 shows its basic execution model. When writing a value to persistent memory, CPU, instead of immediately flushing the corresponding cache line, forwards the cache line address to the software cache to buffer the write. In a parallel program, per-thread caching provides isolation and good scalability. The isolation is important. Each thread independently manipulates its own cache, without interference from others. Scalability is good because the implementation does not require locking.

Each thread combines cache line flushes if the coming cache line is already in its local store. Otherwise, it would replace a stale entry, when its local store is full, with the new cache line. A thread issues a command to the hardware cache to force data of the stale cache line out to NVRAM. Figure 1 shows that the local store of thread 1 is full, and after inserting the new cache line 0x600, thread 1 instructs the hardware cache to force 0x400 out to the NVRAM storage.

The software cache is placed in the faster DRAM, rather than NVRAM. We use Least-Recently-Used (LRU) replacement policy. Traditionally, hardware cache has been optimized for fast reads. For persistent memory, the software cache only stores modified data.

3   Adaptive Write Caching

It would be beneficial if cache capacity is workload-aware. Overly large cache size incurs a long CPU stall at the end of a FASE, when CPU resources are wasted. Too small cache size would cause too many cache line flushes.

We use the miss ratio curve (MRC). MRC shows cache miss ratios over different cache sizes. We choose the size online adaptively, which has relatively small cache miss ratio based on MRC and is not very large to stall CPU too long, as the software cache size. The number of misses is the number of cache line flushes in the software cache.

In this section, we present a reuse-based locality theory to derive MRC. We consider an execution as a sequence of data accesses (writes). A logical time is assigned to each data access. A time window is designated by two data accesses and includes all intervening accesses. The length of a window is the number of accesses it contains.

The reuse locality is measured by the number of data reuses in a time window. Counting the number of intra-window reuses is the same as counting number of reuse intervals that fall within the window. We define the following:

Definition 1 Reuse interval and Intra-window reuse. *The time interval between a data access and its next access to the same datum is defined as a reuse interval. If a reuse interval is enclosed within a window, we say that the window has an intra-window reuse.*

Different windows may contain different numbers of reuses. We define the timescale reuse *reuse(k)* as the average number of intra-window reuses of all windows of length k. We call the length k the timescale parameter. Given any trace, *reuse(k)* is uniquely defined.

From Reuse to Cache Hit Ratio. At any moment t in fully associative LRU cache, the content consists of data referenced by previous k accesses for some k. *reuse(k)* is the average number of reuses in each k consecutive data accesses. It follows that on average, there are k-*reuse(k)* distinct data in these accesses. The next access is a hit if it is a reuse; otherwise, it is a miss. The difference, $reuse'(k) = reuse(k+1) - reuse(k)$, shows the average portion of times that the next access is a reuse. Hence, the hit ratio of cache of size $(k - reuse(k))$ is the derivative of *reuse(k)* at k, as shown in Eq. 1.

$$hr(c) = reuse'(k) = reuse(k+1) - reuse(k) \qquad (1)$$

where $c = k - reuse(k)$. To illustrate, consider an example pattern "*abab...*" that is infinitely repeating. The following table shows discrete values of *reuse(k)* and hit ratio, where c denotes cache size, i.e., k-*reuse(k)*.

k	$reuse(k)$	c	hr
1	0	1	0
2	0	2	1
3	1	2	1
4	2	2	1

Reuse vs. Footprint Locality. Footprint $fp(k)$ is the average number of distinct data accesses in all windows of length k [4]. Hence, it is obvious that $fp(k)$ plus $reuse(k)$ is k. Xiang et al. showed that the miss ratio is the derivative of footprint [4]. Inspired by their work, we can prove that the derivative of reuse is the hit ratio theoretically. The result is mathematically derivable from footprint, so it is not new. However, the formulation is new and has not been considered in past work. The new derivation gives a new linear-time algorithm to calculate cache performance, which we refer to [3]. In addition, it is the first mathematical connection between the theory of locality [4] (data caching) and the theory of liveness [2,3] (memory allocation).

4   Preliminary Results

We implemented the software cache in `Atlas` [1], and used an emulator to use DRAM to simulate NVRAM. The emulator system is a machine shipped with 60 Intel Xeon E7-4890 cores at 2.8GHz, running Linux kernel 3.10. We tested SPLASH2 benchmark suite for single-threaded runs. We chose the best cache size online once we have MRC. We compared our approach, **SC**, with three alternatives:

- **AT**: the table approach used in the state-of-the-art `Atlas` [1].
- **ER**: the eager approach, which flushes cache lines instantly every time a persistent store happens.
- **LA**: the lazy approach, which flushes all cache lines at the end of a FASE.

Table 1. The data flush ratios of different techniques.

Benchmarks	ER	LA	AT	SC	AT/SC	SC/LA
barnes	1.00000	0.00295	0.08206	0.00391	20.987×	1.325×
fmm	1.00000	0.00246	0.01683	0.00328	5.131×	1.333×
ocean	1.00000	0.09203	0.40290	0.16467	2.447×	1.789×
raytrace	1.00000	0.07140	0.13952	0.07918	1.762×	1.108×
volrend	1.00000	0.00219	0.03189	0.00219	14.561×	1×
water-nsquared	1.00000	0.00107	0.05334	0.00411	12.978×	3.748×
water-spatial	1.00000	0.00103	0.07122	0.00157	45.363×	1.524×
average	1.00000	0.02473	0.11396	0.03698	14.747×	1.893×

Table 1 shows the write-back ratios of the four techniques. SC outperforms AT by 15× significantly, as a result of selection of the best cache size. As profiled, these sizes are all different and hence workload-aware. Moreover, SC achieves the best for *volrend*. We also measured performance in execution time for ER, AT, and SC. Over ER, the speedup of SC ranges from 1.4× to 34.2×, with an average of 9.6×. The average speedup over AT is 2.1×. As tested, the online overhead of MRC computation is negligible. LA reaches the lowest possible, 16%, since it maximally combines data flushes. However, since all cache lines are written back at the end of a FASE, CPU resources are wasted and hence performance is extremely bad. For example, for *volrend*, LA is slower than AT by 17.8× in running time.

References

1. Chakrabarti, D.R., Boehm, H.-J., Bhandari, K.: Atlas: leveraging locks for non-volatile memory consistency. In: Proceedings of OOPSLA (2014)
2. Li, P., Ding, C., Luo, H.: Modeling heap data growth using average liveness. In: Proceedings of ISMM (2014)
3. Li, P., Luo, H., Ding, C.: Rethinking a heap hierarchy as a cache hierarchy: a higher-order theory of memory demand (HOTM). In Proceedings of ISMM (2016)
4. Xiang, X., Ding, C., Luo, H., Bao, B.: HOTL: a higher order theory of locality. In: Proceedings of ASPLOS (2013)

Compiler Analysis and Optimization

Polyhedral Compiler Technology in Collaboration with Autotuning Important to Domain-Specific Frameworks for HPC

Mary Hall[1,2] and Protonu Basu[1,2]([envelope])

[1] School of Computing, University of Utah, Salt Lake City, UT 84103, USA
[2] Lawrence Berkeley National Laboratory, Berkeley, CA 94721, USA
pbasu@lbl.gov

Abstract. Domain-specific frameworks – including embedded domain-specific languages and libraries – increase programmer productivity by encapsulating proven manual optimization strategies into software modules or (semi-)automated tools. In such frameworks, optimizations and optimization strategies capitalize on knowledge of the requirements of a particular application domain to achieve high performance and architecture portability. While many strategies have been used to develop domain-specific frameworks, this position paper argues the importance of polyhedral compiler technology and autotuning for important classes of high-performance computing domains. Such an approach has the following advantages over other strategies: (1) composability; (2) software reuse; and, (3) facilitates performance portability.

Keywords: Domain-specific frameworks · Autotuning · Polyhedral compiler technology

1 Introduction

The President's National Strategic Computing Initiative of July 2015 established as its first objective to accelerate the "...delivery of a *capable* exascale computing system that integrates hardware and software capability..." If we look at the architectural diversity among current supercomputers and also look forward a few years, it is clear that a variety of specialized processor architectures (e.g., Nvidia Pascal GPUs vs. Intel Knights Landing many-cores) and memory systems (e.g., NVRAM and Near-Data Processing) will be developed, and different vendors will provide dramatically different hardware solutions. Consequently, attaining high performance of applications across different exascale platforms may require fundamentally different implementations of software: different algorithms, strategies for parallelization, loop order, data layout and mapping, and exploiting SIMD/SIMT. This need for different implementations is at odds with the goal of *performance portability*, whereby the same application performs well across platforms without significant rewriting. A key concern of the organizations targeting future exascale platforms is the high cost of developing and maintaining

© Springer International Publishing AG 2017
C. Ding et al. (Eds.): LCPC 2016, LNCS 10136, pp. 101–105, 2017.
DOI: 10.1007/978-3-319-52709-3_9

performance-portable applications for diverse exascale architectures, including many-core CPUs and GPUs. Thus, by achieving performance portability, we will also dramatically increase programmer productivity.

Over the last several years, many researchers have addressed performance portability using two key approaches. First, *domain-specific frameworks* – including embedded domain-specific languages and libraries – encapsulate proven manual optimization strategies into software modules and (semi-)automated tools that can produce a collection of architecture-specific implementations. Such frameworks achieve high performance because the optimizations employed and the optimization strategy are specialized to the application domain. Second, *autotuning* involves empirically exploring a search space of possible implementations to identify the best implementation for a particular execution context (e.g., architecture and input data set). By automating the process of evaluating alternatives, autotuning mitigates the need for extensive manual tuning.

While both concepts are well established in the research community, they are nevertheless not widely deployed in the development of HPC applications. As the HPC community prepares for exascale, we must begin now to develop and harden the underlying software capability to provide performance portability and increase programmer productivity; this technology must be ready in a few years to be deployed in exascale applications.

In this position paper, we propose an approach that combines both concepts and, like several research compilers for HPC, relies on *polyhedral transformation and code generation*, which represents loop nest computations mathematically as integer sets, composes sequences of transformations, and generates code using polyhedra scanning. Polyhedral compiler technology and autotuning are well suited to work in collaboration with each other. The mathematical representation of polyhedral frameworks allows the compiler to try a variety of optimization strategies and adjust optimization parameters and still count on being able to generate correct code. Conversely, autotuning frees the compiler developer from having to encode the optimization decisions using a one-size-fits-all algorithm buried inside the compiler implementation. Instead, a variety of optimization strategies can be explored, permitting more aggressive exploration of which transformations to apply.

Our approach separates a high-level C/C++/FORTRAN implementation from architecture-specific implementation (OpenMP, CUDA, etc.), optimization, and tuning. Such an approach would enable exascale application developers to express and maintain a single, portable implementation of their computation, legal code that can be compiled and run using standard tools. An autotuning compiler and search framework, in conjunction with expert programmers and other tools, transforms the baseline code into a collection or search space of highly-optimized implementations. Then autotuning is used to explore this search space and derive final implementations that are best-suited for a specific execution context. *We believe such an approach is reaching a level of maturity that it could realistically be deployed in the early 2020s timeframe for exascale, but it will require institutional support and organization of the parallelizing compiler community to achieve this goal.*

The remainder of this position paper illustrates this approach to productivity and performance portability and its advantages over other approaches to domain-specific frameworks. It concludes by describing the challenges in deploying such an approach in HPC exascale applications.

2   Overview of Approach

Although most of the domain-specific framework literature is not examining HPC applications, the use of domain-specific frameworks in HPC dates back multiple decades, including the Tensor Contraction Engine (a domain-specific compiler), Chombo (a domain-specific C++ library), and high-performance libraries for dense linear algebra (BLAS) and sparse solvers (PETSc).

Recent years have seen polyhedral compiler technology maturing and being applied to code beyond kernels, and deployment in widely-used open source compilers such as LLVM and gcc. Nevertheless, it is broadly considered by potential HPC users to be a technology that is too limited in applicability and too hard to understand. Thus, other "simpler" approaches have gained traction in the HPC application community: (1) specialized manually-written libraries; (2) automatically-generated libraries like ATLAS, SPIRAL and FFTW; (3) specialization through C++ template expansion; (4) single-purpose custom DSLs; and, (5) eDSL frameworks that rely on rewriting rules. While all of these approaches have proven useful, they lack the composability and ability to optimize within context that is afforded from polyhedral frameworks. Therefore, we argue that polyhedral frameworks (in conjunction with autotuning) should be a building block for constructing domain-specific optimization frameworks for HPC.

We draw from our experience in working with application developers and applying the CHiLL autotuning compiler framework to HPC applications across a variety of application domains over the last several years. When used for HPC application code, we argue that the following features are valuable.

- *Composable transformation and code generation:* The importance of having a general and robust transformation framework, where different collections of transformations can be optionally used, is that the same tool can be applied to multiple different application domains. For example, in the last three years, CHiLL has targeted stencils and geometric multigrid, tensor contraction, spectral element methods and sparse linear algebra.
- *Extensible to new domain-specific transformations:* New optimizations that can be represented as transformations on loop nest iteration spaces can be added to such a framework and composed with existing transformations. For example, domain-specific transformations for geometric multigrid including expanding ghost zones and partial sums for higher-order stencils have been composed with existing communication-avoiding optimizations such as fusion and parallel wavefront. For sparse matrices, inspector/executor code generation and support for non-affine transformations are composed with existing

tiling, skew, permute, shift and alignment operations. The tensor contraction support does not require new transformations, but only a new tensor-specific decision algorithm.

- *Optimization strategies and parameters exposed to autotuning:* Another requirement is the ability to generate a variety of optimized code that can be explored for different execution contexts. By exposing high-level expression of the autotuning search space as transformation recipes, the compiler writer, an expert programmer or embedded DSL designer can directly express how to compose transformations that lead to different implementations.
- *Search space navigation:* The compiler framework described above provides a way of expressing a search space of different implementations of a computation to target different execution contexts, including architectures, input data sets and phases of a computation. Typically, this search space is prohibitively large to explore in a brute force manner. Thus, autotuning incorporates sophisticated external search space navigation tools that use heuristics and machine learning to accelerate search space exploration and make it feasible. Examples of search space navigation tools used in the HPC community include Orio, Active Harmony and OpenTuner.

3   Deployment Challenges and Research Opportunities

There is a long history of parallelizing compiler technology in the HPC community, and many promising ideas that never made it into practice. Yet combining polyhedral frameworks and autotuning technology is well suited for code generation and optimization required for exascale. There are challenges to make this vision of practical use to HPC application developers; first consider polyhedral frameworks:

- The technology must be robust, widely available and with a long-term maintenance plan. Thus, incorporation into open source compilers with large development teams is needed. There must be a migration path for research advances to move into practice.
- To extend existing open source polyhedral frameworks to support domain-specific systems and autotuning, optimization strategies need to be exposed to the expert programmer and/or domain-specific tool developer.
- The technology must be more broadly applicable. Restricting to loop nest computations is appropriate for HPC, but we must go beyond affine array-based codes; e.g., indirection used in sparse, adaptive and unstructured algorithms, C++ iterators, parallel constructs must be supported.

For autotuning, a number of practical barriers remain:

- Search space navigation must be practical, which becomes more complex as autotuning goals expand.

- Autotuning needs to be part of an application's build process to truly offer performance portability and a path forward. By integrating into Makefiles, autotuning can be repeated after changes to the code or retargeting the application to new platforms or input data sets.
- Co-tuning of multiple related computations is needed to evaluate global optimizations such as data layout.

Acknowledgments. This work has been supported in part by DOE award DE-SC0008682 and NSF award CCF-1564074.

An Extended Polyhedral Model for SPMD Programs and Its Use in Static Data Race Detection

Prasanth Chatarasi$^{(\boxtimes)}$, Jun Shirako, Martin Kong, and Vivek Sarkar

Rice University, Houston, TX 77005, USA
{prasanth,shirako,mkong,vsarkar}@rice.edu

Abstract. Despite its age, SPMD (Single Program Multiple Data) parallelism continues to be one of the most popular parallel execution models in use today, as exemplified by OpenMP for multicore systems and CUDA and OpenCL for accelerator systems. The basic idea behind the SPMD model, which makes it different from task-parallel models, is that all logical processors (worker threads) execute the same program with sequential code executed redundantly and parallel code executed cooperatively. In this paper, we extend the polyhedral model to enable analysis of explicitly parallel SPMD programs and provide a new approach for static detection of data races in SPMD programs using the extended polyhedral model. We evaluate our approach using 34 OpenMP programs from the `OmpSCR` and `PolyBench-ACC` (PolyBench-ACC derives from the PolyBench benchmark suite and provides OpenMP, OpenACC, CUDA, OpenCL and HMPP implementations.) benchmark suites.

Keywords: SPMD parallelism · Data race detection · Polyhedral model · Phase mapping · Space mapping · May happen in parallel relations

1 Introduction

It is widely recognized that computer systems anticipated in the 2020 time frame will be qualitatively different from current and past computer systems. Specifically, they will be built using homogeneous and heterogeneous many-core processors with 100's of cores per chip, and their performance will be driven by parallelism, and constrained by energy and data movement [21]. This trend towards ubiquitous parallelism has forced the need for improved productivity and scalability in parallel programming models. Historically, the most successful runtimes for shared memory multiprocessors have been based on bulk-synchronous Single Program Multiple Data (SPMD) execution models [10]. OpenMP [18] represents one such embodiment in which the programmer's view of the runtime is that of a fixed number of threads executing computations in "redundant" or "work-sharing" parallel modes.

As with other imperative parallel programming models, data races are a pernicious source of bugs in the SPMD model. Recent efforts on static data

© Springer International Publishing AG 2017
C. Ding et al. (Eds.): LCPC 2016, LNCS 10136, pp. 106–120, 2017.
DOI: 10.1007/978-3-319-52709-3_10

race detection include approaches based on symbolic execution [15,23], and on polyhedral analysis [3,24]. Past work on data race detection using polyhedral approaches have either focused on loop level parallelism, as exemplified by OpenMP's `parallel for` construct, or on task parallelism, as exemplified by X10's `async` and `finish` constructs, but not on general SPMD parallelism.

In this paper, we introduce a new approach for static detection of data races by extending the polyhedral model to enable analysis of explicitly parallel SPMD programs.[1] The key contributions of the paper are as follows:

1. An extension of the polyhedral model to represent SPMD programs.
2. Formalization of the May Happen in Parallel (MHP) relation in the extended polyhedral model.
3. An approach for static detection of data races in SPMD programs.
4. Demonstration of our approach on 34 OpenMP programs from the `OmpSCR` and the `PolyBench-ACC` OpenMP benchmark suites.

The rest of the paper is organized as follows. Section 2 summarizes the background for this work. Section 3 motivates the proposed approach for race detection. Section 4 includes limitations of the existing polyhedral model, and the details of our extensions to the polyhedral model to represent SPMD programs. Section 5 shows how the MHP relation can be formalized in the extended model and describes our approach to compile-time data race detection. Section 6 contains our experimental results for data race detection. Finally, Sect. 7 summarizes related work, and Sect. 8 contains our conclusions and future work.

2 Background

This section briefly summarizes the SPMD execution model using OpenMP APIs, as well as an introduction to data race detection, which provides the motivation for our work. Then, we briefly summarize the polyhedral model since it provides the foundation for our proposed approach to static data race detection.

2.1 SPMD Parallelism Using OpenMP

SPMD (Single Program Multiple Data) parallelism [9,10] continues to be one of the most popular parallel execution models in use today, as exemplified by OpenMP for multicore systems and CUDA, OpenCL for accelerator systems. The basic idea behind the SPMD model is that all logical processors (worker threads) execute the same program, with sequential code executed redundantly and parallel code (worksharing, barrier constructs, etc.) executed cooperatively.

In this paper, we focus on OpenMP [18] as an exemplar of SPMD parallelism. The OpenMP `parallel` construct indicates the creation of a fixed number of parallel worker threads to execute an SPMD parallel region. The OpenMP `barrier`

---

[1] An earlier version of this paper was presented at the IMPACT'16 workshop [6], a forum that does not include formal proceedings.

construct specifies a barrier operation among all threads in the current `parallel` region. In this paper, we restrict our attention to textually aligned barriers, in which all threads encounter the same textual sequence of barriers. Each dynamic instance of the same `barrier` operation must be encountered by all threads, e.g., it is not permisible for a barrier in a then-clause of an if statement executed by (say) thread 0 to be matched with a barrier in an else-clause of the same if statement executed by thread 1. We plan to address textually unaligned barriers as part of the future work. However, many software developers believe that textually aligned barriers are better from a software engineering perspective.

The OpenMP `for` construct indicates that the immediately following loop can be parallelized and executed in a work-sharing mode by all the threads in the parallel SPMD region. An implicit barrier is performed immediately after a `for` loop, while the `nowait` clause disables this implicit barrier. Further, a `barrier` is not allowed to be used inside a `for` loop. When the `schedule(`*kind*, *chunk_size*`)` clause is attached to a `for` construct, its parallel iterations are grouped into batches of *chunk_size* iterations, which are then scheduled on the worker threads according to the policy specified by *kind*.

The OpenMP `master` construct indicates that the immediately following region of code is to be executed only by the master thread of the parallel SPMD region. Note that, there is no implied barrier associated with this construct.

2.2 Data Race Detection

Data races are a major source of semantic errors in shared memory parallel programs. In general, a data race occurs when two or more threads perform conflicting accesses (such that at least one access is a write) to a shared location without any synchronization among threads. Complicating matters, data races may occur only in some of the possible schedules of a parallel program, thereby making them notoriously hard to detect and reproduce. A large variety of static and dynamic data race detection techniques have been developed over the years with a wide range of guarantees with respect to the scope of the checking (schedule-specific, input-specific, or general) and precision (acceptable levels of false negatives and false positives) supported. Among these, the holy grail is static checking of parallel programs with no false negatives and minimal false positives. This level of static data race detection has remained an open problem for SPMD programs, even though there has been significant progress in recent years on race detection for restricted subsets of fork-join and OpenMP programs [15, 16, 23], as well as for higher-level programming models [2–4, 24].

2.3 Polyhedral Model

The polyhedral model is a flexible representation for arbitrarily nested loops [12]. Loop nests amenable to this algebraic representation are called *Static Control Parts* (SCoP's) and represented in the SCoP format, which includes four elements for each statement, namely, iteration domains, access relations, the program schedule and dependence polyhedra/relations. In the original formulation of polyhedral frameworks, all array subscripts, loop bounds, and branch conditions in *analyzable* programs were required to be affine functions of loop index variables and global parameters. However, decades of research since then have led to a significant expansion of programs that can be considered analyzable by polyhedral frameworks [8].

Iteration Domain, $\mathcal{D}^S$: A statement S enclosed by m loops is represented by an m-dimensional polytope, referred to as the iteration domain of the statement. Each point in the iteration domain is an execution instance $i \in \mathcal{D}^S$ of the statement.

Access Relation, $\mathcal{A}^S(i)$: Each array reference in a statement is expressed through an access relation, which maps a statement instance i to one or more array elements to be read/written. This mapping is expressed in the affine form of loop iterators and global parameters; a scalar variable is considered to be a degenerate (zero-dimensional) array.

Schedule, $\Theta^S(i)$: The execution order of a program is captured by the schedule, which maps instance i to a logical time-stamp. In general, a schedule is expressed as a multidimensional vector, and statement instances are executed according to the increasing lexicographic order of their timestamps.

Dependence Relation, $\mathcal{D}^{S \rightarrow T}$: Program dependences in polyhedral frameworks are represented using dependence relations that map instances between two statement iteration domains, i.e., $i \in S$ to $j \in T$. These relations are then leveraged to compute a new program schedule that respects the order of the statement instances in the dependence.

3   Motivation

To motivate the proposed approach for static detection of data races, we discuss an explicitly parallel SPMD kernel as an illustrative example.

Illustrative Example. The example shown in Figure 1) is a 2-dimensional Jacobi computation from the OmpSCR benchmark suite [11]. The computation is parallelized using the OpenMP parallel construct with worksharing directives (lines 5, 11) and synchronization directives (implicit barriers from lines 5, 11). The first for-loop is parallelized (at line 5) to produce values of the array uold. Similarly, the second for-loop is parallelized (at line 11) to consume values of the array uold. The reduced error (from the reduction clause at line 11) is updated by only the master thread in the region (lines 26–29). Finally, the entire computation in lines 5–29 is repeated until it reaches the maximum number of iterations (or) the error is less than a threshold value. This pattern is very common in many stencil programs, often with multidimensional loops and multidimensional arrays. Although the worksharing parallel loops have implicit barriers, the programmer who contributed this code to the OmpSCR suite likely overlooked the fact that a master region does not include a barrier. As a result, data races are

```
 1 #pragma omp parallel private(resid, i)//tid-thread id
 2 {
 3     while (k <= maxit && error > tol) { //S1
 4     /* copy new solution into old */
 5 #pragma omp for
 6         for (j=0; j<m; j++)
 7           for (i=0; i<n; i++)
 8             uold[i + m*j] = u[i + m*j];

10         /* compute stencil, residual and update */
11 #pragma omp for reduction(+:error)
12         for (j=1; j<m-1; j++)
13           for (i=1; i<n-1; i++) {
14             resid=(ax*(uold[i-1+m*j] + uold[i+1+m*j]) + ay*(uold[i+m*(j-1)]
15                    + uold[i+m*(j+1)]) + b*uold[i+m*j] - f[i+m*j]) / b;

17             /* update solution */
18             u[i + m*j] = uold[i + m*j] - omega * resid;

20             /* accumulate residual error */
21             error =error + resid*resid;
22           }

24         /* error check */
25 #pragma omp master
26         {
27           k++; //S2
28           error = sqrt(error) /(n*m); //S3
29         }
30     } /* while */
31 } /* end parallel */
```

Fig. 1. A data race between statements S1 (at line 3), S2 (line 27) on variable k and another data race between statements S1 (at line 3), S3 (line 28) on variable **error** in 2-D Jacobi kernel from OmpSCR benchmark suite.

possible in this example since statement S1's (at line 3) read access of variables k, error by a non-master thread can execute in parallel with an update of the same variables performed in statements S2 (at line 27) and S3 (at line 28) by the master thread. These races can be fixed by inserting another barrier immediately after the **master** region.

We observe that existing static race detection tools (e.g., [3,23]) are unable to identify such races since they don't model barriers inside of imperfectly nested sequential loops in the SPMD regions. We also observe that existing dynamic race detection tools such as Intel Inspector XE (2015 Update 1) in its **default** mode miss this true race and hybrid race detection tools such as ARCHER [2] incurred significant runtime overhead to detect this true race. In contrast, our proposed approach using the extended polyhedral model can identify such races at compile-time by effectively capturing execution phases from **barrier** directives via static analysis of SPMD regions.

4   Extended Polyhedral Model for SPMD Programs

In this section, we begin with discussing limitations of the polyhedral model for analyzing SPMD programs. Then, we summarize our extensions to the polyhedral model to support SPMD parallelism.

4.1   Limitations

The polyhedral model is an algebraic representation used in compiler techniques for analysis and transformation of perfectly/imperfectly nested loops in sequential programs. Recent efforts [5] have extended polyhedral modeling techniques to explicitly parallel programs, but assuming the "serial-elision" property i.e., the property that removal of all parallel constructs results in a sequential program that is a valid (albeit inefficient) implementation of the parallel program semantics. Note that SPMD programs don't satisfy the "serial-elision" property because (for example) removing a barrier from an SPMD region would alter the semantics.

An interesting property of an explicitly parallel program is that it specifies a partial execution order unlike a sequential program, which specifies a total order. The schedule mapping (defined in Sect. 2.3) was originally introduced to represent the total order present in a sequential program. However, it can also be used to specify parallelism by assigning the same logical timestamp to multiple statement instances, thereby indicating that they can be executed at the same time. Still, this mapping is not always sufficient to capture the partial order in a SPMD program. Hence, we extend the schedule mapping with space and phase mappings (defined in the following sections) to explicitly capture the partial order.

4.2   Space (Allocation) Mapping, Θ_A^S

Space (Allocation) mapping assigns a processor stamp to a statement instance 'S' that indicates a logical processor id on which the instance has to be executed. For the OpenMP program in Fig. 1, the space mappings for statements S1, S2, and S3 are (tid), (0), and (0) respectively where tid is an iterator from the logical parallel loop (line 1).

As a convenience for computing the space mappings, we (1) Replace the omp parallel region header by a logical parallel loop that iterates over threads, (2) Enclose the body of static scheduled worksharing loop in an if block with the condition on the thread iterator to be a function of lower and upper bounds, the loop chunk size and total number of threads participating in the worksharing loop (the last two are treated as fixed but unknown program parameters), (3) Insert an explicit barrier immediately after the worksharing loop (or) single region if a nowait clause is not specified, (4) Enclose the body of master region in an if block with the condition on the thread iterator to be zero. (Note that these transformations are only performed for the purpose of program analysis, and do not result in changes in the original program.)

Space mapping (physical thread distribution) of a statement instance may contain non-affine and unknown functions when the statement instance is enclosed in an OpenMP single construct or another OpenMP worksharing loop with a static schedule, parametric chunk size and parametric number of threads. However, we conservatively compare name and arguments of space mapping of a thread with other threads to distinguish as two different threads.

4.3   Phase Mapping, Θ_P^S

A key property of the SPMD programs is that their execution can be partitioned into a sequence of phases separated by barriers. It has been observed in past work that statements from different execution phases cannot execute concurrently [26]. Thus, only pairs of data accesses that execute within the same phase need to be considered as potential candidates for data races. The phase mapping assigns a logical identifier, which we refer to as a phase stamp, to each statement instance 'S'. Thus, statement instances are executed according to increasing lexicographic order of their phase-stamps.

Algorithm 1. Computation of phase mappings for statements in a SCoP

---

1 **begin**

    /* Extract initial schedules (time stamps)   */

2   θ^S := Statement schedules from SCoP

3   θ^B := Barrier schedules from SCoP

    /* Compute a map from statements to barriers such that elements
        of statements are lexicographically strictly smaller than
        those of barriers   */

4     $\delta^{S \to B} := \{ \boldsymbol{x} \to \boldsymbol{y} : \theta(\boldsymbol{x}) \prec \theta(\boldsymbol{y}), \boldsymbol{x} \in S, \boldsymbol{y} \in B \}$

    /* Build a map from time stamps of statements to time stamps of
        barriers with lexicographically strictly smaller property   */

5     $\delta^{\theta(S) \to \theta(B)} := (\theta^S)^{-1} \circ \delta^{S \to B} \circ \theta^B$

    /* Extract a map from pairs of statement and barrier timestamps
        to their time difference   */

6     $\delta^{(S,B) \to (\theta(B) - \theta(S))} := \{ (\theta(\boldsymbol{x}) \to \theta(\boldsymbol{y})) \to (\theta(\boldsymbol{y}) - \theta(\boldsymbol{x})) : \boldsymbol{x} \in S, \boldsymbol{y} \in B \}$

    /* Compute a map from each statement time stamp to the time stamp
        of the closest barrier instance for each lexical barrier   */

7     $\beta := dom(lexmin(\delta^{(S,B) \to (\theta(B) - \theta(S))}))$

    /* Compute a map (reachable barriers) from each statement
        instance to the closest barrier instance, among all lexical
        barriers   */

8     $\beta^S := lexmin(\theta^S \circ \beta) \circ (\theta^B)^{-1}$

    /* Compute phase mappings by union of timestamp of the reachable
        barrier instances to each statement instance   */

9   Phase mappings, $\Theta_P^S := \beta^S \circ \theta^B$

10 **end**

Algorithm 1 summarizes the overall approach to compute the phase mappings for statements in a given SCoP by taking regular statement and barriers schedules as input (at lines 2–3 in Algorithm 1). In order to compute the phase mappings, we define reachable barriers for a statement instance 'S' (at line 8 in Algorithm 1) as a set of barrier instances that can be executed after the statement instance 'S' without an intervening barrier instance. For the OpenMP program in Figure 1, reachable barriers for the statement S2 are the implicit barrier instance (at line 9) in the next iteration of `while` loop and the implicit barrier at the end of the `parallel` region (at line 31). The phase mapping for a statement instance (at line 9 in Algorithm 1) is computed as the union of the schedule (timestamp) of all reachable barriers of the statement instance. There exists only one such reachable barrier at run-time for a given dynamic statement instance under the assumption of textually aligned barriers and it would be one (based on the program parameters) from the statically determined set of reachable barriers.

5   Static Data Race Detection

In this section, we begin with workflow of our tool(PolyOMP) for static data race detection. Then, we explain the formalization of MHP relations using the extended polyhedral model and describe our approach to static data race detection.

5.1   PolyOMP Workflow

The overall workflow is summarized in Fig. 2, which is implemented as an extension to the Polyhedral Extraction Tool (PET) [22], and consists of the following components: (1) Conversion from input OpenMP-C program to Clang AST with the help of Clang-omp (version: 3.5) [7] and LLVM (version: 3.5.svn), (2) Conversion from Clang AST to PET AST (defined in [22]) (with the support for `omp parallel`, `for`, `parallel for`, `barrier`, `single`, `master` directives and nested parallel regions), (3)

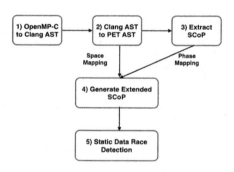

Fig. 2. Overview of PolyOMP

Extract SCoP (refer to Sect. 2.3) from the PET AST, (4) Generate Extended SCoP (SCoP with space and phase mappings) from the PET AST and the SCoP, (5) Perform static race detection to detect races with the help of MHP relations.

5.2   Formalization of May Happen in Parallel (MHP) Relations

May Happen in Parallel (MHP) analysis determines if it is possible for execution instances of two statement instances to execute in parallel [1]. In general, two statement instances S and T can execute in parallel iff both of them are in the same phase of computation (not ordered by synchronization, $\Theta_P^A = \Theta_P^T$) and are executed by different threads ($\Theta_A^S \neq \Theta_A^T$) in the region. Algorithm 2 summarizes the overall steps to build the MHP relation on a given pair of statements S, T.

Algorithm 2. Building MHP relation between statement instances S, T

---

1 **begin**

    /* Extract space and phase mappings of statements S and T   */

2    $\Theta_A^S, \Theta_A^T :=$ Space mappings of S, T

3    $\Theta_P^S, \Theta_P^T :=$ Phase mappings of S, T

    /* Compute a map from S to T such that they are in same phase   */

4    $\delta_{SamePhase}^{S \to T} := \Theta_P^S \; \circ \; (\Theta_P^T)^{-1}$

    /* Compute a map from S to T such that they are on same thread */

5    $\delta_{SameThread}^{S \to T} := \Theta_A^S \; \circ \; (\Theta_A^T)^{-1}$

    /* Compute the cross product of S and T   */

6    $\delta_{CrossProduct}^{S \to T} := dom(\Theta_A^S) \times dom(\Theta_A^T)$

    /* Compute a map from S to T such that they are run on different threads   */

7    $\delta_{DiffThreads}^{S \to T} := \delta_{CrossProduct}^{S \to T} - \delta_{SameThreads}^{S \to T}$

    /* Build MHP relation by intersecting the same phase and different thread maps of S and T   */

8    $\delta_{MHP}^{S \to T} := \delta_{DiffThreads}^{S \to T} \cap \delta_{SamePhase}^{S \to T}$

9 **end**

5.3   Race Detection

Detecting read-write and write-write data races becomes straightforward with the availability of MHP relations. In general, there exists a race between statements S and T on memory location 'x' iff MHP(S, T) is true, and access relations of S and T intersect each other on memory location x and at-least one of them is a write. Our approach considers all possible pairs of the statements in the SCoP and builds race conditions as per the above criteria and solves for the existence of solutions.

Our approach is guaranteed to be exact (with neither false positives nor false negatives) if the input program satisfies all the standard preconditions of the polyhedral model (without any non-affine constructs). Thanks to the PET framework's [22] ability to handle non-affine constructs (in both data subscripts and control flow) elegantly in the form of may-write access relations, our approach now incorporates may-write access relations while computing data races and hence it may induce false positives (but not false negatives) for non-affine programs.

Limitations. The current implementation supports OpenMP constructs such as omp parallel for, parallel for, barrier, single, master directives and nested parallel regions. Our tool currently does not perform any pointer based analysis. However, previous works on pointer analysis can be added as a pre-pass to our race detection stage to enhance the race detection. The support for analyzing SPMD programs with lock-based synchronization and task-based constructs are part of future work.

6   Experimental Evaluation

In this section, we present the evaluation of our approach for static race detection using the extended polyhedral model. Tables 1 and 2 list the number of races discovered by our PolyOMP tool in the OmpSCR and PolyBench-ACC suites, along with the number of different OpenMP constructs in each benchmark. The experiments have been performed on a quad core-i7 (2.2 GHz) machine with 16 GB main memory.

6.1   OmpSCR Benchmarks Suite

OmpSCR, an OpenMP Source Code Repository [11], consists of OpenMP applications written in C, C++ and Fortran. There are 18 OpenMP-C benchmarks in this repository, 6 of which use C structs and pointer arithmetic. Since we defer support for C structs and pointer arithmetic in our current toolchain for future work, our results focus on the remaining 12 OpenMP-C benchmarks in OmpSCR, which are listed in Table 1.

Table 1. Race detection analysis over the subset of OmpSCR benchmark suite. #SPMD / #WS / #Barriers : Number of SPMD regions, Number of worksharing directives in a SPMD region, Number of barriers including implicit. PolyOMP - Detection time / Reported / False +ves : Total time taken to detect races by PolyOMP, Number of reported races, Number of false positives among reported. ARCHER / Intel Inspector XE: Number of races reported.

Benchmark	#SPMD	#WS	#Barriers	PolyOMP			ARCHER	Intel Inspector XE
				Detection time (s)	Reported	False + ves		
Jacobi01	2	1	1	1.38	2	2	0	0
Jacobi02	1	2	2	3.91	2	2	0	0
Jacobi03	1	3	3	1.54	4	2	2	0
Lud	1	1	1	0.30	0	0	0	1
LoopA.bad	1	1	1	0.20	1	0	1	2
LoopA.sol1	2	1	2	0.44	0	0	0	2
LoopA.sol2	1	0	2	1.21	7	7	0	0
LoopA.sol3	1	0	2	1.19	7	7	0	0
LoopB.bad1	1	1	1	0.20	1	0	1	2
LoopB.bad2	1	1	1	0.21	1	0	1	2
LoopB.pipe	1	0	2	2.40	7	7	0	0
C_pi	1	1	1	0.05	0	0	0	1
Total	14	12	19	13.03	32	27	5	10

This benchmark suite contains known races, as reported in prior work on dynamic data race detection in the ARCHER tool [2]. Our evaluation shows that PolyOMP is able to detect all of the documented races in the following applications using the static analysis algorithm in this paper: Jacobi03, LoopA.bad,

LoopB.bad1, LoopB.bad2. All reported races (column Reported) were manually verified. (Note: each reported data race corresponds to a static pair of conflicting accesses). The False +ves column shows the number of reported races that actually are false positives. In addition, we compared our reported races with those reported by ARCHER[2]. Our tool computes races conservatively when unanalyzable control flow or data accesses are present and result in false positive races. This is evident in benchmarks Jacobi01, Jacobi02, Jacobi03, LoopA.sol2, LoopA.sol3 and LoopB.pipe since they contain linearized array subscripts, thereby yielding 27 false positives. However, when the parallel region fully satisfies all the assumptions of standard polyhedral frameworks (e.g., all array accesses and branch conditions must be affine functions of the loop variables) then all reported races are true races. Even though Intel Inspector XE (2015 update 1 with default mode) was able to identify the true races in LoopA.bad, LoopB.bad1 and LoopB.bad2, it failed to detect the races in Jacobi03 (explained in Sect. 3). Furthermore, it reported additional false races on the iterators of parallel loops for benchmarks Lud, LoopA.bad, LoopA.sol1, LoopB.bad1, LoopB.bad2 and C_pi.

6.2 PolyBench-ACC Benchmark Suite

We also use PolyBench-ACC, another benchmark suite partially derived from the standard PolyBench benchmark suite [13]. There are 32 OpenMP-C benchmarks in this suite, for which we were unable to compile 10 benchmarks due to compile-time errors arising from the usage of OpenMP directives in those codes. Thus, our results focus on the remaining 22 OpenMP-C benchmarks in PolyBench-ACC.

All of the benchmarks in this suite have statically analyzable control flow, affine subscripts and completely fit the assumptions of the polyhedral model. found the races to be real. Moreover, our static analysis does not need to resort to conservative estimations for these benchmarks, as they meet all the standard affine requirements.

Currently, we are not aware of any prior work reporting data races in this benchmark suite. Hence, we compared our reported races with those reported by the Intel Inspector XE tool (2015 update 1 with default mode), which (unlike ARCHER) is known to have false negatives even for a given input. Overall, our tool reported a total of 61 races whereas Intel Inspector XE could only find 31 races. The details are presented in Table 2. A table entry marked with the letter "H" indicates that the Intel Inspector XE tool would get into a hang mode for that benchmark, while a table entry marked with the letter "A" indicates that the Intel Inspector XE tool encountered an Application exception for that benchmark. The explanations for the races in the PolyBench-ACC benchmark suite are: (1) The majority of the data races in Cholesky and Gramschmidt originate from conflicting accesses on scalar variables inside the worksharing loops. These races can be fixed by privatizing the scalars; (2) Data races in

---

[2] ARCHER is known to not have any false positives or false negatives for a given input, but may have false negatives for inputs that it has not seen.

Table 2. Race detection analysis over the subset of `PolyBench-ACC` benchmark suite. #SPMD/#WS/#Barriers: Number of SPMD regions, Number of worksharing directives in a SPMD region, Number of barriers including implicit. PolyOMP - Detection time/Reported/False +ves: Total time taken to detect races by PolyOMP, Number of reported races, Number of false positives among reported. Intel Inspector XE: Number of races reported, Hang up (H) and Application exception (A).

Benchmark	#SPMD	#WS	#Barriers	PolyOMP			Intel Inspector XE
				Detection time (s)	Reported	False +ves	
Correlation	1	4	4	2.30	0	0	H
Covariance	1	3	3	1.04	0	0	H
2 mm	1	2	2	0.64	0	0	0
3 mm	1	3	3	1.13	0	0	0
Atax	1	2	2	0.37	2	0	2
Bicg	1	2	2	0.43	2	0	2
Cholesky	1	1	1	0.49	28	0	8
Doitgen	1	1	1	0.54	0	0	0
Gemm	1	1	1	0.34	0	0	0
Gemver	1	4	4	0.75	0	0	0
Gesummv	1	1	1	0.52	0	0	0
Mvt	1	2	2	0.32	0	0	0
Symm	1	1	1	0.64	5	0	5
Syrk	1	2	2	0.39	0	0	0
Syr2k	1	2	2	0.52	0	0	0
Trmm	1	1	1	0.28	1	0	1
Durbin	1	2	2	0.73	6	0	0
Gramschmidt	1	1	1	0.36	12	0	8
Lu	1	1	1	0.33	5	0	5
Convolution-2	1	1	1	0.25	0	0	0
Convolution-3	1	1	1	0.42	0	0	A
Fdtd-ampl	1	1	1	1.62	0	0	0
Total	22	39	39	14.41	61	0	31

`Atax` and `Bicg` are on the common array elements which are updated inside a sequential loop of the SPMD region; (3) Data races in remaining benchmarks arise on shared arrays and on worksharing (parallel) outer loops.

7   Related Work

In this section, we discuss past work related to compile-time detection of data races, and the analysis of textually aligned barriers present in SPMD programs.

7.1   Static Race Detection

There is an extensive literature on identifying races in explicitly parallel programs (at compile-time [3,4,15,16,23,24], run-time [20], and hybrid combinations of both [19]). We focus our discussion on past work of static analysis techniques for identifying data races in SPMD-style parallel programs.

Symbolic approaches have received a lot of attention in analyzing parallel programs, mainly in the context of OpenMP. Yu et al's [23] work checks the consistency of multi-threaded programs with OpenMP directives using extended thread automata (with a tool called Pathg). However, their race detection is only guaranteed for a fixed number of worker threads. Ma et al. [15] use a symbolic execution-based approach (running the program on symbolic inputs and fixed number of threads) to detect data races in OpenMP codes, based on constraint solving using an SMT solver. The data races reported from this toolkit (called OAT) are applicable only to a fixed number of input threads, unlike our approach which allows the number of threads to be unknown.

Polyhedral based approaches have gained significant interest in analyzing parallel programs due to its ability to perform exact analysis on affine programs. Basupalli et al. [3] presented an approach (ompVerify) to detect data races inside a given worksharing loop using polyhedral dependence analysis. However, this approach handled only affine constructs and was limited to worksharing loops, rather than to general SPMD parallel regions. Yuki et al. [24] presented an adaptation of array data-flow analysis to X10 programs with finish/async parallelism. In this approach, the happens-before relations are first analyzed, and the data-flow is computed based on the partial order imposed by happen-before relations. This extended array data flow analysis is used to certify determinacy in X10 finish/ async parallel programs by identifying the possibility of multiple sources of writes for a given read. Their extended work [25] formulated the happens-before relations with X10 clocks in a polyhedral context. This approach provides the race-free guarantee of clocked X10 programs by disproving all possible races. But, it doesn't provide races present in the input program since computing happens-before relations involves polynomials in a general case.

Atzeni et al. [2] introduced a hybrid static+dynamic approach (ARCHER) to achieve high accuracy, low overheads on large applications to detect data races. The static part of ARCHER tool leverages an existing polyhedral dependence analyzer to identify races in a given worksharing loop. Our static approach can be complemented with the dynamic analysis of ARCHER tool to further reduce dynamic overheads as observed for the benchmark in Fig. 1 (refer to Sect. 3).

There has been attention given to the analysis of textually aligned barriers at compile-time. The work by sYelick et. al on concurrency analysis [14] computes MHP relations using a graph-based approach over single-valued expressions. Then, concurrent statements are identified using a depth-first search from a given statement. The MHP relations computed using graph-based approach is conservative since it doesn't analyze statements and barriers at the instance level when they are enclosed in loops, in contrast to the exactness of our approach for affine programs. It also doesn't consider thread-mapping information in computing MHP relations.

8 Conclusions and Future Work

This work is motivated by the observation that software with explicit parallelism is on the rise, and that SPMD parallelism is a common model for explicit parallelism as evidenced by the popularity of OpenMP, OpenCL and CUDA. As with other imperative parallel programming models, data races are a pernicious source of bugs in the SPMD model and may occur only in few of the possible schedules of a parallel program, thereby making them extremely hard to detect dynamically.

In this paper, we introduced a new approach for static detection of data races by extending the polyhedral model to enable analysis of explicitly parallel SPMD programs. We evaluated our technique using 34 OpenMP programs from the OmpSCR and PolyBench-ACC benchmark suites. We formalize the May Happen in Parallel (MHP) relations by adding "space" and "phase" dimensions to the schedule, and is guaranteed to be exact (with neither false positives nor false negatives) for identifying data races if the input program satisfies all the standard preconditions of the polyhedral model.

In summary, our contributions include the following: (1) An extension of the polyhedral model to represent SPMD programs, (2) Formalization of the May Happen in Parallel (MHP) relation in the extended model, (3) An approach for static detection of data races in SPMD programs, and (4) Demonstration of our approach on 34 OpenMP programs from the OmpSCR and PolyBench-ACC benchmark suites.

As future work, we plan to leverage our framework to address problems such as redundant barrier optimization, detection of false sharing patterns, deadlock identification and coupling it with dynamic analysis techniques to prune false positives arising from unanalyzable data accesses, as done in [2,17].

References

1. Agarwal, S., Barik, R., Sarkar, V., Shyamasundar, R.K.: May-happen-in-parallel analysis of X10 programs. In: PPoPP, New York, NY, USA (2007)
2. Atzeni, S., Gopalakrishnan, G., Rakamarić, Z., Ahn, D.H., Laguna, I., Schulz, M., Lee, G.L., Protze, J., Müller, M.S.: Archer: effectively spotting data races in large OpenMP applications. In: IPDPS (2016)
3. Basupalli, V., Yuki, T., Rajopadhye, S., Morvan, A., Derrien, S., Quinton, P., Wonnacott, D.: Polyhedral analysis for the OpenMP programmer. In: Chapman, B.M., Gropp, W.D., Kumaran, K., Müller, M.S. (eds.) IWOMP 2011. LNCS, vol. 6665, pp. 37–53. Springer, Heidelberg (2011). doi:10.1007/978-3-642-21487-5_4
4. Betts, A., Chong, N., Donaldson, A., Qadeer, S., Thomson, P.: GPUVerify: a verifier for GPU Kernels. In: OOPSLA (2012)
5. Chatarasi, P., Shirako, J., Sarkar, V.: Polyhedral optimizations of explicitly parallel programs. In: PACT (2015)
6. Chatarasi, P., Shirako, J., Sarkar, V.: Static data race detection for SPMD programs using an extended polyhedral representation. In: IMPACT (2016)
7. Clang, O.M.P.: CLANG Support for OpenMP 3.1. https://clang-omp.github.io

8. Collard, J.F., Barthou, D., Feautrier, P.: Fuzzy array dataflow analysis. In: Proceedings of the Fifth ACM SIGPLAN Symposium on Principles and Practice of Parallel Programming, PPoPP 1995, pp. 92–101. ACM, New York (1995)
9. Cytron, R., Lipkis, J., Schonberg, E.: a compiler-assisted approach to SPMD execution. In: Supercomputing, Los Alamitos, CA, USA (1990)
10. Darema, F., et al.: A single-program-multiple-data computational model for EPEX/FORTRAN. Parallel Comput. **7**(1), 11–24 (1988)
11. Dorta, A.J., Rodriguez, C., Sande, F.d., Gonzalez-Escribano, A.: The OpenMP source code repository. In: PDP, Washington, DC, USA (2005)
12. Feautrier, P., Lengauer, C.: Polyhedron model. In: Padua, D.A. (ed.) Encyclopedia of Parallel Computing, pp. 1581–1592. Springer, Heidelberg (2011)
13. Grauer-Gray, S., Xu, L., Searles, R., Ayalasomayajula, S., Cavazos, J.: Auto-tuning a High-Level Language Targeted to GPU Codes (2012)
14. Kamil, A., Yelick, K.: Concurrency analysis for parallel programs with textually aligned barriers. In: Ayguadé, E., Baumgartner, G., Ramanujam, J., Sadayappan, P. (eds.) LCPC 2005. LNCS, vol. 4339, pp. 185–199. Springer, Heidelberg (2006). doi:10.1007/978-3-540-69330-7_13
15. Ma, H., Diersen, S.R., Wang, L., Liao, C., Quinlan, D., Yang, Z.: Symbolic analysis of concurrency errors in OpenMP programs. In: ICPP, Washington, DC, USA (2013)
16. Mellor-Crummey, J.: Compile-time support for efficient data race detection in shared-memory parallel programs. In: PADD, New York, NY, USA (1993)
17. O'Callahan, R., Choi, J.D.: hybrid dynamic data race detection. In: Proceedings of PPoPP (2003)
18. OpenMP Specifications. http://openmp.org/wp/openmp-specifications
19. Protze, J., Atzeni, S., Ahn, D.H., Schulz, M., Gopalakrishnan, G., Müller, M.S., Laguna, I., Rakamarić, Z., Lee, G.L.: Towards providing low-overhead data race detection for large OpenMP applications. In: Proceedings of the 2014 LLVM Compiler Infrastructure in HPC (2014)
20. Raman, R., Zhao, J., Sarkar, V., Vechev, M.T., Yahav, E.: Scalable and precise dynamic datarace detection for structured parallelism. In: Proceedings of PLDI (2012)
21. Sarkar, V., Harrod, W., Snavely, A.E.: Software Challenges in Extreme Scale Systems, Special Issue on Advanced Computing: The Roadmap to Exascale, January 2010
22. Verdoolaege, S., Grosser, T.: Polyhedral extraction tool. In: Second International Workshop on Polyhedral Compilation Techniques (IMPACT 2012), Paris, France (2012)
23. Yu, F., Yang, S.C., Wang, F., Chen, G.C., Chan, C.C.: Symbolic consistency checking of OpenMp parallel programs. In: LCTES (2012)
24. Yuki, T., Feautrier, P., Rajopadhye, S., Saraswat, V.: Array dataflow analysis for polyhedral X10 programs. In: Proceedings of PPoPP (2013)
25. Yuki, T., Feautrier, P., Rajopadhye, S.V., Saraswat, V.: Checking Race Freedom of Clocked X10 Programs. CoRR abs/1311.4305 (2013)
26. Zhang, Y., Duesterwald, E., Gao, G.R.: Concurrency analysis for shared memory programs with textually unaligned barriers. In: Adve, V., Garzarán, M.J., Petersen, P. (eds.) LCPC 2007. LNCS, vol. 5234, pp. 95–109. Springer, Heidelberg (2008). doi:10.1007/978-3-540-85261-2_7

Polygonal Iteration Space Partitioning

Aniket Shivam[1]([✉]), Alexandru Nicolau[1], Alexander V. Veidenbaum[1],
Mario Mango Furnari[3], and Rosario Cammarota[2]([✉])

[1] University of California Irvine, Irvine, USA
aniketsh@uci.edu
[2] Qualcomm Research, San Diego, USA
rosarioc@qti.qualcomm.com
[3] ICIB - National Council for Research, Pozzuoli, Italy

Abstract. This work presents a new set of loop transformations to expose and maximize data locality in loop-nests with non-uniform reuse patterns. The proposed set of transformations use the norms of the Polyhedral Model to represent loop-nests and then leverages such a representation to partition the iteration space into polygonally shaped partitions with maximum locality. However, the partitioning algorithm tends to produce partitions with complex geometry (shape) and with progressively smaller number of iterations, which, in practice, introduces much run-time overhead. This work also focuses on containing the number of partitions and properly manage their geometry at run-time, to contain unnecessary overhead. The proposed transformations also exposes loop level parallelism, by grouping together independent iterations, thus improving performance of both serial and parallel execution. In parallel execution a selective mapping of partitions to threads based on the type of reuse these partitions exhibit is proposed.

The proposed transformations show a consistent performance speedup on serial execution (up to 1.2x over Polly) and parallel execution (up to 3.17x over PLuTo) of some loop-nests.

Keywords: Polygonal partitions · Shape and size independent tiling · Temporal locality · Polyhedral model

1 Introduction

Modern compilers, such as LLVM, GNU GCC and Intel ICC perform many loop transformations, such as tiling, strip-mining, fusion and interchange [10], to speedup program execution. Loop transformations, such as tiling [7], focus on grouping iterations (tiles) to improve data locality. Such transformations effectively speedup program execution when loop-nests exhibit uniform reuse distances between loop statements and across loop iterations. Tiles shape and size, determined based on the cache hierarchy organization, are usually constant and repeat during the loop execution to include all the iterations. For example, in a doubly-nested loop where iteration $I_{i,j}$ accesses array index $A_{i-1,j-1}$ and $A_{i+1,j+1}$, the formation of either square or rectangular tiles would help in

© Springer International Publishing AG 2017
C. Ding et al. (Eds.): LCPC 2016, LNCS 10136, pp. 121–136, 2017.
DOI: 10.1007/978-3-319-52709-3_11

improving locality. Tiling ensures that data remains in cache until $I_{i-1,j-1}$ and $I_{i+1,j+1}$ are computed.

However, tiling loop-nests with non-uniform reuse patterns still remains a challenge, due to the impossibility of defining a single set of dependency vectors which can govern a tile size and shape. For example, if iteration $I_{i,j}$ accesses array index $A_{i,j}$ and $A_{i+j,j}$, neither a single fixed-shape tile nor a symmetric tile can ensure improved cache data reuse during the whole execution of the loop-nest. The technique proposed by Meister et al. [9] for partitioning loops works irrespective of reuse pattern, i.e., it is not bound by constraint of shape and size of the tiles or partitions. The price of such a technique, however, is that the management of the boundary condition for the tiles introduces much instruction overhead, which the halt condition of the original partitioning algorithm does not account for.

This work proposes a new set of loop transformations to address the case of loop-nests with non-uniform reuse patterns, and to cope with the management of the execution of tiles of arbitrary shapes. Our proposed technique represents a loop-nest in the norms of the Polyhedral Model and then categorize iterations, i.e., create partitions based on the number of iterations that can linked by the reuse of their accessed data elements. In principle, the process could indiscriminately proceed until all the iterations in the loop belong to a partition. Alternatively, the compilation process may be set to halt at a predefined maximum number of partitions. However, the number of partitions has to be selected appropriately based on the characteristics of the loop-nest and the features of the target architecture to achieve maximum performance. We show that an optimal number of partitions can be determined per loop. Selecting more than the optimal number of partitions would introduce much overhead at run-time, whereas selecting less than the optimal number of partitions would miss a portion of exploitable locality and hence reducing speedup in both cases.

The proposed technique is implemented using the integration of source-to-source optimizer PLuTo[1] with PolyLib[2] library. The performance of the technique is compared against the combination of loop transformations already supported in Polyhedral Frameworks like Polly[3] and like PLuTo [4] (later compiled with ICC). Experimental results show a consistent speedup up to 1.2x w.r.t. Polly on serial execution and up to 3.17x w.r.t. PLuTo on parallel execution.

The rest of the paper is organized as follows: Sect. 2 presents our proposed set of loop transformations. Section 3 presents our experimental setup and results. Section 4 presents and comments on prior and related work. Finally, Sect. 5 summarizes our findings and presents our conclusive remarks.

2 Polygonal Iteration Space Partitioning

The proposed technique for generating the polygonal partitions of a loop-nest is presented in this section.

---

[1] PLuTo: http://pluto-compiler.sourceforge.net.
[2] PolyLib: http://icps.u-strasbg.fr/~loechner/polylib/.
[3] Polly (LLVM Plugin): http://polly.llvm.org.

2.1   Determining Reuse Using the Polyhedral Model

With the polyhedral representation of a nest of loops, a set of mathematical equations can be derived for identifying the data accessed by the references in a statement. For each instance of a statement in the body of a loop-nest, an iteration vector I is defined. For instance, if the enclosed statement accesses the data at a particular position of a multi-dimensional array $\mathbf{A}$, the exact location of the data ($A(I)$) can be calculated as: $A(I) = \mathbf{R} \times I + \mathbf{r}$. The *reference matrix*, R, is based on the coefficient of the iteration variables in the subscript representing the data access in A. Whereas, the *offset vector*, r, represents the constant from the subscript. For a D-dimensional array A, with N being the depth of the loop-nest, R will be a $D \times N$ matrix and r will be a D-dimensional vector identifying an offset in each dimension. To provide a explanatory example, consider the following loop-nest:

```
for (i = -N;  i <= N;  i++)
    for (j = -N;  j <= N;  j++)
        X[i,j] = Y[i,i+j+3] * Y[i+j,j];
```

The reference Y[i,i+j+3] references a two dimensional array Y enclosed in a two dimensional loop-nest. Therefore, R will be a 2×2 matrix, $\begin{pmatrix} 1 & 0 \\ 1 & 1 \end{pmatrix}$. Each row represents the projection of the reference along each dimension of the array, i.e., the value of subscript in each dimension (i and i+j+3). The column represents the coefficient associated with each iteration variable (i and j) of the loop-nest. The offset vector r is a column vector, $\begin{pmatrix} 0 \\ 3 \end{pmatrix}$, representing the offset for reference along every dimension, i.e., the constants in the subscript. An iteration I can be substituted using a column vector (i j). Each reference to the array is an unique combination of (R, r). The pair is represented as Γ to locate the accessed data point by an iteration. Γ is a function which computes the *image* of the polyhedron. In the above loop-nest, the two references to the array Y are written as: $\Gamma_{i,i+j+3} = \begin{pmatrix} 1 & 0 \\ 1 & 1 \end{pmatrix} I + \begin{pmatrix} 0 \\ 3 \end{pmatrix}$ and $\Gamma_{i+j,j} = \begin{pmatrix} 1 & 1 \\ 0 & 1 \end{pmatrix} I + \begin{pmatrix} 0 \\ 0 \end{pmatrix}$.

Suppose, there is reuse of a data by two different references Γ_α and Γ_β in iterations I_α and I_β respectively. Then, the dependence between two iterations can be described using Eq. 1.

$$\Gamma_\alpha = \Gamma_\beta \Leftrightarrow R_\alpha I_\alpha + r_\alpha = R_\beta I_\beta + r_\beta \tag{1}$$

Therefore using Eq. 1, as suggested in [9], the temporal reuse relation or dependence relation, $\mathcal{T}$, between I_α and I_β can be formally represented by Eq. 2.

$$R_\beta^{-1} R_\alpha I_\alpha + R_\beta^{-1}(r_\alpha - r_\beta) = I_\beta \Leftrightarrow T_{\alpha\beta} I_\alpha + t_{\alpha\beta} = I_\beta, \quad \text{if } R \text{ is invertible.} \tag{2}$$

The reuse relation $\mathcal{T}$ is a combination of $(T_{\alpha\beta}, t_{\alpha\beta})$, where $T_{\alpha\beta} = R_\beta^{-1} R_\alpha$ and $t_{\alpha\beta} = R_\beta^{-1}(r_\alpha - r_\beta)$. Substituting a particular iteration in place of I_α yields another iteration (I_β) that reuses the same data. If and only if R is invertible, then T can be computed. Therefore, the *reference matrix* R needs to be an square matrix. This implies that it is critical for the application of this technique that the dimensions of the involved array is same as the depth of the loop-nest. This reduces the applicability to the loops with references that generate an invertible *reference matrix* R and hence an invertible $\mathcal{T}$. However, using R and $\mathcal{T}$ makes it possible to determine if a data accessed by I_β using Γ_β is also accessed by I_α using Γ_α, $I_\alpha = T_{\alpha\beta}^{-1}I_\beta - T_{\alpha\beta}^{-1}t_{\alpha\beta}$. Therefore, the temporal reuse relation $\mathcal{T} = (T, t)$ for the loop-nest in the example is: $T = \begin{pmatrix} 0 & -1 \\ 1 & 1 \end{pmatrix}$ and $t = \begin{pmatrix} -3 \\ 3 \end{pmatrix}$ using Eq. (2). In the example above, to check if the data accessed by an iteration, say i = 2 and j = 1, using reference $\Gamma_{i,i+j+3}$, is also accessed by another iteration using the reference $\Gamma_{i+j,j}$. Substituting the iteration vector by (2,1) in Eq. 2, $\begin{pmatrix} 0 & -1 \\ 1 & 1 \end{pmatrix}\begin{pmatrix} 2 \\ 1 \end{pmatrix} + \begin{pmatrix} -3 \\ 3 \end{pmatrix}$, yields vector $(-4,6)$. Therefore, it can be concluded that iterations $(2,1)$ and $(-4,6)$ have reuse.

2.2   Partitioning Technique

The goal of our proposed technique is to identify and execute non-adjacent partitions of the iteration space in an order such that the data is reused in the cache. For an unoptimized version of the loop-nest, this data would have been flushed out of the cache before its reuse. These partitions are thereafter grouped based on the locality of the data their iterations access. Hence, all the partitions accessing the same set of data are aggregated. Assuming there are two references Γ_α and Γ_β to an array in a single statement in the loop-nest. The primary step is to partition the iteration space ($\mathcal{D}$) in three sets denoted by L, $\mathcal{P}_1$ and $\mathcal{P}_2$.

- $\mathcal{P}_1$ contain iterations that reference the data using Γ_α that another iteration in $\mathcal{D}$ accesses by Γ_β, i.e., these iterations have an *image* in $\mathcal{D}$ using relation $\mathcal{T}$.
- Iterations referencing the data using Γ_β that is also referenced by another iteration in $\mathcal{D}$ using Γ_α form the set $\mathcal{P}_2$. These iterations are the *images* of the iterations in $\mathcal{P}_1$. In other words, they have a *Pre-Image* in $\mathcal{D}$ ($Image(\mathcal{T}^{-1},\mathcal{D})$).
- The rest of the iterations in $\mathcal{D}$, i.e., the iterations that reference the data which is not referenced by another iteration are included in the partition denoted by $\mathcal{L}$. These iterations neither project nor they are projected in $\mathcal{D}$ using $\mathcal{T}$. Hence, $\mathcal{D} = \mathcal{P}_1 + \mathcal{P}_2 + \mathcal{L}$.
  The sets $\mathcal{P}_1$ and $\mathcal{P}_2$ can be further categorized into three subsets named $\mathcal{C}$, $\mathcal{D}_1$ and $\mathcal{D}_2$, in addition to $\mathcal{L}$.
- $\mathcal{C}$: These iterations belong to both $\mathcal{P}_1$ and $\mathcal{P}_2$, i.e., $\mathcal{C} = \mathcal{P}_1 \cap \mathcal{P}_2$. Data accessed by these iterations using both the references (Γ_α and Γ_β) is also accessed by other iterations.
- $\mathcal{D}_1$: These iterations belong to $\mathcal{P}_1$ only, i.e., $\mathcal{D}_1 = \mathcal{P}_1 - \mathcal{C}$ or $\mathcal{D}_1 = \mathcal{P}_1 - \mathcal{P}_2$. The data accessed by Γ_α of these iterations is accessed by other iterations. Data accessed by Γ_β is not reused.
- $\mathcal{D}_2$: These iterations belong to $\mathcal{P}_2$ only, i.e., $\mathcal{D}_2 = \mathcal{P}_2 - \mathcal{C}$ or $\mathcal{D}_2 = \mathcal{P}_2 - \mathcal{P}_1$. Similarly, the data accessed by these iterations using Γ_β is reused, whereas data accessed by Γ_α remains unused.

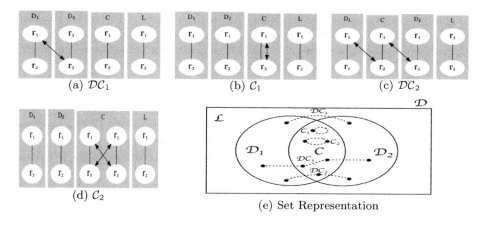

Fig. 1. Classification of iterations - formation of the sets $\mathcal{DC}_1$, $\mathcal{C}_1$, $\mathcal{DC}_2$, $\mathcal{C}_2$.

After categorizing the iterations based on the reuse of their accessed data, a further sub-categorization is performed such that each subset is executed in a specific order to improve the temporal locality. That is, iterations having reuse among them and forming smaller partitions ($\mathcal{DC}_k$ and $\mathcal{C}_k$) are linked together. Figure 1 shows a graphical illustration of how iterations are categorized.

- $\mathcal{DC}_1$: $\mathcal{D}_1$ iterations that link to $\mathcal{D}_2$ iterations by $\mathcal{T}$, i.e., $\mathcal{DC}_1 = \mathcal{D}_1 \cap \mathcal{T}^{-1}(\mathcal{D}_2)$.
- $\mathcal{C}_1$: $\mathcal{C}$ iterations that are linked to themselves by $\mathcal{T}$, i.e., $\mathcal{T}(\mathcal{C}_1) = \mathcal{T}^{-1}(\mathcal{C}_1)$.
- $\mathcal{DC}_2$: $\mathcal{D}_1$ iterations that link to $\mathcal{C}$ iterations that link to $\mathcal{D}_2$ iteration, i.e., $\mathcal{D}_1$ iterations that link to $\mathcal{D}_2$ iterations by $\mathcal{T}^2$, $\mathcal{DC}_2 = \mathcal{D}_1 \cap \mathcal{T}^{-1}(\mathcal{C}) \cap \mathcal{T}^{-2}(\mathcal{D}_2)$.
- $\mathcal{C}_2$: The remaining $\mathcal{C}$ iterations that form cyclic-link with one other iteration in $\mathcal{C}$, i.e., $\mathcal{C}$ iterations that are linked to themselves by $\mathcal{T}^2$, $\mathcal{C}_2 = \mathcal{C} \cap \mathcal{T}^{-1}(\mathcal{C}) \cap \{I \in \mathcal{C} | T^2 I + Tt + t = I\} - \mathcal{C}_1$.
  After k repetitions of the previous steps:
- $\mathcal{DC}_k$: $\mathcal{D}_1$ iterations that link to chain of $k - 1$ $\mathcal{C}$ iterations and at the end link to a $\mathcal{D}_2$ iteration by $\mathcal{T}^k$, i.e., $\mathcal{DC}_k = \{I \in \mathcal{D}_1 | Tt + t \in \mathcal{C}, T^2 I + Tt + t \in \mathcal{C}, ..., T^k I + T^{k-1}t + ... + Tt + t \in \mathcal{DC}_2\}$.
- $\mathcal{C}_k$: The remaining $\mathcal{C}$ iterations that are linked to themselves by $\mathcal{T}^k$ forming a cyclic-link of k $\mathcal{C}$ iterations, i.e., $\mathcal{C}_k = \{I \in \mathcal{C} | Tt + t \in \mathcal{C}, T^2 I + Tt + t \in \mathcal{C}, ..., T^k I + T^{k-1}t + ... + Tt + t = \mathcal{C}\} - \{\mathcal{C}_1 + ... + \mathcal{C}_{k-1}\}$.

These repetitive steps generate partitions based on the number of iterations that can linked by reuse of their accessed data elements. This partitioning technique requires a halting condition such that the number of steps of the algorithms, k, can be determined and so does determines the number of partitions that it creates. As mentioned in [9], the value of k can be chosen as: (a) If after the kth repetition of the algorithm, the entire iteration space ($\mathcal{D}$) is completely partitioned. At this point $\mathcal{T}^k$ is an identity matrix, where $\mathcal{T}$ is represented as $\begin{pmatrix} T & t \\ 0..0 & 1 \end{pmatrix}$, and (b) If value of k is preset, the algorithm stops after the k repetitions and put the rest of the iterations in $\mathcal{C}_{k+1}$.

The partitions categorized as either $\mathcal{DC}_i$ or $\mathcal{C}_i$, where $1 \leq i \leq k$, are disjoint partitions spread across the iteration space. Therefore, the partitions labeled as $\mathcal{DC}_i$ can be numbered based on the position of their containing iterations in the chain. In the $\mathcal{DC}_i$ partitions, the first partition containing only $\mathcal{D}_1$ iterations are labeled as $\mathcal{DC}_i^0$. The next $i-1$ partitions containing $\mathcal{C}$ iterations are labeled as $\mathcal{DC}_i^1$, $\mathcal{DC}_i^2$,...,$\mathcal{DC}_i^{i-2}$ and $\mathcal{DC}_i^{i-1}$. The last partition in the chain containing $\mathcal{D}_2$ iterations is labeled as $\mathcal{DC}_i^i$. The same naming paradigm is followed for $\mathcal{C}_i$ partitions. These i partitions are labeled as $\mathcal{C}_i^0$, $\mathcal{C}_i^1$,...,$\mathcal{C}_i^{i-2}$ and $\mathcal{C}_i^{i-1}$. The number of iterations in the partitions of similar type is always equal, since the iterations in the successive partitions are the *images* of the iterations in the previous partition.

2.3   Orchestrating Formation of the Partitions

Premature Halting. An indiscriminate application of the algorithm introduce overhead at run-time due to large number of small sized partitions, which is not considered in the halting conditions defined above. The increase in the number of partitions increases the control statement overhead in the restructured loop-nest. Therefore, in the partitions with very few iterations the gain in performance from better locality is overshadowed by the control overhead needed to manage such partitions.

We introduced a termination method for the algorithm so that the control statement overhead does not overshadow the speedup gained through maximizing locality, by predicting the minimum tile size. Specially in loop-nests where the longest chain of linked iterations is very long, i.e., T^k generates an identity matrix for a very high value of k, say k_{max}, it is critical to find an optimal value of $k < k_{max}$ to protect gained speedup from increasing control overhead. This is applicable to most loop-nests with one dimensional non-uniform reuse pattern. Therefore, the algorithm is halted after partitioning for T^k and the remaining iterations form partition $\mathcal{C}_{k+1}$. From our experiments, it can be deduced that the algorithm must be halted if the number of iterations in newly generated partitions is below 25×25, .i.e., 625 iterations.[4]

Multi-level Tiling. The partitions generated on each repetition of the technique are labeled as $\mathcal{DC}_i$ and $\mathcal{C}_i$, where $1 \leq i \leq k$. Partitions labeled as $\mathcal{DC}_i$ or $\mathcal{C}_i$ are set of separate and distantly located partitions of the iteration space. The execution order of these partitions influences the improvement in locality or improved cache hit-miss ratio at a certain cache level. A single partition targets the improvement in locality in the smallest cache with the least expensive data transfer cost, ideally L1 cache. The set of partitions in $\mathcal{DC}_i$ or $\mathcal{C}_i$ targets a larger cache that can be either L2 or L3 cache. This technique guarantees that for loops with non-uniform reuse pattern, the cost in terms of time spent in fetching data for reuse is reduced by making it available in closest possible cache level.

---

[4] The number of integer points contained by a parameterized polyhedron is computed using the Ehrhart Polynomials as implemented in PolyLib.

Locality on Parallel Execution of the Partitions. Loop-nests without any loop-carried dependences can be executed in parallel without any constraints. But tiling such loops can improve the performance by improving locality so that the cost of data transfer is reduced. During parallel execution more fetches from private memory and lesser fetches from the shared memory improves the performance. Scheduling similar partitions (either a $\mathcal{DC}_i$ or $\mathcal{C}_i$, $1 \leq i \leq k$) on the same thread achieves the improvement in locality, since each thread finds the required data in private memory.

2.4   Multi-reference Statements

We also extend the technique to statements with multiple references to the array and also to stencil computations that exhibit fixed pattern reuse in multiple directions. Every pair of temporal reuse relations lead to different partitions which on combining would generate a single partition. Reuse along multiple directions create a complex network of iterations linked by $\mathcal{T}$, therefore it is important to eliminate reuse relations such that iterations do not link to themselves by either $\mathcal{T}$ or $\mathcal{T}^2$. For example, the reuse vector $v_{i,j-1}$ and $v_{i,j+1}$ link themselves by $\mathcal{T}^2$. Therefore, one of them must be eliminated. Also, $v_{i,j}$ must be eliminated since it links to itself by $\mathcal{T}$. One drawback of the original algorithm is that some pairs of reuse vectors produce partitions which consume the entire iteration space like $v_{i,j+1}$ and $v_{i+1,j}$. These pairs are eliminated. The aim is to find the '*pair*' (best set of two references) from all the references that generate the best possible partitions for maximizing locality.

Another heuristics to choose the *pair* is to select it based on the amount of reuse in the partitions that it creates. A **reuse count function** as shown in Eq. 3 is used to predict the amount of reuse in the partitions can be appended in the original technique. This step involves choosing the best *pair* out of every set of two references - from those left after eliminating the redundant references - based on the amount of reuse that can be calculated from size of $\mathcal{DC}$s and $\mathcal{C}$s sets. When the algorithm is prematurely halted to reduce control statement overhead as described in the previous section, the residual iterations that form $\mathcal{C}_{k+1}$ are not counted towards the reuse.

$$Reuse(\Gamma_\alpha, \ \Gamma_\beta) = \sum_{i=1}^{k} i \times |\mathcal{DC}_i^0| + \sum_{i=1}^{k} i \times |\mathcal{C}_i^0| \tag{3}$$

This technique can also be extended to multiple statements enclosed in a loop-nest. Since, reuse of data from an array might occur between references spanning across multiple statements. These multiple references can be reduced to the best *pair* of references exploiting the maximum locality.

2.5   Code Generation Paradigm

The code generation for these partitions begins by analyzing the polyhedron representation for each partition. This polyhedron representation contains the constraints (boundary hyperplanes) that define the affine boundaries for the partitions. These constraints are then scanned using the Fourier-Motzkin algorithm implemented in PolyLib and also using tools like CLooG [3]. CLooG generates code by scanning the polyhedrons and performs the union of distinct polyhedron to produce code with the least control statement overhead. The work in [9] suggests a methodology to scan just the initial partition from each category, i.e., $\mathcal{DC}_i^0$ for the $\mathcal{DC}_i$ type partitions and $\mathcal{C}_i^0$ for $\mathcal{C}_i$ type partitions. The next steps is to derive the subscripts for the next iterations in the link using the reuse relation $\mathcal{T}$. Let, I, a column vector, represent the iterations in the $\mathcal{DC}_i^0$. The subscript for the iterations in the following partitions $\mathcal{DC}_i^1$, $\mathcal{DC}_i^2$,..., $\mathcal{DC}_i^i$ are derived from $\mathcal{T}(I)$, $\mathcal{T}^2(I)$,..., $\mathcal{T}^i(I)$ respectively. The locality is exposed in the successive statements since there is reuse between I and $\mathcal{T}(I)$ iteration, then in $\mathcal{T}(I)$ and $\mathcal{T}^2(I)$ iteration, etc. This methodology is efficient unless the value of k is high in which case it enormously expands the code size. The loop-nest for $\mathcal{DC}_i$ and $\mathcal{C}_i$ partitions encloses $i+1$ and i statements respectively. For some value of k, the code will have a minimum of k loop-nests for either $\mathcal{DC}$ or $\mathcal{C}$ type partitions and maximum of $k \times 2$ (k $\mathcal{DC}$ plus k $\mathcal{C}$) loop-nests. Each of them containing statements between 0 and k. For a higher value of k, a better solution is to find the union of the polyhedron representing a type of partitions ($\mathcal{DC}_i$ or $\mathcal{C}_i$) to generate code. Also, since each partition in $\mathcal{DC}_i$ or $\mathcal{C}_i$ type partitions contain equal iterations, they tend to form similar geometries. These geometries are recurring patterns and hence code generation for them requires slight modification in the boundary conditions of the control statements. These modification can be captured to form a basis for iterating through each partition of a particular type. Hence, reducing the total count of loop-nests in the code.

An important part of the speedup comes from re-partitioning the generated partitions to reduce boundary check overheads. This is performed by computing these partial partitions and scanning them so as compute multiple partitions in a single loop. The entire partitioning technique is shown in Algorithm 1.

For generating parallel code, we propose the use of OpenMP® Sections. It allows the *selective mapping* of a certain type of partitions onto a single thread. This improves the locality in each thread which in turn reduces the fetching of same data from shared memory on multiple threads. These sections are dynamically scheduled to achieve load balancing. However, the generation of a schedule for parallel execution of polygonal partitions of a loop-nest with non-uniform data dependence remains a challenge. Because if the execution of partitions as per the technique violates any data dependence, then modifying the execution order without violating dependence disrupts locality.

3   Experiments and Results

For evaluating our technique, we choose four cases in which the corresponding loop-nests exhibit different reuse patterns. These styles are: (a) **Two Dimensional Non-Uniform Reuse** in which the reuse pattern varies along both dimensions of a two dimensional iteration space; (b) **One Dimensional Non-Uniform Reuse** in which the reuse pattern varies along a single dimension;

Algorithm 1. Polygonal Tile Generation

1: **Input**: A loop-nest with potential reuse on a dataset (array).
2: Eliminate set of references that link iterations to themselves by either $\mathcal{T}$ or $\mathcal{T}^2$. (Sect. 2.4)
3: **for** each set of two references (Γ_α, Γ_β) to the array **do**
4:     Define the Reuse Relation $\mathcal{T}$ using the two references Γ_α and Γ_β.
5:     Generate coarse partitions of the iteration space ($\mathcal{D}$):
    $\mathcal{P}_1$ ($Image(\mathcal{T},\mathcal{D})$), $\mathcal{P}_2$ ($Image(\mathcal{T}^{-1},\mathcal{D})$) and $\mathcal{L}$ (No reuse).
6:     Categorize $\mathcal{P}_1$ and $\mathcal{P}_2$ into: $\mathcal{C}=\mathcal{P}_1 \cap \mathcal{P}_2$, $\mathcal{D}_1=\mathcal{P}_1 - \mathcal{P}_2$ and $\mathcal{D}_2=\mathcal{P}_2 - \mathcal{P}_1$.
7:     **while** $\mathcal{D}$ is not completely partitioned **do**
8:         Create partitions ($\mathcal{DC}_i$ and $\mathcal{C}_i$) that have iterations linked by relation $\mathcal{T}^i$.
9:         **if** Iterations in the generated partitions is below 25×25 **then**
10:            $k = i$ (Since the algorithm is halted, k is set to i.)
11:            Put rest of the iterations in $\mathcal{C}_{k+1}$.
12:            break
13:         **end if**
14:         Increment i.
15:     **end while**
16: **end for**
17: Remove the set of references that produce a single partition which consume the entire iteration space. (Sect. 2.4)
18: On the remaining set of references, apply the **Reuse Count Formula** (Eq. 3) to estimate the amount of reuse.
19: Choose the *pair* having the maximum reuse in their polygonal partitions for code generation.
20: Scan the polygonal partitions using the Fourier-Motzkin algorithm to generate the boundaries for the partitions.
21: Use the code generation tools like CLooG with modifications so as to generate array subscripts using the function $\mathcal{T}^i(I)$.
22: **Output**: Polygonally tiled iteration space that improves data locality.

(c) **Symmetric or Uniform Reuse** in which the reuse is generally among neighboring iterations along a certain direction(s); (d) **Multiple References** in which loop-nests contains multiple references to an array in a single statement, e.g., as seen in benchmark suites like PolyBench[5].

The compiled codes are analyzed for performance on Intel's Sandy-Bridge Core i7-2600 CPU @ 3.40 GHz. The processor has 4 cores (8 threads) with 32 KB L1 I/D cache, 1024 KB L2 cache and 8 MB LLC. Hardware performance counters were analyzed for measuring performance metrics.

3.1   Case 1: Two Dimensional Non-uniform Reuse Pattern

In the loop-nest shown in Fig. 2, the references to the array Y can be represented as: $\Gamma_{i,\ i+j+3} = \begin{pmatrix} 1 & 0 \\ 1 & 1 \end{pmatrix} \mathbf{I} + \begin{pmatrix} 0 \\ 3 \end{pmatrix}$, $\Gamma_{i+j,\ j} = \begin{pmatrix} 1 & 1 \\ 0 & 1 \end{pmatrix} \mathbf{I} + \begin{pmatrix} 0 \\ 0 \end{pmatrix}$. Therefore, the

---

[5] PolyBench/C 4.1: http://web.cse.ohio-state.edu/~pouchet/software/polybench/.

```
for  (i = -N;  i <= N;  i++)
    for  (j = -N;  j<= N;  j++)
        X[i,j] = Y[i,i+j+3] * Y[i+j,j];
```

Fig. 2. Case 1: Loop-nest with two dimensional non-uniform reuse

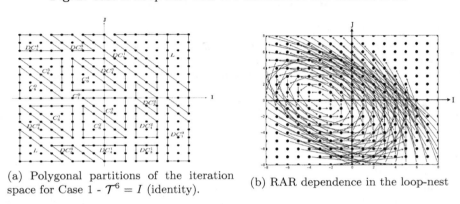

(a) Polygonal partitions of the iteration space for Case 1 - $\mathcal{T}^6 = I$ (identity).

(b) RAR dependence in the loop-nest

Fig. 3. Partitions of the iteration space in Case 1.

temporal reuse relation $\mathcal{T} = (T, t)$ can be calculated using Eq. 2, where $T = \begin{pmatrix} 0 & -1 \\ 1 & 1 \end{pmatrix}$ and $t = \begin{pmatrix} -3 \\ 3 \end{pmatrix}$. For this case k comes out to be 6, since T^6 is an identity matrix. Therefore, the partitioning process would terminate after six repetitions of the core algorithm. The remaining iterations in $\mathcal{C}$ are placed in partition $\mathcal{C}_6$ as described in the technique. The graphical representation of the partitioned iteration space is shown in Fig. 3a [9]. The partitioning algorithm generates a fixed number of partitions, which is independent of the input size. Hence, the partitions generated from this technique are scalable with the dataset size. Since, the maximum value of k is 6, it generates a small number of partitions which suggests that the control statement overhead will have negligible effect on

```
for  (i = -N;  i <= -4;  i++) {
    for  (j = MAX(-N+3,-i-N-3);  j <= -i-N-1;  j++) {
        X[i][j]           = Y[i][i+j+3] * Y[i+j][j];
        X[-j-3][i+j+3]    = Y[-j-3][i+3] * Y[i][i+j+3];
        X[-i-j-6][i+3]    = Y[-i-j-6][-j] * Y[-j-3][i+3];
        X[-i-6][-j]       = Y[-i-6][-i-j-3] * Y[-i-j-6][-j];
        X[j-3][-i-j-3]    = Y[j-3][-i-3] * Y[-i-6][-i-j-3];
    }
}
```

Fig. 4. Index calculation for $\mathcal{DC}_4$ using reuse relation($\mathcal{T}$).

performance. Therefore, there is no need to apply the halting condition described in Sect. 2.3 in this case. Hence, the maximum value must be chosen to obtain the finest partitions with the maximum reuse.

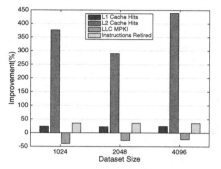

Fig. 5. Case 1: % Improvement in L1, L2, LLC and Instructions Retired Counters

The code shown in Fig. 4 presents the application of the function $\mathcal{T}^i(\mathbf{I})$ where $0 \leq i \leq 6$, as mentioned in Sect. 2.5, to compute array subscripts for disjoint but equivalent $\mathcal{DC}_4$ partitions. This optimization reduces the control statement overhead, as well as increases the temporal locality due to consecutive data accesses in subsequent iterations. Also, because of this there are less memory accesses and therefore there is a constant 35% decrease in instruction count. Figure 5 shows the increase in cache hits.

The serial code optimized using the technique shows up to 1.19x speedup (Fig. 11a). For parallel execution, each type of partition is executed on a different thread using OpenMP® Sections so as to maximize data reuse on a core. On parallel execution the speedup is even higher (up to 3.17x) as shown in Fig. 11b due to the *selective mapping* of the partitions. Polly and PLuTo generate rectangular tiles for the given program, since both of them do not use the information from RAR dependence to optimize code for locality, unlike the proposed technique. Experimental results show scalability of performance with the input size because even though the number of partitions remains constant, the size of the partitions scales with the input size.

3.2 Case 2: One Dimensional Non-uniform Reuse Pattern

```
for (i = –N; i <= N; i++)
    for (j = –N; j<= N; j++)
        X[i,j]= Y[i,j] + Y[i,i+j+N];
```

Fig. 6. Loop-nest with one dimensional non-uniform reuse

The references to array Y for this case, shown in Fig. 6, are: $\Gamma_{i,\,j} = \begin{pmatrix} 1 & 0 \\ 0 & 1 \end{pmatrix} \mathbf{I} + \begin{pmatrix} 0 \\ 0 \end{pmatrix}$, $\Gamma_{i,\,i+j+N} = \begin{pmatrix} 1 & 0 \\ 1 & 1 \end{pmatrix} \mathbf{I} + \begin{pmatrix} 0 \\ N \end{pmatrix}$. Therefore, the temporal reuse relation $\mathcal{T} = (T, t)$, assumes the following form, according to Eq. 2: $T = \begin{pmatrix} 1 & 0 \\ -1 & 1 \end{pmatrix}$, $t = \begin{pmatrix} 0 \\ -N \end{pmatrix}$. For this case, the maximum value of k is too high. It is dependent on the variable N, which is a representation of the dataset size, as such: $T^k = \begin{pmatrix} 1 & 0 \\ -k & 1 \end{pmatrix}$, $t = \begin{pmatrix} 0 \\ -kN \end{pmatrix}$.

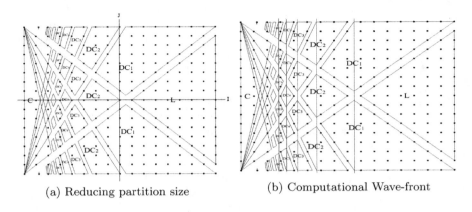

(a) Reducing partition size   (b) Computational Wave-front

Fig. 7. Partitions of the iteration space in Case 2.

Since the reuse is along the dimension J, refer to Fig. 7a, the maximum value that k can reach is $2N - 1$. As the algorithm moves towards $-I$ direction, it forms smaller partitions. This leads to the drawback of the original algorithm. As described in the Sect. 2.3, an optimal value for k must be chosen such that the achievable speedup is not diminished by the excessive control statement overhead. Therefore, the algorithm must halt as soon as tile size reduces below 25×25 iterations. This is deduced from the experimental data as shown in Fig. 8a. The optimal value of k was found to be around 30 in a small dataset ($N = 1024$), 40 in a medium dataset ($N = 2048$), and 60 in a large dataset ($N = 4096$). If

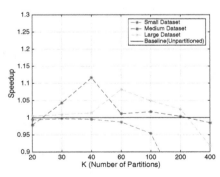

(a) Speedup vs Number of Partitions.

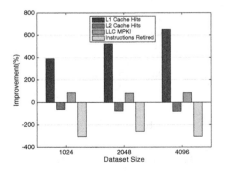

(b) % of Improvement in L1 and L2 hits, LLC misses and Instructions Retired

Fig. 8. Case 2: Optimal number of partitions and improvement in counters

a value of k is chosen to be lower than the optimal value, the loop execution experiences a performance degradation due to low locality exploitation. On the other hand, if a value of k is chosen to be larger than the optimal value, the loop execution experiences a performance degradation due to control statement overhead.

Another important contribution to the achieved speedup comes from a code generation optimization which is discussed in Sect. 2.5. If partitions are executed similarly as in Case 1, the control statement overhead will inhibit achieve the maximum speedup achievable. By further splitting and executing them in a variable step wave-front (Fig. 7b), the control overhead is reduced because the loop boundary conditions are simplified. This method does not conform to the originally proposed method of computing partitions of similar reuse pattern together inside single loop nest. This wave-front method execute different partition types together inside the outer-most loop. It also improves spatial locality due to reuse on same cache-line for multiple partition-types. The increase in cache hits as shown in Fig. 8b is evident of improvement in locality.

On serial execution, the maximum speedup of 1.13x is achieved for the medium dataset (Fig. 11a). Whereas, on parallel execution the speedup improves with the size of the dataset reaching maximum of 2.27x (Fig. 11b).

3.3   Case 3 (Seidel-2D) and Case 4 (Jacobi-2D): Uniform Reuse Pattern and Multiple References

Partial loop−nests exposing reuse

```
for (i = 1; i < N; i++) {                for (i = 1; i < N; i++) {
    for (j = 1; j< N; j++) {                 for (j = 1; j< N; j++) {
    A[i][j]=(A[i-1][j-1]+A[i-1][j]+             B[i][j]=(A[i][j]+
        A[i-1][j+1]+A[i][j-1]+                      A[i][j-1]+
        A[i][j]+A[i][j+1]+                          A[i][j+1]+
        A[i+1][j-1]+A[i+1][j]+                      A[i+1][j]+
        A[i+1][j+1])/9.0;                           A[i-1][j])*0.2;
    }                                        }
}                                        }
```

(a) Seidel-2D   (b) Jacobi-2D

Fig. 9. Loop-nest with uniform reuse pattern and multiple references

Case 3 and 4 are stencil benchmarks taken from the PolyBench. Case 3 (Seidel stencil) from Fig. 9a has multiple references in 8 directions. Therefore, the heuristics mentioned in Sect. 2.4 must be applied to choose the best two references for creating partitions. The reuse vectors $v_{i,j-1}$ and $v_{i,j+1}$ link themselves by $\mathcal{T}^2$. Therefore, one of the reuse relations must be eliminated. The same applies to $(v_{i-1,j-1}, v_{i+1,j+1}), (v_{i-1,j}, v_{i+1,j})$ and $(v_{i+1,j-1}, v_{i-1,j+1})$.

Reference $v_{i,j}$ must also be removed since its combination with any other v generates multiple equivalent partitions along v. Therefore, references $v_{i,j+1}$, $v_{i+1,j+1}$, $v_{i+1,j}$, $v_{i+1,j-1}$ and $v_{i,j}$ must be eliminated. Also, some pairs of reuse vectors produces partitions which consume the entire iteration space, i.e., the two references $(v_{i-1,j-1}, v_{i,j-1})$ link every iteration in the domain. Therefore, this pair of references must be eliminated in addition to the pairs $(v_{i-1,j}, v_{i-1,j-1})$,

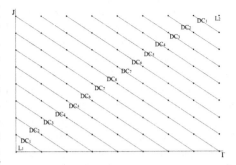

Fig. 10. Partitions for stencils

$(v_{i-1,j}, v_{i-1,j+1})$ and $(v_{i-1,j-1}, v_{i-1,j+1})$. Finally, $v_{i,j-1}$ and $v_{i-1,j}$ are left and they create the partitioning as shown in Fig. 10.

The two stencils show different performance results due to different amount of reuse among iterations in the partitions. In the case of Seidel-2D, there is more reuse between consecutive iterations inside a single sub-partition than Jacobi-2D, due to additional reuse on $v_{i+1,j-1}$ and $v_{i-1,j+1}$ in Seidel-2D.

3.4 Improvement in Performance

Serial Execution. The performance of the polygonally tiled code, compiled with LLVM (flags: -O3 -fno-inline-functions), is compared against Polly - an optimizer for LLVM - optimized code (flags: -O3 -polly -polly-vectorizer = stripmine -fno-inline-functions, tile size = 32×32). The lack of benchmarks exhibiting non-uniform reuse pattern in standard benchmarks suites like SPEC CPU and Polybench restricts the comparison of our technique to the existing techniques.

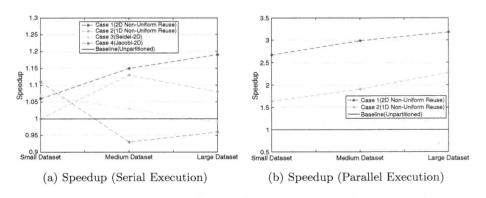

(a) Speedup (Serial Execution)   (b) Speedup (Parallel Execution)

Fig. 11. Performance improvement

Parallel Execution. The polygonally tiled code is compared for performance against the code optimized using PLuTo-0.11.4 (flags: --tile --parallel --diamond-tile, tile size = 32×32) that generate OpenMP® code. PLuTo is chosen for parallel execution because it generates better schedules for regular tiles on parallel execution and supports diamond tiling. Both codes are compiled with Intel's ICC-15.0.4 compiler (flags: -O3 -xHost -ansi-alias -ipo -fp-model precise -fno-inline-functions) and are executed across 8 threads.

4   Related Work

Loop tiling, its variants and combination with other loop transformations [7,12,13] aim to optimize data locality along with other objectives, e.g., exhibiting loop level parallelism [1,14]. Tiling techniques are concentrated on partitioning the iteration space into group of iterations (tiles) of similar shape and size. The factors determining the size of tiles may depend on memory hierarchy, cache capacities, etc. When execution proceeds tile by tile, reuse distances are no longer a function of the problem size, but a function of the tile size.

Optimal Tile Size and Parametrized Tiling. Determining the tile size at compile-time usually produce suboptimal solution since the cache sizes for the target architecture are not known in many situations. Parameterized tiling techniques [8,11] have shown that it is possible to get comparable performance and parallelism [6] as compared to statically compile-time generated tiled loop-nests. However, tiling the loops with non-uniform reuse pattern is still a challenge due to the inability of defining a single set of dependency vectors which can govern a tiling size and pattern. Whereas, in our technique the size of the tiles is solely determined by the reuse pattern of the loop-nest.

Modern Tiling Geometries. In addition to the variable sized tiles, some recent work on the exploration of newer tiling geometries have shown some promise, especially for stencil computations. The work in [2] shows that diamond-shaped tiles - when executed in parallel - can achieve concurrent start for the tiles which might not have been possible with regular rectangular/parallelogram tiles. Tiling in the shape of variable-sized Hexagons [5] provides better locality and concurrent execution of tiles for parallel architectures like GPUs. But, varying tile shapes for better locality has not received similar attention. The polygonal tiling technique presented in this work is not bound to a specific tile shape. Instead, tile shapes are determined based on the iteration space's reuse pattern.

5   Conclusion

In this work, a polygonal tiling technique is presented, which is not constrained to either the shape or the size of tiles that needs to be pre-determined. The shapes and sizes are governed by the reuse pattern of the loop-nests. The proposed technique partitions the iteration space and schedule the partitions to maximize locality.

Our experiments on a set of loops exhibiting either non-uniform or uniform reuse patterns show that a significant portion of the achievable speedup is missed when applying traditional loop tiling to such loops. Speedup is significant for loops with non-uniform reuse pattern on serial execution as shown in the case studies. Benefits of the presented polygonal tiles is even greater for multi-threaded execution for such loops. High speedup (up to 3.17x) is achieved and it consistently improves on increasing the input size.

Acknowledgments. We would like to thank Benoît Meister and Vincent Loechner for providing us with their implementation which laid the foundation for this work. This work was supported in part by NSF award XPS 1533926.

References

1. Agarwal, A., et al.: Automatic partitioning of parallel loops and data arrays for distributed shared-memory multiprocessors. TPDS **6**(9), 943–962 (1995)
2. Bandishti, V., et al.: Tiling stencil computations to maximize parallelism. In: SC 2012, pp. 40:1–40:11. IEEE Computer Society Press, Los Alamitos (2012)
3. Bastoul, C.: Code generation in the polyhedral model is easier than you think. In: PACT 13, Juan-les-Pins, France, pp. 7–16, September 2004
4. Bondhugula, U., et al.: A practical automatic polyhedral program optimization system. In: PLDI, June 2008
5. Grosser, T., et al.: Hybrid hexagonal/classical tiling for GPUs. In: CGO 2014, pp. 66:66–66:75. ACM, New York (2014)
6. Hartono, A., et al.: DynTile: parametric tiled loop generation for parallel execution on multicore processors. In: IPDPS 2010, pp. 1–12, April 2010
7. Irigoin, F., Triolet, R.: Supernode partitioning. In: POPL 1988, pp. 319–329. ACM, New York (1988)
8. Kim, D., et al.: Multi-level tiling: M for the price of one. In: SC 2007, pp. 1–12, November 2007
9. Meister, B., Loechner, V., Clauss, P.: The polytope model for optimizing cache locality. Technical report, Technical report RR 00–03, ICPS-LSIIT (2000)
10. Padua, D.A., Wolfe, M.: Advanced compiler optimizations for supercomputers. Commun. ACM **29**(12), 1184–1201 (1986)
11. Renganarayanan, L., et al.: Parameterized tiled loops for free. In: PLDI 2007, pp. 405–414. ACM, New York (2007)
12. Wolfe, M.: Iteration space tiling for memory hierarchies. In: Proceedings of the Third SIAM Conference on Parallel Processing for Scientific Computing, pp. 357–361. SIAM, Philadelphia (1989)
13. Wolfe, M.: More iteration space tiling. In: SC 1989, pp. 655–664. ACM, New York (1989)
14. Xue, J.: Loop Tiling for Parallelism. Kluwer Academic Publishers, Norwell (2000)

Automatically Optimizing Stencil Computations on Many-Core NUMA Architectures

Pei-Hung Lin[1]([✉]), Qing Yi[2], Daniel Quinlan[1],
Chunhua Liao[1], and Yongqing Yan[2]

[1] Lawrence Livermore National Laboratory, Livermore, CA 94550, USA
lin32@llnl.gov
[2] University of Colorado, Colorado Springs, CO 80918, USA

Abstract. This paper presents a system for automatically supporting the optimization of stencil kernels on emerging Non-Uniform Memory Access (NUMA) many-core architectures, through a combined compiler + runtime approach. In particular, we use a pragma-driven compiler to recognize the special structures and optimization needs of stencil computations and thereby to automatically generate low-level code that efficiently utilize the data placement and management support of a C++ runtime on top of NUMA API, a programming interface to the NUMA policy supported by the Linux kernel. Our results show that through automated specialization of code generation, this approach provides a combined benefit of performance, portability, and productivity for developers.

1 Introduction

Modern architectures increasingly use a large number of cores to boost application performance. To reduce the cost of using a global bus to support cache coherence, these cores are typically decomposed into a hierarchy of NUMA nodes, illustrated in Fig. 1(a). Figure 1(b) shows the widely varying memory latencies across the eight NUMA cores in a single compute node. To attain high performance, applications need to be aware of these different latencies to reduce the overhead of remote data accesses. In addition to the obvious performance benefit, such a design offers potential portability to future architectures, which may no longer support cache coherence across different NUMA nodes.

It is well known that significant developer effort is required to decompose an application into separate memory spaces and then explicitly reference remote data based on their locations. Instead of burdening developers with the effort, which degrades their productivity, we propose an automated approach, where user applications are written using a conventional SMP programming model, e.g., OpenMP [18], and a compiler is used to automatically translate the high level specifications down to a lower level implementation that explicitly manages local and remote memory references and by invoking a runtime library, flexibly manages the distribution and relocation of data.

© Springer International Publishing AG 2017
C. Ding et al. (Eds.): LCPC 2016, LNCS 10136, pp. 137–152, 2017.
DOI: 10.1007/978-3-319-52709-3_12

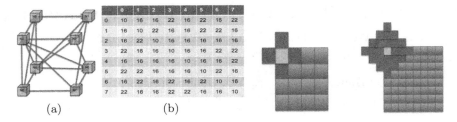

(a)   (b)

Fig. 1. AMD 6380 CPU: (a) NUMA
hierarchy; (b) Latency distance matrix

Fig. 2. Stencil distance in a 2D representation

This paper presents such a compiler and runtime combination for an important class of scientific kernels, the stencil computations, which are generally considered one of the most fundamental kernels of scientific simulations and are widely used in solving problems such as partial differential equations. As illustrated by Fig. 2, a typical stencil kernel iteratively modifies each element of a regular grid based on values of its neighboring elements. The number of neighbors in the computation can vary significantly depending on the distances of the neighbors and the dimension of the grid.

The regular structures of the stencils make them ideal candidates for high performance computing on the latest ccNUMA (cache coherent NUMA) architectures, which use inter-node communication between cache controllers to support cache coherence across cores. A principle to obtaining high performance on such systems is to have each core perform local computations most of the time and to limit cache coherence induced traffic among neighboring nodes, thereby avoiding traffic congestion. Such constraints are naturally satisfied by decomposing the underlying grid of a stencil kernel, e.g., the one in Fig. 2, into blocks so that the composition of the grid matches the underlying topology of the NUMA cores. Then, each block of data, together with the computation that modifies it, can be permanently allocated to its corresponding NUMA core, eliminating global data movements and maintaining a consistent level of locality throughout.

We have developed a pragma-driven compiler and a runtime library to accomplish the above for stencil computations. The compiler is designed to recognize the special structures of stencil computations and thereby to automatically generate low-level C code that explicitly distinguishes local and remove memory references to efficiently utilize the underlying data placement and management scheme supported by a runtime library on top of NUMA APIs (libnuma) [12]. We show that through automated specialized code generation for stencils, our approach provides a combination of good performance, architecture portability, and productivity for developers. Our technical contributions include:

– We present how to use specialized code generation to take advantage of the structures of stencil codes and thereby automatically provide advanced optimization support for these kernels on NUMA architectures.

– We study the implications of varying optimization schemes for ccNUMA and demonstrate the importance of coordinated compiler and runtime support.

The rest of the paper is organized as follows. Section 2 presents the programming interface of our system. Sections 3 and 4 present our stencil compiler and runtime library. Section 5 presents experimental results. Section 6 discusses related work. Section 7 summarize our conclusions.

```
1: #pragma stencil s1 time <t> array [X*Y] <A0,Anext>
2: for (t = 0; t < timesteps; t++) {
3:    if (t%2 == 0) { old_a = A0; a = Anext; }
4:    else {a = A0; old_a = Anext; }
5: #pragma stencil s1 data <i,j> array <old_a,a>  halo <-1,1> <-1,1> copy_halo
6:    for (int i = 1; i < X-1; i++)
7:       for (int j = 1; j < Y-1; j++)
8:          old_a[i][j] = (a[i-1][j]+a[i+1][j]) + a[i][j-1] + a[i][j+1]))/4.0;
9: }
```

Fig. 3. Example: 2-D stencil with the optimization pragma

2   The Programming Interface

The programming interface of our system includes a set of pragma notations, illustrated by lines 1 and 5 of Fig. 3, to describe various properties of a stencil. Each pragma identifies an immediately following loop as part of a stencil computation to be optimized, by specifying the following properties of the stencil.

– A name that uniquely identifies the stencil kernel, so that multiple pragmas can be used to collectively define a single stencil. For example, both pragmas in Fig. 3 use $s1$ as the stencil name, with line 1 specifying the time dimension of the stencil, and line 5 the data dimensions.
– The time dimensions of the stencil, expressed using the notation $time$ $<v_0 \ldots v_m>$, where each $v_i (i = 0, \ldots, m)$ specifies the index variable of a loop that enumerates a time dimension of the stencil. In Fig. 3, the time dimension is enumerated by the t loop at line 2 and specified inside the pragma at line 1.
– The data dimensions of the stencil, expressed using the notation $data$ $<v_0 \ldots v_n>$, where each $v_i (i = 0, \ldots, n)$ specifies the index variable of a loop that enumerates different elements of a stencil data dimension. In Fig. 3, the data dimensions are enumerated by the i and j loops at lines 6–7 and are specified inside the pragma at line 5.
– The names and dimension sizes of the arrays used to store the stencil data, specified using the notation $array [d_1 * \ldots * d_m] <a_0, \ldots, a_l>$, where $d_1 * \ldots * d_m$ defines the dimensionality (m) of the stencil, the size of each dimension, and the name $a_i (i = 0, \ldots, l)$ of each array, as illustrated by the [X*Y] $<A0, Anext>$ and $<old\_a, a>$ declarations at line 1 and line 5 of Fig. 3.

- The neighboring references used to update each element of the stencil, specified using the notation $halo <l_0, r_0> \ldots <l_n, r_n>$, where each $<l_i, r_i>$ (i = $1, \ldots, n$) specifies the neighbors from the left (l_i) and right (r_i) of data dimension i. For example, the simple stencil in Fig. 3 uses four neighbors, one from each side of each dimension, to update each element.
- Optimization configurations, e.g., $halo\_copy$ or $halo\_no\_copy$ (the default option) to indicate whether to pre-copy values of the neighboring references to local variables before using them to update halo regions of each core.

Each pragma defines the immediately following loops as new components of the stencil. Pragmas with the same identifier, which can span multiple procedures, are required to collectively satisfy the following constraints.

- If a stencil has multiple pragmas, the data dimensions must be nested inside the time dimensions. In particular, when across procedures, each inner pragma must be inside a procedure invoked by the body of an outer one, and the function that contains the inner pragma must not be invoked elsewhere for other purposes (a function specialization pre-transformation can be applied by the compiler to automatically support this property).
- Each pragma may introduce a set of arrays used to store the stencil data. All stencil arrays must have the same size, and when multiple sets of arrays are introduced, each inner declaration introduces a set of new names aliased to those introduced by the outer pragmas.
- When modifying each element at subscript $(v_0, \ldots, v_n)$ of a stencil array, the computation only uses elements from the other arrays that are within the neighborhood of $(v_0+l_1, \ldots, v_n+l_n)$ and $(v_0+r_1, \ldots, v_n+r_n)$, where (l_i, r_i)i = $0, \ldots, n$ is the hallo region of each dimension.

The compiler relies on the above properties to ensure safety and profitability of optimizations. In particular, if the stencil modifies an array a_i by reading only neighbors from the other arrays, no synchronization is needed when using OpenMP to parallelize the data dimension loops within each time step. On the other hand, if a_i is modified by reading its own neighborhood, additional synchronizations are needed to make sure up-to-date values of a_i are used. Our system currently support only the first case (a.k.a. the jacobi type of stencils).

3   The Stencil Compiler

Figure 4 shows the algorithm implemented by our compiler to automatically convert an annotated stencil kernel into its lower level implementation (llustrated in Fig. 5) through the following three steps inside function *transform-stencil*.

- Data placement: decompose and copy the data onto the proper NUMA cores, illustrated by lines 2–7 of Fig. 5, which create two new arrays of type MulticoreArray<float>, a distributed array type defined in our runtime library with pre-allocated data on the NUMA cores, and then concurrently copy the original data into these distributed arrays. The original stencil code is then modified to use the new arrays, named _Anext and _A0 In Fig. 5.

transform-stencil (*p* : stencil pragma, input: stencil code to modify)
1:    *t*=time_loop(*p*); *arr*=stencil_arrays(*p*,*t*); insert gen-distribution(p,arr) before *t* in input;
      for each array *a* ∈ *arr* **do**: replace *a* with *multicore_arr(a)* in *t*; **enddo**;
      for each function g called inside *t* and parameter *x* of *g* s.t. *x* ∈ *stencil_arrays(p)* **do**
         replace *x* with multicore_array(x) in *g*; **enddo**
2:    *d* = data_dims(*p*); *local*=gen-stencil-local(*p*, *d*); *edges*=gen-stencil-boundaries(p,local,d);
      replace *outermost_loop(d)* with gen_manycore_compute(local, edges) in input;
      if configured to do so **then** apply_aray_copying_opt(input, stencil_arrays(p,d), hallo(p)) **endif**
3: insert gen-data-collection(p, arr) after *t* in input;

gen-stencil-local(*p*: stencil pragma, *d*: stencil data dimensions)
2.1: res = copy(outermost_loop(d));
2.2: **for each** loop *l* ∈ *d* **do**:
      local_l = replace stencil_size(*l*) with local-size(*p*, *l*) in *l*; replace *l* with *local_l* in *res*; **enddo**
2.3: **for each** *a*[*sub*] ∈ *res* s.t. *a* ∈ *stencil_arrays(p)* **do**: replace a[sub] with local_ref(a[sub]); **enddo**
      return *res*;

gen-stencil-boundaries(*p*: stencil pragma, *local*: local computation, *d*: stencil data dimensions)
      res=empty; cdims = ∅;
      for each loop *l* : for *i* = *lo_i*..*hi_i* ∈ *d* s.t. halo(*p*, *l*) = (*halo_l*, *halo_r*) **do**
2.4: *left_l* = *right_l* = empty;
2.5: **for each** iteration *v* of *l* s.t. *lo_i* + *halo_l* ≤ *v* ≤ *lo_i* **do**
      left_v = replace *i* with *v* in copy(body_of *l*); append *left_v* to the end of *left_l*; **enddo**
      for each iteration *v* of *l* s.t. *hi_i* ≤ *v* ≤ *hi_i* + *halo_r* **do**
      right_v = replace *i* with *v* in copy(body of *l*); append *right_v* to the end of *right_l*; **enddo**
2.6: left_edge=replace *l* with *left_l* in copy(local); right_edge = replace *l* with *right_l* in copy(local);
2.7: **for each** *a*[*sub*] in *left_edge* s.t. *a* ∈ *stencil_arrays(p)* and offset(sub,l) < *lo_i* **do**
      replace *a*[*sub*] with *remote_stencil_from_left(r)*; **enddo**
      for each *a*[*sub*] in *right_edge* s.t. *a* ∈ *stencil_arrays(p)* and offset(sub,l) > *hi_i* **do**
      replace *a*[*sub*] with *remote_stencil_from_right(r)*; **enddo**
2,8: append gen-stencil-boundaries(*p*,*left_edge*,*cdims*) with conditional at the end of res;
      append gen-stencil-boundaries(*p*,*right_edge*,*cdims*) with conditional at the end of res;
      cdims = *cdims* ∪ {*l*};
      enddo
      return res;

Fig. 4. Algorithm: transforming stencil computations

- Many-core computing: deploy the NUMA cores, which have been pre-allocated with stencil data in the constructor of the MulticoreArrays at line 2 of Fig. 5, to each concurrently update their pre-allocated data (lines 14–18 of Fig. 5).
- Data collection: copy the distributed data at each NUMA core back to the original stencil arrays, illustrated at lines 21–24 of Fig. 5.

The data placement and collection steps serve the purposes of copying data back and forth between the original and the distributed stencil arrays. They represent the most significant overhead of the parallelization optimization and are placed outside of the outermost time loop of the annotated stencil computation, so that the overhead can be amortized when the computation is repeated many times (which is typical in practice). As summarized at lines 16–17 of Fig. 5, the many-core computing step extracts the following two components of the computation to be performed on each NUMA core.

The inner stencil, which modifies and reads only data that are on the local core, illustrated by lines 3–5 of Fig. 6. The inner stencil is extracted by invoking the *gen-stencil-local* algorithm in Fig. 4, which includes three steps: (2.1) make a copy of the outermost data dimension loop, e.g., loop i in Fig. 3, which represents a single time step iteration of the stencil; (2.2) modify the copy so that the upper

```
 1:  /* initialize local arrays and their dimensions on each core*/
 2:  MulticoreArray<float> _Anext(nz,ny,nx,CORE_NUM,0,true), _A0(nz,ny,nx,CORE_NUM,0,true);
 3:  int numberOfCores = _A0.get_numberOfCores();
 4:  #pragma omp parallel for private(i,j,k)
 5:  for (int core = 0; core < numberOfCores; core++) {
 6:        ... copy Anext and A0 into _Anext and _A0 ...
 7:  }
 8:  MulticoreArray<float>* _old_a, *_a;
 9:  #pragma stencil s1 time <t>  array <_A0,_Anext>
10:  for (t = 0; t < timesteps; t++) {
11:     if (t%2 == 0) { _old_a = _A0; _a = _Anext; }
12:     else {_a = _A0; _old_a = _Anext; }
13:     #pragma stencil s1 data<i,j> array<_old_a,_a>  halo<-1,1><-1,1> dist<blocked>
14:     #pragma omp parallel for private(i,j,k)
15:     for (int core = 0; core < numberOfCores; core++) {
16:     ...compute 2D stencil on the local arrays of each core ...
17:     ...compute boundary values by communicating with the neighbors ...
18:     }
19: }
20:  #pragma omp parallel for private(i,j,k)
21:  for (int core = 0; core < numberOfCores; core++) {
22:        ... copy _Anext and _A0 back into Anext and A0 ...
23:  }
```

Fig. 5. Example: structure of lower-level implementation of Fig. 3

bound of each data dimension (e.g., X and Y in Fig. 3) is replaced with the size of the local portion of the dimension (e.g., $c.sz0$ and $c.sz1$ in Fig. 6); and (2.3) replace references to the global stencil arrays (e.g., _old_a and a in Fig. 5) to instead use their local copies (e.g., _old_a_local and _a_local in Fig. 6).

The stencil boundaries, which modify data located at either end of a data dimension and need to read data from the neighboring cores to correctly perform the updates. These boundary computations are extracted by invoking the *gen-stencil-boundaries* algorithm in Fig. 4. Since two boundaries at both ends must be considered for each data dimension, 2^n cases are generated for a stencil of n dimensions. As example, the boundary cases of the two-dimensional stencil in Fig. 3 are illustrated at lines 6–23 of Fig. 6. The algorithm in Fig. 4 uses a variable $cdims$ to keep track of all the data dimensions already processed and uses two variables, $left_l$ and $right_l$, to store computations that modify either end (left or right) of each data dimension l (step 2.4). Each boundary case is extracted from loop l by removing the loop and replacing its index variable with an iteration number in the left or right halo region of the dimension (step 2.5). Next, the original l loop in the inner stencil is replaced with a corresponding boundary case to generate $left\_edge$ and $right\_edge$, which contain unrolled halo iterations of l on the left and right boundaries respectively (step 2.6). Then, step 2.7 replaces the stencil array references that are outside the local core with remote references that explicitly fetch the data from the neighboring cores. Finally, for each stencil boundary computation already generated and saved in $left\_edge$ and $right\_edge$, invoke the *gen-manycore-stencil-boundary* function again to generate computations at the corners of multiple distributed data dimensions (step 2.8), which need to access remote data from two or more neighbors. All boundary

```
1:  float *_a_local = (*_a).arr_ptrs[core], *_old_a_local = (*_old_a).arr_ptrs[core];
2:  Core<float>& c = (*_a).core_info[core];
3:  for (i=1; i<c.sz0-1; i=i+1) /* computation with only local references */
4:    for (j=1; j<c.sz1-1; j=j+1)
5:      _old_a_local[i+j*c.sz0] = (_a_local[i-1+j*c.sz0] + _a_local[i+1+j*c.sz0] +
                                   _a_local[i+(j-1)*c.sz0] +_a_local[i+(j+1)*c.sz0])/4.0;
6:  if (!c.is_leftmost_core[0]) /* left boundary computation at dimension 0*/
7:    for (j=1; j<c.sz1-1; j=j+1)
8:      _old_a_local[j*c.sz0] = ((*_a).arr_ptrs[c.l_neighbor[0]] [(c.l_sz0-1)+j*c.l_sz0]
         +_a_local[(1+j*c.sz0]+_a_local[(j-1)*c.sz0] +_a_local[(j+1)*c.sz0])/4.0;
9:  if (!c.is_rightmost_core[0]) /* right boundary computation at dimension 0*/
10:   for (j=1; j<c.sz1-1; j=j+1)
11:     _old_a_local[c.sz0-1+j*c.sz0] = (_a_local[c.sz0-2+j*c.sz0]+(*_a).arr_ptrs[c.r_neighbor[0]]
         [1+j*c.r_sz0] +_a_local[c.sz0-1+(j-1)*c.sz0] +_a_local[c.sz0-1+(j+1)*c.sz0])/4.0;
12: if (!c.is_leftmost_core[1]) /* left boundary computation at dimension 1*/
13::   for (i=1; j<c.sz0-1; i=i+1)
14:     _old_a_local[i] = _a_local[i-1] +_a_local[i+1]
         +(*_a).arr_ptrs[c.l_neighbor[1]] [i+(c.l_sz0-1)*c.l_sz0]+_a_local[i+c.sz0)/4.0;
15:   if (!c.is_leftmost_core[0]) /* if core is additionally on the boundary at dimension 0 */
16:     { ...... left-left corner computation ... }
17:   if (!c.is_rightmost_core[0]) /* if core is additionally on the boundary at dimension 0 */
18:     { ...... right-left corner computation ... }
19: if (!c.is_rightmost_core[1]) /* right boundary computation at dimension 1*/
20:   for (i=1; i<c.sz0-1; i=i+1)
21:     _old_a_local[i+(c.sz1-1)*c.sz0] = (_a_local[i-1+(c.sz1-1)*c.sz0]+_a_local[i+1+(c.sz1-1)*c.sz0]
         +_a_local[i+(c.sz1-2)*c.sz0] +(*_a).arr_ptrs[c.r_neighbor[1]][i])/4.0;
22:   if (!c.is_leftmost_core[0]) /* if core is additionally on the left boundary at dimension 0 */
23:     { ...... left-right corner computation ... }
24:   if (!c.is_rightmost_core[0]) /* if core is additionally on the right oundary at dimension 0 */
25:     { ...... right-right corner computation ... }
```

Fig. 6. Example: local and boundary computation per core

cases are then wrapped inside a sequence of if conditionals, shown at lines 6, 9, 12, 15, 17, 19, 22, and 24 in Fig. 6, before being appended to the result.

The low-level implementation in Fig. 6 is essentially the result of numerous splitting and unrolling transformations to the nested data dimension loops of the stencil. Each split loop nest contains a unique combination of local and remote data references, with each remote reference triggering a data movement between a pair of neighboring cores. Two benefits are offered by such an implementation. First, the implementation knows and explicitly enumerates the exact location of each data item and thus incurs no runtime address translation overhead and requires no cache coherency support from the hardware. Second, the separation of different combinations of local vs. remote references allows additional optimization opportunities, e.g., by prefetching the remote references explicitly, shown as the last operation of step (2) of the algorithm in Fig. 4. The complexity of the low-level implementation, while nearly impossible for a developer to manually manage, is easily managed by compilers by recursively enumerating all the boundary cases, as demonstrated, enhancing application portability.

4   Runtime Support

Our runtime library provides a C++ abstraction, the *MulticoreArray* templated class used at line 2 of Fig. 5, to support NUMA-aware stencil computation. The abstraction internally integrates the thread decomposition and scheduling support in OpenMP with data placement support through libnuma. Each OpenMP thread is bound to a hardware core, through the system library $sched\_setaffinity()$. The NUMA topology is referenced by the runtime for the binding of OpenMP thread and hardware core, and libnuma is invoked in the constructor of the abstraction to allocate a distributed stencil array of the desired data dimensions, with its internal data placed onto a pre-specified number of different hardware cores. To minimize remote memory access latency, neighboring stencil data are allocated either on hardware cores located inside the same NUMA node, or cores that belong to adjacent NUMA nodes. Halo region copying is supported to help developers manage data movement across cores.

4.1 Thread Decomposition and Management Using OpenMP

Our runtime allows the number of hardware cores to be used for each data dimension of the stencil to be specified when invoking the constructor of the MulticoreArray abstraction. If unspecified, the maximal number of cores that match the underlying system topology is used. and each core is allocated with blocks of distributed data to be used for later computation. The runtime relies on libnuma to retrieve NUMA distances, a relative distance in the machine topology between two NUMA nodes, among all available NUMA nodes. A multidimensional topology can be constructed with the available NUMA information.

Based on the core numbers to be used for each stencil dimension, the runtime use the $omp\_set\_num\_threads()$ and omp $parallel$ for clause to setup the parallelization environment. The system call $sched\_setaffinity()$ is used to enforce CPU affinity and bind the CPU core to a designated OpenMP thread. For example, given a fully parallelized configuration using 64 OpenMP threads on a 64-core machine, OpenMP threads with ID 0 to 7 will be bound to hardware cores with ID 0 to 7. These 8 hardware cores reside in NUMA node 0 according to the NUMA information from the hardware specification. This thread binding is different from the default OpenMP support, which binds an OpenMP thread to any available hardware core based on the system status. In contrast, our runtime exerts full control in the thread scheduling for the many-core hardware.

4.2 NUMA-aware Data Placement

Our runtime uses internal data structures inside the $MulticoreArray$ abstraction to decompose a stencil array into a collection of sub-arrays. Each sub-array separately stores the stencil data to be operated in a designated thread and is stored in a continuous memory space on a hardware core, together with additional information about the size of the local data and pointers to data that belong to its neighboring threads. Multi-dimensional distribution is used to distribute blocked data to the sub-arrays. By default, each sub-array (except the last one) contains the same number of distributed elements. The runtime then evenly assigns sub-arrays to OpenMP threads based on the sub-array IDs and OpenMP thread IDs. Sub-arrays with adjacent ID numbers are assigned to the same NUMA node or adjacent NUMA nodes when possible. After the assignment, the function *numa_alloc_local()* from libnuma is called by each thread to allocate memory space for the distributed data, thereby enforcing all the distributed data are allocated to their designated OpenMP threads and hardware cores/NUMA nodes. When the number of sub-arrays is more than the available hardware cores, our runtime assigns multiple sub-arrays with neighboring IDs to the same OpenMP thread. This again enforces that adjacent sub-arrays are allocated to the same or neighboring NUMA nodes to reduce memory references crossing NUMA nodes. All the threads use the *numa_alloc_** functions from libnuma to allocate local memory for their data.

Data elements inside a *MulticoreArray* object can be accessed in two different ways: (1) through a high-level interface that allows data to be accessed based on their locations in the original stencil arrays using subscript notations, with the subscripting operator internally translating the global coordinates to the appropriate sub-arrays and local subscripts within the subarrays; and (2) through the low-level interface, which directly references the sub-array pointers and their local elements and is therefore much more efficient. The high-level interface is provided to the developers for convenience, while the low-level interface is used by our compiler, illustrated in Fig. 6, to ensure efficiency of the generated code.

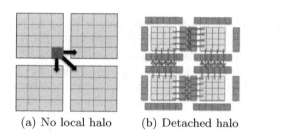
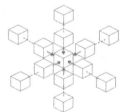

(a) No local halo   (b) Detached halo

Fig. 7. Halo management   **Fig. 8.** 3D Stencil

Our runtime is specialized for the NUMA architecture and is different from the default OpenMP runtime in two key aspects: (1) it decomposes data based on the NUMA topology to minimize exchanges across NUMA nodes, whereas OpenMP uses the first-touch policy; and (2), it supports multi-dimensional data decomposition, with data elements in each decomposed sub-array residing in adjacent memory spaces for better spacial locality. Through the pragma-driven programming interface, our combined runtime and compiler support allows developers to inject domain-specific knowledge into the data and computation decomposition process to maximize application performance.

4.3   Halo Data Management

As stencil data are distributed onto different cores and updated concurrently, each thread needs data from its neighbors to update elements on the boundaries of its local block. These neighboring data are called halo regions of each thread. Our system supports two approaches to managing halo regions, illustrated in Fig. 7. The first approach (shown in Fig. 7(a)) keeps the halo regions in the remote memory, and the second (Fig. 7(b)) replicates the remote data on the local core. The different storage forms impact the performance of the computation by changing when the remote data is fetched (e.g., just in time before they are used vs. far ahead of time using detached halo). Further, hardware with small cache capacity may prefer no local halo storage to save space. The first halo management approach, with computation fetching halo data remotely from the neighboring cores, is adopted by the compiler generated code shown in Fig. 6.

5   Experimental Results

We implemented our stencil compiler by combining the POET program transformation language [24] with the ROSE C/C++ compiler [19]. The compiler is evaluated by using it to automatically generate low-level implementations for four 3D stencil kernels, with 7-point, 13-point, 19-point, and 25-point updates respectively. In particular, each kernel repetitively modifies two 3D stencil arrays of the same size, with each element of one array modified using neighboring elements of the other. The 7-point stencil updates each element using two neighboring elements from each dimension of the other array, as illustrated by the 2D stencil code in Fig. 3. The 13-point stencil updates each element using four neighboring elements of each dimension, as illustrated in Fig. 8, and so on. Each kernel has a baseline OpenMP implementation, where a single OpenMP parallel for pragma is used to parallelize the outermost data dimension loop of each stencil. In contrast, the implementation generated by our compiler (the stencilOpt version) parallelizes all the data dimensions of the stencil instead of just the outermost one as the preferred configuration. Further, each stencil array is placed explicitly on the appropriate NUMA cores, and system-level affinity binding is used to ensure each thread only modifies its local data. The baseline OpenMP implementations have their data distributed among NUMA nodes following the first-touch policy. The OpenMP thread affinity is also setup in OpenMP environment. In contrast, the stencilOpt implementations use the data distribution strategy described in Sect. 4.2.

All kernel implementations are evaluated on a 64-core AMD 6380 workstation comprised of four sockets (16 cores per socket). Each core has a 16 KB L1 data cache, and every two cores share a 2 MB L2 cache memory. Every 8 cores form a NUMA node and share a 8 MB L3 cache. The NUMA distance matrix in Fig. 1 shows the relative memory latencies among the different NUMA nodes, and Fig. 1(a) shows the structure of the NUMA hierarchy. All implementations were compiled on the machine using gcc with –O2 option. Each implementation is evaluated five times, and its average performance is reported. The performance variations across different runs are generally under 3%.

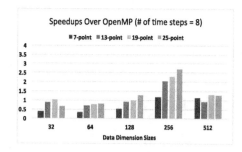 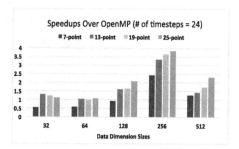

Fig. 9. Speedups attained by our compiler over baseline OpenMP implementations

5.1   The Overall Performance

Figure 9 shows the speedups attained by using our compiler to automatically generate low-level implementations (the *stencilOpt* implementation) for the four 3D stencil kernels, when the size of each data dimension ranges from 32 to 512 and the number of time iterations from 8 to 24. From these results, when the number of time iterations is 24, our *stencilOpt* implementation were able to perform better than the OpenMP implementation in all cases except for the 7-point stencil, which has the fewest neighboring data references, where the stencilOpt implementation performed worse than the OpenMP one when the problem sizes are ≤128. When the number of neighboring references increases, the stencilOpt implementation has uniformly attained a speedup, ranging from factors of 1.1 to 3.7, over the OpenMP implementation. In most cases when the problem size or the number of neighboring references increases, so does the performance speedup over the OpenMP implementation. The overall results indicate that the stencilOpt implementation can manage memory and neighboring core communications much better than the baseline OpenMP implementation, indicating the effectiveness of NUMA-aware data placement by our runtime.

When the number of time iterations equals 8, the speedups attained by stencilOpt generally follow a similar pattern but are much worse than the *time* = 24 cases. This is because when many fewer iterations of the stencil computation are repeated, there are insufficient reuses of the distributed stencil arrays to compensate for the extra overhead of constructing the distributed stencil arrays and copying back and forth between the original stencil arrays and the distributed ones. When amortized at least 24 times, which are much smaller than the number of time iterations in realistic applications, the overhead is no longer a significant factor in performance, and significant speedups can be attained.

5.2   Impact of Execution Configurations

Figure 10 compares the performance of the OpenMP and stencilOpt implementations when using different numbers of threads for the 7-point stencil kernel when the array size is 256^3 and when the computation is repeated 24 times. The

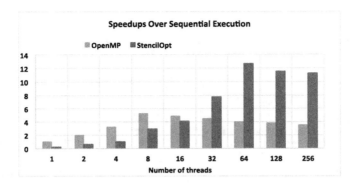

Fig. 10. Impact of thread configurations on 24 time iterations of 256^3 7-point stencil

OpenMP implementations use the default OpenMP policy to schedule these threads onto different hardware cores. On the other hand, the stencilOpt implementations explicitly bind the threads to individual hardware cores to match the actual topology of the stencil when possible, e.g., by parallelizing all data dimensions to form a $n \times n \times n$ topology. From Fig. 10, the best performance by OpenMP is attained when using only 8 out of the 64 cores available on the machine. When more than 8 threads are used, the performance goes down due to network congestions created by the data exchanges among the randomly assigned cores. In contrast, the StencilOpt implementation is able to fully utilize the 64 cores available on the machine to attain close to a factor of 13 speedup over the sequential implementation, compared to a factor of 5 by OpenMP attained when using 8 cores. Although the stencilOpt implementation incurs more significant overhead than the OpenMP baseline, as demonstrated when using fewer than 16 cores, the benefit of better data placement and communication management outweighs the cost when using at least 32 cores.

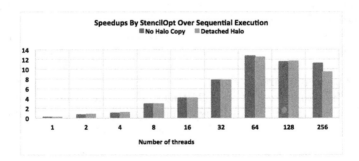

Fig. 11. Impact of halo copying on 24 time iterations of 256^3 7-point stencil

5.3   Implications of Halo Management

Figure 11 compares the performance of stencilOpt implementations when using detached halo management vs. using no explicit halo management, which is the default option used in Sects. 5.1 and 5.2. In particular, the compiler supports detached halo management by prefetching all the remote memory references into local arrays before using the local copies in the actual computation. The main benefit of pre-fetching halo regions is to enable each core reuse its local copies within a single time step. However, the more remote memory references are involved, the larger memory footprint each thread needs to hold all the local copies, and the large footprints may incur additional cache misses when the memory demand is high. For the 256^3 7-point stencil with 24 time iterations, the performance of stencilOpt either with or without halo copying is similar to each other for a majority of cases except when using 256 threads, where since each hardware core needs to host 4 threads, each thread has a smaller cache allocation which is insufficient to hold all the local copies.

Note that halo copying is often used to simplify the complexity of software development when manually implementing stencil computations on distributed memory platforms, as it is impractical to manually enumerate the different combinations of local and remote references as shown in the automatically generated code in Fig. 6. Using a compiler + runtime combined approach make it unnecessary to hardcode this optimization into the high level source code of the computation, therefore promoting application productivity and portability.

6   Related Work

Existing work has recognized the importance of extending OpenMP compilers to support NUMA architectures to attain high performance. For example, Bircsak et al. [2] investigated user-supplied page migration and data layout directives. Chapman et al. [6] evaluated various ways that OpenMP may be used for performance-oriented programming on ccNUMA Architechtures. Huang et al. [11] worked on enabling locality-aware computing in OpenMP by allowing the developer to manipulate data locations hierarchically. The directives we propose are specially tailored for using NUMA aware OpenMP to support the optimization needs of stencil computations and are therefore not intended as part of the general programming model of OpenMP.

Previous research on optimizing stencil computations have mostly focused on enhancing their data locality and parallelism in concert [7,8,13,20,22,23] for multi-core or GPU platforms. These approaches span both manual and automatic code optimizations as well as automated performance prediction and tuning of the optimization configurations (e.g., blocking factors). Bondhugula et al. [4] developed an automated framework that performs parallelization and locality optimizations of stencil codes using the polyhedral model. Liu and Li [15] presented an asynchronous algorithm for reducing synchronization costs and improving locality in stencil computations. Christen et al. [7] presented a strategy for improving locality and exploiting parallelism in a stencil code appearing in a Bio-heat equation targeting the Cell BE and Nvidia GPUs. Our work also includes an automated source-to-source compiler for stencil computations. However, we target many-core NUMA architectures and aim to provide a directive driven framework to support the automated cache management for stencil computations on such architectures.

Datta et al. [9, 10] presented an auto-tuning approach to search for the best optimizations for stencil codes, including their data distribution schemes for NUMA systems, However, their NUMA-aware strategy relies on the first-touch memory policy to perform a page-based distribution. Shaheen and Strzodka [21] focus on spatial-temporal data locality, parallelization, regular memory access, and data-to-core affinity to provide efficient temporal blocking schemes for stencil computations running on ccNUMA systems. Our NUMA-aware decomposition and distribution is driven by topological features of both the stencil arrays and the NUMA hierarchy. In addition to data-to-core affinity, our distribution considers minimizing the overhead by selecting remote access links with the least memory latencies.

Bolosky et al. [3] explored the relations between kernel-based NUMA management policies and multiprocessor memory architectures. Various research efforts have focused on performance evaluation on NUMA architecture using programming models such as OpenMP [6, 17] or MPI [14]. Navarro et al. [16] used Locality Communication Graph (LCG) to represent the data locality and used compiler techniques to generate efficient loop iteration/data distribution for NUMA machines. Other research efforts have focused on thread and memory placement [1], data distribution, migration, and replication [5]. This paper present a NUMA study over the latest multi-core NUMA CPUs.

7   Conclusion

This paper presents a pragma-driven special purpose optimizing compiler to automatically convert stencil computations in scientific applications to low-level implementations that invoke a runtime library to explicitly manage the data placement and remote memory references on NUMA many-core architectures. Our automatically optimized code have consistently outperformed OpenMP implementations that use first-touch policies to schedule the computations. We show that through automatically specialized code generation for stencils, our approach provides a combination of good performance, architecture portability, and productivity for developers.

Acknowledgment. This work was performed under the auspices of the U.S. Department of Energy by Lawrence Livermore National Laboratory under Contract DE-AC52-07NA27344. LLNL-CONF-697198.

References

1. Antony, J., Janes, P.P., Rendell, A.P.: Exploring thread and memory placement on numa architectures: Solaris and Linux, UltraSPARC/FirePlane and Opteron/HyperTransport. In: Robert, Y., Parashar, M., Badrinath, R., Prasanna, V.K. (eds.) HiPC 2006. LNCS, vol. 4297, pp. 338–352. Springer, Heidelberg (2006). doi:10.1007/11945918_35
2. Bircsak, J., Craig, P., Crowell, R., Cvetanovic, Z., Harris, J., Nelson, C.A., Offner, C.D.: Extending OpenMP for NUMA machines. In: ACM/IEEE 2000 Conference Supercomputing, pp. 48–48. IEEE (2000)
3. Bolosky, W.J., Scott, M.L., Fitzgerald, R.P., Fowler, R.J., Cox, A.L.: NUMA policies and their relation to memory architecture. In: ACM SIGARCH Computer Architecture News, vol. 19, pp. 212–221. ACM (1991)
4. Bondhugula, U., Hartono, A., Ramanujan, J., Sadayappan, P.: A practical automatic polyhedral parallelizer and locality optimizer. In: PLDI 2008: Proceedings of the 2008 ACM SIGPLAN Conference on Programming Language Design and Implementation, pp. 101–113, New York, USA (2008)
5. Bull, J.M., Johnson, C.: Data distribution, migration and replication on a cc-NUMA architecture. In: Proceedings of the Fourth European workshop on OpenMP (2002)
6. Chapman, B., Patil, A., Prabhakar, A.: Performance oriented programming for NUMA architechtures. In: Eigenmann, R., Voss, M.J. (eds.) WOMPAT 2001. LNCS, vol. 2104, pp. 137–154. Springer, Heidelberg (2001). doi:10.1007/3-540-44587-0_13
7. Christen, M., Schenk, O., Neufeld, E., Messmer, P., Burkhart, H.: Parallel data-locality aware stencil computations on modern micro-architectures. In: IPDPS 2009: Proceedings of the 2009 IEEE International Symposium on Parallel and Distributed Processing, pp. 1–10, Washington, DC, USA (2009)
8. Datta, K., Murphy, M., Volkov, V., Williams, S., Carter, J., Oliker, L., Patterson, D., Shalf, J., Yelick, K.: Stencil computation optimization and auto-tuning on state-of-the-art multicore architectures. In: Proceedings of the 2008 ACM/IEEE Conference on Supercomputing (SC 2008) (2008)
9. Datta, K., Murphy, M., Volkov, V., Williams, S., Carter, J., Oliker, L., Patterson, D., Shalf, J., Yelick, K.: Stencil computation optimization and auto-tuning on state-of-the-art multicore architectures. In: Proceedings of the 2008 ACM/IEEE conference on Supercomputing, p. 4. IEEE Press (2008)
10. Datta, K., Williams, S., Volkov, V., Carter, J., Oliker, L., Shalf, J., Yelick, K.: Auto-tuning the 27-point stencil for multicore. In: Proceedings of iWAPT2009: The Fourth International Workshop on Automatic Performance Tuning (2009)
11. Huang, L., Jin, H., Yi, L., Chapman, B.: Enabling locality-aware computations in OpenMP. Sci. Prog. 18(3), 169–181 (2010)
12. Kleen, A.: A NUMA API for Linux. Novel Inc (2005)
13. Krishnamoorthy, S., Baskaran, M., Bondhugula, U., Ramanujam, J., Rountev, A., Sadayappan, P.: Effective automatic parallelization of stencil computations. SIGPLAN Not. 42(6), 235–244 (2007)
14. Li, S., Hoefler, T., Snir, M.: NUMA-aware shared-memory collective communication for MPI. In: Proceedings of the 22nd International Symposium on High-Performance Parallel and Distributed Computing, pp. 85–96. ACM (2013)

15. Liu, L., Li, V.: Improving parallelism and locality with asynchronous algorithms. In: PPoPP 2010: Proceedings of the 15th ACM SIGPLAN symposium on Principles and Practice of Parallel Programming, New York, NY, USA, pp. 213–222. ACM (2010)
16. Navarro, A., Zapata, E., Padua, D.: Compiler techniques for the distribution of data and computation. IEEE Trans. Parallel Distrib. Syst. **14**(6), 545–562 (2003)
17. Nikolopoulos, D. S., Papatheodorou, T. S., Polychronopoulos, C. D., Labarta, J., et al.: Is data distribution necessary in OpenMP? In: Proceedings of the 2000 ACM/IEEE Conference on Supercomputing, p. 47. IEEE Computer Society (2000)
18. OpenMP: Simple, portable, scalable SMP programming. http://www.openmp.org (2006)
19. Quinlan, D., et al.: ROSE Compiler Infrastructure. http://www.rosecompiler.org/
20. Rivera, G., Tseng, C.-W.: Tiling optimizations for 3D scientific computations. In: Supercomputing 2000: Proceedings of the 2000 ACM/IEEE Conference on Supercomputing, Washington, DC, USA (2000)
21. Shaheen, M., Strzodka, R.: NUMA aware iterative stencil computations on many-core systems. In: 2012 IEEE 26th International Parallel and Distributed Processing Symposium (IPDPS), pp. 461–473. IEEE (2012)
22. Song, Y., Li, Z.: New tiling techniques to improve cache temporal locality. In: PLDI 1999: Proceedings of the ACM SIGPLAN 1999 Conference on Programming Language Design and Implementation, New York, NY, USA, pp. 215–228 (1999)
23. Song, Y., Xu, R., Wang, C., Li, Z.: Data locality enhancement by memory reduction. In: Proceedings of the 15th ACM International Conference on Supercomputing, Sorrento, Italy (2001)
24. Yi, Q.: POET: a scripting language for applying parameterized source-to-source program transformations. Softw. Pract. Exp. **42**(6), 675–706 (2012)

Formalizing Structured Control Flow Graphs

Amit Sabne$^{(\boxtimes)}$, Putt Sakdhnagool, and Rudolf Eigenmann

Purdue University, West Lafayette, IN 47907, USA
{asabne,psakdhna,eigenman}@purdue.edu

Abstract. Structured programs are believed to be easier to understand, and compiler friendly [5,10,45]. However, compilers do not process the source programs directly; they instead work on control flow graphs (CFGs) of the programs. Unfortunately, there is little formalization of structured CFGs. This paper shows how the lack of formalization has led to varying interpretations of structured CFGs. The paper next presents new formalization of structured CFGs which eliminates the ambiguity. Structured CFGs gain importance as they ease compiler optimizations, decompilation, and help reduce the performance degradation caused by thread divergence on SIMD units. The paper elaborates on these benefits. It also shows that compilers, both front-ends and back-ends, may generate unstructured CFGs from structured program sources, which necessitates mechanisms to obtain structured CFGs from unstructured ones.

Keywords: Control Flow Graphs (CFGs) · Structured programming · Structured CFGs · Irreducible CFGs

1 Introduction

Structured programming is a paradigm where programs are written using just three base constructs [12,45], namely, (i) sequence of statements, (ii) **if**-then-**else** blocks, and (iii) loops. Structured programming was sought for many reasons, two important ones being readability of the program [10,45] and ease of analyzing the control flow [5,45]. While optimizing programs, compilers operate on the control flow graph (CFG) of the program, which is usually built upon an intermediate representation (IR), and not on the program source itself. A CFG is a directed graph wherein the nodes represent basic blocks and the edges represent control flow paths [5]. Because compilers work on CFGs, structuredness of CFGs becomes a more important consideration than the structuredness of the program sources. The existing notion of structured programming assumes that compiler-generated CFGs of structured programs are structured. A key insight of this paper is that structured CFGs do not follow directly from structured program source codes.

The prevalent notion [14,39] of structured CFGs considers three base patterns similar to the structured program constructs mentioned above. They comprise a sequence (Fig. 1a), a selection (Fig. 1b), and a loop (Fig. 1c). We argue that such

© Springer International Publishing AG 2017
C. Ding et al. (Eds.): LCPC 2016, LNCS 10136, pp. 153–168, 2017.
DOI: 10.1007/978-3-319-52709-3_13

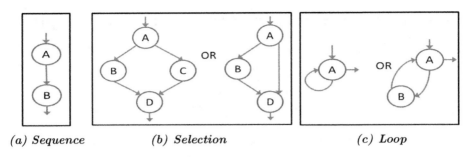

(a) Sequence   *(b) Selection*   *(c) Loop*

Fig. 1. Pictorially represented base structured patterns

pictorial depiction of base patterns alone is insufficient and leads to imprecision. The "definition" fails to clearly distinguish a structured CFG from an unstructured one. Consider the CFGs in Fig. 2, which do not show any obvious matching to the base patterns. Creating structured CFGs contrasts with structured programming, where just by looking for the presence of unstructuring-causing constructs, such as `goto` and `break` statements, unstructuredness can be easily detected. The difficulty in doing the same in CFGs arises because the pictorial representations of the base structured patterns do not show how to compose the patterns into larger CFGs or decompose large CFGs.

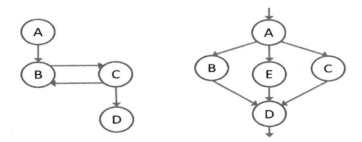

Fig. 2. Are these CFGs structured? The base patterns in Fig. 1 fail to answer.

The central contribution of this paper is to formalize structured control flow graphs. The paper does so by providing formal definitions of the base structured patterns. It then presents a conceptual framework, called *folding*, that replaces base structured patterns identified by the formalization with single nodes. The repeated application of folding determines whether a given CFG is structured or not.

The rest of this paper is organized as follows: Sect. 2 presents preliminary CFG concepts. Section 3 elaborates the insufficiencies of past work in defining structured control flow graphs. Section 4 presents definitions that represent various phenomena in CFGs and describes our formalizations of structured control flow graphs. Structured CFGs ease compiler optimizations and decompilation. They lower the penalty of divergent execution on SIMD units. Section 5 details these benefits. Section 6 elaborates avenues open for research. Section 7 presents results showing the existence of unstructuredness in compiler-generated control flow graphs. Section 8 concludes the paper.

2   Preliminaries

This section presents common definitions and concepts applicable to CFGs that lay foundations of this work.

Definition 1. *Path: A path between nodes A and B is an ordered list of adjacent edges and vertices. The list begins with an out-edge of A, and ends with an in-edge of B.*

Definition 2. *Condition Node: Any node with two or more out-edges is called a condition node.*

Definition 3. *Region: The region between two nodes (edges) A and B contains all nodes and edges that are present on any path from A to B. Such nodes and edges are said to be internal to the region.*

Definition 4. *Dominator: A node (edge) P is a dominator of a node (edge) Q if every path from the entry node of the CFG that reaches Q has to pass through P.*

Each node or edge dominates itself. Each dominator of a given node (edge), except itself, is said to be a *strict* dominator of the node (edge).

Definition 5. *Post-dominator: A node (edge) Q is a post-dominator of a node (edge) P if every path from P to the exit node of the CFG has to pass through Q.*

Each node or edge post-dominates itself. Each post-dominator of a given node (edge), except itself, is said to be a *strict* post-dominator of the node (edge). The dominator (post-dominator) relationships allow construction of a dominator (post-dominator) tree of the CFG, wherein the parent of a node is its strict dominator (post-dominator). The parent node of a given node in the post-dominator tree is known as the immediate post-dominator (IPDOM) of that node.

Definition 6. *Single-entry-single-exit (SESE) region: The region between two nodes (edges) A and B is SESE if all of the following are true:*

- *A dominates B*
- *B post-dominates A*
- *Every cycle containing A also contains B and vice versa.*

A node (edge) is a SESE region by itself. Each base pattern in Fig. 1 represents a SESE region. For the selection pattern (Fig. 1b), node A is the entry and node D is the exit. For the loop pattern (Fig. 1c), node A is the entry as well as the exit. In Fig. 3, region between D and E is not SESE, while the region between B and E is.

Definition 7. *Loop condition node, loop path:* *A given condition node N is said to be a loop condition node, if there is a simple path (all nodes along the path have in/out-degree of one) that originates and ends at N. We refer to any such path as a loop path.*

Next, we describe the transformations that determine if a CFG is reducible or not. We attribute the definitions to Hecht and Ullman [20].

Definition 8. *T1:* *T1 is a transformation that removes an edge from a node onto itself.*

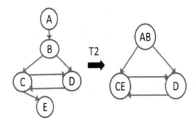

Fig. 3. Example of an irreducible CFG

Definition 9. *T2:* *If a node B has a single predecessor node A, then transformation T2 replaces nodes A and B with a single node C. Predecessors of A become the predecessors of C. Successors of A or B become successors of C.*

Definition 10. *Reducible CFG:* *A CFG is reducible iff it becomes a single node through repeated applications of T1 and T2, otherwise, it is said to be **irreducible**.*

Figure 3 shows an example of an irreducible CFG, where neither T1 nor T2 can be applied.

3 Previous Work on Defining Structuredness

This section outlines previous work on defining structured programs and CFGs. As mentioned in the introduction, much prior work attempts to define structuredness at the program source level [10,12,45]. Even in the terminology

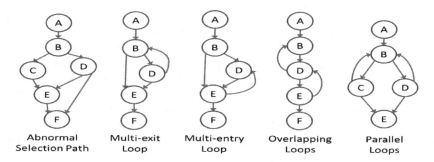

Fig. 4. Base patterns for unstructuredness, from Williams [39]

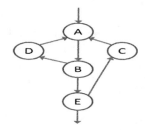

Fig. 5. This CFG is considered structured in [8], although it maps to no structured program!

used while describing structured programming, there is ample ambiguity, e.g., Knuth [28] suggests structured programs can have `goto` statements, while Morreti et al. [31] consider programs with `case` statements to be structured too. Many researchers [6,7,14,19,34] only used loosely-defined notion of structured programming. Furthermore, as Sect. 7 will show, compilers can turn structured programs into unstructured CFGs. It therefore becomes essential to define structuredness of CFGs.

The first attempt of defining structured control flow graphs was from Williams [39], who suggested that structured CFGs are composed of the base patterns in Fig. 1, and unstructured CFGs must comprise one of the five patterns of unstructuredness shown in Fig. 4. Later, Oulsnam [32] presented similar patterns of unstructuredness. However, the lack of formalization in the definition means that sophisticated pattern matching must be done to assess the CFG structuredness, toward which no algorithms were provided. E.g., the CFG on the left in Fig. 2 neither matches base structured patterns in Fig. 1, nor the base unstructured patterns in Fig. 4.

The latest attempt of defining structured CFGs is from Anantpur et al. [8]. However, their definition, although formal, does not truly capture the notion of structured CFGs. Their definition recognizes unstructuring as scenarios where (i) there exists an incoming/outgoing edge from a loop, or (ii) an edge exists between a condition node and a node with multiple in-edges where there is no dominator/post-dominator relationship between the two nodes. This definition departs from the base patterns. Consider the CFG in Fig. 5, where all nodes are strongly connected, with a common entry node, A. All nodes thus belong to the same loop [3], meaning that the first condition is satisfied. Node A is the only multiple in-edge node, but it dominates all other nodes. Hence the second condition is satisfied too. Thus, this CFG will be considered structured in [8], in spite of having no mapping to a high-level structured program.

Therefore, it is essential to formalize the notion of structured CFGs in a way that enables an algorithmic mapping to the three high-level program constructs used in structured programming.

4   Formalizing Structured CFGs

In this section, we formalize the notion of structured CFGs. We start by providing formal definitions for the base structured patterns. Next we introduce the conceptual framework of *folding*, which decomposes CFGs into base patterns. The section introduces terminology to define elements of a CFG, and proves that structured CFGs are always reducible.

Restrictions on CFGs Considered: We consider CFGs with single entry and exit nodes. There are no infinite loops, i.e., there exists a path from each node in the CFG to the exit node. Symmetrically, each node in the CFG can be reached from the entry node. **Also, the maximum in-degree and out-degree for all nodes is two.** Generality is maintained since a CFG with any in-degree or out-degree can be converted into a CFG with a maximum in-degree and out-degree of two.

We begin by defining structured selection and loop condition nodes (nodes with two out-edges).

Definition 11. *Structured selection condition node, selection body:* *A condition node N is a structured selection condition if for every path from N to its IPDOM, the region between the first and last edges is SESE. Therefore, the region between the structured selection condition and its IPDOM is SESE as well, which is said to be its selection body.*

Definition 12. *Structured loop condition node, loop body:* *A structured loop condition node is a loop condition node where there exists a SESE region between one of its out-edges and in-edges. This SESE region is called the loop body.*

Definition 13. *Unstructured condition node:* *If a condition node is neither a structured selection condition node, nor a structured loop condition node, then it is an unstructured condition node.*

Examples: Node A in the base selection pattern (Fig. 1b) is a structured selection condition. Node A in the base loop pattern (Fig. 1c) is a structured loop condition, with edge A→A being both the entry and exit edge of the SESE region (left figure) or edge A→B being the entry edge and the edge B→A being the exit edge of the SESE region (right figure). For condition node A in Fig. 6a, G is the IPDOM. A→B→E→G is one path from A to G, on which the region between the first and last edges is not SESE. Hence, A is not a structured selection node. Similarly, for no out-edge and in-edge pair of A, there exists a SESE region. Therefore, A is not a structured loop condition node either. Hence, A is an unstructured condition. On the other hand, in Fig. 6b, nodes U and T are structured selection conditions, while VZ is a structured loop condition node.

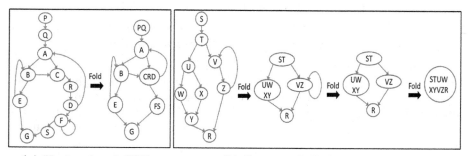

(a) **Unstructured CFG**   (b) **Structured CFG**

Fig. 6. Maximal folding

Now, we present formal definitions for the **base structured patterns** shown in Fig. 1.

Definition 14. Base Pattern of Sequence: *Two nodes, A and B, along with an edge A→B are said to form a sequence if B is the sole successor of A, and A is the sole predecessor of B.*

Definition 15. Base Pattern of Selection: *The pattern of selection contains a structured selection condition node, its IPDOM, and the selection body. The selection body must contain at least one node, and any path from the selection condition node to the IPDOM can have at most one node.*

Definition 16. Base Pattern of Loop: *The pattern of loop contains a structured loop condition node, the loop body, and the entry and exit edges of the loop body. The loop body can contain at most one node.*

To determine if a CFG is structured, we introduce a new concept, called *folding*.

Definition 17. Folding: *Folding is a process of replacing a base structured pattern with a single node in the CFG. During folding, any edge not belonging to the base pattern, but having its source (sink) node in the base pattern, is redirected so that the newly created single node is its source (sink).*

Definition 18. *Maximal Folding:* *Maximal folding repeatedly applies folding to a CFG until no more base structured patterns exist.*

The above formalization of base structured patterns removes ambiguity and trivialises the process of folding. Implementing folding simply requires looking for base patterns formed on each node, which is a constant time operation. Thus, maximal folding is $\mathcal{O}(n)$, where n is the number of nodes in the CFG. Figure 6 shows examples of structured and unstructured CFGs and their maximally folded equivalents.

Definition 19. *Completely Foldable CFG:* *If a maximally folded CFG contains a single node, then the CFG is called completely foldable.*

Definition 20. *Structured CFG:* *A CFG is said to be structured iff it is completely foldable. Otherwise, it is called an* **unstructured CFG.**

Complete foldability, i.e., structuredness, implies that the CFG is composed of the base structured patterns. While reducibility eases CFG analysis, it does not determine if the CFG is structured or not. E.g., the CFG in Fig. 6a is reducible, but is unstructured. Also, a structured CFG does not imply structuredness of all condition nodes. E.g. in Fig. 6b, Z is an unstructured condition node by itself.

Theorem 1. *Structured CFGs are reducible.*

Proof. Since a structured CFG is completely foldable, the idea here is to show that each base structured pattern is reducible. As shown in Fig. 7a, a sequence can be reduced into a single node by applying T2. Figure 7b shows that the repeated application of T2 can reduce the base selection pattern, while Fig. 7c shows that application of T2 (if the loop is not a self loop), or T1 (if the loop is a self loop) can reduce the base loop pattern. The process of folding replaces a base structured pattern with a single node. Since each base pattern can be reduced by T1 and/or T2, it follows that instead of folding a base pattern, one can apply T1 and/or T2, and a continued application would result in a CFG containing a single node, implying reducibility.

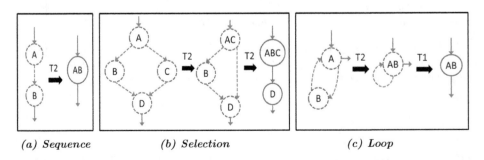

(a) Sequence   *(b) Selection*   *(c) Loop*

Fig. 7. Reducibility of base patterns: Dashed nodes and edges belong to the base structured patterns formalized in this paper

Corollary 1. *Every irreducible CFG is unstructured.*

Proof. Follows directly from Theorem 1.

Lemma 1. *In a maximally folded CFG that can not be completely folded, there must be at least one unstructured condition node.*

Proof. Let us assume that all condition nodes in a CFG are either structured selection conditions or structured loop conditions. Then, there must be some (innermost) condition node whose body does not have a condition node. There are two possibilities for this node:

Case 1: Structured Selection Condition: In this case, there can only be two distinct, simple paths originating at this node that reach its IPDOM, since there are no condition nodes in the selection body. By the definition of a structured condition node, nodes on each of these paths are dominated by their first edge, and hence none of their nodes can have two in-edges. Therefore both these paths can only contain nodes with a single predecessor and a single successor, however, as the CFG is maximally folded, there can at most be one node on either of these two paths. Hence, the selection condition node, its IPDOM, and, the selection body would match the base structured selection pattern.

Case 2: Structured Loop Condition: In this case, this node's loop body can only have nodes with a single predecessor and a single successor. With a similar argument as in case 1, the loop body can only have at most one node. Hence, the loop condition node, the loop body, and its entry and exit edges would match the base structured loop pattern.

Thus, in both cases, a base structured pattern would exist in the CFG, which is a contradiction. Hence, a maximally folded, but not completely folded CFG must have an unstructured condition node.

5   Significance of Structured Control Flow Graphs

Structured control flow graphs ensure that the CFGs are reducible (Theorem 1). Irreducibility is a condition where one or more loops in a CFG have more than one entry points. Irreducible CFGs are difficult to analyze. Many compiler analyses and transformations take place only if the CFG is reducible [11,24–26,30,36,44]. Dataflow analyses are known to be faster on reducible CFGs [22]. Even the standard compilers, such as gcc and llvm, do not optimize irreducible loops. Several research projects have shown cases where specialized approaches had to be taken, simply to cater to irreducible CFGs [23,27,41]. Ensuring structuredness of CFGs will eliminate the need for such passes.

A well-known measure of control flow complexity is the number of *knots* [42] it contains. A knot is an unavoidable crossing of two edges in a CFG. Structured CFGs have no knots, and rank low on complexity. This simplicity also comes into play in program decompilation. Structured CFGs can always be mapped to high-level program sources, e.g., consider a Java bytecode with irreducibility,

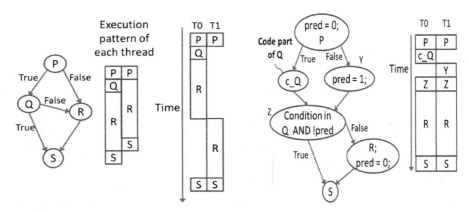

(a) *Unstructured CFG execution on a 2-wide SIMD*

(b) *Equivalent Structured CFG execution*

Fig. 8. Reducing the penalty of divergent execution on SIMD units using structured CFGs

which cannot be translated to Java source code since representing irreducibility requires goto statements that are not supported in Java.

Unstructured CFGs may result in slow execution on SIMD units. Consider the CFG shown in Fig. 8a, where nodes P and Q are unstructured condition nodes. For the two involved threads, T0 and T1, and for their shown execution pattern shown in Fig. 8a, condition P behaves divergently, i.e., the two threads execute different branch targets. Such divergent execution is handled using a mechanism called reconvergence stack [43], wherein the diverged threads resume joint execution only at the IPDOM of the divergent node. The node R, which is computationally expensive, gets executed twice in this mechanism. A structured equivalent of the CFG, shown in Fig. 8b, however, achieves combined execution of node R from both the threads, lowering the overall execution time. In the structured version of the CFG, the diverging threads at P are reconverged as early as possible, by introducing a new IPDOM node Z for P. This transformation requires additional predicate variables and branch instructions. In structured CFGs, threads diverged on a condition cannot execute the same node before they reconverge at the IPDOM, which is the key reason for the reduction in divergent execution.

6   Avenues for Research

Most unstructured-to-structured program converters work on the program source [4,6,7,9,10,19,34,38,45]. Compilers, however, work on CFGs, which are internal representations. Various compiler passes are known to create unstructured CFGs, e.g., short-circuiting, inlining [43], jump threading, and tail-call elimination [37]. Program source-level techniques can not remove such unstructuredness. Therefore, CFG structuring techniques become essential.

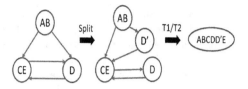

Fig. 9. Node Splitting: D' is a copy of D

The available unstructured-to-structured conversion techniques, both those operating at the source level, and those operating at the CFG level [33, 40] resort to a mechanism called Node Splitting [3, 21] to deal with irreducible CFGs. This technique duplicates code to remove irreducibility. Node Splitting operates on any node with at least two predecessors. This node is duplicated, and each predecessor keeps a copy of this node. The out-edges of each copy are directed to the same nodes as in the original graph. In Fig. 9, splitting just one node results in a reducible CFG.

However, such node duplication can cause exponential code size blowup. Consider Fig. 10, which contains overlapping irreducible loops (Loop1: H→E→F→H and Loop2: H→G→H). In such a scenario, the CFG generated by Node Splitting would contain four copies of G, and two copies each of nodes F and H. Carter et. al. [13] proved that reducible CFGs generated by Node Splitting can get exponentially larger.

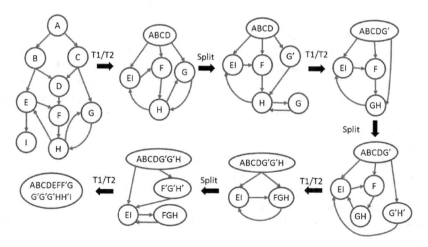

Fig. 10. Blowup caused by Node Splitting: Four copies of G, two copies each of F and H

Due to the exponential blowup property of Node Splitting, paired with the rarity of irreducible CFGs, standard compilers such as gcc and llvm forgo Node Splitting, and loose out on optimizing irreducible codes. This behaviour of static analyzers is exploited by software obfuscators. Software obfuscation intends to make it practically impossible for an attacker to statically determine program properties. To do so, it changes the nature of the code while retaining the functionality. A common obfuscation technique inserts dummy edges in the CFG to make it irreducible [13,16,17]. Malwares often insert fake irreducibilities, making it difficult for static analyzers to detect them, as the equivalent reducible CFGs would be exponentially larger. A research challenge is therefore to convert irreducible CFGs into reducible ones without facing code explosion.

The second challenge is of reducing the divergent execution penalty on SIMD units [35]. While many irreducible-to-reducible converters induce code duplication, some unstructured-to-structured CFG converters duplicate code even when the CFG is reducible [45]. Duplicating code fundamentally removes the possibility of improving code performance on SIMD units. On the other hand, the predicate-based mechanism in Fig. 8b can improve the execution, without needing duplication. However, generic techniques to achieve such transformation are required. Furthermore, it is not quite known if such predicate-based approach would still face code explosion [13,15]. Our ongoing work [1] offers a predicate-based generic mechanism to convert unstructured CFGs into structured ones, with only a polynomial code growth.

7   Unstructuredness in Compiler-Generated CFGs

We now show how compilers can induce unstructuredness in CFGs, even when the source program is structured. We performed our experiments with the LLVM [29] compiler (Version 3.8). Prior to determining whether a given CFG is structured or not, we convert it into an equivalent CFG where the in-degree and out-degree of each node is at most 2.

Table 1 shows unstructuredness in the C implementation [2] of the NAS parallel benchmarks [18]. Although few functions in these applications have source-level unstructuredness, i.e., the unstructuredness caused by constructs such as break, goto, continue etc., the compiler front-end generated CFGs have higher occurrences of unstructuredness. Applications MG, LU, SP, and BP have no source-level unstructuredness; yet, the front-end generated CFGs for some functions in these applications are unstructured. Program source-level structuring techniques [6,7,9,10,19,34,45] cannot cater to such unstructuredness. Furthermore, optimized CFGs can be seen to contain more functions with unstructured CFGs, which is a result of the compiler transformation passes. Benchmarks CG and LU are exceptions; the LLVM compiler inlined unstructured functions in the optimized versions, leading to a reduction in the total number of unstructured functions.

Table 1. Unstructuredness of CFGs in NAS Benchmarks: Even the functions with structured source code can have unstructuredness in the compiler front-end generated CFG. Optimized CFGs are more likely to possess unstructuredness.

Benchmark	#Functions	#Functions with unstructured constructs	#Functions with unstructured CFGs generated from front-end	#Functions with Unstructured CFGs after -O3
CG	16	1	3	2
FT	25	2	3	5
EP	10	1	1	1
MG	26	0	2	7
LU	27	0	3	2
SP	31	0	4	4
IS	13	2	1	1
BT	34	0	1	4

8 Conclusion

This paper has identified that structured programs do not necessarily imply structured CFGs. Many previous definitions of structured CFGs have led to ambiguities. The paper has formalized the notion of structured CFGs by presenting formal definitions for the three base structured patterns that compose a structured CFG. It introduced a conceptual framework of folding, which replaces base structured patterns with single nodes, and helps determine whether or not a given CFG is structured. The paper described the importance of CFG structuredness, namely, (i) guaranteeing reducibility which results in better compiler optimizations, (ii) ease of decompilation, and (iii) help reduce the performance degradation caused by thread divergence on SIMD units. The paper also presented insufficiencies of the available unstructured-to-structured CFG converters that result in excessive code duplication. Finally, experimental results showed that both compiler front-ends and compiler transformation passes can induce unstructuredness in programs.

References

1. Control flow structuring without code explosion [Under Submission]
2. Omni OpenMP benchmarks (2016). http://www.hpcs.cs.tsukuba.ac.jp/omni-comp iler/download/download-benchmarks.html. Accessed 11 Mar 2016
3. Aho, A.V., Sethi, R., Ullman, J.D.: Compilers: Principles, Techniques, and Tools. Addison-Wesley Longman Publishing Co., Inc., Boston (1986)
4. Allen, F.E., Cocke, J.: A program data flow analysis procedure. Commun. ACM **19**(3), 137 (1976). http://doi.acm.org/10.1145/360018.360025
5. Allen, F.E.: Control flow analysis. In: Proceedings of a Symposium on Compiler Optimization, pp. 1–19. ACM, New York (1970). http://doi.acm.org/10.1145/800028.808479

6. Allen, J.R., Kennedy, K., Porterfield, C., Warren, J.: Conversion of control dependence to data dependence. In: Proceedings of the 10th ACM SIGACT-SIGPLAN Symposium on Principles of Programming Languages, POPL 1983, pp. 177–189. ACM, New York (1983). http://doi.acm.org/10.1145/567067.567085
7. Ammarguellat, Z.: A control-flow normalization algorithm and its complexity. IEEE Trans. Softw. Eng. **18**(3), 237–251 (1992). http://dx.doi.org/10.1109/32.126773
8. Anantpur, J., R., G.: Taming control divergence in GPUs through control flow linearization. In: Cohen, A. (ed.) CC 2014. LNCS, vol. 8409, pp. 133–153. Springer, Heidelberg (2014). doi:10.1007/978-3-642-54807-9_8
9. Ashcroft, E.A., Manna, Z.: The translation of 'go to' programs to 'while' programs. In: IFIP Congress, no. 1, pp. 250–255 (1971)
10. Baker, B.S.: An algorithm for structuring flowgraphs. J. ACM **24**(1), 98–120 (1977). http://doi.acm.org/10.1145/321992.321999
11. Blackham, B., Heiser, G.: Sequoll: A framework for model checking binaries. In: 2013 IEEE 19th Real-Time and Embedded Technology and Applications Symposium (RTAS), pp. 97–106, April 2013
12. Böhm, C., Jacopini, G.: Flow diagrams, turing machines and languages with only two formation rules. Commun. ACM **9**(5), 366–371 (1966). http://doi.acm.org/10.1145/355592.365646
13. Carter, L., Ferrante, J., Thomborson, C.D.: Folklore confirmed: reducible flow graphs are exponentially larger. In: Conference Record of POPL 2003: The 30th SIGPLAN-SIGACT Symposium on Principles of Programming Languages, New Orleans, Louisisana, USA, 15-17 January 2003, pp. 106–114 (2003). http://doi.acm.org/10.1145/640128.604141
14. Chapin, N., Denniston, S.P.: Characteristics of a structured program. SIGPLAN Not. **13**(5), 36–45 (1978). http://doi.acm.org/10.1145/953395.953398
15. Collberg, C., Nagra, J.: Surreptitious Software: Obfuscation, Watermarking, and Tamperproofing for Software Protection, 1st edn. Addison-Wesley Professional, Boston (2009)
16. Collberg, C., Thomborson, C., Low, D.: A taxonomy of obfuscating transformations (1997)
17. Collberg, C., Thomborson, C., Low, D.: Manufacturing cheap, resilient, and stealthy opaque constructs. In: Proceedings of the 25th ACM SIGPLAN-SIGACT Symposium on Principles of Programming Languages, POPL 1998. ACM, New York (1998). http://doi.acm.org/10.1145/268946.268962
18. Division, N.A.S.: NAS Parallel Benchmarks (2016). https://www.nas.nasa.gov/publications/npb.html/. Accessed 11 March 2016
19. Erosa, A., Hendren, L.: Taming control flow: a structured approach to eliminating goto statements. In: Proceedings of the 1994 International Conference on Computer Languages, pp. 229–240, May 1994
20. Hecht, M.S., Ullman, J.D.: Characterizations of reducible flow graphs. J. ACM **21**(3), 367–375 (1974). http://doi.acm.org/10.1145/321832.321835
21. Hecht, M.S.: Flow Analysis of Computer Programs. Elsevier Science Inc., New York (1977)
22. Hecht, M.S., Ullman, J.D.: Analysis of a simple algorithm for global data flow problems. In: Proceedings of the 1st Annual ACM SIGACT-SIGPLAN Symposium on Principles of Programming Languages, POPL 1973, pp. 207–217., ACM, New York (1973). http://doi.acm.org/10.1145/512927.512946

23. Hepp, S., Brandner, F.: Splitting functions into single-entry regions. In: Proceedings of the 2014 International Conference on Compilers, Architecture and Synthesis for Embedded Systems, CASES 2014, pp. 17:1–17:10. ACM, New York (2014). http://doi.acm.org/10.1145/2656106.2656128

24. Hundt, R., Raman, E., Thuresson, M., Vachharajani, N.: Mao – an extensible micro-architectural optimizer. In: Proceedings of the 9th Annual IEEE/ACM International Symposium on Code Generation and Optimization, CGO 2011, pp. 1–10. IEEE Computer Society, Washington, D.C. (2011). http://dl.acm.org/citation. cfm?id=2190025.2190077

25. Kalvala, S., Warburton, R., Lacey, D.: Program transformations using temporal logic side conditions. ACM Trans. Program. Lang. Syst. **31**(4), 14:1–14:48 (2009). http://doi.acm.org/10.1145/1516507.1516509

26. Kandemir, M., Banerjee, P., Choudhary, A., Ramanujam, J., Shenoy, N.: A global communication optimization technique based on data-flow analysis and linear algebra. ACM Trans. Program. Lang. Syst. **21**(6), 1251–1297 (1999). http://doi.acm.org/10.1145/330643.330647

27. Kleinsorge, J.C., Falk, H., Marwedel, P.: Simple analysis of partial worst-case execution paths on general control flow graphs. In: Proceedings of the Eleventh ACM International Conference on Embedded Software, EMSOFT 2013, pp. 16:1–16:10. IEEE Press, Piscataway (2013). http://dl.acm.org/citation.cfm? id=2555754.2555770

28. Knuth, D.E.: Structured programming with go to statements. ACM Comput. Surv. **6**(4), 261–301 (1974). http://doi.acm.org/10.1145/356635.356640

29. Lattner, C., Adve, V.: LLVM: a compilation framework for lifelong program analysis & transformation. In: Proceedings of the International Symposium on Code Generation and Optimization: Feedback-Directed and Runtime Optimization, CGO 2004, p. 75. IEEE Computer Society, Washington, D.C. (2004). http:// dl.acm.org/citation.cfm?id=977395.977673

30. Matosevic, I., Abdelrahman, T.S.: Efficient bottom-up heap analysis for symbolic path-based data access summaries. In: Proceedings of the Tenth International Symposium on Code Generation and Optimization, CGO 2012, pp. 252–263. ACM, New York (2012). http://doi.acm.org/10.1145/2259016.2259049

31. Moretti, E., Chanteperdrix, G., Osorio, A.: New algorithms for control-flow graph structuring. In: Fifth Conference on Software Maintenance and Reengineering, CSMR 2001, Lisbon, Portugal, 14–16 March 2001, pp. 184–187 (2001). http:// dx.doi.org/10.1109/.2001.914984

32. Oulsnam, G.: Unravelling unstructured programs. Comput. J. **25**(3), 379–387 (1982). http://dx.doi.org/10.1093/comjnl/25.3.379

33. Oulsnam, G.: The algorithmic transformation of schemas to structured form. Comput. J. **30**(1), 43–51 (1987). http://dx.doi.org/10.1093/comjnl/30.1.43

34. Ramshaw, L.: Eliminating go to's while preserving program structure. J. ACM **35**(4), 893–920 (1988). http://doi.acm.org/10.1145/48014.48021

35. Sabne, A.J., Lin, Y., Grover, V.: Confluence analysis and loop fast-forwarding for improving SIMD execution efficiency, 21 January 2014, uS Patent Ap. 14/160,426

36. Shankar, A., Sastry, S.S., Bodík, R., Smith, J.E.: Runtime specialization with optimistic heap analysis. SIGPLAN Not. **40**(10), 327–343 (2005). http://doi.acm.org/10.1145/1103845.1094837

37. Stanier, J., Watson, D.: A study of irreducibility in C programs. Softw. Pract. Experience **42**(1), 117–130 (2012). http://dx.doi.org/10.1002/spe.1059

38. Unger, S., Mueller, F.: Handling irreducible loops: optimized node splitting versus DJ-graphs. ACM Trans. Program. Lang. Syst. **24**(4), 299–333 (2002). http://doi.acm.org/10.1145/567097.567098
39. Williams, M.H.: Generating structured flow diagrams: the nature of unstructuredness. Comput. J. **20**(1), 45–50 (1977). http://dx.doi.org/10.1093/comjnl/20.1.45
40. Williams, M.H., Ossher, H.L.: Conversion of unstructured flow diagrams to structured form. Comput. J. **21**(2), 161–167 (1978)
41. Wimmer, C., Franz, M.: Linear scan register allocation on SSA form. In: Proceedings of the 8th Annual IEEE/ACM International Symposium on Code Generation and Optimization, CGO 2010, pp. 170–179. ACM, New York (2010). http://doi.acm.org/10.1145/1772954.1772979
42. Woodward, M., Hennell, M., Hedley, D.: A measure of control flow complexity in program text. IEEE Trans. Softw. Eng. **5**(1), 45–50 (1979)
43. Wu, H., Diamos, G., Wang, J., Li, S., Yalamanchili, S.: Characterization and transformation of unstructured control flow in bulk synchronous GPU applications. Int. J. High Perform. Comput. Appl. **26**(2), 170–185 (2012). http://dx.doi.org/10.1177/1094342011434814
44. Xie, Y., Aiken, A.: Saturn: a scalable framework for error detection using Boolean satisfiability. ACM Trans. Program. Lang. Syst. **29**(3), Article No. 16 (2007). http://doi.acm.org/10.1145/1232420.1232423
45. Zhang, F., D'Hollander, E.H.: Using hammock graphs to structure programs. IEEE Trans. Softw. Eng. **30**(4), 231–245 (2004). http://dx.doi.org/10.1109/TSE.2004.1274043

Dynamic Computation and Languages

Automatic Vectorization for MATLAB

Hanfeng Chen$^{(\boxtimes)}$, Alexander Krolik, Erick Lavoie, and Laurie Hendren

School of Computer Science, McGill University, Montréal, Canada
{hanfeng.chen,alexander.krolik,erick.lavoie}@mail.mcgill.ca,
hendren@cs.mcgill.ca

Abstract. Dynamic array-based languages such as MATLAB provide a wide range of built-in operations which can be efficiently applied to all elements of an array. Historically, MATLAB and Octave programmers have been advised to manually transform loops to equivalent "vectorized" computations in order to maximize performance. In this paper we present the techniques and tools to perform automatic vectorization, including handling for loops with calls to user-defined functions. We evaluate the technique on 9 benchmarks using two interpreters and two JIT-based platforms and show that automatic vectorization is extremely effective for the interpreters on most benchmarks, and moderately effective on some benchmarks in the JIT context.

Keywords: Vectorization · Promoted shape analysis · MATLAB · Elementwise functions · Vectorizing user-defined functions

1 Introduction

Vectorization is a mature field which has been studied for decades. However, there are new challenges and opportunities for using vectorization concepts to speed up array-based programming languages such as MATLAB [8]. The key insight is that many operations in MATLAB support both individual element operations, such as $op(a(i))$, as well as elementwise (vectorized) versions that apply op to all elements in an array using just one call, $op(a)$. When a call is made to a built-in operation over an entire array, the underlying implementation can then utilize highly tuned and parallelized libraries. For example, Math-Works began supporting multithreading on elementwise functions in MATLAB 7.4 (R2007a).[1] Thus, it becomes beneficial to replace loops that apply operations on individual elements with one or more vectorized statements, where the operations are now applied to entire vectors or arrays. Indeed, this is standard advice given to MATLAB and Octave [12] programmers as a way of hand optimizing their programs.[2,3]

---

[1] http://www.mathworks.com/matlabcentral/answers/95958-which-matlab-functions-benefit-from-multithreaded-computation.

[2] http://www.mathworks.com/help/matlab/matlab_prog/vectorization.html.

[3] http://wiki.octave.org/FAQ#Porting_programs_from_Matlab_to_Octave.

© Springer International Publishing AG 2017
C. Ding et al. (Eds.): LCPC 2016, LNCS 10136, pp. 171–187, 2017.
DOI: 10.1007/978-3-319-52709-3_14

In this paper we present an approach and tool (Mc2Mc)[4] that automatically detects loops that can be vectorized and automatically produces output MATLAB code with vectorized instructions replacing the loops. In addition to handling loops with built-in MATLAB operations, we also allow loops which call user-defined functions by providing an analysis that determines if user-defined functions have the appropriate elementwise behaviour. Furthermore, we support if-conversion to allow even user-defined functions with conditionals.

We have implemented Mc2Mc based on the McLAB front-end and Tamer infrastructure [4,9], and have used our implementation to study 9 benchmarks on two interpreter-based systems and two JIT-based systems. In the interpreter cases, the automatic vectorizer led to very large speedups on some benchmarks and moderate speedups for others, with geometric mean speedups of 19.1x for Octave 4.0 and 7.65x for MATLAB 2013 (JIT off). However, with systems supporting JITs, such as MATLAB 2013a (1st gen JIT on) and MATLAB 2015b (2nd gen JIT which is always on), the effect of vectorization is mixed with geometric mean speedups of 1.02 and 0.77 respectively. There are still benchmarks which benefit from over 10x speedup, however other benchmarks have loops which are handled very effectively by the JIT, and vectorization can drastically hurt performance. Thus, it no longer makes sense for a MATLAB programmer to hand vectorize all of his/her code. However, our automatic vectorization system would allow a programmer or execution engine to try various strategies and identify those which benefit from vectorization.

The main contributions of this work are:

- We present a tool (Mc2Mc) that automatically transforms scalar MATLAB programs to equivalent vector form;
- We propose an interprocedural promoted shape analysis to determine if scalar code can be modified to vector form in loops and user-defined functions;
- We evaluate the performance of automatic vectorization on 9 benchmarks over 4 different execution engines.

In the rest of the paper we first provide more background about key features of MATLAB in Sect. 2. We then provide a description of our techniques with an overview of our approach in Sect. 3; a more detailed look at two key components, promoted shape propogation in Sect. 4 and our handling of user-defined functions in Sect. 5; and an outline the two final phases, data dependence analysis in Sect. 6 and the actual vectorization in Sect. 7. Finally we provide our experimental evaluation in Sect. 8, related work in Sect. 9 and conclude in Sect. 10.

2   Motivation and Background

MATLAB provides many features which enable vectorization. In this section, we provide an introduction to those features, and a motivating example for our vectorization transformation.

---

[4] https://github.com/sable/mc2mc

Matrix Indexing: Matrix indexing provides a way to retrieve a collection of array elements with one operation. Figure 1(a) shows a **for** loop which accesses items of array m one at a time, and Fig. 1(b) shows the equivalent matrix indexing version, which accesses all the items at indices stored in v. Also note that in Fig. 1(b), the pre-allocation of array r is not needed.

```
m = rand(1,n);
r = zeros(1,4);
v = [3,7,6,4];                    m = rand(1,n);
for i=1:4                         v = [3,7,6,4];
    r(i) = m(v(i));               r = m(v);
end
```
(a) One element at a time   (b) All elements using matrix indexing

Fig. 1. A **for** loop and equivalent using matrix indexing

Colon Operator: The colon operator is mainly used to create vectors, subscript arrays and specify for iterations.[5]

Creating Vectors: The expression j:k generates a vector from j to k if j is less than k. With an additional parameter i, the expression j:i:k produces a vector from j to k with the stride i.

Subscripting Arrays: Matrix indexing can be introduced with the colon operator, such as m(1:n) where $n \leq length(m)$. Moreover, m(:) denotes all elements of m.

Iterating a for-loop: A simple for-loop header is for i=1:n, which indicates that the for body should be executed once for every value of i in [1,n].

For Loop Vectorization: The main topic of this paper is automatic for loop vectorization. To motivate this, we provide a small example in Fig. 2. Function *foovec* is a vectorized version of *foo*. Both the original and vectorized versions call the same user-defined function *bar*. This may seem strange, since *foovec* is passing *bar* a vector, whereas the original *foo* was passing *bar* a scalar. However,

```
function foo(n)
    A=rand(1,n);
    B=zeros(1,n);          function foovec(n)
    C=zeros(1,n);              A=rand(1,n);      function [z] = bar(x)
    for i=1:n                  B=bar(A);             t=x+1;
        B(i)=bar(A(i));        C=sqrt(1:n);          z=sin(x);
        C(i)=sqrt(i);      end                   end
    end
end
```

Fig. 2. Example vectorization

---
[5] http://www.mathworks.com/help/matlab/ref/colon.html?searchHighlight=colon.

because all of the statements in *bar* work on both scalars and vectors in the right way, *bar* can be called from the vector code, and *bar* will return a vector of values. One important part of our work is automaticially identifying such vectorizable user-defined functions.

To automatically vectorize the loop there are several things to check. Firstly, we must apply some standard dependence tests. Secondly, for each built-in function called from the loop body, such as *sqrt*, we must ensure that it has appropriate elementwise behaviour. Finally, for each user-defined function called from the body of the loop, such as *bar*, we must ensure that the body of the called function contains only vectorizable statements. Finally, the resulting vectorized program can be cleaned up, in this case the unneeded initialization of B is removed.

3   Overall Structure of the Vectorizer

We have implemented our approach in a tool, Mc2Mc, which given a MATLAB program, automatically identifies vectorizable sections and transforms scalar code to the equivalent vector form. An overview of the workflow of Mc2Mc can be found in Fig. 3.

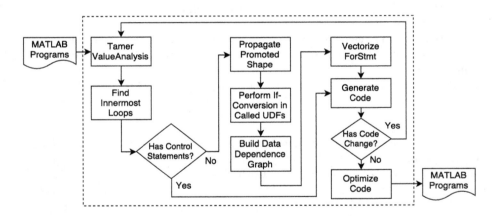

Fig. 3. The workflow of Mc2Mc.

The workflow begins by parsing input MATLAB programs into TameIR, a low-level representation used for analysis of MATLAB programs. The Tamer framework provides a set of interprocedural value analyses for shape information [6], as well as use-define and define-use chains that are used in later sections of the vectorizer. Once the initial analyses have been completed, the inner loops of the input program are collected for input to the vectorization algorithm. The vectorization algorithm thus uses an inside-out approach for handling loop nests [11]. Since the control flow of loops with nested if statements is not well suited for vectorization, only loops without such control statements are considered further.

Next, our new interprocedural promoted shape analysis is performed, determining whether scalar code can be correctly modified to an equivalent vector form. By propagating shapes through user-defined functions we expose additional areas for vectorization beyond built-in functions. While a user-defined function may not contain loops, nested if statements are permitted. A function is only considered vectorizable if all conditions and branches can be expressed in equivalent vector form. Promoted shape propagation is discussed in greater detail in Sect. 4 while user-defined functions and if-conversion are covered in Sect. 5.

Candidate statements for vectorization are then checked for dependencies that prevent vectorization. If no dependencies are found for a particular statement, the vectorized code can then be generated. Since the vectorization algorithm uses an inside-out approach, the pipeline may need to be rerun to handle nested loops and if statements in user-defined functions. Once a fixed point is reached, the newly vectorized code is statically optimized to remove unnecessary colon operators. In addition, dynamic checks are inserted to further reduce the performance impact of using the colon operators.

4   Promoted Shape Analysis

The promoted shape analysis is an interprocedural analysis that identifies the expressions in the body of a for loop that (1) have a scalar value that is derived directly or transitively from the loop index and that (2) can safely be promoted from a *scalar* form to a *vector* form, derived directly or transitively from the entire range of the loop index.

An expression (in a statement) can be promoted safely to a vector form if it performs the same operations on the values represented by variables that compose the expression over the entire range of the loop index.

In order to determine which expressions can be promoted safely, we perform a fixpoint analysis on the shape of variables. Initially, the loop index is first promoted from a scalar shape to a *promoted* shape, of the same shape as the entire loop index range. The promoted shape therefore represents a tentative replacement of the loop index variable scalar value with a vector that contains its entire range. All other variables shapes are initialized to *scalar*, *non-scalar*, or *unknown* ($\perp$) with the precise shape coming from the Tamer ValueAnalysis. The shape information is then propagated through every statement of the loop body and modified according to the effect of a statement's operation. The previous scalar shape of the output variables of a statement might be replaced with a promoted shape if the operation of a statement is compatible with the promoted shape of its input variable(s). If the operation is incompatible, the shape of the output variable will become $\top$.

Once the fixpoint is reached, all the statements that use a variable with a shape of $\top$ cannot be safely converted to vector form and therefore need to stay in the body of the for loop. All the others can potentially be moved outside of the loop body and the expressions that use variables with a promoted shape can be promoted to their vector form, as long as no dependency exist between the different statements (see Sect. 6).

In the remainder of this section, we first provide an explanation of the shape abstraction we use. We then explain which operations are compatible with a shape promotion. We finally provide the key parts of our promoted shape analysis in pseudocode.

4.1 Shape Abstractions

There are five abstractions summarized in Table 1. The initial variable with an unknown shape is denoted by $\bot$. The scalar shape S is considered because it can be extended in the context of elementwise operations. For the non-scalar N, it means the shape is neither a promoted shape nor a scalar. It is fine to have N in array indexing when the index is a scalar since the output of the array indexing is a scalar. For a promoted shape P, it is initialized by loop iterators and then propagated to variables. The $\top$ means there is no safe promoted shape for vectorization.

Table 1. Definitions of abstractions

Type	Description
$\bot$	An unknown shape
S	A scalar which is not promoted
N	A non-scalar which is not promoted
P	A promoted shape
$\top$	A shape cannot be vectorized

Note that a *promoted* shape represents a promotion from a scalar to a one-dimensional array. However some operations such as multidimensional array indexing (e.g. $A(i,i)$) may return a two-dimensional array when the i index variable is promoted (e.g. $A(1{:}n,1{:}n)$) rather than the diagonal of the matrix in the original loop. The expression is therefore not compatible with a promoted shape because it returns different values after the promotion. However, promotion along a single dimension (e.g. $A(i,j)$ to $A(1{:}n,j)$) is possible if the shape of the array is compatible.

4.2 Compatible Operations

A unary function F satisfies the property of elementwise operations when it holds $\hat{R} = \overrightarrow{F}(\hat{A})$, where the $\overrightarrow{F}$ is a vectorizable function, the $\hat{A}$ denotes the promoted input parameter and the $\hat{R}$ denotes the promoted return value. A *promoted operation* is introduced in $A \rightarrow \hat{A}$ when a dimension in A is expanded to k_0, where $k_0 > 1$. That means $\hat{A}$ and A have the same number of dimensions, but $|\hat{A}| = k_0 \times |A|$, where the $|A|$ is its cardinality. Let $\rho(\hat{A})$ denote the new dimension (i.e. k_0). Let $\hat{A} = \{A_1, A_2, \ldots, A_n\}$ and $\hat{R} = \{R_1, R_2, \ldots, R_n\}$, where $\rho(\hat{A}) = \rho(\hat{R}) = n$, so that $\hat{R} = \overrightarrow{F}(\hat{A}) \Leftrightarrow [\{R_1, R_2, \ldots, R_n\}] = F(\{A_1, A_2, \ldots, A_n\})$.

A built-in function (BIF), which satisfies the property of elementwise operation, is vectorizable. For a unary built-in function F_u, it can be described as $\hat{R} = \overrightarrow{F_u}(\hat{A})$. However, a binary function F_b has three possible cases in vectorization. They are 1) $\hat{R} = \overrightarrow{F_b}(\hat{A}, B)$; 2) $\hat{R} = \overrightarrow{F_b}(A, \hat{B})$; and 3) $\hat{R} = \overrightarrow{F_b}(\hat{A}, \hat{B})$, where the A and B denote input arguments. It should be noted that the lengths of the argument A and B must agree in the third case.

User-defined functions are also compatible with input arguments in vector form under some conditions. An interprocedural sub-analysis, described in Sect. 5, is performed when a user-defined function is called from the body of a for loop to determine if the input arguments can indeed be promoted.

4.3 Key Parts of the Analysis

Initialization. The analysis starts from the innermost for loops. The variables in the body of the innermost for loops are initialized with one of the abstractions in Table 1. The loop index variables of all statements in the body of for loops are initialized to the promoted shape. All other variables are initialized to the scalar or non-scalar shape obtained from the Tamer ValueAnalysis. The pseudocode is provided in Algorithm 1.

Algorithm 1. Initialization

Data: a statement
Result: each variable with a promoted shape
1 **foreach** *variable var in the statement* **do**
2   **if** *var.promotedShape has not been initialized* **then**
3   **if** *the statement is from a for-loop* **then**
4   **if** *var is the loop iterator* **then**
5   *var.promotedShape* ←from a scalar to a vector (i.e. loop's range);
6   **else**
7   **if** *the shape of var is a scalar* **then**
8   *var.promotedShape* ←*Scalar*;
9   **else**
10   var.promotedShape ←*Non-scalar*;

Promoted Shape Propagation in Statements. There are three important major cases for the propagation of the flow information, with the first case further sub-divided in three cases, as listed in Algorithm 2.

The first major case is a call to a function. A function call may target a built-in function or a user-defined function. For the BIFs, we separate them into two groups: elementwise built-in functions (eBIFs) and non-elementwise built-in functions (nBIFs). The eBIFs are compatible with a vector form under some conditions while most nBIFs are not. We therefore do not consider nBIFS and their return value is always $\top$. The rules for unary and binary eBIFs are defined in Tables 2 and 3 separately. In the Table 3, the N_d returns N if both have the same non-scalar promoted shape otherwise $\top$ and the P_d returns P if both have the same promoted shape otherwise $\top$. User-defined functions are covered in Sect. 5.

Table 2. The propagation rule for unary eBIFs

eBIF	$\bot$	S	N	P	$\top$
Output	$\bot$	S	N	P	$\top$

Table 3. The propagation rule for binary eBIFs

eBIF	$\bot$	S	N	P	$\top$
$\bot$	$\bot$	$\bot$	$\top$	$\top$	$\top$
S	$\bot$	S	N	P	$\top$
N	$\bot$	N	N_d	$\top$	$\top$
P	$\top$	P	$\top$	P_d	$\top$
$\top$	$\top$	$\top$	$\top$	$\top$	$\top$

The second major case concerns array indexing statements. For both *ArrayGetStmt* and *ArraySetStmt*, the promoted shape of the index variable needs to be the same as the shape of the array. Or the *ArraySetStmt* accepts a promoted shape P on the left-hand side and a promoted shape S on the right-hand side. In the *ArrayGetStmt* case, if so, the returned value's shape is set to *promoted*, otherwise it is set to $\top$.

The last major case, with the CopyStmt, trivially copies the shape of the left-hand side variable to the right-hand side variable.

4.4　An Example of Promoted Shape Analysis

To illustrate the promoted shape analysis, consider the loop from the function *needle* in the NW benchmark, as given in Fig. 4(a). In this example, *input_itemsets* is a matrix and *penalty* is a scalar. We would like to use our promoted shape analysis determine if the loop can be converted to vector form.

Our Mc2Mc tool first converts the code to a lower-level three-address style TameIR, as shown in Fig. 4(b). This means that each statement will now have at most one operation, which simplfies the subsequent analysis.

Figure 4(c) shows the result of the promoted shape analysis after each statement in the loop body. The loop iterator is used to get initial promoted shape. At program point 2, the `minus` is an eBIF which takes a promoted shape P (i.e. i) and a promoted shape S (i.e. 1). The output of the eBIF returns a promoted shape P for the variable `mc_t1`. Variable `mc_t1` and its promoted shape are then included in the flow set. The next statement has a unary BIF, `uminus`, which returns the same promoted shape as `mc_t1`. At program point 4, the variable *penalty* has a promoted shape S so that the eBIF `times` returns a promoted shape P. At program point 5, the array indexing on the left-hand side

Algorithm 2. Promoted shape propagation

```
1  PropagateStmt(assignStmt, inSet)
2  |   (lhs, rhs) ←assignStmt;
3  |   ps ←⊤ ;
4  |   if the assignStmt is a CallStmt then
5  |   |     op ←rhs.getFunctionName();
6  |   |     args ←rhs.getArguments();
7  |   |     if op is a unary eBIF then
8  |   |     |    ps ←UnaryFunctionTable(op, args[1].ps);
9  |   |     else if op is a binary eBIF then
10 |   |     |    ps ←BInaryFunctionTable(op, args[1].ps, args[2].ps);
11 |   |     else if op is a UDF then
12 |   |     |_   ps ←PropagateUDF(op, args, inSet);
13 |   else if the assignStmt is an ArrayGetStmt then
14 |   |     ps ←GetArrayIndexShape(rhs, lhs);
15 |   else if the assignStmt is an ArraySetStmt then
16 |   |     ps ←GetArrayIndexShape(lhs, rhs) ;
17 |   else if the assignStmt is a CopyStmt then
18 |   |_    ps ←CopyPromotedShape(rhs.ps) ;
19 |   genSet(assignStmt) = {(lhs,ps)} ;
20 |   killSet(assignStmt) = {any tuple contains lhs};
21 |   outSet(assignStmt) = (inSet(assignStmt) - killSet(assignStmt)) ∪
   |   genSet(assignStmt);
22 |   return outSet
```

```
% penalty is a scalar
% input_itemsets is a matrix
for i = 2:max_rows
  input_itemsets(i,1)=-(i-1)*penalty;
end
```

(a) Original loop

```
[1] for i = (2 : max_rows);
[2] [mc_t1] = minus(i, 1);
[3] [mc_t2] = uminus(mc_t1);
[4] [mc_t3] = times(mc_t2, penalty);
[5] input_itemsets(i, 1) = mc_t3;
[6] end
```

(b) TameIR

```
[1] {(i,P)}
[2] {(i,P),(mc_t1,P)}
[3] {(i,P),(mc_t1,P),(mc_t2,P)}
[4] {(i,P),(mc_t1,P),(mc_t2,P),
    (mc_t3,P)}
[5] {(i,P),(mc_t1,P),(mc_t2,P),
    (mc_t3,P),(input_itemsets,N)}
```

(c) Flow sets

```
i=2:max_rows;
input_itemsets(i,1)=-(i-1).*penalty;
```

(d) Final vectorized code

Fig. 4. An example of promoted shape analysis

is a one-dimension promotion and the variable mc_t3 has the same promoted
shape. Therefore, the assignment is safe and the promoted shape of the variable
input_itemsets is set to N. Finally, the analysis returns the set of promoted
shape information. If a set of statements has no promoted shape ⊤ and there are

no cyclic dependences, the statements can be vectorized safely. We then perform a final aggegration step on the TameIR, to produce back a MATLAB vectorized statement, as shown in Fig. 4(d).

5   Handling User Defined Functions

One of the key contributions of our approach is that we can vectorize loops which contain calls to user-defined functions (UDFs). The key insight is that if the body of the UDF contains only vectorizable statements, then the calling code can use the UDF as a vectorized operation. Since some UDFs contain conditional if statements, we have also developed a MATLAB-specific if-conversion to convert control dependence expressed as if statements into equivalent vectorized statements without control dependences.

5.1   Promoted Shape Analysis for UDFs

When the promoted shape analysis encounters a call to a UDF, the initial promoted shapes are propogated from the arguments of the call to the parameters of the called UDF. The promoted shape analysis is then used to propogate promoted shapes to all statements in the body of the UDF. At the end of the dataflow analysis, the return values are checked before they are copied back to the caller site. If any return value is neither a scalar nor a promoted shape, then the UDF is not vectorizable and all return values are set to $\top$ and then returned.

Since UDFs may include conditionals, we must extend the promoted shape analysis to handle conditional control flow. The key addition is that we apply the promoted shape analysis to each branch of the conditional, and then merge the results. More precisely, let $op2$ be the function for binary eBIFs defined in Table 3, ps_1 and ps_2 are promoted shape from two different branches, and ps_{cond} is the promoted shapes of the condition of the if. The $merge$ operator gets a new promoted shape with the following equation.

$$merge(ps_1, ps_2, ps_{cond}) = op2(op2(ps_{cond}, ps_1), op2(ps_{cond}, ps_2));$$

If a UDF is called multiple times from different caller sites, we follow a simple rule to solve the possible conflicting results from the analysis. The rule is that a UDF is kept the same no matter the changes in input arguments if the UDF is still vectorizable with the new arguments. Otherwise, the UDF is not vectorizable despite its prior result.

5.2   If-Conversion for UDFs

Some UDFs contain if statements, which would normally interfere with vectorization. However, there are some if statements which can be transformed into vectorized statements, using primitive vector operations available in MATLAB to combine results from the then and else branches.

Consider the example from the *CNDF* function of the *Blackscholes* (BS) benchmark, given in Fig. 5(a). The original code, with explicit control flow cannot be vectorized, because when *InputX* is promoted from a scalar to a vector, the if condition will execute only once instead of once per item in the vector. However, the computation can be converted to vector form as shown in Fig. 5(b). The trick is to create a boolean vector of 0's and 1's containing the results of the condition, and then to use this to select the appropriate values by multiplying by 1 for all values that should come from the then branch (and 0 otherwise). The same trick, with the negative conditions are used for the else branch. Then the two vectors are combined, giving all the results for both branches.

```
if InputX < 0
    InputX = - InputX;          thenCond = InputX < 0;
    sign = 1;                   elseCond = not(thenCond);
else                            InputX = thenCond.*(-InputX) + elseCond.*InputX;
    sign = 0;                   sign = thenCond.*1 + elseCond.*0;
end
    (a) Original if-structure              (b) After if-conversion
```

Fig. 5. If-conversion from the CNDF function of the BlackScholes (BS) benchmark

In general, if-conversion takes place when promoted shape can be safely propagated through the if-structure. Equivalently, the promoted shape must successfully propagate the new code after if-conversion. TameIR provides a simple if-structure with only then- and else-block. We first identify the variables which will be used in both the then- and else-block. We then analyze both branches using input flow. For variables which are used only in one block, there are two cases: (1) only used within block; or (2) remain after the if-block. The variables in (1) can be kept the same while the variables in (2) must multiply with its corresponding mask (i.e. *cond* or ∼*cond*).

6 Data Dependence Analysis

Besides promoted shape information, we consider the possible dependence between statements. It is the key problem for program vectorization. We investigate the exact test, the GCD test [1], to tell whether data dependence exists. If two statements cannot be decided by this test, we conservatively assume they have data dependence. Furthermore, a dependence graph is built on the result of the test. We split the graph into subgraphs in which each node connects but there is no connection between subgraphs. A subgraph is a directed graph. The Tarjan's algorithm [13] for finding strong connected components is adopted to identify possible acyclic subgraphs. Given an acyclic subgraph with no variable having promoted shape ⊤, we are able to get the topological order of each node in the subgraph with a topological sort. When vectorizing, the topological ordering is used to order the equivalent vector statements.

7   Vectorization and Optimization

The statements in a loop are separated into two groups: (1) vectorizable statements in a topological order and (2) non-vectorizable statements in a sequential order. For the first group, the loop range is extracted and each statement is vectorized and inserted above the loop. For the second group, the statements are not vectorizable and thus remain as is. If all statements are vectorizable, the resulting loop is empty and can be removed.

7.1   Special Cases

Function Replacement. MATLAB programs may contain many arithmetic operators, some of which can have different meanings depending on the operand types. Multiplication (∗) for instance can either be an arithmetic or matrix multiplication. In MATLAB, a built-in function *mtimes* provides matrix multiplication while *times* performs an elementwise operation. With the Tamer Value-Analysis, we can generate improved code by using the faster elementwise function where possible. This replacement also applies to division (*mrdivide* vs. *rdivide*) and power (*mpower* vs. *power*).

Idioms for Reductions. MATLAB programs also commonly use patterns within loops, especially accumulation [2]. Using cycles from the dependence graph, common patterns can be replaced using the equivalent reduction operation. MATLAB provides a built-in reduction function *sum* for accumulation. The Mc2Mc tool is able to detect this idiom and generate vectorized code with the *sum* function.

Special Built-in Functions. Some built-in functions are excluded from the promoted shape analysis since they are not elementwise functions. However, they can be analyzed to expose further vectorization opportunities. We identify two such functions below.

Colon: Since we adopt an iterative method to vectorize loops from innermost to outermost, the generated code from a previous iteration may contain multiple calls to the colon operator. Since the colon operator is not elementwise, it is not included in the initial promoted shape analysis. To expose further vectorization, we give the return variable of a colon operator promoted shape N. This allows vectorization of outer loops which require full promoted shape information.

Transpose: Since the promoted shape of the function argument may be either a row or column vector and the vectorized function may require a particular shape to be semantically equivalent, we use the *transpose* built-in function to transform the inputs as needed.

7.2   Code Optimization with Dynamic Checks

Since indexing using a colon operator has an impact on the performance of vectorization, we explore dynamic checks to reduce the overhead caused by the redundant array indexing. If a colon indexing covers all elements in an array, the colon indexing can be replaced with an array name to improve performance. Only the left-hand side of an assignment statement is considered for the dynamic checks.

8   Evaluation

To study the performance of our automatic vectorization we have performed experiments on a diverse set of benchmarks on four different execution engines.

8.1   Experimental Setup

The experiments were done on a desktop with an i7-3820 3.60 GHz (eight cores) CPU and 8 GB RAM running Ubuntu 14.04 TLS. We selected four execution engines. We used two interpreters: Octave 4.0, which is an open-source interpreter and MATLAB 8.1 (R2013a) with the JIT turned off. We used two JIT-based systems: MATLAB 8.1 (R2013a) which has a 1st-generation JIT, and MATLAB 8.6 (R2015b) which has a newer 2nd-generation JIT. Each benchmark was executed 5 times and the mean execution time is reported. We used the Wu-Wei Benchmarking Toolkit to perform the experiments.[6] The source code of these experiemnts is available on GitHub.[7]

There are total nine benchmarks chosen for the experiments, taken from the Ostrich benchmark set which provides multi-language versions of benchmarks covering a wide range of numerical categories (Dwarfs).[8]

Back-Propagation (BP): a method of training artificial neural networks. It provides an interactive algorithm to update the weights in the given network.
Black-Scholes (BS): a computationally intensive algorithm which is used to calculate the price for a portfolio of European options analytically with the Black-Scholes partial equation (PDE).
Capacitance (CAPR): computes the capacitance of a transmission line using finite difference and Gauss-Seidel iteration.
Crank-Nicholson (CRNI): computes the Crank-Nicholson solution to the one-dimensional heat equation.
Fast Fourier Transform (FFT): computes FFT on a random data set as input.
Monte-Carlo simulation (MC): approximates the value of π.
Needleman-Wunsch (NW): calculates optimal global alignment of two DNA sequences.
Page-Rank (PR): link analysis algorithm.
Sparse Matrix-Vector Multiplication (SPMV): compressed sparse row (CSR) format multiplication between a sparse matrix and a vector.

---

[6] https://github.com/Sable/wu-wei-benchmarking-toolkit/.
[7] https://github.com/Sable/lcpc16-analysis.
[8] https://github.com/Sable/Ostrich.

8.2   Experimental Results

To study the performance influence caused by the code vectorization, we compared the original MATLAB code with the automatically vectorized code. To produce the vectorized code we used our tool to identify and transform loops which could be vectorized, and we replaced the original loops with the automatically generated vector code.

Overall Performance. The results of our experiments are given in Table 4. There are four multicolumns, one for each execution engine. For each of these there are three columns: time for the original code, time for the automatically vectorized code, and speedup which is the ratio of *orig_time/vect_time*. We also provide the geometric mean speedup for each execution engine. A speedup of k means that the vectorized version was k times faster than the original loop version. In Table 4 we have shown all speedups ≥ 1 as bold blue numbers. For each benchmark (i.e. each row in the table) we show the time of fastest version over all the execution engines as bold italic red numbers.

Table 4. Times (in seconds) and Speedups (SU) (orig. time/vect. time)

Benchmark	Octave 4.0 (interpreter)			MATLAB 2013a (interpreter)			MATLAB 2013a (1st gen JIT)			MATLAB 2015b (2nd gen JIT)		
	orig. time	vect. time	vect. SU	orig. time	vect. time	vect. SU	orig. time	vect. time	vect. SU	orig. time	vect. time	vect. SU
BP	1855	*0.83*	**2235**	138.4	2.76	**50.1**	6.18	3.00	**2.06**	2.18	3.09	0.71
BS	97.1	0.20	**485.5**	28.84	0.14	**206**	4.84	0.13	**37.2**	1.35	*0.09*	**15.0**
CAPR	207.6	203.7	**1.02**	14.63	14.4	**1.02**	0.43	0.51	0.84	*0.23*	0.29	0.79
CRNI	2452	1075	**2.28**	248.7	119.7	**2.08**	7.67	40.9	0.19	*3.05*	3.66	0.83
FFT	80.88	76.2	**1.06**	12.95	13.0	**1.00**	3.83	7.05	0.54	*1.25*	2.13	0.59
NW	981.3	733	**1.34**	57.09	40.3	**1.42**	2.43	1.97	**1.23**	*1.12*	1.17	0.96
PR	511.3	5.00	**102.3**	49.75	1.95	**25.5**	1.28	1.16	**1.10**	*1.08*	1.15	0.94
MC	535.3	*0.35*	**1529**	128.3	0.59	**217.5**	3.75	0.55	**6.82**	0.93	0.46	**2.02**
SPMV	117.6	197.3	0.60	17.73	33.8	0.52	0.26	12.8	0.02	*0.20*	14.5	0.013
Geo Mean			**19.1**			**7.65**			**1.02**			0.77

The results are very interesting and show the relative importance of vectorization for different types of execution engines and show that although vectorization can lead to huge speedups, it is not always beneficial.

For the two interpreters we see excellent speedups due to vectorization. In the case of Octave we see speedups of 2235x for BP and 1529x for MC. In fact, these vectorized versions are the fastest overall, beating even the 2nd-generation JIT in MATLAB 2015b. The speedups for MATLAB 2013a (interpreter) are also quite impressive. However, the results also show that even with interpreters it is not always worth vectorizing, as illustrated by the slowdowns for SPMV. In this case the vectorized loop is the inner loop of the main computation, and the main compuation outer loop is not vectorizable. The inner loop executes on a vector of size 2, and thus is not a good candidate for vectorization.

In the case of the JIT execution engines, the results are more nuanced. Some benchmarks show only a small performance improvement, and others have small performance degradations. However, there still exist benchmarks where vectorization can give good speedups, namely BS and MC. Vectorization of BS gives 37.2x speedup for MATLAB 2013a (1st gen JIT) and 15x for MATLAB 2015b (2nd gen JIT). The reason is that the two benchmarks successfully achieve loop vectorization and UDF vectorization. The called UDFs are fully vectorized. The function invocations in BS are more complex than MC. Therefore, it is more difficult for the JIT to exploit possible parallelsim while our vectorizer achieves this. However, with the JITs there can be even more drastic performance degradations due to vectorization, as can be seen by the slowdown of SPMV. It would seem that vectorizing an inner loop that has very few iterations not only introduces overheads to that inner loop, but also likely interferes with the JIT's ability to generate efficient code for the entire loop nest.

9   Related Work

While vectorization is a mature field, there is no universal method for transforming scalar programs into vector form. Existing approaches either use user input, automated analyses or a combination of the two.

User-Guided Vectorization. Tian et al. implemented vector extensions to C and C++, allowing the Intel C++ compiler to produce efficient SIMD instructions without requiring low-level programming [14]. Using in-code directives, entire user-defined functions can be vectorized in addition to for loops yielding significant performance improvements. In constrast, our implementation allows vectorization of user-defined functions without code annotations. Klemm et al. also explored directive based vectorization by introducing non-vendor specific SIMD constructs to OpenMP [5]. Since not all loops can be automatically vectorized, experimental results show that using annotations improves performance over an existing production auto-vectorizing compiler. While evaluating the effectiveness of auto-vectorizing compilers, Maleki et al. also confirmed that production compilers can handle many synthetic benchmarks but have difficulty automatically vectorizing real world applications [7]. In our work, results show that auto-vectorization can still provide significant performance increases to substantial benchmarks, but that performance degredation is also possible, especially with modern MATLAB JITs.

A mixed user-automatic approach to vectorization has been implemented for MATLAB. Since vectorization of MATLAB code requires matrix sizes and shapes, Birkbeck et al. allow user shape annotations to guide the auto-vectorization techniques [2]. Additionally, a pattern based approach transforms common code patterns to the equivalent MATLAB built-in. Our implementation uses the same principles for vectorization, but can automatically infer the necessary shapes instead of using annotations.

Array Programming Languages. Array programming languages such as R and MATLAB are also important candidates for vectorization. Menon and Pingali showed that source-to-source transformations of MATLAB, including vectorization, can significantly improve program performance [10]. Vectorization allows better exploitation of the underlying hardware and reduces the interpreter overhead of repeatedly iterating the loop body. However, their exploration used hand-optimized programs and did not consider function vectorization as in our implementation. Chauhan and Kennedy introduced two optimizations: *procedure vectorization* and *procedure strength reduction*, which improved the performance of real digital signal processing applications [3]. The idea of *procedure vectorization* is similar to our approach to UDFs, replacing a function call inside a loop by a single function call with vectorized arguments. However, their transformation is achieved by hand while we present an automatic method for handling UDFs.

The R programming language provides a popular built-in function *lapply* which runs a given function on a list of input. By replacing the looping execution of *lapply* with a vectorized version of the supplied function, Wang et al. achieved meaningful speedups [15]. However, their implementation is both limited to *lapply* and can also generate inequivalent vector code from if statements due to the semantics of the R *ifelse* built-in function. Our work accepts more general input, and generates equivalent vector code when vectorizing if statements.

10   Conclusions and Future Work

We have presented an automated technique to detect and transform loops to vectorized code in MATLAB. Our approach introduces a new promoted shape propogation analysis which is used to identify vectorizable statements and user-defined functions.

We have implemented our approach as the Mc2Mc tool and used it to experiment with 9 diverse benchmarks over 4 different execution engines. From our experimental results we conclude that our automatic vectorizer can find and transform loops in a wide range of benchmarks. The vectorized code is usually faster, and sometimes three orders of magnitude faster, on interpreted engines. There is less benefit for vectorizing on JIT systems, but there still exist benchmarks where excellent speedups can be achieved by vectorizing. Our results also show that the general advice of "vectorize to improve performance" is not always true, especially in the JIT settings where vectorizing can interfere with the JIT.

In our future work we would like to integrate our automatic vectorizer into a MATLAB or Octave IDE, so programmers could selectively vectorize loops. We would also like investigate automatic and profile-driven techniques for deciding when vectorization is beneficial, and perhaps also develop some "unvectorizing" techniques for converting vectorized code to loops when vector code is deemed to be less efficient.

Acknowledgments. We would like to thank the McLAB group for providing the analysis framework, Tamer. This work was supported, in part, by NSERC.

References

1. Allen, R., Kennedy, K.: Automatic translation of Fortran programs to vector form. ACM Trans. Program. Lang. Syst. **9**(4), 491–542 (1987)
2. Birkbeck, N., Levesque, J., Amaral, J.N.: A dimension abstraction approach to vectorization in Matlab. In: CGO, pp. 115–130 (2007)
3. Chauhan, A., Kennedy, K.: Reducing and vectorizing procedures for telescoping languages. Int. J. Parallel Prog. **30**(4), 291–315 (2002)
4. Dubrau, A.W., Hendren, L.J.: Taming MATLAB. In: OOPSLA, pp. 503–522 (2012)
5. Klemm, M., Duran, A., Tian, X., Saito, H., Caballero, D., Martorell, X.: Extending OpenMP* with vector constructs for modern multicore SIMD architectures. In: Chapman, B.M., Massaioli, F., Müller, M.S., Rorro, M. (eds.) IWOMP 2012. LNCS, vol. 7312, pp. 59–72. Springer, Heidelberg (2012). doi:10.1007/978-3-642-30961-8_5
6. Li, X., Hendren, L.J.: Mc2FOR: A tool for automatically translating MATLAB to FORTRAN 95. In: CSMR-WCRE, pp. 234–243 (2014)
7. Maleki, S., Gao, Y., Garzarán, M.J., Wong, T., Padua, D.A.: An evaluation of vectorizing compilers. In: PACT, pp. 372–382 (2011)
8. MathWorks: MATLAB. http://www.mathworks.com/
9. McLAB: The McLAB tools for compiling MATLAB (2016). http://www.sable.mcgill.ca/mclab/
10. Menon, V., Pingali, K.: A case for source-level transformations in MATLAB. In: DSL, pp. 53–65 (1999)
11. Muraoka, Y.: Parallelism exposure and exploitation in programs. Ph.D. thesis, Univ. of Ill. at Urbana-Champaign, Dept. of Comp. Sci. UMI(71–21189), February 1971
12. Octave: GNU Octave. https://www.gnu.org/software/octave/
13. Tarjan, R.E.: Depth-first search and linear graph algorithms. SIAM J. Comput. **1**(2), 146–160 (1972)
14. Tian, X., Saito, H., Girkar, M., Preis, S., Kozhukhov, S., Cherkasov, A.G., Nelson, C., Panchenko, N., Geva, R.: Compiling C/C++ SIMD extensions for function and loop vectorizaion on multicore-simd processors. In: IPDPS, pp. 2349–2358 (2012)
15. Wang, H., Padua, D.A., Wu, P.: Vectorization of apply to reduce interpretation overhead of R. In: OOPSLA, pp. 400–415 (2015)

Analyzing Parallel Programming Models for Magnetic Resonance Imaging

Forest Danford[1]([✉]), Eric Welch[1], Julio Cárdenas-Ródriguez[2],
and Michelle Mills Strout[1]

[1] Department of Computer Science, University of Arizona, Tucson, USA
{fdanford,welche,mstrout}@email.arizona.edu
[2] Department of Medical Imaging, University of Arizona, Tucson, USA
cardenaj@email.arizona.edu

Abstract. The last several decades have been marked by dramatic increases in the use of diagnostic medical imaging and improvements in the modalities themselves. As such, more data is being generated at an ever increasing rate. However, in the case of Magnetic Resonance Imaging (MRI) analysis and reports remain semi-quantitative, despite reported advantages of quantitative analysis (QA), due to prohibitive execution times. We present a collaborator's QA algorithm for Dynamic Contrast-Enhanced (DCE) MRI data written in MATLAB as a case study for exploring parallel programming in MATLAB and Julia. Parallelization resulted in a 7.66x speedup in MATLAB and a 72x speedup in Julia. To the best of our knowledge, this comparison of Julia's performance in a parallel, application-level program is novel. On the basis of these results and our experiences while programming in each language, our collaborator now prototypes in MATLAB and then ports to Julia when performance is critical.

Keywords: MATLAB · Julia · Parallel programming languages · Parallel applications · Medical imaging · Dynamic Contrast-Enhanced MRI

1 Introduction

Over the last 30 years there has been a dramatic increase in the usage of Magnetic Resonance Imaging (MRI) and other imaging modalities in the research and medical communities [26,27]. Simultaneously, there have been substantial improvements to the underlying technologies themselves that allow for images to be captured at significantly higher spatial and temporal resolutions. One of the consequences of these improvements has been a massive increase in the amount of data being generated [17]. For scientists and clinicians, this has often translated to making the difficult decision to forgo a truly quantitative analysis (QA) and instead sub-sample the available data to perform analyses and generate reports within an acceptable time frame. One application that currently suffers this

---

F. Danford and E. Welch—Authors contributed equally

© Springer International Publishing AG 2017
C. Ding et al. (Eds.): LCPC 2016, LNCS 10136, pp. 188–202, 2017.
DOI: 10.1007/978-3-319-52709-3_15

plight is Quantitative Analysis (QA) model-based Dynamic Contrast-Enhanced MRI (DCE MRI) [21]. DCE MRI is used to visualize and characterize cancerous tumors in animal models and humans. The results can be used to predict patient-specific response to anticancer drugs and provide insight for new drug discovery [10, 20]. DCE MRI is thus highly valuable to clinical oncologists and scientists. Our work in this study was in collaboration with a medical imaging researcher who had developed a serial implementation of DCE MRI analysis code written in MATLAB that had an unacceptable run time unless it used dramatically sub-sampled datasets ($\geq$ 50x). For example, evaluating the QA algorithm on a breast cancer dataset [11] was estimated to take approximately six months, which is not practical.

To understand the volume of data being generated, it is valuable to briefly summarize the workflow of a DCE MRI experiment. Two separate regions, the volume containing the tumor and a volume containing normal vascular tissue (known as the reference region; in our case the leg), must be imaged continuously for several minutes. The MRI machine generates a 2-dimensional double array of intensities (at a specified spatial resolution) for every time point captured during the imaging time frame. These volumes must be imaged twice - first as a baseline to determine the tissue's innate relaxation properties (T_R volume), and then many times after the injection of a gadolinium-based contrast agent (CA). The CA's properties cause a change in the relaxation properties of the tissue, translating to different voxel intensities. These changes in signal intensity over time are used to calculate the CA's concentration, which is run through to a non-linear least squares computation to estimate the permeability of the tumor [20]. For more information, we refer readers to [5].

The computationally expensive portion of the QA DCE MRI algorithm lies in the non-linear fitting step, which must be performed for each voxel containing tissue in the image volume. Even in our heavily sub-sampled dataset, thousands of non-linear least square problems must be solved. Analysis of the original serial MATLAB code revealed that the majority of the workload could be computed in an embarrassingly parallel fashion, as each spatial point in the volume is independent of the others.

Given that the original code was already implemented in MATLAB and the popularity of the language in the biomedical engineering community, the straightforward approach to solving the performance problem was to implement an equivalent parallel implementation using the *Parallel Computing Toolbox* (PCT) in MATLAB. However, this only improved performance on a by 7.66x using 12 cores at best. Therefore, we decided to do a case study where we implemented a version in a newer language called Julia [4]. With Julia, we were able to achieve an approximately 72x performance improvement over the serial MATLAB implementation.

This paper makes the following contributions:

- We analyze the serial algorithm and identify areas where parallelization is expected to increase performance.

- We provide a more substantial benchmark for the Julia programming language (previous publications only include microbenchmark results) via quantitative performance data for the MATLAB and Julia versions.
- We provide a comparison of the process of writing parallel code in MATLAB and Julia based on our experiences in this case study.

Based on the significant increase in performance observed in the Julia implementations (22x speedup for the serial version and 72x speedup in the parallel version), our medical imaging researcher's group has begun to translate their performance critical code to Julia.

The remainder of the paper is organized as follows: Sect. 2 contains a thorough description of the serial code and the experimental methodology. Sections 3 and 4 discuss the MATLAB and Julia languages and implementations. Section 5 details our results, Sect. 6 presents related work, and Sect. 7 concludes.

2   Analysis of the Serial MATLAB Code

The QA DCE MRI code consists of the following five tasks:

1. Loading the data
2. Segmenting the tissue from the background
3. Calculating T_1 time (seconds) on a per-voxel basis via non-linear least squares curve fitting to its phenomenological equation
4. Calculating the change in R_1 as a function of time
5. Estimating the relative permeability between the tumor and muscle tissue (R^{Ktrans}) using the linear reference region model and evaluating the goodness-of-fit via the R^2 value.

The original serial algorithm was revised to remove all unnecessary operations (e.g. those done solely to produce human-interpretable images) and the standards recommended by The MathWorks were enforced [31]. This resulted in about a 1.67x speedup (execution time of 46.33 ± 1.33 seconds vs. 77.36 ± 4.22 seconds). This simplified version, whose execution time is profiled in Fig. 1, is used as the baseline for all comparisons presented in the paper. The remainder of this section analyzes the performance of the serial MATLAB implementation and describes each task in more detail.

2.1   Experimental Methodology

The execution times reported are the average of five runs ± their standard deviation measured after a warm up run whose time was not included. This allows just-in-time (JIT) compilation to complete and parallel workers to initialize in both languages to avoid comparing compiler speeds and efficiencies, and instead provide a comparison of the performance of the computation in each language. Given that these are one-off costs that are amortized over many datasets, the contribution to the overall run time becomes negligible. All speedups reported are comparisons of the T_1 calculation (see Sect. 2.2).

Execution times were obtained by submitting jobs to a PBS scheduling system on a high-performance computing cluster consisting of Lenovo NeXtScale nx360 M5 compute nodes with Xeon Haswell E5-2695 V3 Dual 14-core processors operating at 2.3 GHz. The dataset used for benchmarking the various implementations consisted of 5 time points, each composed of a 128×128 array of doubles. MATLAB 2015b and Julia v.0.4.3 were used for these experiments.

Timing information in MATLAB was obtained using the built-in `tic`/`toc` construct. These values were validated against MATLAB's built-in code profiler and were not found to be significantly different.

Step	Time (seconds)	
	Tumor	Leg
Load data	0.122 ± 0.003	
Segmentation	0.028 ± 0.019 sec	0.014 ± 0.003
T_1 calculation	34.055 ± 1.231	10.932 ± 0.211
ΔR_1 calculation	0.018 ± 0.001	0.007 ± 0.000
K^{trans} via RRM	1.151 ± 0.021	
Total run time	46.329 ± 1.335	

Fig. 1. Execution time for main tasks of serial MATLAB implementation.

2.2 Performance Bottleneck: T_1 Calculation

As shown in Fig. 1, the T_1 calculation accounts for approximately 97% of the total run time on average. The disparity between the run time of the tumor and leg volume arises due to the difference in the number of tissue voxels present post-segmentation (3199 voxels vs. 1083 voxels). If we account for this difference, it appears that the execution time for this function scales linearly, so there is nothing intrinsically different about the tumor. In this task, each voxel from the T_R volume is fit to the following phenomenological equation to solve for T_1:

$$S(t) = M_z(1 - e^{-T_R/T_1(t)}) \tag{1}$$

via MATLAB's built-in non-linear least squares solver, `lsqcurvefit`. As the calculations performed for each voxel is independent and the two T_R volumes are independent, they can be computed in an embarrassingly parallel fashion. Parallelization efforts were focused on this function for the MATLAB and Julia implementations and as such speedup results consider this section only.

2.3 Other Tasks

The raw output from the MRI machine is pre-processed into an array of doubles that are stored in a MATLAB `.mat` file and a `csv` format for the Julia implementation. MATLAB's built-in command `load()` takes virtually no time (Fig. 1), and the same is true of Julia's `readdlm` function.

Segmentation is performed using MATLAB's built-in k-means clustering algorithm (kmeans). A 1-D vector containing all voxels is provided as input and the function categorizes each voxel as either tissue or background. MATLAB's built-in implementation of Otsus method to determine the gray-scale threshold for binarization was also explored, but k-means generated the best mask (results omitted). The k-means algorithm in the clustering package of JuliaStats generated identical masks. The run time of this task is also negligible.

After T_1 is calculated, two equations are combined to describe R_1 ($\propto$ CA concentration) as a function of time, T_1, and T_R:

$$R_1(t) = -\frac{1}{T_R} \cdot \ln(1 - S(t)e^{-T_R \cdot R_1(0)/S(0)}) \tag{2}$$

As this is a straightforward calculation that takes a negligible amount of time, we do not parallelize it. At this point, concentration as a function of time is known — that is, we have solved the non-linear relationship between voxel intensity and CA concentration for both tissue volumes. The reference region model (RRM) [5] is used to calculate the permeability of the CA, K^{trans}, and the R^2 value on a voxel-by-voxel basis for the tumor tissue via a linear least squares fitting with non-negativity constraints (lsqnonneg). Despite each voxel being independent, the function runs for a short enough time that overhead costs would likely outweigh parallelization gains.

2.4 Performance Analysis Summary

To summarize, the tumor and reference region voxels are entirely independent and are processed identically until the calculation of K^{trans}. Additionally, in all tasks that process the segmented tissue voxels, the calculations performed on each voxel are independent, and can therefore be computed in an embarrassingly parallel fashion. Analysis of the computations that occur within these tasks does not reveal anything inherent to the code that would result in one language handling the computation preferentially.

3   MATLAB Implementations

The DCE MRI algorithm was parallelized in MATLAB by a graduate student who had several years of experience working with MATLAB and the *Parallel Computing Toolbox* (PCT) in the biomedical domain. Using the PCT, a 7.66x speedup over the serial code was achieved for the T_1 calculation.

3.1 MATLAB Background

Because most scientists do not receive formal software engineering training [2], MATLAB's ease of use (e.g. weak and dynamic typing system, lack of need to declare dimensions, etc.) and trusted libraries have made it a popular language for scientific computing applications [9,23]. Additionally, the core intentions of MATLAB's parallel programming model (the PCT) were to extend the aforementioned traditional strengths of MATLAB onto the cluster via first-class language constructs to deal with embarrassingly parallel problems [24]. This allows users to easily utilize multicore processors, GPUs and clusters with minimal modification of code or impact on readability.

However, MATLAB is not as performant as other programming languages, especially those used for parallel programming [4]. MATLAB worker threads that execute concurrent computation are heavyweight, and the PCT is proprietary and has limited scalability [15]. Additionally, the dynamic and complex typing system results in significant overhead [1,8,14]. Despite these drawbacks, in the realm of scientific computing, time to solution, readability, portability, and maintainability often trump pure performance [2], so MATLAB is utilized significantly [14].

As a bridge, continuous and significant work has been done on static analysis, ahead of time speculation, JIT compilation, and automatically porting existing code to more performant languages [1,9,13,15,16]. While automatically ported code makes sacrifices in terms of both the highly human-interpretable syntax and interactive nature of MATLAB, The MathWorks has adopted some of the other techniques, and as of release 2015b MATLAB is now entirely JIT compiled [29,30]. Based on selected case studies [30] and comparing the benchmarks performed by the Julia language creators on MATLAB 2011a [4] to MATLAB 2015b (http://julialang.org/), it appears that this has had a predominantly positive impact on performance.

3.2   Parallelization Using the Parallel Computing Toolbox

For the DCE MRI application, the T_1 calculation was rewritten so that every voxel was fit in parallel, while the tissue was processed serially (version 1). Modifications to the serial code were minimal and consisted of slicing variables [18] and changing the `for` to a `parfor` in the function shown in Fig. 2. As nested parallelism is not supported in MATLAB, version 2 consisted of restructuring the code to process both the tissues and voxels in parallel.

Table 1 contains the execution time, speedup, and efficiency for the parallelized versions as a function of the number of cores provided to the MATLAB

Table 1. Summary of parallel MATLAB implementations

# cores	Version 1			Version 2		
	Runtime (seconds)	Speedup	Efficiency	Runtime (seconds)	Speedup	Efficiency
1	49.58 ± 1.90	0.93x	93.17%	50.09 ± 2.42	0.92x	92.21%
2	26.96 ± 0.18	1.71x	85.66%	25.26 ± 0.50	1.83x	91.44%
4	14.57 ± 0.14	3.17x	79.25%	13.86 ± 0.55	3.33x	83.30%
8	8.37 ± 0.20	5.52x	69.01%	7.95 ± 0.19	5.81x	72.64%
12	6.03 ± 0.14	7.66x	63.85%	6.17 ± 0.10	7.49x	62.43%

parallel pool for the T_1 calculation. Versions 1 and 2 using 12 cores were the most performant and achieved a 7.66x speedup at 63.85% efficiency and a 7.49x speedup at 62.43% efficiency respectively. The execution time of versions 1 and 2 were not found to be statistically different as determined by a Two-Sample Kolmogorov-Smirnov test (kstest2) at a p-value of .05. On average, it took 10.27 ± 1.48 seconds to initialize the parallel pool, which is nearly 45% of the total execution time (for all sections) of the fastest version.

4   Julia Implementations

The DCE MRI algorithm was converted from MATLAB to Julia by a graduate student who never worked with MATLAB or Julia, had no experience with medical imaging, and had no prior experience with parallel computing. Thanks to several features of the two languages, this process was straightforward, as was the parallelization of the T_1 calculation, which ultimately resulted in a 72x speedup over the serial MATLAB code. Julia v0.4.3 was used and timing information was obtained using the @time macro as per the recommended best practices.

4.1   Julia Background

Julia was designed specifically for numerical and scientific computing, and has a syntax similar to languages such as MATLAB and R, but has been shown to outperform such dynamically-typed languages on microbenchmarks, often achieving performance comparable to C and Fortran [4]. Julia's creators have indicated that the language's speed is accounted for by its robust type inference system, multiple dispatch, and high-performance LLVM-based JIT compiler that generates optimized, on-the-fly native machine code directly [3].

Julia features built-in parallel capability [3], and although it is still in pre-release, its user base has created a significant number of native libraries for the language [25], as well as interfaces to commonly utilized libraries from other languages such as NLopt.

4.2   Serial Julia Implementation

The run time of the T_1 calculation in the serial Julia implementation was 2.07 ± 0.01 seconds, roughly a 22x speedup over the serial MATLAB version. Because MATLAB and Julia were designed for programmability and are thoroughly documented, it was easy to investigate MATLAB functions and determine how to implement them in Julia. Indeed, Julia seems to liberally "borrow" features from many other languages, including MATLAB, and we found that many MATLAB functions, such as the matrix manipulation function reshape, have been implemented in Julia with nearly identical syntax and semantics (Fig. 5).

When required MATLAB functions had no equivalent in the Julia standard library, it was easy to locate third-party, open-source libraries providing the needed functionality. This occurred in the segmentation task — Julia did not

MATLAB

```
% Normalize signal
Signal = masked_T1_vTR ./
    repmat(max(masked_T1_vTR, [], 2), 1,
    numTimePoints);

% Set curve fitting parameters
x0 = [1.2, 3.0];
lb = [1, 1];
ub = [2, 5];

% Define model function
T1vTRfunc = @(pars, xdata) pars(1) .*
    (1 - exp(-xdata./pars(2)));

% Do curve fitting on per voxel basis
for q = 1:numSignalPixels
    [beta, ~, resid, ~, ~, ~, J] =
        lsqcurvefit(T1vTRfunc, x0, TR,
        Signal(q, :)', lb, ub, options);
    T1vTR.map(q) = beta(2);
end
```

Julia

```
for q in 1:size(indices,1)
    Signal = T1vTR_Images[indices[q],:]
    Signal ./= maximum(Signal)

    # Create solver and set objective function
    model = Model(solver=NLoptSolver(
        algorithm=:LN_COBYLA))
    @defVar(model, beta[1:2])
    @setNLObjective(model, Min, sum{(Signal[i]-
        beta[1]*(1-exp(-TR[i]/beta[2])))^2, i=1:N})

    # add constraints and initial guess
    @addNLConstraint(model, beta[1] >= lb[1])
    @addNLConstraint(model, beta[1] <= ub[1])
    @addNLConstraint(model, beta[2] >= lb[2])
    @addNLConstraint(model, beta[2] <= ub[2])
    setValue(beta[1], x0[1])
    setValue(beta[2], x0[2])

    status = solve(model)
    T1vTR_Map[indices[q]] = getValue(beta[2])
end
```

Fig. 2. Curve-fitting function in MATLAB and Julia

have a built-in k-means function. However, because Julia features a package manager, typing the command Pkg.add("Clustering.jl") at the Julia command prompt immediately downloaded the latest version of the library Clustering.jl from a github repository (https://github.com/JuliaStats/Clustering.jl), and provided the use of its kmeans function, which had the same syntax as MATLAB's implementation. For the task involving least-squares curve fitting, a function from the JuliaOpt package LsqFit.jl that appeared to mirror MATLAB's lsqcurvefit was inadequate, as it did not allow for bounds on the solution. An interface allowing Julia to call the NLopt library, NLopt.jl, was used instead (Fig. 2).

A few MATLAB functions involved in the permeability estimation step, such as cumtrapz and nans, were not present in Julia, but it was straightforward to simply implement them.

4.3   Parallelization of Julia Implementation

Julia allows for a variety of approaches to parallel programming, but for the embarrassingly parallel computations required in this application, a simple shared memory model was sufficient. We utilized a special Julia datatype designed for this purpose, called a SharedArray, which is accessible by multiple processors. The demonstration code for SharedArrays in the Julia documentation provided a clear blueprint for our implementation. Following this example, the key steps were to copy data from several arrays into SharedArrays, and create two kernels that: (1) determined which voxels to process on each processor, and (2) ran the appropriate subset of the least-squares curve-fitting calculations on each processor.

Index determination kernel

```
@everywhere function my_range(shared_indices)
    idx = indexpids(shared_indices)
    if idx == 0
        return 0:1
    end
    n_chunks = length(procs(shared_indices))
    splits = [round(Int, s) for s in linspace(0, size(shared_indices, 1), n_chunks+1)]
    return splits[idx]+1 : splits[idx+1]
```

(a) Kernel to divide indices in SharedArray to be processed on different processors

Serial curve-fitting in Julia

```
for q in 1:size(indices,1)
    Signal = T1vTR_Images[indices[q],:]
    Signal ./= maximum(Signal)
    T1vTR_Map[indices[q]] =
        calculate_T1(Signal, TR)
end
```

Parallel curve-fitting kernel run on each worker

```
for q in my_range
    Signal = T1vTR_Images[indices[q],:]
    Signal ./= maximum(Signal)
    T1vTR_Map[indices[q]] =
        calculate_T1(Signal, TR)
end
```

(b) Serial vs. Parallel curve-fitting function in Julia

Fig. 3. Functions involved in serial and parallel curve fitting in Julia

The first of these (Fig. 3a), which was essentially copied from the Julia documentation [32], partitions a collection of indices into equal-sized groups for each processor. The second (Fig. 3b) merely substitutes an iteration over all voxel indices for an iteration over the indices assigned to the worker running the kernel.

As shown in Table 2, the parallelization produces gains of up to 3.24x over the serial Julia implementation, with reasonable efficiency.

Table 2. Summary of parallel Julia implementations

# Cores	Execution time (seconds)	Speedup relative to serial Julia	Total efficiency
1	2.63 ± 0.37	0.79x	78.56%
2	1.47 ± 0.07	1.41x	70.53%
4	1.03 ± 0.09	2.01x	50.37%
8	0.71 ± 0.01	2.92x	36.51%
12	0.64 ± 0.06	3.24x	27.00%

5   Results

In this section, we evaluate our implementations of the researcher's algorithm in terms of performance and reliability, and report on differences in programmability between MATLAB and Julia. We find that rewriting the algorithm in Julia resulted in performance gains exceeding those of using the MATLAB PCT.

5.1   Performance

Quantitative performance metrics were generated for the parallel MATLAB, serial Julia, and parallel Julia implementations for the T_1 calculation. The most performant version of parallel MATLAB achieved a speedup of 7.66x with 63.85% efficiency. As shown in Fig. 4, the serial version of Julia achieved a 22.32x speedup compared to the serial MATLAB version, a 72.32x speedup with parallelism, and a 9.44x speedup when comparing the fastest parallel Julia implementation with the fastest parallel MATLAB implementation. However, MATLAB exhibits substantially more efficient parallelism compared to Julia (Tables 1 and 2).

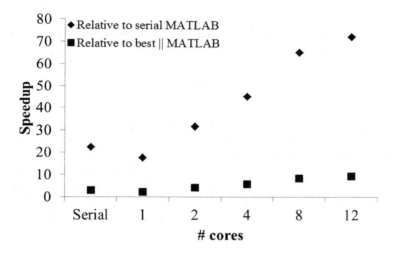

Fig. 4. Speedup of Julia implementations relative to MATLAB implementations

5.2   Reliability

The results obtained with Julia were comparable to those obtained with MAT-LAB. The T_1 calculation results obtained from Julia had insignificant numerical differences compared to the original MATLAB implementation: within the 1,083 signal pixels in the leg, the root mean square error (RMSE) was 7.90e-4 and the maximum absolute difference (MAD) was 0.0108; within the 3,199 signal pixels of the tumor, the RMSE was 9.07e-4 and the MAD was 0.0347. For the final $R^{K_{trans}}$ calculation, the RMSE was 2.31e-3 and the MAD was 0.0744.

5.3   Programmability

MATLAB and Julia are similar in terms of syntax (Fig. 5) and expressiveness. The serial MATLAB and Julia implementations contain 292 and 244 source lines of code (SLOC) respectively. The fastest parallel implementation in MATLAB contains 239 SLOC compared to Julia's 284 SLOC. Productivity was also comparable after familiarity was gained with Julia — in both languages it took approximately 1.5 h to parallelize the algorithm. This was somewhat surprising given the differences in familiarity with the languages and parallelism. The graduate student who learned MATLAB and Julia in tandem did not find either language particularly more difficult to understand than the other — however, he was simply translating MATLAB code to Julia code, as opposed to prototyping purely in Julia.

Mask extraction code in MATLAB

```
[x,y,z] = size(data);
data_mtx = reshape(data, x*y, z);
k = 2
kmeans_group_index = kmeans(data_mtx, k);
group_index_noise = kmeans_group_index(1);
mask = reshape(kmeans_group_index ~=
group_index_noise, x, y);
```

Mask extraction code in Julia

```
(x,y,z) = size(data)
data_mtx = reshape(data, x*y, z)
k = 2
kmeans_group_index = kmeans(data_mtx', 2)
group_index_noise = kmeans_group_index.assignments[1]
mask = reshape([d == group_index_noise ? 0 : 1
    for d in kmeans_group_index.assignments], x, y)
```

Fig. 5. k-means mask extraction code in MATLAB and Julia

One difference between the languages is that Julia's error messages initially appear cryptic, often including information about types that the programmer did not specify, but were inferred during JIT compilation. In Fig. 6, an error arises because `size(out)` returns a `Tuple` type, while the colon operator expects the right-hand operand to be an integer. In MATLAB, comparable code runs with no error, since the colon simply uses the first element of the 2×1 array returned by `size`. MATLAB was generally found to be more "forgiving" than Julia.

```
julia> function seq(a, b)
           out = zeros(b-a)
           for i in 1:size(out)
               out[i] = a+i
           end
           out
       end
seq (generic function with 1 method)

julia> seq(2,4)
ERROR: MethodError: `colon` has no method matching colon(::Int64, ::Tuple{Int64})
Closest candidates are:
  colon{T<:Real}(::T<:Real, ::Any, ::T<:Real)
  colon{A<:Real,C<:Real}(::A<:Real, ::Any, ::C<:Real)
  colon{T}(::T, ::Any, ::T)
  ...
 in seq at none:3
```

Fig. 6. A typical Julia error message

Moreover, MATLAB's Code Analyzer will infer and warn the programmer if, for instance, there is code that would distribute a large array to many parallel workers, while Julia does not provide warnings of this type. More broadly, the

MATLAB IDE was felt to be more convenient and powerful than using a Julia the Juno IDE (http://junolab.org/) or a Jupyter Notebook (http://jupyter.org/).

Another difficulty that arose when implementing the algorithm in Julia was locating a library that would provide the same functionality as MATLAB's lsqcurvefit function. The fact that a Julia library function with the same name had been written, but which used a different algorithm that did not allow bounds constraints, was troubling.

In spite of these hurdles, our experience suggests that learning Julia is comparable to learning a dynamically-typed programming language.

5.4   Limitations

Our implementations in the two languages used different algorithms for performing the fitting for the T_1 calculation: the MATLAB lsqcurvefit function used the Trust-Region-Reflective Least Squares Algorithm from the Optimization Toolbox, while the Julia version used a modified version of Powell's implementation of the COBYLA algorithm in the NLopt library. In order to ensure that the execution times were not different due to this distinction, the original MATLAB implementation was altered to solve the non-linear fitting using the NLopt library with the same parameters and objective function that the Julia implementation did. The T_1 calculation took 80.53 ± 0.41 seconds using NLopt (compared to 52.40 ± 0.65 seconds using lsqcurvefit). The numerical differences between the two implementations were insignificant: The voxels in the leg had an RMSE of 3.63e-04 and MAD of 4.25e-03, and the tumor had an RMSE of 3.75e-04 and MAD of 1.06e-02. Since MATLAB is proprietary software, it is difficult to determine the source of the performance differences observed in a detailed fashion.

6   Related Work

To the best of our knowledge this is the first comparison of the performance of two implementations of the linear reference region model (LRRM) for the analysis of DCE MRI data. Smith et al. [25] recently described DCEMRI.jl, a Julia implementation of the commonly used Tofts model for DCE MRI, and compared it briefly against implementations in IDL [22] and R language [28]. DCEMRI.jl was reported to be 24X faster than DCE@urLAB; both implementations used the Levenberg— Marquardt algorithm (LMA). Additionally, DCEMRI.jl was reported to be 10X faster than dcemriS4, but this is not a straight comparison because dcemriS4 uses a Bayesian hierarchical approach for curve fitting that is more demanding than the LMA.

Much research has been done on compiling and automatically parallelizing MATLAB [6, 7, 12, 19]. We did not compare the Julia and MATLAB parallel implementations against what the most active MATLAB compiler project, McLab at McGill, can perform and this is future work. One important consideration in the selection of Julia was that it is a programming environment that is gaining significant community support. For the medical imaging research community to switch to a new programming platform, the platform will need to show signs of significant community support and longevity.

A review of the literature found no references comparing Julia's performance to that of other languages for the same algorithm in an authentic parallel programming application (i.e. beyond microbenchmarks).

7   Conclusion

Although the initial MATLAB code processed the benchmark data set on the order of minutes, a typical experiment for a medical imaging researcher often includes more and larger images, taken from dozens of patients, and may take weeks to run. The 72x speedup achieved using Julia would reduce weeks to hours, removing a significant constraint on researchers. Based on our experience while writing this paper, Julia appears to be a very attractive, emergent programming language for scientific computing.

As a result of our work on the DCE MRI algorithm, and his subsequent investigations into Julia, the research scientist has adopted the following model: (1) prototype and validate in MATLAB, (2) use MATLAB to identify bottlenecks, (3) port performance-critical portions of code to Julia. Taking into account the results of this case study, we feel that it would not be difficult for other research groups (who have already navigated the MATLAB learning curve) to similarly utilize Julia. Furthermore, since none of the performance gains found in this study resulted directly from the use of MRI data, it seems likely that other scientific computing applications could be prototyped rapidly in MATLAB, then efficiently ported to Julia for high-throughput applications. The DCE MRI code in both languages can be found at github.com/fdanford/LCPC2016_MATLAB_Julia/.

Acknowledgments. An allocation of computer time from the UA Research Computing High Performance Computing (HPC) and High Throughput Computing (HTC) at the University of Arizona is gratefully acknowledged by the authors.

References

1. Almási, G., Padua, D.: MaJIC: compiling matlab for speed and responsiveness. In: ACM SIGPLAN Notices, vol. 37, pp. 294–303. ACM (2002)
2. Basili, V.R., Carver, J.C., Cruzes, D., Hochstein, L.M., Hollingsworth, J.K., Shull, F., Zelkowitz, M.V.: Understanding the high-performance-computing community: a software engineer's perspective. IEEE Softw. **25**(4), 29 (2008)
3. Bezanson, J., Edelman, A., Karpinski, S., Shah, V.B.: Julia: a fresh approach to numerical computing. arXiv preprint arXiv:1411.1607 (2014)
4. Bezanson, J., Karpinski, S., Shah, V.B., Edelman, A.: Julia: a fast dynamic language for technical computing. arXiv preprint arXiv:1209.5145 (2012)

5. Cárdenas-Rodríguez, J., Li, X., Whisenant, J.G., Barnes, S., Stollberger, R., Gore, J.C., Yankeelov, T.E.: The basic principles of dynamic contrast-enhanced magnetic resonance imaging. In: Bammer, R. (ed.) MR & CT Perfusion Imaging: Clinical Applications and Theoretical Principles, chapter 31. Lippincott Williams & Wilkins, Philadelphia (2016)
6. Casey, A., Li, J., Doherty, J., Chevalier-Boisvert, M., Aslam, T., Dubrau, A., Lameed, N., Aslam, A., Garg, R., Radpour, S., Belanger, O.S., Hendren, L., Verbrugge, C.: McLab: an extensible compiler toolkit for MATLAB and related languages. In: Proceedings of the Third C* Conference on Computer Science and Software Engineering, C3S2E 2010, pp. 114–117. ACM, New York (2010)
7. Chauhan, A., Kennedy, K.: Optimizing strategies for telescoping languages: procedure strength reduction and procedure vectorization. In: Proceedings of the 15th ACM International Conference on Supercomputing, New York, pp. 92–102 (2001)
8. Chevalier-Boisvert, M., Hendren, L., Verbrugge, C.: Optimizing MATLAB through just-in-time specialization. In: International Conference on Compiler Construction, pp. 46–65. Springer, Heidelberg (2010)
9. De Rose, L., Padua, D.: Techniques for the translation of MATLAB programs into FORTRAN 90. ACM Trans. Program. Lang. Syst. (TOPLAS) 21(2), 286–323 (1999)
10. DeGrandchamp, J.B., Whisenant, J.G., Arlinghaus, L.R., Abramson, V.G., Yankeelov, T.E., Cardenas-Rodrguez, J.: Predicting response before initiation of neoadjuvant chemotherapy in breast cancer using new methods for the analysis of dynamic contrast enhanced MRI (DCE MRI) data. In: International Society for Optics and Photonics, SPIE Medical Imaging, pp. 978811–978811, March 2016
11. DeGrandchamp, J.B., Whisenant, J.G., Arlinghaus, L.R., Abramson, V.G., Yankeelov, T.E., Cárdenas-Rodríguez, J.: Predicting response before initiation of neoadjuvant chemotherapy in breast cancer using new methods for the analysis of dynamic contrast enhanced MRI (DCE MRI) data. In: Proceedings of SPIE, pp. 9788:978811–978811-10 (2016)
12. DeRose, L., Gallivan, K., Gallopoulous, E., Marsolf, B., Padua, D.: A MATLAB compiler and restructurer for the development of scientific libraries and applications. In: Preliminary Proceedings of the 8th International Workshop on Languages and Compilers for Parallel Computing, pp. 18.1–18.18, May 1995
13. Doherty, J., Hendren, L., Radpour, S.: Kind analysis for MATLAB. ACM SIGPLAN Not. 46(10), 99–118 (2011)
14. Dubrau, A.W., Hendren L.J.: Taming MATLAB, vol. 47. ACM (2012)
15. Kumar, V., Hendren, L.: Compiling MATLAB for high performance computing via x10. Sable Technical report 03 (2013)
16. Li, X., Hendren, L.: Mc2FOR: a tool for automatically translating MATLAB to FORTRAN 95. In: 2014 Software Evolution Week-IEEE Conference on Software Maintenance, Reengineering and Reverse Engineering (CSMR-WCRE), pp. 234–243. IEEE (2014)
17. Markonis, D., Schaer, R., Eggel, I., Müller, H., Depeursinge, A.: Using mapreduce for large-scale medical image analysis. arXiv preprint arXiv:1510.06937 (2015)
18. MathWorks. Matlab parallel computing toolbox users guide (2016). www.mathworks.com/help/pdf_doc/distcomp/distcomp.pdf. Accessed 20 May 2016
19. Menon, V., Pingali, K.: A case for source-level transformations in MATLAB. In: Proceedings of the 2nd Conference on Domain-Specific Languages, pp. 53–66. USENIX Association, Berkeley, 3–5 1999

20. O'Connor, J.P., Jackson, A., Parker, G.J., Jayson, G.C.: DCE-MRI biomarkers in the clinical evaluation of antiangiogenic and vascular disrupting agents. Br. J. Cancer **96**(2), 189–195 (2007)

21. O'Connor, J.P.B., Tofts, P.S., Miles, K.A., Parkes, L.M., Thompson, G., Jackson, A.: Dynamic contrast-enhanced imaging techniques: CT and MRI. Br. J. Radiol. 84(2) (2011)

22. Ortuño, J.E., Ledesma-Carbayo, M.J., Simões, R.V., Candiota, A.P., Arús, C., Santos, A.: Dce@ urlab: a dynamic contrast-enhanced mri pharmacokinetic analysis tool for preclinical data. BMC Bioinform. **14**(1), 1 (2013)

23. Radpour, S., Hendren, L., Schäfer, M.: Refactoring MATLAB. In: Jhala, R., Bosschere, K. (eds.) CC 2013. LNCS, vol. 7791, pp. 224–243. Springer, Heidelberg (2013). doi:10.1007/978-3-642-37051-9_12

24. Sharma, G., Martin, J.: MATLAB: a language for parallel computing. Int. J. Parallel Prog. **37**(1), 3–36 (2009)

25. Smith, D.S., Li, X., Arlinghaus, L.R., Yankeelov, T.E., Welch, E.B.: DCEMRI.jl: a fast, validated, open source toolkit for dynamic contrast enhanced MRI analysis. PeerJ **3**, e909 (2015)

26. Smith-Bindman, R., Miglioretti, D.L., Johnson, E., Lee, C., Feigelson, H.S., Flynn, M., Greenlee, R.T., Kruger, R.L., Hornbrook, M.C., Roblin, D., Solberg, L.I., Vanneman, N., Weinmann, S., Williams, A.E.: Use of diagnostic imaging studies and associated radiation exposure for patients enrolled in large integrated health care systems, 1996–2010. JAMA **307**(22), 2400–2409 (2012)

27. Smith-Bindman, R., Miglioretti, D.L., Larson, E.B.: Rising use of diagnostic medical imaging in a large integrated health system. Health Aff. **27**(6), 1491–1502 (2008)

28. Whitcher, B., Schmid, V.J., et al.: Quantitative analysis of dynamic contrast-enhanced and diffusion-weighted magnetic resonance imaging for oncology in r. J. Stat. Softw. **44**(5), 1–29 (2011)

29. Matlab execution engine. http://www.mathworks.com/products/matlab-matlab-execution-engine/. Accessed 26 Aug 2016

30. Loren on the art of matlab: Run code faster with the new matlab execution engine. http://blogs.mathworks.com/loren/2016/02/12/run-code-faster-with-the-new-matlab-execution-engine/. Accessed 26 Aug 2016

31. Techniques to improve performance. http://www.mathworks.com/help/matlab/matlab_prog/techniques-for-improving-performance.html

32. Parallel computing - julia language 0.4.7 predocumentation. http://docs.julialang.org/en/release-0.4/manual/parallel-computing/. Accessed 11 July 2016

The Importance of Efficient Fine-Grain Synchronization for Many-Core Systems

Tongsheng Geng[1]([✉]), Stéphane Zuckerman[2], José Monsalve[2],
Alfredo Goldman[1], Sami Habib[3], Jean-Luc Gaudiot[1], and Guang R. Gao[2]

[1] PArallel Systems and Computer Architecture Lab,
Department of Electrical Engineering and Computer Science,
University of California, Irvine, USA
{tgeng,gaudiot}@uci.edu, gold@ime.usp.br
[2] Computer Architecture and Parallel Systems Laboratory,
Department of Electrical and Computer Engineering,
University of Delaware, Newark, USA
{szuckerm,josem}@udel.edu, ggao.capsl@gmail.com
[3] Computer Engineering Department, Kuwait University, Al-khalidiya, Kuwait
sami_habib@me.com

Abstract. Current shared-memory systems can feature tens of processing elements. The old assumption that coarse-grain synchronization is enough in a shared-memory system thus becomes invalid. To efficiently take advantage of such systems, we propose to use fine grain synchronization, with event-driven multithreading. To illustrate our point, we study a naïve 5-point 2D stencil kernel. We provide several synchronization variants using our fine-grain multithreading environment, and compare it to a naïve coarse-grain implementation using OpenMP. We conducted experiments on three different many-core compute nodes, with speedups ranging from 1.2× to 1.75×.

1 Introduction

In the past decade, the number of processing elements (PEs) found in general-purpose high-performance processors has increased between fourty and a hundred times, as demonstrated by, *e.g.*, Intel®'s Xeon and IBM®'s POWER8 processors. Further, so-called accelerators have reached even higher PE counts in recent years.

In the meantime, the programming models and program execution models (PXMs) used by application scientists are mostly the same: MPI is used for inter-node communication, and OpenMP is still favored for shared-memory computations. However, while the OpenMP standard has evolved to include finer-grain tasks with OpenMP 3, and even provide ways to define task-dependence graphs in OpenMP 4 [6], a large majority of application programmers still rely on a coarse-grain style to express parallelism, *i.e.*, they mostly use constructs tied to parallel `for` loops, which in turn require the use of global barriers.

While the core count remained low in compute nodes, this approach was still reasonable. However as we explained above, assuming a low core count is

© Springer International Publishing AG 2017
C. Ding et al. (Eds.): LCPC 2016, LNCS 10136, pp. 203–217, 2017.
DOI: 10.1007/978-3-319-52709-3_16

not realistic anymore. Synchronization usually leverages the use of atomic operations, which can seriously hamper performance in a multi-core, multi-socket environment. In particular, memory-bound workloads tend to tax the interconnection network linking sockets together. In general, high-performance based synchronization constructs rely on some sophisticated variation of busy-waiting (potentially mitigated with a sleep policy) which can hog the memory subsystem, as the system software designer expects contention to be low and the workload to be well-balanced—particularly in the case of embarrassingly parallel algorithms and programs. Specifically, memory-bound workloads may suffer from load imbalance due to saturated resources, *e.g.*, FPUs shared by multiple PEs, or contention on a given memory level. One such example is the use of partial differential equation iterative solvers for linear equation systems, in particular the application of Jacobi or Gauss-Seidel methods to a linear system by resorting to a stencil-based iterative solver: every element of an n-dimensional grid depends on its immediate neighbors, and potentially more remote ones. Such algorithms are used in a multitude of applications, *e.g.*, to solve Laplace equations used in heat conduction and computational fluid dynamics solvers.

In this paper, we propose to demonstrate the need for fine-grain synchronization even in the presence of rather coarse-grained workload partitioning. We compare the coarse-grain parallelization of a 5-point stencil application implemented with OpenMP to several variants using a fine-grain event-driven execution model. While there are various ways to optimize stencil codes, our intent is to demonstrate that in a dependence-heavy context, yet with a uniform amount of work per thread, *fine-grain synchronization matters*, even in "regular" general-purpose systems[1].

Our experiments show that even with a simple hierarchical scheme, the reduction in atomic operations and memory traffic in general benefits the overall execution of the program. We then further modify our variant so that parallel tasks only communicate with their neighbors. The process itself is made easier thanks to the integration in the task-definition semantics of event dependencies. Moreover, while we hand-coded our stencil computations using an implementation of the Codelet Model, the process to parallelize such a workload in a hierarchical manner is rather systematic and easy to follow.

We run our experiments on three different types of machines featuring ×86 processors, with a different number of processing elements per chip, but also a different number of sockets per node. Our results show an improvement of up to 1.75× on the speedup obtained with OpenMP.

Section 2 presents the codelet model and its runtime implementation, which we used to carry our experiments. Section 3 describes our approach to parallelize our stencil application. Section 4 describes our experimental results. Section 5 describes other work related to fine-grain multithreading and stencil computations. Finally, we conclude in Sect. 6.

---

[1] Note that we do *not* claim that our own environment is better than OpenMP 4.

2   The Codelet Model

The Codelet Model [21] is a fine-grain event-driven program execution model which targets current and future multi- and many-core architectures (A short introduction is available at http://www.capsl.udel.edu/codelets.shtml). In essence, it is inspired by dataflow models of computation [8].

2.1   General Principles

Codelets: Definition and Firing Rules. The quantum of execution is the *codelet*, a fine-grain task that executes a sequence of machine instructions until completion, and runs on a von Neumann type of computation core. A codelet *fires* when all its dependencies (data and resource requirements) are met. A codelet cannot be preempted while it is firing, *i.e.*, while it is executing on a computation core.

Codelet Graphs and Threaded Procedures. Each time a codelet produces data items or releases a shared resource, it signals the other codelets that depend on such data item(s) and/or resource(s). Such a group of codelets and their dependencies can be modeled as a directed graph called a *codelet graph* (CDG). In general, a given CDG statically specifies the dependencies between the codelets it contains.

A *Threaded Procedure* (TP) is a container that comprises a CDG and data to be accessed by the codelets it contains. A TP is essentially an asynchronous function: once it has invoked a TP, its caller resumes its execution. The TP itself can run anywhere on the machine once it has been scheduled for execution.

2.2   The Codelet Abstract Machine

The codelet model relies on a Codelet Abstract Machine (CAM), which models a general purpose many-core architecture with two types of cores: synchronization units (SUs) and computation units (CUs). A CAM is composed of clusters of cores: each cluster contains at least one SU, one or more CUs, and some local memory. Clusters are grouped together to form a chip, which itself has access to some memory modules. Multiple chips can be grouped into a node, and multiple nodes form a full machine. At each level of the hierarchy, an interconnection network is assumed in order to allow for memory transfers.

A CAM is meant to be mapped on real hardware: the number of clusters, and computation units per cluster will be directly influenced by the actual hardware architecture on which a codelet program should be running. Further, different configurations may be used on the same target hardware, depending on the nature of the application.

2.3   A Codelet Runtime System

Our work relies on DARTS, a faithful implementation of the codelet model [19]. It targets shared-memory nodes (there is no distributed memory implementation at the time of this writing). DARTS executes on regular multi-core chips and assigns a role to each core: a core is either a synchronization unit or a computation unit.

3   Applying Fine-Grain Parallelism to Embarrasingly Parallel Problems

This section describes how we started from an OpenMP coarse-grain implementation of a simple, naive 5-point stencil computation and reproduced its overall structure using a codelet runtime system, to gradually refine the stencil code parallelization and leverage finer-grain synchronization.

3.1   Basic Implementation of a Parallel Coarse-Grain 5-Point Stencil

The code presented in Listing 1.1 is a naïve OpenMP version of a coarse-grain multithreaded 5-point stencil computation. To simplify the problem, we do not consider the convergence test and only rely on a given number of time steps. This version of the stencil code privatizes everything, so that each thread can perform all computations (including pointer swapping and moving forward to the next time step). The computation itself is located in a parallel `for` loop (see line 15). We removed the implicit barrier at the end of the loop so that threads that finish processing their own iteration chunk may proceed to swap their source and destination pointers for the next time step. The only required synchronization is the global barrier (line 17) before looping to the next iteration in the `while` loop, to ensure that all threads have properly swapped their array pointers before resuming the computation.

```
void    stencil_5pt(double* restrict dst,     double* restrict src,       1
                    const size_t     n_rows, const size_t     n_cols,      2
                    size_t           n_steps)                              3
{                                                                          4
   typedef double (*Array2D)[n_cols];                                      5
# pragma omp parallel default(none) shared(src, dst) \                     6
            firstprivate(n_rows, n_cols, n_tsteps)                         7
   {                                                                       8
      Array2D  D = (Array2D) dst, S = (Array2D) src;                       9
      size_t n_ts  = n_tsteps;                                            10
      while (n_ts-- > 0) {                                                11
#        pragma omp for nowait                                            12
         for (size_t i=1; i<n_rows-1; ++i)                                13
            for (size_t j=1; j<n_cols-1; ++j)                             14
               D[i][j] = 0.25 * (S[i-1][j]+S[i+1][j] + S[i][j-1]+S[i][j+1]);  15
         SWAP_PTR(&D,&S);                                                 16
#        pragma omp barrier                                               17
      }                                                                   18
   }                                                                      19
}                                                                         20
```

Listing 1.1. Naïve 5-Point Stencil kernel—OpenMP version. Everything has been privatized, but threads can only proceed to the next time step if they all have swapped their array pointers.

We first adapted the code of Listing 1.1 to our DARTS framework. The definition of codelets and threaded procedures is shown in Listing 1.2. The codelets are defined with default dependence counts (0 for Compute, and 2 for Barrier), but they can be overriden when they are effectively instantiated. The Stencil TP is essentially a C++ `struct` which allocates the right amount of codelets for a given cluster of cores, and holds the data which the codelets can access.

Table 1. Codelet Model macros and their meaning.

Keyword	Description
DEF_TP	Defines a new threaded procedure
DEF_CODELET	Defines a new codelet
DEF_CODELET_ITER	Defines a new codelet with a specific ID
SYNC	Signals a codelet within the same TP frame
SIGNAL	Signals a codelet in another TP frame
SIGNAL_CODELET	Signals a codelet from a TP setup phase
LOAD_FRAME	Loads the threaded procedure frame
FIRE(CodeletName)	Code to run when CodeletName is fired
INVOKE(TPName,...)	Invokes a new TP from a codelet

The listing of the first variant we implemented, which we call Naive in our experiments (see Sect. 4), is not shown here due to lack of space. The Compute codelet proceeds to execute the stencil operation for one time step over a chunk of the data. When it is done firing, it signals the Barrier codelet, which collects all the signals of all firing Computes. Barrier then proceeds to invoke a new Stencil TP where the source and destination arrays are swapped in the parameters list, and the time step is decreased. This variant performs poorly compared to OpenMP, as we require DARTS to allocate a new codelet graph for each new time step. The second variant still implements a coarse-grain synchronization scheme, but this time, it has Compute codelets reset their dependence count when they are fired. Barrier signals the end of the computation if there are no more time steps, or it resets itself, and then signals Compute codelets. The code is provided in Listing 1.3[2].

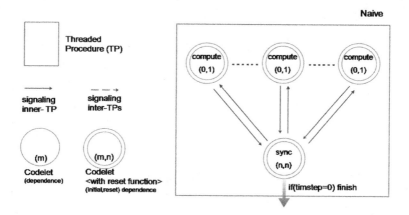

Fig. 1. A coarse-grain version of a naïve stencil computation. Each codelet resets itself if there are remaining iteration steps.

---

[2] Obviously, as we are writing directly using a runtime system API, the code has to be more verbose than its OpenMP counterpart.

The various keywords emphasized in bold red are macros defined to simplify the writing of DARTS programs. A short description of the various keywords is provided in Table 1. A graphical illustration of the codelet program (Naïve Stencil-DARTS with reset function) is shown in Fig. 1.

```
DEF_CODELET_ITER ( Compute, 0, NO_META_DATA );                  1
DEF_CODELET      ( Barrier, 2, NO_META_DATA );                  2
DEF_TP(Stencil) {                                               3
// Data                                                         4
  double *dst, *src;                                            5
  size_t  n_rows, n_cols, n_tsteps;                             6
// Code                                                         7
  Compute* compute;                                             8
  Barrier  barrier;                                             9
                                                                10
  Stencil(double* restrict p_dst,    double* restrict p_src,    11
            size_t          p_nRows, size_t           p_nCols,  12
            size_t          p_nTSteps)                          13
  : dst(p_dst), src(p_src)                                      14
  , n_rows(p_nRows), n_cols(p_nCols), n_tsteps(p_nTSteps)       15
  , compute(new Compute[g_nCU])                                 16
  , barrier(g_nCU,g_nCU,this,NO_META_DATA)                      17
  {                                                             18
    for (size_t cid = 0; i < g_nCU; ++cid) {                    19
      compute[cid] = Compute{1,1,this,NO_META_DATA,cid};        20
      SIGNAL_CODELET(compute[cid]);                             21
    }                                                           22
  }                                                             23
};                                                              24
```

Listing 1.2. Coarse-Grain 5-Point Stencil kernel—DARTS version. **Stencil** TP definition and its associated codelets.

```
FIRE(Compute) {                                                1
  LOAD_FRAME(Stencil);                                         2
  typedef double (*Array2D)[n_cols];                           3
  Array2D D = (Array2D) FRAME(dst), S = (Array2D) FRAME(src);  4
  const size_t n_rows = FRAME(n_rows), n_cols = FRAME(n_cols), 5
               n_steps = FRAME(n_steps);                       6
                                                               7
  size_t cid = getID(), // current codelet's ID                8
         lo  = lower_bound(n_cols,cid),                        9
         hi  = upper_bound(n_cols,cid);                        10
                                                               11
  RESET(compute[cid]);                                         12
  for (size_t i = lo; i < hi-1; ++i)                           13
    for (size_t j = 1; j < n_cols-1; ++j)                      14
      D[i][j] = 0.25 * (S[i-1][j]+S[i+1][j] + S[i][j-1]+S[i][j+1]); 15
  SYNC(barrier);                                               16
  EXIT_TP();                                                   17
}                                                              18
                                                               19
FIRE(Barrier) {                                                20
  LOAD_FRAME(Stencil);                                         21
  if ( FRAME(n_tstep) == 0 ) SIGNAL(done), EXIT_TP();          22
                                                               23
  RESET(barrier);                                              24
  for (size_t i = 0; i < g_nCU; ++i) SYNC(compute[i]);         25
  EXIT_TP();                                                   26
}                                                              27
```

Listing 1.3. Coarse-Grain 5-Point Stencil kernel—DARTS version. Codelets reset themselves until the last iteration step is reached.

3.2   Description of Parallel Stencil Computation Variants

Distributing the Computation Over Multiple Clusters in the Codelet Abstract Machine. The code presented in Listing 1.3 is sufficient in case we map a codelet abstract machine (CAM) which features only a single Synchronization Unit (SU, see Sect. 2). However, this configuration centralizes all codelet graph creations onto a single processing element. Further, it creates a single unique synchronization object which will be accessed by all codelets to signal the end of their computation. This will force the whole compute node to serialize memory accesses when performing the synchronization step. As a result, we implemented a new variant inspired by the very first naïve one, which partitions the codelet graph into sub-graphs, and each contained within its own threaded procedure featuring a local **Barrier** codelet, and each confined to a given cluster of cores to maintain locality. Note that, following the original code, new TPs *are* invoked for each new time step in the computation. However, to avoid paying the cost of dynamically allocating the various codelets involved per cluster, the same array of codelets is passed from invocation to invocation: the codelets are destroyed only once the last iteration step has been reached. Figure 2 provides a high-level view of the resulting codelet graph.

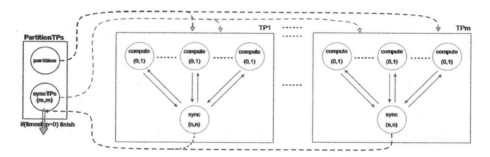

Fig. 2. A medium-grain version of a naive 5-point stencil computation. The computation is decomposed into several sub-codelet graphs, allowing a machine to hold multiple synchronization units for a better workload balance.

Toward a Finer-Grain Approach. Our goal is to allow portions of work to proceed with the next iteration step, as long as the shared rows they require to update their portion of the matrix are up-to-date. We are still decomposing the work along the rows of the matrices, but this time, each codelet simply signals its neighbors when it is done updating the rows they depend on to move to the next iteration step. Hence, some codelets may proceed to update the system at step S_{t+1} while others are still finishing step S_t. Figure 3 provides a diagram of the resulting codelet graph. In this case, we create a single TP holding the whole codelet graph, where all dependencies are statically determined. The stress on the memory subsystem is not expected to be excessive, since signals are now only sent between "neighboring" cores, thus confining atomic operations to PEs that are physically close.

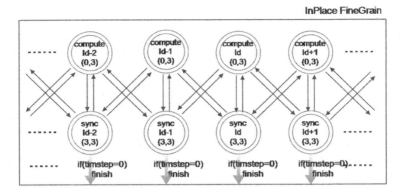

Fig. 3. A fine-grain version of a naive stencil computation. A single TP is generated, which holds the full codelet graph. Codelets only signal the neighbors which read and write shared rows.

Reducing the Stencil Computation's Footprint. The fine-grain approach we followed in the previous section also makes it easier to reduce the memory footprint of the computation. Rather than systematically using two matrices to iteratively compute new values at each time step (subsequently requiring to exchange array pointers), it is possible to allocate a small buffer per codelet in each invoked TP. Each buffer must be large enough to hold a set of at least three full rows in the matrix. The original naive loop thus becomes more complex, as each codelet must now first write the new values of the system to its local buffer first, then must write the newly updated row(s) back to the original matrix. However, this scheme lends itself well to fine-grain synchronization. Indeed, as Fig. 3 only features TPs, codelets, and their dependencies, but not the actual code or data that are held in the TP frames, then it is also an adequate representation of an "in-place" version of a fine-grain version of an *n*-point stencil computation. However, this version suffers from the same limitation as the previous fine-grain variant: it requires to invoke a single threaded procedure, thus forcing the codelet abstract machine to be mapped with a single SU for the whole machine, and, in turn, to accept that all TP creations will involve a potentially heavy serial step.

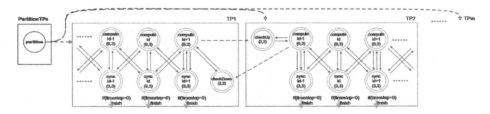

Fig. 4. A fine-grain in-place version of a naïve stencil computation. Multiple TPs can be generated, which hold a portion of the overall codelet graph. Codelets only signal the neighbors which read and write shared rows. A single matrix is required.

Hence, a final refinement is to allow for the distribution of the fine-grain "in-place" variant over multiple TPs. While the previous variants, including the initial fine-grain one, were relatively easy to implement, this specific implementation requires some careful coding when setting up the overall codelet graph, as codelets will reset themselves and signal each other not only within the same TP frame, but also *across* frames. However, the basic structure remains the same, and it clearly can be automated by a compiler. The resulting codelet graph is shown in Fig. 4. In this last variant, each codelet graph features three types of codelets: `Compute` performs the actual computation, as before. The `CheckDown` and `CheckUp` codelets are signaled when rows shared by "upper" and/or "lower" neighbors are ready to be updated. In turn, they also signal other compute codelets to let them know that the rows they are sharing with their neighbors are cleared for reading.

4   Experimental Results

4.1   Experimental Setup

The hardware platforms characteristics are described in Table 2.

Table 2. Compute nodes characteristics. "PE" = "Processing element." L2 and L3 caches are all unified. Hyperthreaded cores feature two threads per core. Platform A features 64 GiB of DRAM; architectures B and C feature 128 GiB.

Platform	Processor type	# Sockets	# PEs per Socket	Total PEs	L1D (KiB)	L2 (KiB)	L3 (MiB)	Comments
A	Intel Sandy Bridge	2	16	32	32	256	20	Private L2; hyper-threading
B	Intel Sandy Bridge	4	12	48	32	256	15	Private L2; hyper-threading
C	AMD bulldozer interlagos	4	12	48	16	2048	12	L2 & FPU are shared by 2 cores

Table 3 provides the information related to the system software running on each compute node where we ran our experiments. Each platform offers a relatively varied system software layer, with compilers and OS kernels being slightly (or even widely) different from node to node. All experiments are run by pinning threads to a given processing element (hardware thread or core), by setting the `OMP_PROC_BIND` environment variable to `true` (for OpenMP). `DARTS` automatically pins its work queues to the underlying processing elements.

Table 3. System software stack used for the experiments.

Platform	Linux distribution	Kernel version	GCC version
A	CentOS 7.1	3.10.0	4.8.3
B	Ubuntu 14.04.3 LTS	3.13.0	4.8.4
C	Scientific Linux 6.1	2.6.32	4.9.3

4.2 Experimental Protocol

We ran seven different variants of our stencil code: Seq is our baseline and is a benchmark that runs sequentially; OMP runs the same code as Seq with added OpenMP directives; Naive is a single threaded procedure implementation of the stencil computation (see Sect. 3.1), NaiveTPsPtr implements the same logic as Naive, but distributes the work across several TPs; FineGrain implements the fine-grain synchronization scheme described in Sect. 3.2; InPlace implements our in-place strategy to run the stencil computation, using a single TP; and InPlaceTPs implements the same in-place variant, but distributes the computation across multiple TPs which then must issue inter-TP signals to satisfy dependencies.

We ran our experiments using the following protocol: (1) All stencil computations run for 30 time steps, (2) Each variant instance is run 20 times to increase the stability of the run, then the accumulated times are averaged after removing the 2 most extreme values (min and max), and (3) Each binary containing a variant is run 10 times from the command line, and we average the accumulated times once again (this is due to system-induced noise in sequential, codelet, or OpenMP variants—in particular for small input sizes).

4.3 Results

The results for strong scaling are shown in Fig. 5. The default CAM is used in the case of DARTS, which maps compute units

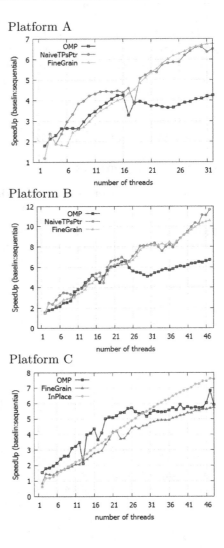

Fig. 5. 5-point 2D stencil. Strong scaling for a 3000×3000 input matrix. The baseline is the pure sequential code. We only show the two best performing DARTS variants.

to PEs that are physically close to each other. As a result, we do not use the entirety of the available aggregated cache capacity. In the OpenMP case, we used OMP_PROC_BIND, to make sure that threads are pinned to a given PE. However they are assigned in a more random fashion (left to the discretion of the OpenMP runtime and the OS), thus making better use of the overall caches. Still, when resources start to be saturated, *i.e.*, when more than half of the processing elements are used, and start to compete for FPUs, caches, *etc.*, the DARTS variants outperform the OpenMP version. As the PE count increases, so does the performance gap.

Platform A

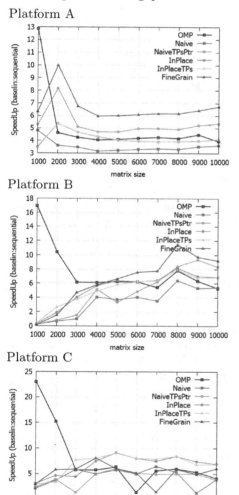

Platform B

Platform C

Fig. 6. 5-point stencil computation. Weak scaling. The baseline is the pure sequential code.

In the weak scaling case, the results for all variants are shown in Fig. 6. As with the strong scaling case, FineGrain and NaiveTPsPtr achieve the best performance on Intel-based architectures (A and B), with speedups reaching up to 1.75× compared to OpenMP. The OpenMP variant has a clear advantage over DARTS when the workload fits in the caches (*i.e.*, when the matrix size is 1000, or possibly 2000, as it still partially fits in the caches). In the OpenMP case, loops are statically scheduled, thus ensuring that the same PE processes the same chunk of data, thus minimizing cache misses. In contrast, codelets in DARTS can be run by any PE belonging to the same cluster of cores. Hence a given data chunk may be processed by different PEs over two successive iteration steps, resulting in additional cache trashing.

Once the data grows beyond the capacity of L3 caches, DARTS gets the upper hand: the finer-grain variants either issue "local" atomic operations between neighbors (as with the FineGrain variant), or at least provide a hierarchical way to maintain some locality within their cluster of cores, thus reducing the overall memory traffic. In particular in the Intel compute nodes (Platforms A and B), the inclusive nature of the caches allows the hardware to recognize when a given memory location is owned by the "local" L3, and thus avoids a costly request for ownership across sockets.

Unfortunately, Platform C features exclusive caches, thus forcing the hardware to issue a broadcast to flush write buffers across the whole node, as it does not know which other caches own a copy of the data [17].

4.4 Discussion

Coarse-grain synchronizations (*e.g.*, barriers) tend to be implemented with a single memory location. This has several negative consequences: (1) all processing elements issue an atomic operation to the same location, forcing the other PEs to flush their write buffers, sometimes more than once; (2) there is a "natural" contention due to the target single location. By contrast, finer-grain synchronization makes use of more locations with better locality effects. Write buffer flushes still occur, but tend to be limited to writing back in L3 (at least in the Intel case). In addition, codelets can better exploit the "slack" that exists when a core is done running a thread, due to their event-driven nature.

Finer-grain synchronization clearly *does* provide better results on general-purpose many-core systems, as shown in Figs. 5 and 6. However, which variant works best varies significantly depending on which platform we run our tests. On Intel-based compute nodes, our most refined variants did not perform very well in the end: the InPlace and InPlaceTPs variants underperformed compared to their most simple counterparts, and even compared to the coarse-grain OpenMP version. We attribute this to too naive an implementation: while the InPlace variant does require less memory than the original code, its implementation is too simplistic: it makes use of dynamic allocation each time a computation codelet is being fired, which in turn invokes the OS to perform the allocation itself. As most codelets are fired within a very small time range, some serialization while trying to access the OS's memory allocator results in wasted time. As Intel-based nodes feature inclusive caches, the data can only be as big as the L3s of the system.

By contrast, as Platform C is AMD-based, caches are exclusive: the aggregated size of the L2 caches equals the aggregated size of the L3s, effectively doubling the overall size of the data that can be held in the caches. It also helps with the InPlace and InPlaceTPs variants, as the local buffer allocated for the fine-grain update of the matrix is held in a separate cache than the original matrix. This is compared to the naïve, 2-array version which requires to constantly read and write from and to memory through the L1 and L2 caches. The AMD system also relies on write-through L1D caches (compared to Intel's write-back L1Ds), which allows for a better utilization of the L1D (there is roughly four times more reads than writes in the stencil computation).

Moreover, as we intended to show the benefits of "pure" fine-grain synchronization, without resorting to classical loop transformations, such as tiling or loop skewing, even the allocation of just three complete rows is enough to quickly fill L1D caches. For example, our smallest input size for a matrix, 1000×1000, requires three rows of a thousand elements to implement the current in-place variants. However, this represents already 2/3 of the L1D cache of the Intel-based compute nodes, and overflows into the L2 cache in the case of the AMD compute node. Hence, to obtain an efficient in-place variant, additional blocking and tiling techniques are required. We intend to explore this research venue, but to be fair to coarse-grain models, we must do the same for the naïve OpenMP code.

5   Related Work

Fine-Grain Multithreading Program Execution Models. In recent years, several attempts at providing more dynamic ways to create parallel work have been proposed. Many such attempts are inspired by dataflow models of computation. Among them, we can mention Concurrent Collection [11], an implementation of dynamic macro-dataflow. It has shown encouraging results, including on stencil-like computations [14]. XKaapi [9], OCR [15], and SWARM [12] all propose a dataflow (or even codelet) inspired way to deal with multithreading. However, they do not provide an explicit way to group dataflow tasks to ensure they execute on a specific portion of the hardware (for example, to maintain spacial and temporal locality), contrary to DARTS (which uses threaded procedures to enforce codelet grouping). Other frameworks provide fine-grain multithreading without being directly tied to dataflow. Chief among them are Cilk [5] and Habanero [3].

Finally, the latest version of the OpenMP standard proposes a way to describe task dependencies in a program [6], by describing dataflow-like dependencies in the code. The resulting task dependence graph is obtained in a fully dynamic manner. By contrast, DARTS's codelet graphs tend to dynamically allocate chunks of codelets which feature statically-defined dependencies.

Frameworks and Transformations for Stencil Computations. While this paper's intent is to advocate for finer-grain synchronization for large-scale general-purpose compute nodes, and uses stencil kernels only as an example, we provide a short description of related techniques and frameworks to optimize stencil computations.

Classical loop optimization techniques provide very efficient ways to improve sequential stencil computation. Loop tiling, locality optimization and parallelization are the main methodology to improve stencil computation performance. Loop tiling [1] manipulates hyperplanes from the iteration space to determine the tile shapes for a given computation, as well as the scheduling order. Further transformations include diamond tiling [2,4]. More recently, the manipulation of the iteration space has led to better work scheduling for many-core devices. For example, Shrestha *et al.* propose to perform transformations on the iteration space using jagged-tiling to allow for a better concurrent start for processing tiles in parallel [18].

Pochoir is a domain-specific language relying on Cilk that allows the user to specify a given type of stencil computation to be generated automatically for parallel execution [20]. Kamil *et al.* [7,10] propose a code generation and auto-tuning framework for stencil computations targeted at multi- and many-core processors. Muranushi and Makino introduced the PiTCH tiling method [16], which leverages a temporal blocking methodology which can achieve a target's optimal memory bandwidth ratio well-suited for multidimensional stencil computations. Lesniak introduced a block-based wave-front synchronization technique for parallel stencil calculation [13].

6   Conclusion and Future Work

We have presented a study of a dependence-heavy application to advocate for finer-grain and hierarchical synchronization in current high-performance general purpose many-core compute nodes. Leveraging a runtime system implementation of a fine-grain event-driven execution model, we have devised several variants to study the best way to leverage fine-grain synchronization, and demonstrated that by using finer-grained synchronization, even embarrassingly parallel workloads can see their performance improve by up to 1.75× using regular work distribution among cores.

Our future work includes rewriting the original naïve OpenMP code using OpenMP 4.5's task dependence constructs, and compare the resulting performance with our own environment's. While the fine-grain variants we have presented in this paper were hand-written, most of them can be implemented in a compiler, using a syntax close or identical to OpenMP 4's. We are in the process of developing a compiler that translates OpenMP code to fine-grain event-driven tasks, and generates automatically a multi-level synchronization scheme—we believe OpenMP's programming model is enough to express parallelism, but that the Codelet Model provides a better program execution model.

Acknowledgments. This research is based upon work supported by the National Science Foundation, under awards XPS-1439165 and XPS-1439097.

References

1. Ancourt, C., Irigoin, F.: Scanning polyhedra with DO loops. SIGPLAN Not. **26**(7), 39–50 (1991)
2. Bandishti, V., Pananilath, I., Bondhugula, U.: Tiling stencil computations to maximize parallelism. In: Proceedings of the International Conference on High Performance Computing, Networking, Storage and Analysis, SC 2012. IEEE Computer Society Press, Salt Lake City (2012)
3. Barik, R., et al.: The Habanero multicore software research project. In: Proceedings of the 24th ACM SIGPLAN Conference Companion on Object Oriented Programming Systems Languages and Applications, OOPSLA 2009. ACM, Orlando (2009)
4. Bertolacci, I.J., et al.: Parameterized diamond tiling for stencil computations with chapel parallel iterators. In: Proceedings of the 29th ACM on International Conference on Supercomputing, ICS 2015. ACM, Newport Beach (2015)
5. Blumofe, R.D., et al.: Cilk: an efficient multithreaded runtime system. J. Parallel Distrib. Comput. **37**(1), 55–69 (1996)

6. OpenMP Architecture Review Board. OpenMP Application Program Interface version 4.0 (2013)
7. Christen, M., Schenk, O., Burkhart, H.: PATUS: a code generation and autotuning framework for parallel iterative stencil computations on modern microarchitectures. In: 2011 IEEE International Parallel Distributed Processing Symposium (IPDPS) (2011)
8. Dennis, J.B.: First version of a data flow procedure language. In: Robinet, B. (ed.) Programming Symposium. LNCS, vol. 19, pp. 362–376. Springer, Heidelberg (1974). doi:10.1007/3-540-06859-7_145
9. Gautier, T., et al.: XKaapi: a runtime system for data-flow task programming on heterogeneous architectures. In: 2013 IEEE 27th International Symposium on Parallel Distributed Processing (IPDPS) (2013)
10. Kamil, S., et al.: An auto-tuning framework for parallel multicore stencil computations. In: 2010 IEEE International Symposium on Parallel Distributed Processing (IPDPS) (2010)
11. Knobe, K.: Ease of use with concurrent collections (CnC). In: Hot Topics in Parallelism (2009)
12. Lauderdale, C., Khan, R.: Towards a codelet-based runtime for exascale computing: position paper. In: Proceedings of the 2nd International Workshop on Adaptive Self-Tuning Computing Systems for the Exafop Era, EXADAPT 2012. ACM, London (2012)
13. Lesniak, M.: PASTHA: parallelizing stencil calculations in Haskell. In: Proceedings of the 5th ACM SIGPLAN Workshop on Declarative Aspects of Multicore Programming, DAMP 2010. ACM, Madrid (2010)
14. Liu, C., Kulkarni, M.: Optimizing the LULESH stencil code using concurrent collections. In: Proceedings of the 5th International Workshop on Domain-Specific Languages and High-Level Frame-Works for High Performance Computing, WOLFHPC 2015. ACM, Austin (2015)
15. Mattson, T., et al.: OCR: the open community runtime interface. Technical report, June 2015. https://xstack.exascaletech.com/git/public
16. Muranushi, T., Makino, J.: Optimal temporal blocking for stencil computation. Procedia Comput. Sci. 51, 1303–1312 (2015). International Conference on Computational Science, ICCS 2015 Computational Science at the Gates of Nature
17. Schweizer, H., Besta, M., Hoefler, T.: Evaluating the cost of atomic operations on modern architectures. Technical report ETH Zurich, Department of Computer Science (2015)
18. Shrestha, S., Manzano, J., Marquez, A., Feo, J., Gao, G.R.: Jagged tiling for intratile parallelism and fine-grain multithreading. In: Brodman, J., Tu, P. (eds.) LCPC 2014. LNCS, vol. 8967, pp. 161–175. Springer, Heidelberg (2015). doi:10.1007/978-3-319-17473-0_11
19. Suettlerlein, J., Zuckerman, S., Gao, G.R.: An implementation of the codelet model. In: Wolf, F., Mohr, B., Mey, D. (eds.) Euro-Par 2013. LNCS, vol. 8097, pp. 633–644. Springer, Heidelberg (2013). doi:10.1007/978-3-642-40047-6_63
20. Tang, Y., et al.: The pochoir stencil compiler. In: Proceedings of the Twenty-Third Annual ACM Symposium on Parallelism in Algorithms and Architectures, SPAA 2011. ACM, San Jose (2011)
21. Zuckerman, S., et al.: Using a "codelet" program execution model for exascale machines: position paper. In: Proceedings of the 1st International Workshop on Adaptive Self-Tuning Computing Systems for the Exaflop Era, EXADAPT 2011. ACM, San Jose (2011)

Optimizing LOBPCG: Sparse Matrix Loop and Data Transformations in Action

Khalid Ahmad$^{(\boxtimes)}$, Anand Venkat, and Mary Hall

University of Utah, Salt Lake City, UT 84112, USA
{khalid,anandv,mhall}@cs.utah.edu
http://ctop.cs.utah.edu/ctop/

Abstract. Sparse matrix computations are widely used in iterative solvers; they are notoriously memory bound and typically yield poor performance on modern architectures. A common optimization strategy for such computations is to rely on specialized representations that exploit the nonzero structure of the sparse matrix in an application-specific way. Recent research has developed loop and data transformations for sparse matrix computations in a polyhedral compilation framework. In this paper, we apply these and additional loop transformations to a real application code, the LOBPCG solver, which performs a Sparse Matrix Multi-Vector (SpMM) computation at each iteration. The paper presents the transformation derivation for this application code and resulting performance. The compiler-generated code attains a speedup of up to 8.26× on 8 threads on an Intel Haswell and 30 GFlops; it outperforms a state-of-the-art manually-written Fortran implementation by 3%.

1 Introduction

Sparse matrix computations arise in numerous engineering and science applications. Sparse matrices are represented by data structures that store only nonzero elements, with additional auxiliary structures to identify the corresponding row and column of each element [1,2]. Consider the representative sparse matrix-vector multiplication (SpMV), a performance bottleneck in solving sparse linear systems and eigenvalue problems because it is performed hundreds or thousands of times during a single execution of an application [3]. Frequent indirection through auxiliary arrays and a lack of data reuse lead to low computational intensity, i.e. number of arithmetic operations per memory reference [4]. There is extensive prior work dealing with the development, optimization, and improving the performance of parallel SpMV kernels for both multi-core and many-core architectures, e.g. [1,3,5–9]. One common strategy is to specialize a sparse matrix representation to exploit the nonzero structure of the sparse matrix and thus reduce memory accesses and simplify the generated code. This approach usually involves using an optimized library that converts to the desired representation from a standard format such as Compressed Sparse Row (CSR) or Coordinate (COO).

© Springer International Publishing AG 2017
C. Ding et al. (Eds.): LCPC 2016, LNCS 10136, pp. 218–232, 2017.
DOI: 10.1007/978-3-319-52709-3_17

While ideally a compiler can be used to perform these optimizations and data transformations, compilers have been severely limited in their ability to optimize sparse matrix computations due to the indirection that arises in indexing and looping over just the nonzero elements. This indirection gives rise to *non-affine* subscript expressions and loop bounds; i.e., array subscripts and loop bounds are no longer linear expressions of loop indices. A common way of expressing such indirection is through *index arrays* such as, for example, array B in the expression A[B[i]]. Code generators based on polyhedra scanning are particularly restricted in the presence of non-affine loop bounds or subscripts [10–14]. As a consequence, most parallelizing compilers either give up on optimizing such computations, or apply optimizations very conservatively.

Recent work has developed non-affine support and loop and data transformations in a polyhedral transformation and code generation framework and shown to be effective in optimizing SpMV for multicores and GPUs [15]. In this paper, we demonstrate that such compiler technology can be extended so that it is suitable for the far more complex support required by real applications. We apply our compiler transformations to optimize the Locally Optimal Block Preconditioned Conjugate Gradient (LOBPCG) solver [16]. Specifically, an important kernel within LOBPCG is the sparse matrix multi-vector multiplication (SpMM), which is a generalization of the SpMV kernel in which a sparse m-by-n matrix A is multiplied by a tall and narrow dense n-by-k matrix B (k << n). SpMM is used in a variety of sparse matrix computations such as those using block Krylov subspace methods for solving several linear systems simultaneously as well as obtaining several eigen pairs of eigenvalue problems, e.g. [17–24]. Other applications that require SpMM operations include: (i) aerodynamic design optimization [25], (ii) the search engine PageRank algorithm, and (iii) atmospheric modeling [24]. A characteristic of SpMM is that arithmetic intensity is significantly higher than SpMV if access to the sparse matrix can be reused by the vectors, as clarified in Table 1. In the table, *nnz* refers to the number of nonzero elements and n is the number of columns in the sparse matrix; k is the number of dense vectors.

The remainder of the paper will demonstrate the applicability of prior loop and data transformations and the new challenges that arise in optimizing LOBPCG for very large matrices that characterize the application in which it is used [16]. The novel contributions of the paper are as follows: (1) we apply these transformations to automatically generate an inspector that produces a new matrix representation, *compressed sparse block (CSB)*, starting from a standard *compressed sparse row (CSR)*; (2) we generate an optimized SpMM,

Table 1. Arithmetic intensity of SpMV and SpMM.

	SpMV	k independent SpMV	SpMM
Flops	2 * nnz	2k * nnz	2k * nnz
Words moved	nnz + 2n	k * nnz +2k * n	nnz + 2k * n

implemented for a symmetric matrix by computing both SpMV and SpMV^T (transposed SpMV) [1]; (3) we identify additional optimizations to reduce the data movement for indexing expressions and optimize AVX SIMD execution; and, (4) we demonstrate the collection of optimizations that lead to a 3% performance gain over the manually-written state-of-the-art Fortran implementation [16].

The remainder of the paper is organized as follows. The next two sections provide background on the CSR, COO and CSB storage formats, inspector/executor, the compiler approach and the LOBPCG solver. Section 4 provides the compiler derivation of the optimized inspector and executor. We then discuss the experimental setup and provide a performance comparison of the compiler-generated code and the manual code. Section 6 discusses related work. Finally, we conclude this work with a summary of contributions and ideas for possible future work.

2   Background

The remainder of the paper relies on understanding sparse matrix storage formats based on the example dense format (Fig. 1), inspector/executor paradigm and an overview of the compiler approach, all briefly described in this section.

2.1   Storage Formats

Coordinate Storage Format (COO). COO is often used as the entry format in sparse matrix packages [1,26]. In COO, a *data* vector stores the nonzero elements of the matrix and two integer vectors, *row* and *column*, store the row and column indices of the corresponding nonzero elements in the *data* vector. Although nonzero elements and their corresponding indices can be stored in any order, they are usually stored by ascending row order. The amount of required storage is proportional to the number of nonzero elements. Figure 2 shows an example of storing a matrix using COO.

Compressed Sparse Row (CSR). Like COO, CSR (see Fig. 3) stores the nonzero elements of the matrix in a *data* array and column indices in an integer array. The third array stores pointers to the beginning of each row of the matrix in the

11	12	13	14	0	0
0	22	23	0	0	0
0	0	33	34	35	36
0	0	0	44	45	0
0	0	0	0	0	56
0	0	0	0	0	66

Fig. 1. A 6*6 example sparse matrix.

data | 11 | 12 | 13 | 14 | 22 | 23 | 33 | 34 | 35 | 36 | 44 | 45 | 56 | 66 |

row index | 0 | 0 | 0 | 0 | 1 | 1 | 2 | 2 | 2 | 2 | 3 | 3 | 4 | 5 |

column index | 0 | 1 | 2 | 3 | 1 | 2 | 2 | 3 | 4 | 5 | 3 | 4 | 5 | 5 |

Fig. 2. The COO representation.

data	11	12	13	14	22	23	33	34	35	36
							44	45	56	66

row pointer	0	4	6	10	12	13	14

column index	0	1	2	3	1	2	2	3	4	5	3	4	5	5

Fig. 3. The CSR representation.

data	11	12	22	13	14	23	33	34	44	35	36	45	56	66

blkptr	0,0	0,1	1,1	1,2	2,2

row index	0	0	1	0	0	1	0	0	1	0	0	1	0	1
column index	0	1	1	0	1	0	0	1	1	0	1	0	1	1

Fig. 4. The CSB representation.

data and *columns* arrays. The *rowpointers* array is of size N+1, where N is the number of matrix rows. The last element in the *rowpointer* array contains the total number of nonzero elements in the matrix. CSR requires less storage for row indices. In addition, the *rowpointer* array allows for easy computations of some quantities of interest for a matrix such as the number of nonzero elements in a row $i = ptr[i+1] - ptr[i]$ and the total number of nonzero elements $ptr[N+1]$.

Compressed Sparse Block (CSB). In the CSB format, matrix A is partitioned into small blocks and each block is treated as a COO matrix. CSB consists of three arrays *blkptr*, *indices*, and *data*. Array *blkptr* is a two-dimensional array storing the offset of the first nonzero of each block. The *indexarray* stores the concatenated row and column indices of nonzeros in a block; in Fig. 4, *row* and *columnindices* are shown separately. Array *data* stores nonzeros. In CSB, a row (column) of blocks is designated as a blockrow (blockcolumn).

2.2   Inspector/Executor

A general technique to analyze data accesses through index arrays and consequently reschedule or reorder data at run time employs an *inspector/executor* paradigm whereby the compiler generates *inspector* code to be executed at run-time that can collect the index expressions and then an *executor* employs specific optimizations that incorporate the run-time information [27–30]. These inspector/executor optimizations have targeted parallelization and communication [28, 31] and data reorganization [32–36].

2.3   Overview of Approach

In this paper, we employ an inspector in conjunction with data transformations to convert a symmetric matrix from CSR to CSB format, and generate an optimized, parallel executor for the CSB representation. The generation of both optimized inspector and executor is performed by the CHiLL polyhedral transformation and code generation framework. CHiLL's operations are driven by a transformation recipe which specifies the functions and loops to optimize and the transformations to apply.

Recent work has extended CHiLL to support non-affine computations that incorporate indirection through index arrays [15, 37, 38]. CHiLL is able to tolerate and maninputate non-affine loop bounds and array access expressions using the abstraction of *uninterpreted function symbols*, expanding on their use in Omega [11]. Data transformations are composed with standard and non-affine transformations in [15] to convert between matrix formats and realize optimized executors by introducing transformations used in this paper, described as follows:

- *make-dense* takes as input a set of non-affine array index expressions and introduces a guard condition and as many dense loops as necessary to replace the non-affine index expressions with affine accesses. The *make-dense* transformation enables further affine loop transforamtions such as tiling.
- *compact* and *compact-and-pad* are *inspector-executor* transformations; an automatically generated inspector gathers the iterations of a dense loop that are actually executed and the optimized executor only visits those iterations. The executor represents the transformed code that uses the compacted loop, which can then be further optimized.
- Using *compact-and-pad*, the inspector also performs a data transformation, inserting explicit zeros when necessary to correspond with the optimized executor. In this paper, *compact-and-pad* is used to reorder the data, but does not add zeros.

In the remainder of the paper, we will describe LOBPCG and then present how these transformations and others are used to derive an optimized implementation.

3   LOBPCG

LOBPCG is a subspace iteration method which starts with an initial guess about the eigenvectors and refines the guess at each iteration of the solver [16]. It is used in the Many-body Fermion Dynamics for nuclei (MFDn) application to study the structure of light nuclei. At the heart of LOBPCG lies SpMM, which multiplies a sparse matrix with multiple dense eigenvectors. Due to the very large size of the input matrix used, the symmetry of the matrix is exploited to store only half of the matrix entries to optimize for memory footprint. Since the matrix is symmetric, performing SpMM using the entire matrix is accomplished by SpMM over half of the symmetric matrix, followed by an additional transposed SpMM (SpMM^T) over the same half (Fig. 5).

```
for(i=0; i<n; i++)                    for(i=0; i<n; i++)
  for(j=index[i]; j<index[i+1]; j++)  for(j=index[i]; j<index[i+1]; j++)
    for(k=0; k<m ; k++)                 for(k=0; k<m; k++)
      y[i][k]+= A[j]*x[col[j]][k];        y[col[j]][k]+= A[j]*x[i][k];
```

(a) SpMM code using CSR format.   (b) SpMM^T code using CSR format.

Fig. 5. SpMM for symmetric matrix requires a matrix representation suitable for two separate computations.

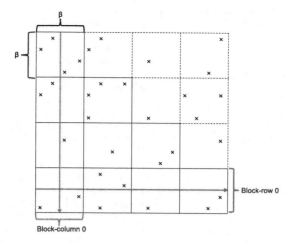

Fig. 6. Parallelization strategy using CSB format. Nonzeros are represented by crosses. Input matrix is blocked into $\beta \times \beta$ blocks. Blocks with dotted boundaries represent symmetric portion of matrix which is not stored. SpMM is parallelized by block rows, while transposed SpMM is parallelized by block columns.

SpMM can be trivially parallelized using CSR format by computing each row computation in parallel. However computing the SpMM^T in parallel using the CSR format is difficult due to write conflicts on the output vector when the row computations are parallelized. The Compressed Sparse Column (CSC) format might be ideal for parallelization of SpMM^T, but then a similar problem would arise for computing SpMM using CSC.

The CSB format solves this problem by blocking the actual matrix dimensions into square blocks of $\beta \times \beta$. It then determines the nonzeros falling in each block and stores them in the COO format in addition to storing the start and end offsets of each block. Now, SpMM can be parallelized by block rows since they do not have any write conflicts and SpMM^T can be parallelized by block column without conflicts. This strategy is illustrated in Fig. 6. Block-column-wise parallelization for SpMM^T is indicated by a vertical line while block-row-wise parallelization is indicated by a horizontal line. The tiles with dotted boundaries are actually not stored but serve to illustrate that the actual matrix is symmetric.

4   Compiler Approach

This section describes how make-dense and compact-and-pad are used to derive the parallel SpMM implementation for symmetric matrices using CSB format, which will be integrated into LOBPCG. The complete CHiLL transformation recipe is shown in Fig. 7. In this section, we focus on the effects of *make-dense*

```
source: csb_v2.c # SpMM              compact(0,[3,4],[A_prime], 0, [A])
procedure: csb
format : rose                        distribute([0,1,2,3], 1)
loop: 0                              permute(1,1,[2,1])

original()                           #OpenMP code generation
remove_dep(0,1)                      mark_omp_threads(0,[0])
fuse([0,1], 2)                       mark_omp_threads(1,[0])
split_with_alignment(0,1,4096)       mark_omp_threads(2,[0])
split_with_alignment(1,1,4096)       mark_omp_threads(3,[0])

make_dense(0,2,k)                    # simd code generation
known(lb == 0)                       mark_pragma(0,4, simd)
known(ub == 2412565)                 mark_pragma(1,4, simd)
known(n == 2412469)                  mark_pragma(2,3, simd)
                                     mark_pragma(3,3, simd)
#tile outer row and col loops by 4096
tile(0,2,4096,1,counted)             #set number of OpenMP threads
tile(0,2,4096,1,counted)             omp_par_for(1,1,8)

#normalize tiled loops               known(index_ < index__)
shift_to(0,4,0)                      known(m > 1)
shift_to(0,3,0)
```

Fig. 7. CHiLL script for SpMM based on the CSB format.

and *compact-and-pad*[1], and describe additional optimizations needed to further reduce the memory footprint and exploit SIMD execution.

4.1   Compiler-Generated Inspector to Derive CSB Representation

To expose the dense loops that correspond to the actual dimensions of the matrix, the *make-dense* transformation is firstly called on the SpMM code yielding the intermediate code shown in Fig. 8(a). Next, tiling is applied to the two outermost loops to yield the $\beta \times \beta$ blocks in CSB. Here β is the tiling factor in Fig. 8(b).

Finally *compact-and-pad* is applied to the consecutive third and fourth loop levels (i, l), which are treated as a single logical loop level. The input sparse matrix is also reorganized by compact-and-pad into a new layout reflecting the updated traversal order of the nonzeros. Additionally the *offset_index*, *expl_index_1* and *expl_index_2* arrays are populated.

The generated inspector is shown in Fig. 8(c). The offset of each $\beta \times \beta$ block into the array of nonzeros is stored in _P_DATA1. Each entry of the array _P1 corresponds to a single block, and the block's nonzeros are stored as a linked list because the size of the matrix is unknown. For each nonzero, its block is

---

[1] Both compact and compact-and-pad use variations of the CHiLL compact command; a matrix is provided as an argument for compact-and-pad.

```
for(i=0; i < n; i++)
  for(l=0; l < n; l++)
    for(j=index[i]; j < index[i+1]; j++)
      for(k=0; k < m ; k++)
        if(l == col[j])
          y[i][k]+= A[j]*x[l][k];
```

(a) SpMM after make-dense.

```
for(ii=0; ii < n/beta; ii++)
  for(ll=0; ll < n/beta; ll++)
    for(i=0; i < beta; i++)
      for(l=0; l < beta; l++)
        for(j=index[ii*beta + i]; j < index[ii*beta+i+1]; j++)
          for(k=0; k < m ; k++)
            if(ll*beta + l == col[j])
              y[ii*beta + i][k]+= A[j]*x[ll*beta + l][k];
```

(b) SpMM after tiling.

```
for (ii = 0; ii <= 587; ii += 1)
    for (ll = 0; ll <= 589; ll += 1) {
        _P1[590 * ii + ll] = 0;
        _P_DATA1[590 * ii + ll + 1] = 0;
    }
  for (ii = 0; ii <= 587; ii += 1)
    for (i = 0; i <= 4095; i += 1)
      for (j = index_(4096 * ii + i); j <= index__(4096 * ii + i) - 1; j += 1) {
        ll = (col[j] - 0) / 4096;
        l = (col[j] - 0) % 4096;
        _P_DATA5 = ((struct a_list *)(malloc(sizeof(struct a_list ) * 1)));
        _P_DATA5 -> next = _P1[590 * ii + ll];
        _P1[590 * ii + ll] = _P_DATA5;
        _P1[590 * ii + ll] -> A = 0;
        _P1[590 * ii + ll] -> col_[0] = i;
        _P1[590 * ii + ll] -> col_[1] = l;
        chill_count_1 += 1;
        _P_DATA1[590 * ii + ll + 1] += 1;
        _P1[590 * ii + ll] -> A = A[j];
    }
  for (ii = 0; ii <= 587; ii += 1) {
    if (ii <= 0) {
      _P_DATA2 = ((unsigned short *)(malloc(sizeof(unsigned short ) * chill_count_1)));
      _P_DATA3 = ((unsigned short *)(malloc(sizeof(unsigned short ) * chill_count_1)));
      A_prime = ((float *)(malloc(sizeof(float ) * chill_count_1)));
    }
    for (ll = 0; ll <= 589; ll += 1) {
      _P_DATA5 = _P1[590 * ii + ll];
      for (newVar0 = 1 - _P_DATA1[590 * ii + ll + 1]; newVar0 <= 0; newVar0 += 1) {
        _P_DATA2[_P_DATA1[590 * ii + ll] - newVar0] = _P_DATA5 -> col_[0];
        _P_DATA3[_P_DATA1[590 * ii + ll] - newVar0] = _P_DATA5 -> col_[1];
        A_prime[(_P_DATA1[590 * ii + ll] - newVar0) * 1] = _P_DATA5 -> A;
        _P_DATA5 = _P_DATA5 -> next;
      }
      _P_DATA1[590 * ii + ll + 1] += _P_DATA1[590 * ii + ll];
    }
  }
}
```

(c) SpMM generated inspector code.

Fig. 8. Steps of generating the inspector.

identified using the indices *ii* and *ll*. These indices specify the entry of _P1, whose linked list is appended with the nonzero. The row and column offsets within the block correspond to indices i and l and are stored in the linked list fields col_[0] and col_[1] respectively. The total count of nonzeros is stored in chill_count_1 and the individual nonzero count of each block is stored in the corresponding entry in _P1. Once all nonzeros have been gathered, the offset and explicit index arrays are allocated within the memory for the right size. The data is then copied from the linked list to the arrays and, the offset of each block is updated using _P_DATA1.

4.2   Optimized Executor

The effect of compact-and-pad additionally results in an optimized executor. The generated CSB code was parallelized using OpenMP directives across block rows for SpMM and block columns for SpMM^T. For transposed SpMM, the two outermost loops were permuted so that the resulting code would be traversed by block columns. A further optimization that reduced the memory footprint of index arrays was declaring the row and column index arrays, or *expl_index_1* and *expl_index_2* within a $\beta \times \beta$ block to be short data type. To detect that the size of the index array used did not exceed the maximum allocatable size with 16 bits, the loop bounds and array access expressions were queried during *compact-and-pad* to verify the maximum possible value of the array index expression.

```
#pragma omp parallel  private(ii,ll,i,k)
{
  #pragma omp for  schedule(dynamic,1)
  for(ii=0; ii < n/beta; ii++)
    for(ll=0; ll < n/beta; ll++)
      for(i=offset_index[ii][ll]; i < offset_index[ii][ll+1]; i++)
        #pragma simd
        for(k=0; k < m ; k++)
          y[ii*beta + expl_index_1[i]][k]+= A[i]*x[ll*beta + expl_index_2[i]][k];
}
```

(a) Final SpMM parallelized code.

```
#pragma omp parallel  private(ii,ll,i,k)
{
  #pragma omp for  schedule(dynamic,1)
  for(ll=0; ll < n/beta; ll++)
    for(ii=0; ii < n/beta; ii++)
      for(i=offset_index[ii][ll]; i < offset_index[ii][ll+1]; i++)
        #pragma simd
        for(k=0; k < m ; k++)
          y[ii*beta + expl_index_2[i]][k]+= A[i]*x[ll*beta + expl_index_1[i]][k];
}
```

(b) Final SpMM^T parallelized code.

Fig. 9. Optimized parallel executors.

Also, the innermost loop of SpMM does not carry a dependence, and is data parallel, and hence is parallelized with the SIMD pragma annotation for further performance benefits. The pragma annotation is supplied via the transformation interface with the loop level for the annotation, and the code generator inserts the pragma at this loop level. The final parallelized codes for SpMM and $SpMM^T$, containing SIMD pragmas are shown in Fig. 9.

5 Experimental Evaluation

In this section, we measure performance of the generated combined SpMM and $SpMM^T$ executor code, and compare its performance to the manual FORTRAN implementation in [16].

5.1 Methodology

The experiments were performed on an Intel i7-4770 (Haswell) CPU with 256 KB L1 cache, 1 MB L2 cache, 8 MB L3 cache, and 32 GB of memory. The clock rate is 3.40 GHz frequency, with 4 physical cpu cores and 8 threads. The Intel version 15.0.0 compilers were used: the Fortran compiler for the manual code and the C compiler for the generated code.

Because our goal is to examine performance in the context of realistic engineering and scientific problems that are used by MFDn, we consider large matrices arising from the finite element discretization. Half of our application specific test sparse matrix is generated by the original Fortan code in [16]. The matrix has 2412469 rows, 2412566 columns and contains 429895762 nonzero elements stored in single precision to reduce the total size of the file, which makes it easier to handle and less time-consuming to read during program execution.

To obtain reliable timing measurements, each computation is run 100 times, and the median value is recorded. The initialization of the codes are not included in the timings as in a real world situation the environment can be set up once and then reused for a large number of calculations. Performance in GFLOPs can be calculated using the following equation, where nnz is number of nonzeros, nvd is the number of dense vectors, and t is execution time in seconds.

$$GFLOPs = (nnz * 4 * nvd)/(t * 10^9)$$

5.2 Performance Measurements

We show the performance in two ways. In Fig. 10, we examine performance as a function of the number of dense vectors and threads using a beta value of 4096. We used a number of different dense vectors $= \{1, 4, 8, 12, 16, 24, 32, 48, 64, 80, 96\}$ and a number of threads $= \{1, 2, 4, 6, 8, 10\}$. As k increases, we see a significant performance improvement which benefits from parallelization up until about $k = 16$, and then the reuse becomes difficult to fully exploit. For larger values of k, the best performance is achieved on fewer threads.

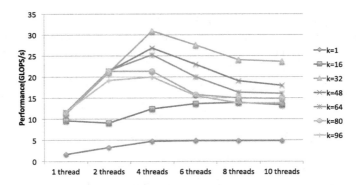

Fig. 10. Performance in GFLOPs of generated implementations for varying numbers of dense vectors and threads.

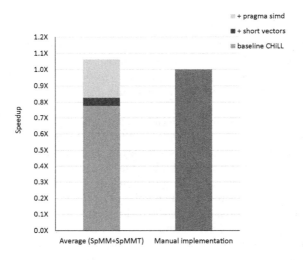

Fig. 11. Speedup attributed to different optimizations in the generated code as compared to the manually-written Fortran code.

Figure 11 shows the increase in speedup due to using each optimization from the previous section. We used a fixed blocking factor 4096 in this graph and compute an average speedup from the results of the previous section. The baseline generated code achieves only 0.77× of the performance of the manual Fortran code. By using 16-bit indices for the row and column index arrays (short vector), and inserting the SIMD pragma, the compiler is able to achieve even better performance than the original Fortran code, a speedup of 1.03×. We attribute this difference to simplifications in the indexing that arise in the compiler implementation.

6   Related Work

The majority of literature describes optimized SpMV implementations and strategies targeting different architectures. However, work on SpMM and SpMM^T is not as prevalent.

6.1   Application-Specific Approaches

Applications such as biconjugate and quasi-minimal residual iterative linear solvers require computing both SpMV and SpMV^T (transposed SpMV) [1]. Generally this problem is solved by transposing the sparse matrix and then performing regular SpMV, and, intuitively this is expensive in space and data movement. Buluc et al. developed the CSB storage format to compute SpMV and SpMV^T at the same time and requires similar storage to CSR or CSC [39]. This representation was then used as part of parallel SpMM and SpMM^T by Aktulga et al. [16].

6.2   Compiler Approaches

Some compiler approaches begin with a dense abstraction of a sparse matrix computation; these compilers then generate sparse data representations during code generation, placing a burden on the compiler to optimize away the sometimes orders of magnitude difference in performance between dense and sparse implementations [40–42]. To our knowledge, the only prior compiler approach that starts with a sparse computation and derives new sparse matrix representations is that of Wijshoff et al. [43]. They convert code with indirect array accesses and loop bounds into dense loops that can then be converted into sparse matrix code using the MT1 compiler [44,45].

7   Conclusion and Future Work

This paper demonstrated the effectiveness of compiler-generated code for SpMM, when used in the context of the LOBPCG solver on a real-world scientific application at the scale of a problem that fits on a single socket. The key finding is that compiler-generated C code can outperform manual code written in Fortran. We discovered the importance of 16-bit index arrays and AVX SIMD execution to match the manual code's performance. We found out that the performance benefits when using multiple vectors trails off when the vector becomes too large.

As a continuation of this work, we are exploring the generation of CUDA code, which was not attempted by the application developers. Our future work also includes comparing against the extended CSB implementation for GPUs described in [46] to our implementation.

References

1. Saad, Y.: Iterative Methods for Sparse Linear Systems. SIAM, Philadelphia (2003)
2. Montagne, E., Ekambaram, A.: An optimal storage format for sparse matrices. Inf. Process. Lett. **90**(2), 87–92 (2004)
3. Bell, N., Garland, M.: Implementing sparse matrix-vector multiplication on throughput-oriented processors. In: Proceedings of the Conference on High Performance Computing Networking, Storage and Analysis, p. 18. ACM (2009)
4. Im, E.-J., Yelick, K.A.: Optimizing the Performance of Sparse Matrix-Vector Multiplication. University of California, Berkeley (2000)
5. Anzt, H., Tomov, S., Dongarra, J.: Implementing a sparse matrix vector product for the sell-C/sell-C-σ formats on NVIDIA GPUs
6. Kreutzer, M., Hager, G., Wellein, G., Fehske, H., Bishop, A.R.: A unified sparse matrix data format for modern processors with wide SIMD units (2013). arXiv preprint arXiv:1307.6209
7. Lowell, D., Godwin, J., Holewinski, J., Karthik, D., Choudary, C., Mametjanov, A., Norris, B., Sabin, G., Sadayappan, P., Sarich, J.: Stencil-aware GPU optimization of iterative solvers. SIAM J. Sci. Comput. **35**(5), S209–S228 (2013)
8. Choi, J.W., Singh, A., Vuduc, R.W.: Model-driven autotuning of sparse matrix-vector multiply on GPUs. ACM SIGPLAN Not. **45**(5), 115–126 (2010)
9. Williams, S., Bell, N., Choi, J., Garland, M., Oliker, L., Vuduc, R.: Sparse matrix-vector multiplication on multicore and accelerators. In: Scientific Computing with Multicore and Accelerators, pp. 83–109 (2010)
10. Ancourt, C., Irigoin, F.: Scanning polyhedra with DO loops. In: ACM SIGPLAN Symposium on Principles and Practice of Parallel Programming, April 1991
11. Kelly, W.A.: Optimization within a unified transformation framework. Ph.D. dissertation, University of Maryland, December 1996
12. Quilleré, F., Rajopadhye, S.: Generation of efficient nested loops from polyhedra. Int. J. Parallel Program. **28**(5), 469–498 (2000)
13. Vasilache, N., Bastoul, C., Cohen, A.: Polyhedral code generation in the real world. In: Proceedings of the 15th International Conference on Compiler Construction, March 2006
14. Chen, C.: Polyhedra scanning revisited. In: Proceedings of the 33rd ACM SIGPLAN Conference on Programming Language Design and Implementation, PLDI 2012, pp. 499–508, June 2012
15. Venkat, A., Hall, M., Strout, M.: Loop and data transformations for sparse matrix code. In: Proceedings of the 36th ACM SIGPLAN Conference on Programming Language Design and Implementation (2015)
16. Aktulga, H.M., Buluc, A., Williams, S., Yang, C.: Optimizing sparse matrix-multiple vectors multiplication for nuclear configuration interaction calculations. In: 2014 IEEE 28th International Parallel and Distributed Processing Symposium, pp. 1213–1222. IEEE (2014)
17. Yamazaki, I., Dong, T., Solcà, R., Tomov, S., Dongarra, J., Schulthess, T.: Tridiagonalization of a dense symmetric matrix on multiple GPUs and its application to symmetric eigenvalue problems. Concurr. Comput.: Pract. Exp. **26**(16), 2652–2666 (2013)
18. Yamazaki, I., Tadano, H., Sakurai, T., Ikegami, T.: Performance comparison of parallel eigensolvers based on a contour integral method and a Lanczos method. Parallel Comput. **39**(6), 280–290 (2013)

19. Campos, C., Roman, J.E.: Strategies for spectrum slicing based on restarted Lanczos methods. Numer. Algorithms **60**(2), 279–295 (2012)
20. Meerbergen, K., Vandebril, R.: A reflection on the implicitly restarted Arnoldi method for computing eigenvalues near a vertical line. Linear Algebra Appl. **436**(8), 2828–2844 (2012)
21. Morgan, R.B., Nicely, D.A.: Restarting the nonsymmetric Lanczos algorithm for eigenvalues and linear equations including multiple right-hand sides. SIAM J. Sci. Comput. **33**(5), 3037–3056 (2011)
22. Jiang, W., Wu, G.: A thick-restarted block Arnoldi algorithm with modified Ritz vectors for large eigenproblems. Comput. Math. Appl. **60**(3), 873–889 (2010)
23. Baker, A.H., Dennis, J.M., Jessup, E.R.: On improving linear solver performance: a block variant of GMRES. SIAM J. Sci. Comput. **27**(5), 1608–1626 (2006)
24. Bai, Z., Demmel, J., Dongarra, J., Ruhe, A., van der Vorst, H.: Templates for the Solution of Algebraic Eigenvalue Problems: A Practical Guide, vol. 11. SIAM, Philadelphia (2000)
25. Pinel, X., Montagnac, M.: Block Krylov methods to solve adjoint problems in aerodynamic design optimization. AIAA J. **51**(9), 2183–2191 (2013)
26. Bell, N., Garland, M.: Efficient sparse matrix-vector multiplication on CUDA. Nvidia technical report NVR-2008-004, Nvidia Corporation (2008)
27. Mirchandaney, R., Saltz, J.H., Smith, R.M., Nico, D.M., Crowley, K.: Principles of runtime support for parallel processors. In: Proceedings of the 2nd International Conference on Supercomputing, pp. 140–152 (1988)
28. Rauchwerger, L., Padua, D.: The LRPD test: speculative run-time parallelization of loops with privatization and reduction parallelization. In: Proceedings of the ACM SIGPLAN Conference on Programming Language Design and Implementation, PLDI 1995 (1995)
29. Ravishankar, M., Eisenlohr, J., Pouchet, L.-N., Ramanujam, J., Rountev, A., Sadayappan, P.: Code generation for parallel execution of a class of irregular loops on distributed memory systems. In: Proceedings of SC 2012, November 2012
30. Basumallik, A., Eigenmann, R.: Optimizing irregular shared-memory applications for distributed-memory systems. In: Proceedings of the Symposium on Principles and Practice of Parallel Programming (2006)
31. Saltz, J., Chang, C., Edjlali, G., Hwang, Y.-S., Moon, B., Ponnusamy, R., Sharma, S., Sussman, A., Uysal, M., Agrawal, G., Das, R., Havlak, P.: Programming irregular applications: runtime support, compilation and tools. Adv. Comput. **45**, 105–153 (1997)
32. Ding, C., Kennedy, K.: Improving cache performance in dynamic applications through data, computation reorganization at run time. In: Proceedings of the ACM SIGPLAN Conference on Programming Language Design, Implementation, pp. 229–241. ACM, New York, May 1999
33. Mitchell, N., Carter, L., Ferrante, J.: Localizing non-affine array references. In: Proceedings of the International Conference on Parallel Architectures and Compilation Techniques (PACT), pp. 192–202, October 1999
34. Mellor-Crummey, J., Whalley, D., Kennedy, K.: Improving memory hierarchy performance for irregular applications using data and computation reorderings. Int. J. Parallel Program. **29**(3), 217–247 (2001)
35. Han, H., Tseng, C.-W.: Exploiting locality for irregular scientific codes. IEEE Trans. Parallel Distrib. Syst. **17**(7), 606–618 (2006)

36. Wu, B., Zhao, Z., Zhang, E.Z., Jiang, Y., Shen, X.: Complexity analysis and algorithm design for reorganizing data to minimize non-coalesced memory accesses on GPU. In: Proceedings of the 18th ACM SIGPLAN Symposium on Principles and Practice of Parallel Programming PPoPP 2013 (2013)
37. Venkat, A., Shantharam, M., Hall, M., Strout, M.M.: Non-affine extensions to polyhedral code generation. In: Proceedings of Annual IEEE/ACM International Symposium on Code Generation and Optimization, CGO 2014 (2014)
38. Kaleem, R., Venkat, A., Pai, S., Hall, M., Pingali, K.: Synchronization trade-offs in GPU implementations of graph algorithms. In: 30th IEEE International Parallel and Distributed Processing Symposium (2016)
39. Buluç, A., Fineman, J.T., Frigo, M., Gilbert, J.R., Leiserson, C.E.: Parallel sparse matrix-vector and matrix-transpose-vector multiplication using compressed sparse blocks. In: Proceedings of the Twenty-First Annual Symposium on Parallelism in Algorithms and Architectures, pp. 233–244. ACM (2009)
40. Bik, A., Wijshoff, H.A.: Advanced compiler optimizations for sparse computations. In: Supercomputing 1993 Proceedings, pp. 430–439, November 1993
41. Pugh, W., Shpeisman, T.: SIPR: a new framework for generating efficient code for sparse matrix computations. In: Proceedings of the Eleventh International Workshop on Languages and Compilers for Parallel Computing, August 1998
42. Mateev, N., Pingali, K., Stodghill, P., Kotlyar, V.: Next-generation generic programming and its application to sparse matrix computations. In: Proceedings of the 14th International Conference on Supercomputing, Santa Fe, New Mexico, USA, pp. 88–99, May 2000
43. Spek, H.L.A., Wijshoff, H.A.G.: Sublimation: expanding data structures to enable data instance specific optimizations. In: Cooper, K., Mellor-Crummey, J., Sarkar, V. (eds.) LCPC 2010. LNCS, vol. 6548, pp. 106–120. Springer, Heidelberg (2011). doi:10.1007/978-3-642-19595-2_8
44. Bik, A.J.C., Wijshoff, H.A.G.: On automatic data structure selection and code generation for sparse computations. In: Banerjee, U., Gelernter, D., Nicolau, A., Padua, D. (eds.) LCPC 1993. LNCS, vol. 768, pp. 57–75. Springer, Heidelberg (1994). doi:10.1007/3-540-57659-2_4
45. Bik, A.J.C., Wijsho, H.A.G.: Automatic data structure selection and transformation for sparse matrix computations. IEEE Trans. Parallel Distrib. Syst. $7(2)$, 109–126 (1996)
46. Tao, Y., Deng, Y., Mu, S., Zhang, Z., Zhu, M., Xiao, L., Ruan, L.: GPU accelerated sparse matrix-vector multiplication and sparse matrix-transpose vector multiplication. Concurr. Comput.: Practice Exp. $27(14)$, 3771–3789 (2015)

GPUs and Private Memory

LightHouse: An Automatic Code Generator for Graph Algorithms on GPUs

G. Shashidhar[✉] and Rupesh Nasre[✉]

IIT Madras, Chennai, India
{shashi,rupesh}@cse.iitm.ac.in

Abstract. We propose LightHouse, a GPU code-generator for a graph language named Green-Marl for which a multicore CPU backend already exists. This allows a user to seamlessly generate both the multicore as well as the GPU backends from the same specification of a graph algorithm. This restriction of not modifying the language poses several challenges as we work with an existing abstract syntax tree of the language, which is not tailored to GPUs. LightHouse overcomes these challenges with various optimizations such as reducing the number of atomics and collapsing loops. We illustrate its effectiveness by generating efficient CUDA codes for four graph analytic algorithms, and comparing performance against their multicore OpenMP versions generated by Green-Marl. In particular, our generated CUDA code performs comparable to 4 to 64-threaded OpenMP versions for different algorithms.

1 Introduction

Processing big graphs in a reasonable time requires huge computing power as well as ability to perform operations in parallel. Unfortunately, graph algorithms are notoriously difficult to optimize and parallelize. The main source of difficulty in graph algorithms stems from a technicality called *irregularity*. Graph algorithms are irregular because their memory access, control-flow and communication patterns cannot be predicted at compile time (as they depend upon the nature of the input graph, which is unavailable during compilation).

In the last decade, we made a substantial progress in understanding graphs and their access patterns in various algorithms. It has been shown that graph algorithms indeed have a good amount of parallelism [8]. However, the analysis and the parallelization techniques developed for *regular* programs (such as dense matrix algebra) need not be best suited for graph-based computation [15]. Graph algorithms are more amenable to dynamic processing, rather than compile-time static processing performed for regular programs.

Over the years, researchers have optimized parallel graph processing for multi-cores [9,10,19], GPUs [3,13], CPU clusters [1,12], and for heterogeneous combination of these [5]. However, several of these codes can only be used and modified by experts alone. Domain experts from various fields such as astronomy, physics, chemistry and biological sciences, who are not experts in high-performance computing, often cannot directly utilize the proposed techniques.

© Springer International Publishing AG 2017
C. Ding et al. (Eds.): LCPC 2016, LNCS 10136, pp. 235–249, 2017.
DOI: 10.1007/978-3-319-52709-3_18

One of the interesting approaches to allow non-experts to program in a domain is using domain-specific languages (DSLs). DSLs have been quite successful in various fields, such as matrix computations using MATLAB, string processing using regular expressions, and statistical processing using R. In a similar spirit, DSLs have been developed for graph algorithms with a hope for non-experts to achieve reasonable performance without worrying about the intricacies of the hardware platform or parallel execution. Unfortunately, graph DSLs are currently limited to one type of platform. For instance, a graph DSL Green-Marl [6] has a backend to generate code for multi-core CPUs, but is unsuitable for GPUs. Efficient code-generation for GPUs is challenging due to separate memories of CPUs and discrete GPUs (variables need to be defined, copied and accessed appropriately in the generated code), GPUs being more suitable for hierarchical computation spanning individual thread, warps, thread-blocks and GPU threads (the compiler should be able to identify scenarios where such a hierarchical code can be generated), lack of logical locks (which are routine in CPU libraries), and generating code for various data structures using arrays and offsets rather than pointers. We highlight and address these challenges in this work. Following are our main contributions.

- We create a GPU backend for a graph DSL. In this process, we exploit various architectural features of the GPU, and develop techniques to map the high-level language constructs to efficient backend processing. While we use CUDA as the target language, the techniques developed are general enough to be applicable to other GPU languages as well.
- To reduce the learning curve for a programmer, we use the language specification of an existing DSL called Green-Marl, instead of developing a new language. Green-Marl already has an OpenMP backend for multi-core execution. This also provides us with an opportunity to compare the efficiency of LightHouse-generated GPU code with a well-optimized CPU backend.
- We overcome several GPU-centric challenges (separate memories, hierarchical computation, SIMD execution, etc.) by optimizing the abstract syntax tree, and illustrate the efficacy of our compiler by generating four graph algorithms: computing bipartite matchings, finding single-source shortest paths, computing page-rank, and calculating conductance of a graph. Our experimental evaluation reveals that the performance of the generated CUDA code considerably varies compared to that of the multi-core CPU version (comparable to 4 to 64-threaded OMP version), but overall, provides a productive way to generate code for GPUs.[1]

2   Green-Marl Language Specification

In this section we introduce the constructs of the Green-Marl language. Green-Marl has constructs that can be used to describe many graph analytic algorithms. The language does not allow graph mutation, that is, the graphs are static. It

---

[1] LightHouse code is available at http://pace.cse.iitm.ac.in/tools.php.

supports basic types such as nodes and edges as well as operations on collections (such as a set of nodes or a sequence).

Algorithms in Green-Marl have a single procedure with input graph as argument along with the properties defined on the nodes and the edges of the graph. The procedure returns a value or a property. The basic data types such as int, bool, float are supported as property types. Nodes and Edges are also supported as basic collection types in Green-Marl. To access individual elements in the collections, Green-Marl supports iterators. In particular, it provides node and edge iterators to navigate the graph. The order in which the graph elements are traversed is decided by the collection type (a set or a sequence).

```
1   Procedure triangle_counting(G: Graph): Long // Return value type
2   {
3       Long T;
4       Foreach(v: G.Nodes) {
5         Foreach(u: v.Nbrs) (u > v) {
6           Foreach(w: v.Nbrs) (w > u) {
7             If ((w.HasEdgeTo(u))) {
8               T = 0;
9             }
10          }
11        }
12      }
13      Return T;
14  }
```

One of the advantages of the Green-Marl syntax is that most of the code is sequential, which is very intuitive for the programmer. Parallelism is implicitly specified using a foreach construct. Combined with iterators, the foreach loop allows a compiler to assign tasks to different processing workers (iterations mapped to threads). Green-Marl follow the fork-join style of parallel execution.

At line 4 of triangle_counting procedure, a set of parallel executions is created starting the execution of the loop-body. At line 5, each running parallel execution creates more parallel executions and waits for their completion at line 11. Each of the outer parallel executions continues after line 11 and exits at line 13. The scope of the iterators used inside a foreach statement is only within the statement body.

The parallel execution style of Green-Marl has data races on the location read from and written to concurrently. Green-Marl provides *reduction* statements to provide determinism on some operations.

```
1   reducedValue += expr;
```

expr values computed by all the parallel executions are reduced to reducedValue such that the result would be the same as computed sequentially. The reduction operation can be +, *, min, max, bitwise AND and OR. reducedValue should be read only after all the parallel executions have finished the execution of the reduction statement. Node and Edge properties can also be reduced.

```
1   Foreach(n: G.Nodes)
2       Foreach(t: n.Nbrs)
3           n.A += t.B;
```

The property B is reduced into property A. The frontend of the Green-Marl provides syntax checking to identify any conflicts in the locations being read in expr and written to in reducedValue. In addition to the normal reduction statement, Green-Marl provides constructs to gather values in the context which minimized or maximized the expression.

Output of the Green-Marl compiler *gm_comp* is a C++ code annotated with OpenMP pragmas. This code needs to be compiled with another code containing the main entry point to generate the final application.

Green-Marl Frontend: The front end provides the syntax checks and parallel semantics checks, and generates an Abstract Syntax Tree (AST). The higher level description of the program helps in identifying possible problems in the parallel program semantics like data-races. For instance, consider this code:

```
1    Node_Prop<Int> A;  // node property
2    Foreach(n: G.Nodes)
3       Foreach(t: n.Nbrs)
4          n.A = t.A;
```

At line 4, the iterators t and n are used to update the node property A. The property A is written through iterator n and read through iterator t. At this point, there is no guarantee that n and t could not create a data conflict on A; that is, n in one thread and t in another may refer to the same node leading to a race. The frontend analysis finds that at line 3, iterator t is defined on n's neighbors. The analysis reduces iterator t to random access along n. At this point there is a write by n and the random access read by reduction from t. A data conflict exists between iterator t and n on the node property A. The compiler issues errors on identifying such conflicts. After parsing and checking of the input specification, the front end generates an AST representing various constructs defined in the Green-Marl language.

Green-Marl Optimizations: A set of architecture independent transformations is applied on the AST: (i) Perform loop fusion which combines two foreach loops that have the same type of iterator and no loop-carried dependence. (ii) Combine assignments that are running on the same iterator type into a single parallel loop. (iii) Hoist the temporary property definition out of the sequential loop to save the repeated allocations and deallocations. (iv) Convert the reduction inside a sequential loop to a normal assignment. (v) Move a reduction to the outermost parallel loop just after the definition/declaration of the target symbol. If there is no such loop then the compiler converts the reduction to a normal assignment. The output of this phase is a modified AST which is transformed by the above mentioned optimizations.

Green-Marl Backend: The existing backend currently generates OpenMP code for multi-core CPU processing. The backend traverses the AST and generates parallel for construct for the outermost foreach loop. For single value reductions, atomic construct is utilized, while for multi-value assignments, a lock-based code gets generated. Note that generating such a lock-based code for GPUs is not an option due to inefficient execution of locks in the presence of hundreds of thousands of threads. Further, reductions on GPUs can be accomplished by a hierarchical computation across warps and threads-blocks. This demands careful management of cooperation across threads. Finally, the generated C++ procedure may contain temporary as well as global variables. Temporaries get converted to thread-local variables, while global variables can be directly accessed by OpenMP threads. However, in CUDA, the globals from CPU are not directly accessible on GPUs (unless unified memory is used for storing data). This demands identifying the locations of variables' access as well as their definitions. If the two devices are different, the compiler needs to insert code to explicitly transfer such variables across the two devices.

3   GPU Code Generation

This section presents the challenges that LightHouse faces for efficient GPU code-generation of the Green-Marl language specification. Apart from translating the usual constructs, LightHouse primarily involves four subtasks, which we discuss in the following subsections.

3.1   Identifying Parallel Regions

This phase selects the part of the code to be run on the GPU. The Foreach construct specifies parallelism implicitly. LightHouse generates a kernel corresponding to the parallel loop. Only the outermost Foreach is selected to be run on the GPU in parallel. For instance, for the code shown in Fig. 1, the outer Foreach on line 6 gets converted to a kernel which contains the body of the loop. Thus, loop iterations are executed by concurrently running threads. The inner Foreach on line 7, on the other hand, gets compiled into a sequential for loop executed by each thread within its kernel code.

```
1   Procedure Test (G: Graph,
2       A: N_P<Int>, root: Node) {
3
4       N_P<Int> B;
5       Int rootValue;
6       Foreach (n: G.Nodes) {
7           Foreach (s: n.Nbrs) {
8               n.B = n.A + s.A;
9           }
10      }
11      rootValue = root.B;
12  }
```

Symbol	Type	Parent	Allocate in
G	Graph		GPU
A	NP< Int >		GPU
B	NP< Int >		GPU
n	Node::I	G	GPU
s	Node::I	n → G	GPU
root	Node		CPU
rootValue	Int		CPU

Fig. 1. Green-Marl example

Fig. 2. Symbol table for the program in Fig. 1

3.2   Identifying Variable Location

Unlike in the CPU backend, LightHouse needs to identify the variable location (whether on CPU or GPU). This is decided by a static pass which relies on a *use-def* analysis to find out the variables read and written to at different instructions in the program. LightHouse maintains a symbol table which is populated with variables and their type information. All the variables inside the parallel regions have to be accessible to the GPU. These variables are allocated in the GPU (global) memory. Variables of primitive data types can be passed as parameters to the kernel. Variables that need to be in the GPU memory are marked to have a *GPU Scope*. In addition, a variable written in the GPU kernel but used in the CPU code needs to be transferred to the CPU. For instance, Fig. 2 shows the symbol table for the Green-Marl program in Fig. 1. The variables accessed inside the foreach loop at line 6 need to be accessed in the GPU. This includes Graph G, Node properties A and B, and Node iterators n and s. The iterator n traverses all the nodes of G, and s traverses the neighbors of those nodes.

Each outermost `foreach` loop defines a new *scope* for the GPU. All the variables accessed in the `foreach` loop have to be declared and defined inside the GPU scope. Node and Edge properties are converted to arrays. These arrays are allocated space in GPU's global memory and are sent as kernel launch parameters. Temporary variables used inside the foreach loops are declared inside the kernel and are added to the lexicographic scope of the kernel. Variables which are defined and used outside the kernel are added to the CPU (Global) scope.

For the variables in the Global scope that are also accessed inside the foreach loop, LightHouse creates a copy in the GPU Global memory. It modifies the variable accesses inside the kernel to the corresponding copies in the GPU scope.

3.3 Generating Indices for Memory Accesses

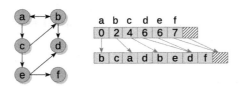

Fig. 3. Graph in CSR format

The input graph is stored in Compressed Sparse Row Format (CSR) which consists of two arrays (another array for weights). The row array R has the adjacency list of all the nodes in the graph. The column array C has the indices into the row array for the starting index of the adjacency list for each node. Figure 3 shows an example graph in the CSR format. For each iterator the index pattern based on the CSR format needs to be generated for CUDA threads. The parent information of the iterator in the symbol table is used to generate the index values.

For instance, consider the code snippet: Foreach(n: G. **Nodes**)... In this code, n is an iterator on all the nodes in the graph. Running this `foreach` loop in a fully parallel manner on GPU assigns one node to each CUDA thread. The corresponding index pattern generated is as follows.

```
1   n = threadID ;
2   if (n > numNodes)
3      return ;
```

Here n is the node id being processed by a thread, derived from the unique id threadID of the thread, computed in CUDA as blockIdx.x * blockDim.x + threadIdx.x. Similarly for the pattern below,

```
1   Foreach (n: G.Nodes)
2     Foreach (s: n.Nbrs)
3       ...
```

the inner **foreach** loop is converted into a sequential loop. Iterator **s** goes over all the neighbors of **n**. The generated code is:

```
1   n = threadID;
2   if (n > numNodes)
3     return;
4   for (i = C[n]; i < C[n+1]; i++) {
5     s = R[i];
6     ...
```

Similar patterns are defined for in/out neighbors and in/out edge iterators.

3.4   Generating Code for Reduction Statements

Green-Marl provides min, max, add, mult, or, and, inc reduction constructs.
LightHouse converts these reduction operations to atomic operations on GPU.

```
1   Int T = 0;
2   Node src, dst;
3   Foreach (s: G.Nodes)
4     Foreach (t: s.Nbrs)
5       T<src, dst> max= s.A + t.A<s, t>;
```

The assignment at line 5 performs a max-reduction of the expression s.A + t.A to variable T and assigns the corresponding node ids to src and dst.

```
1    int T = 0;
2    GPUMemCpy(GPU_T, T, HostToDevice);
3    KernelCall<<<LaunchPara>>>(C, R, A);
4    GPUMemCpy(from, GPU_from, DeviceToHost);
5    GPUMemCpy(to, GPU_to, DeviceToHost);
6
7
8    KernelCall(C, R, A) {
9      s = threadID;
10     if(s > NumNodes)
11       return;
12     for(i = C[n]; i < C[n + 1]; i++) {
13       t = R[i];
14       expr = s.A + t.A;
15       atomicMax(&GPU_T, expr);
16       if(localExpr < expr) {
17         localExpr = expr;
18         localFrom = s;
19         localTo = t;
20       }
21     }
22     SoftwareBarrier();
23     if(localExpr == GPU_T)
24       chooseThread = threadID;
25     SoftwareBarrier();
26     if(chooseThread == threadID) {
27       GPU_from = localFrom;
28       GPU_to = localTo;
29     }
30   }
```

Fig. 4. Code for multiple atomic assignment

The language definition of Green-Marl demands evaluation of line 5 in an atomic manner. That is, assignments to T, src and dst must be seen by other threads as happening together. We call its type as *multiple atomic assignment statement*. On CPUs, the Green-Marl OpenMP backend uses logical locks to implement multiple atomic assignments. CUDA neither has a support for such a statement type, nor is it feasible to use locks in the presence of hundreds of thousands of concurrent threads. For efficiency, we implement such reductions using software barrier and atomics. Figure 4 shows the CUDA code generated for *multiple atomic assignment statement*. All the threads store the expression to be reduced (line 14) and perform an atomic minimum (or maximum) on the target global value (line 15). If the new expression value is lesser (respectively, larger) than the previously computed value, then the values of the sub-expressions are stored into local variables (line 17–19). All the threads synchronize at the end of the `foreach` loop (line 22) and compare their individual local copies of reduction expressions with the reduced value. Threads having the same value are the potential threads which might have written the reduced value. According to the language semantics, one of these potential threads must assign the reduced value. All the potential threads write their `threadID` to a unique location (line 24) and only one of the writes gets reflected at the end. This thread is chosen to write its value of local sub-expressions to the global value (lines 26–28). This ensures that only one of the potential threads which had reduced the value to its minimum/maximum also writes the corresponding sub-expressions to the global location.

Lines 22 and 25 use a call to `SoftwareBarrier()` which implements a global barrier across all the threads on the GPU. A global barrier is a synchronization primitive that guarantees that all threads from all the thread-blocks belonging to a kernel reach a specific point in the code before any thread may progress beyond that point. CUDA supports a barrier at the thread-block level (`syncthreads`). However, a global barrier (across thread blocks) needs to be emulated in software. We implement it without using atomics [13, 21].

4   Program Optimizations

In this section we present three important GPU-specific optimizations that are implemented in `LightHouse` to improve the performance of the generated CUDA code. The optimizations work with the control-flow graph and the def-use chains.

4.1   Eliminating Atomics

Reduction of a boolean value can be implemented without using atomics by initializing a value to the reduction variable and set the variable based on the condition. As only one thread is enough to change the value of the reduction variable, subsequent reduction does not change the semantics of the program.

```
atomicOr(&A, val);              atomicAnd(&A, val);
becomes                         becomes
// initialized outside kernel   // initialized outside kernel
A = false;                      A = true;
....                            ....
if (val) A = true;              if (!val) A = false;
```

In the above translated code, there is a data race on A, but the threads participating in the race set A to the same value. So, the race is benign. In case of multiple assignment statement, a sub-expression of type boolean can be assigned similar to the above code without using the software barriers. This gets rid of the limitation of the software barrier which demands all threads participating in the barrier to be resident (which reduces concurrency).

4.2   Loop Collapsing

Typical implementations of graph algorithms are *vertex-centric*, that is, a vertex is assigned to a thread and the thread operates on all its neighbors. When the input graph's degree-distribution is rather uniform, as in road networks, a vertex-centric algorithm assigns almost equal amount of work per thread. However, for a graph with skewed degree-distribution, as in social networks, a vertex-centric algorithm suffers from high load-imbalance [2,22]. The problem is exacerbated on GPUs as warp-threads execute in SIMD fashion. One way to remove the load imbalance is to make the algorithm *edge-centric*, that is, transform the traversal on neighbors of all the nodes to traversal on all the edges. One thread is assigned to work on one edge which creates evenly balanced workload and hence improved parallelism. In CSR representation of the graph, each thread accesses contiguous memory locations on the edge list. CUDA combines such contiguous memory accesses from a warp into a single global memory access (called as memory coalescing). This increases the memory bandwidth of the process and results in better performance.

		Foreach(e:G.**Edges**) {
Foreach(s:G.**Nodes**)	becomes	s = e.FromNode();
Foreach(t:s.**Nbrs**)		t = e.ToNode();

From Green-Marl language perspective, such a transformation can be depicted as shown on the above. In this code, *FromNode* and *ToNode* are API that return end-points of an edge. Such an approach needs an array of edges rather than the CSR format. However, converting a vertex-centric algorithm to an edge-centric version may change synchronization requirements. For instance, in a *pull-based* implementation a thread operating on a vertex reads-in attributes from its in-neighbors and updates the current vertex's attribute. In such an approach, each vertex is being written to by only one thread, and hence threads need not synchronize their writes. However, when such a pull-based implementation is combined with edge-centric version, single-writer guarantee cannot be enforced, necessitating synchronization. Typically, for simple attributes (such as distance of a vertex or pagerank value), an atomic instruction suffices for correct execution (e.g., atomicMin for the shortest paths computation).

4.3   Full Device Occupancy

We also studied the effect of occupancy in the context of graph algorithms, by generating codes with full-occupancy and otherwise. We observed in our experiments that although occupancy is useful, its effect is limited in the case of graph algorithms and gets overshadowed by other effects such as launch configuration, memory coalescing, and thread-divergence.

4.4   Limitations of LightHouse

Although our code generator is automated, it can be improved in multiple aspects, such as generating code for heterogeneous systems, supporting graph mutation (would need changes in the language), reducing synchronization among threads, and optimizations using GPU shared memory.

5   Experimental Evaluation

We added a CUDA backend to Green-Marl to read the AST and generate GPU code as detailed in the previous sections. Thus, for the same graph algorithm specification, we are now able to generate both OpenMP as well as CUDA codes. This allows us to faithfully compare the performances of the generated programs.

Table 1. Benchmark graphs and baseline performance

Graph	#Nodes (millions)	#Edges (millions)	OpenMP 1-thread (in msec)				
			MATCH	SSSP	COND	PAGERANK GATHER	PAGERANK PROPAGATE
Epinions	0.076	0.509	11	11	1	48	139
LiveJournal	4.848	68.994	1432	1347	50	11818	21119
Pokec	1.633	30.623	273	1073	16	6267	8563
Orkut	3.073	117.185	687	3779	46	10724	20945
USA	23.947	57.709	1705	>35 min	125	14312	26886

5.1   Experimental Setup

We generated CUDA and OpenMP codes for four graph analytic algorithms: bipartite matching (MATCH), single-source shortest paths (SSSP), page-rank (PAGERANK), and conductance (COND) of a graph. MATCH is a matching algorithm where a random edge is selected as matching between two nodes. The algorithm returns one of the maximal matchings and not the maximum matching. Because of the randomness the algorithm can be run in parallel. SSSP computes the shortest paths in a directed graph from a designated source vertex, and uses a variant of Bellman-Ford algorithm. PAGERANK calculates the importance of each node in the graph using the following formula.

$$PageRank(n) = \frac{(1-d)}{NumNodes} + d * \sum_{t \in IncomingNodes(n)} \frac{PageRank(t)}{OutDegree(t)} \quad (1)$$

COND identifies how *well-knit* a graph is based on the degree distribution. The four algorithms test various aspects of our code-generator: MATCH involves testing data parallelism, SSSP tests generation of multi-atomic assignment, PAGERANK tests floating-point operations, while COND tests reductions and conditional evaluation of expressions.

Table 1 shows the benchmark graphs used in our evaluation along with their sizes in terms of the number of nodes and number of edges. The sizes range from 0.5 million edges (for Epinions) to 117 million edges (for orkut). All the graphs are obtained from SNAP [11]. The last columns of the table also show execution time of single-threaded OpenMP version for the three graph algorithms. We use it as a baseline for comparison of multi-threaded OpenMP and CUDA versions. We also compare our generated SSSP code against hand-optimized CUDA versions from LonestarGPU [3] and Totem [5]. Each algorithm implementation is run in CUDA and OpenMP frameworks with 1, 4, 8, 16 and 64 threads. The benchmarks for OpenMP are run on an Intel XeonE5-2650 v2 machine with 32 cores clocked at 2.6 GHz with 100 GB RAM, 32 KB of L1 data cache, 256 KB of L2 cache and 20 MB of L3 cache. The machine runs CentOS 6.5 and 2.6.32-431 kernel, with GCC version 4.4.7 and OpenMP version 4.0. The CUDA code is run on Tesla K40C device which has 2880 cores clocked at 745 MHz with 12 GB of global memory. The GPU device is connected to the same CPU device. CUDA_OPT is the baseline version with Eliminating Atomics and Loop Collapsing enabled. The execution time is taken after all the data necessary for computation is copied to respective memories till the procedure ends.

5.2 Experimental Results

Figure 5a shows the speedup obtained by the OpenMP and CUDA versions of **MATCH** compared to the single-threaded OpenMP version. We observe that CUDA_OPT considerably outperforms the OMP version's maximum performance. The algorithm has a nested Foreach loop which goes over neighbors of all nodes. CUDA_OPT converts this nested Foreach loop into a single Foreach-on-edge loop. Further, it converts the reduction of a boolean variable inside the nested Foreach loop to a normal assignment. Its high speedup is due to less conflicts across threads and load-balanced task distribution.

Figure 5b shows the results for **COND**. We observe that the OpenMP version performs considerably better and scales well, achieving a speedup of 9.3× for orkut. COND has atomics-based reductions to a variable from all the nodes of the graph which turn out to be slightly expensive in the presence of massive multithreading such as GPUs. Nonetheless, CUDA_OPT performs reasonably good and is comparable to 4-threaded OpenMP version.

PAGERANK is run with damping factor $d = 0.85$ and error tolerance of 0.0001 for maximum 40 iterations. It can be implemented both as a gathering or a propagating approach. In the former, every node gathers the pagerank of its incoming nodes to calculate its own pagerank. An advantage of gathering is that it does not need atomic writes, as every node is owned by a single thread. Figure 5c shows Pagerank results, which indicate that OpenMP scales well with number of threads. In case of CUDA, gather-based code improves synchronization, but also increases load-imbalance, as each thread needs to sequentially process all the incoming neighbors. On the other hand, in propagation-based code, every node propagates its pagerank to its outgoing nodes. The propagation demands atomics, but due to CUDA_OPT's node-based to edge-based optimization, the load-balance improves, leading to better performance, as shown in Fig. 5d.

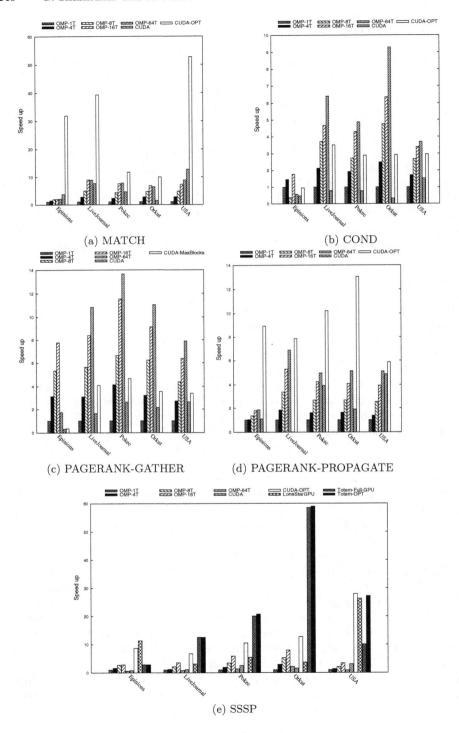

(a) MATCH

(b) COND

(c) PAGERANK-GATHER

(d) PAGERANK-PROPAGATE

(e) SSSP

Fig. 5. Performance of MATCH, SSSP, PAGERANK and COND on input graphs

Figure 5e shows the speedup obtained by the OpenMP and the CUDA versions of **SSSP** compared to the single-threaded OpenMP version. We observe that, in contrast to MATCH, the OpenMP version performs better in case of SSSP up to 16 threads (8× speedup). In comparison, our CUDA version performs consistently better for each graph. SSSP has a nested `Foreach` loop to propagate the distance value to all its neighbors. Along with minimizing the distance, each iteration marks the neighbors for propagation in the next iteration. Due to the irregular nature of the graphs and the algorithm, the number of conflicts on a memory location and load-imbalance increases with the number of threads. CUDA_OPT converts the traversal of neighbors of all nodes into edge-traversal which enables more parallelism. Totem's peak performance is achieved when all the graph nodes are processed on the GPU. It is hand-tuned to minimize the synchronization usage. In addition, automated code-generation of `LightHouse` has its bookkeeping overheads, which can be overcome by adding more architecture-independent optimizations to `LightHouse`.

Overall, we illustrate that `LightHouse` was able to generate well-performing CUDA versions from the same high-level description of the graph algorithms.

6 Related Work

Green-Marl [6] is a DSL for graph analytic algorithms running on shared memory systems. We explain Green-Marl's language features and code-generation briefly in Sect. 2. We use Green-Marl's specification as our language syntax. This allows us to retain existing productivity of the programmer. Further, in our experience, Green-Marl's syntax is intuitive (close to algorithmic description), well-defined and easy to learn; thus making it ideal for new domain experts.

Elixir [16] is a system for synthesizing irregular algorithms on multi-core platforms. Programmers specify the parallel computation as a set of *operators*, which is executed by multiple threads. Efficient execution of operators necessitates a good scheduling, which is often application dependent. Therefore, Elixir also provides a flexibility of specifying *schedules*, which could be customized as per the needs of an application. This allows generation of multiple implementations of the same algorithm (operator). Elixir also performs auto-inferencing to identify the next set of graph elements (nodes or edges) to be processed from the specification. An extension of Elixir [17] uses planning to generate schedules as well as synchronization automatically. Compared to Elixir, Green-Marl's syntax does not involve schedule specification and `LightHouse` targets GPUs which pose different challenges as discussed throughout the paper.

Halide [18] is a DSL for image processing. It provides a set of filters and a pipelined execution, where the output of one filter acts as input to the other. Users can write their own filters and alter the schedule to achieve the best results. Halide programs are restricted to stencils, in which the memory access pattern is *regular* (known at compile-time). Similar to our goal, Halide generates code for multiple platforms such as GPUs and heterogeneous CPU+GPU combination. `LightHouse` differs from the Halide compiler because the access patterns of graph algorithms are *irregular*, requiring dynamic parallelization techniques. This means that the related optimizations in case of graph algorithms need to be deferred until run-time.

While there are only a few DSLs for irregular codes, there are several library-based platforms and parallelization frameworks proposed for processing graph algorithms. Galois [10] is a C++ framework for writing multi-core graph algorithms. A salient feature of Galois is that it supports morph algorithms also, wherein the graph structure changes. Ligra [19] is a framework for parallelizing input-dependent programs, such as graph algorithms. LonestarGPU [3] and Totem [5] are frameworks for GPU and heterogeneous implementations of graph algorithms respectively. Medusa [24] is a C/C++ library-based approach to parallelize graph algorithms on multiple GPUs. GPU code generators for sparse matrix-vector multiplication [20] are also relevant.

Graph algorithms [10,15] have been shown to bear enough parallelism especially in the context of distributed [2,4,14] and heterogeneous systems [5]. G-Streamline is a software-based runtime approach to eliminate control-flow and memory-access irregularities from GPU programs [23]. DyManD is an automatic runtime system for managing recursive data structures (like trees) on GPUs [7]. Our work does not replace these existing approaches, but instead, complements them by allowing the optimizations to be generated automatically.

7   Conclusion

We proposed techniques for efficient GPU code generation of graph algorithms from their high-level description. We reused an existing graph analytics DSL, Green-Marl, as the front-end and added a CUDA backend called LightHouse. It had to overcome several challenges specific to GPUs due to separate memories, thread-hierarchy and SIMD processing on GPUs. We discussed unique issues encountered in GPU code generation compared to those in CPU code generation. We illustrated the effectiveness of our approach by generating CUDA code for four graph algorithms and comparing their performance against that of their OpenMP versions generated by Green-Marl. The performance benefits reveal that DSLs provide an effective way of developing parallel algorithms.

References

1. Bader, D.A., Madduri, K.: Designing multithreaded algorithms for breadth-first search and st-connectivity on the Cray MTA-2. In: ICPP 2006, pp. 523–530 (2006)
2. Buluç, A., Madduri, K.: Parallel breadth-first search on distributed memory systems. In: SC 2011, pp. 65:1–65:12. ACM (2011)
3. Burtscher, M., Nasre, R., Pingali, K.: A quantitative study of irregular programs on GPUs. In: IISWC 2012, pp. 141–151. IEEE Computer Society (2012)
4. Checconi, F., Petrini, F., Willcock, J., Lumsdaine, A., Choudhury, A.R., Sabharwal, Y.: Breaking the speed, scalability barriers for graph exploration on distributed-memory machines. In: SC 2012, pp. 13:1–13:12 (2012)

5. Gharaibeh, A., Costa, L.B., Santos-Neto, E., Ripeanu, M.: A yoke of oxen and a thousand chickens for heavy lifting graph processing. In: PACT 2012 (2012)
6. Hong, S., Chafi, H., Sedlar, E., Olukotun, K.: Green-Marl: a DSL for easy and efficient graph analysis. In: ASPLOS 2012, pp. 349–362 ACM (2012)
7. Jablin, T.B., Jablin, J.A., Prabhu, P., Liu, F., August, D.I.: Dynamically managed data for CPU-GPU architectures. In: CGO 2012. ACM (2012)
8. Kulkarni, M., Burtscher, M., Inkulu, R., Pingali, K., Casçaval, C.: How much parallelism is there in irregular applications? In: PPoPP 2009, pp. 3–14 (2009)
9. Kulkarni, M., Pingali, K., Ramanarayanan, G., Walter, B., Bala, K., Chew, L.P.: Optimistic parallelism benefits from data partitioning. SIGARCH Comput. Archit. News **36**(1), 233–243 (2008)
10. Kulkarni, M., Pingali, K., Walter, B., Ramanarayanan, G., Bala, K., Chew, L.P.: Optimistic parallelism requires abstractions. PLDI **42**(6), 211–222 (2007)
11. Leskovec, J., Sosič, R.: SNAP: a general purpose network analysis and graph mining library in C++, June 2014. http://snap.stanford.edu/snap
12. Madduri, K., Bader, D., Berry, J., Crobak, J.: An experimental study of a parallel shortest path algorithm for solving large-scale graph instances. In: ALENEX (2007)
13. Nasre, R., Burtscher, M., Pingali, K.: Morph algorithms on GPUs. In: PPoPP 2013. ACM (2013)
14. Pearce, R., Gokhale, M., Amato, N.M.: Multithreaded asynchronous graph traversal for in-memory and semi-external memory. In: SC 2010, pp. 1–11 (2010)
15. Pingali, K., Nguyen, D., Kulkarni, M., Burtscher, M., Hassaan, M.A., Kaleem, R., Lee, T.-H., Lenharth, A., Manevich, R., Méndez-Lojo, M., Prountzos, D., Sui, X.: The tao of parallelism in algorithms. In: PLDI 2011, pp. 12–25. ACM (2011)
16. Prountzos, D., Manevich, R., Pingali, K.: Elixir: a system for synthesizing concurrent graph programs. In: OOPSLA 2012, pp. 375–394. ACM (2012)
17. Prountzos, D., Manevich, R., Pingali, K.: Synthesizing parallel graph programs via automated planning. In: PLDI, pp. 533–544. ACM (2015)
18. Ragan-Kelley, J., Barnes, C., Adams, A., Paris, S., Durand, F., Amarasinghe, S.: Halide: a language and compiler for optimizing parallelism, locality, and recomputation in image processing pipelines. In: PLDI 2013, pp. 519–530. ACM (2013)
19. Shun, J., Blelloch, G.E.: Ligra: A lightweight graph processing framework for shared memory. In: PPoPP, pp. 135–146. ACM (2013)
20. Venkat, A., Shantharam, M., Hall, M., Strout, M.M.: Non-affine extensions to polyhedral code generation. In: Proceedings of Annual IEEE/ACM International Symposium on Code Generation, Optimization, CGO 2014, pp. 185:185–185:194. ACM, New York (2014)
21. Xiao, S., Feng, W.: Inter-block GPU communication via fast barrier synchronization. In: IPDPS, pp. 1–12. IEEE (2010)
22. Yoo, A., Chow, E., Henderson, K., McLendon, W., Hendrickson, B., Catalyurek, U.: A scalable distributed parallel breadth-first search algorithm on blueGene/L. In: ICS, p. 25. IEEE Computer Society (2005)
23. Zhang, E.Z., Jiang, Y., Guo, Z., Tian, K., Shen, X.: On-the-fly elimination of dynamic irregularities for GPU computing. In: ASPLOS. ACM (2011)
24. Zhong, J., He, B.: Medusa: simplified graph processing on GPUs. IEEE Trans. Parallel Distrib. Syst. **25**(6), 1543–1552 (2014)

Locality-Aware Task-Parallel Execution on GPUs

Jad Hbeika$^{(\boxtimes)}$ and Milind Kulkarni

Purdue University, West Lafayette, USA
{jhbeika,milind}@purdue.edu

Abstract. GPGPUs deliver high speedup for regular applications while remaining energy efficient. In recent years, there has been much focus on tuning irregular, task-parallel applications and/or the GPU architecture in order to achieve similar benefits for irregular applications running on GPUs. While most of the previous works have focused on minimizing the effect of control and memory divergence, which are prominent in irregular applications and which degrade the performance, there has been less attention paid to decreasing cache pressure and hence improving performance of applications given the small cache sizes on GPUs.

In this paper we tackle two problems. First we extract data parallelism from irregular task parallel applications, which we do by subdividing each task into sub tasks at the CPU side and sending these sub tasks to the GPU for execution. By doing so we take advantage of the massive parallelism provided by the GPU. Second, to mitigate the memory demands of many tasks that access irregular data structures, we schedule these subtasks in a way to minimize the memory footprint of each warp running on the GPU. We use our framework with 3 task-parallel algorithms and show that we can achieve significant speedups over optimized GPU code.

1   Introduction

GPGPUs have proven themselves to be a cost-effective way of accelerating applications. The single-instruction, multiple-thread (SIMT) execution model of GPUGPUs provides massive amounts of parallelism while remaining energy efficient. The hardware of the GPU is limited to keep power consumption low. Most prominently, the SIMT execution model requires that all threads in a *warp* perform the same instruction at the same time to enjoy parallelism; if different threads do different work, some threads sit idle and parallelism is lost. Second, there is relatively little hardware support for hiding latency—the core cannot execute instructions out of order, nor are there forwarding networks to help mitigate the penalty of long-latency instructions—instead, the GPU relies on massive multithreading to hide latency, keeping hundreds or even thousands of threads in context to swap in and out during long-latency operations. Perniciously, this means that not only does the GPU *support* massive parallelism, it *needs* massive parallelism for effective execution. Finally, caches are small compared to their

© Springer International Publishing AG 2017
C. Ding et al. (Eds.): LCPC 2016, LNCS 10136, pp. 250–264, 2017.
DOI: 10.1007/978-3-319-52709-3_19

CPU counterparts, especially when considered on a per-thread basis (thousands of threads spread a <1 MB cache very thin!)

As a result of these limitations, not all applications can execute efficiently on GPUs. GPUs are well-suited to *regular, data-parallel* applications, where the well-structured computation is performed on different pieces of data. In these applications, the similarity of the computations performed in parallel means that there are not substantial penalties for executing in a SIMT manner. Moreover, the data-parallel nature of the application means that it is easy to generate enough parallelism to fill the GPU, allowing for effective multithreading.

However, for *task* parallel applications, where parallelism arises from independent, distinct tasks that run simultaneously, GPUs are not nearly as attractive a target. First, the fork-join nature of task parallelism does not map well to standard GPU programming models such as CUDA [11] or OpenCL [9]. Second, even if there is data parallelism in these applications (either because individual tasks have data parallel work, or because there is some parallel outer loop in the application), there may not be enough parallelism to effectively use the GPU's resources. Third, even *if* the tasks of the program could be mapped to the GPU, the limited memory subsystem of the GPU can lead to poor performance in data-heavy tasks.

There has been recent work on turning task parallelism into data parallelism to map task-parallel applications to hardware (including GPUs) that is made for data parallelism [5,12,13]. These proposals either require hardware changes [5, 12] or target fine-grained data parallelism in SIMD units [13]. None of these approaches consider locality.

In this paper, we propose a *locality-aware, task-queue* abstraction for mapping task-parallel applications to GPUs. The basic approach is to expand task parallel work *on the CPU* to generate a large number of tasks. These tasks are then inserted into one or more task queues according to the type of computation they perform and, crucially, the locality properties of the tasks. These queues are then merged into a single queue that is sent to the GPU, where they are executed in a data-parallel manner, with each task executing to completion on the GPU. This model has several features. First, by expanding out the task-parallel work on the CPU, we avoid needing to handle task-parallelism on the GPU; instead, once execution begins on the GPU, it is purely data parallel. Second, because the task queues are partitioned based on operation type, the tasks that execute simultaneously are computationally similar, promoting efficient SIMT execution. Finally, the locality-aware nature of the queues promotes tasks in the same queue having overlapping memory footprints, reducing cache pressure and hence improving performance relative to a locality-unaware approach.

We evaluate this queue abstraction on three applications: a task-parallel implementation of the fast multipole method, and two data mining applications that feature a mix of data-parallelism and task-parallelism, nearest-neighbor and two-point correlation. In all three cases, we demonstrate that our locality-aware approach delivers better performance than a locality-agnostic one. For the mixed applications, not only do we show that our locality-aware approach is better than the locality-agnostic approach, but we also show that in the absence of very large amounts of data parallelism (for example, only 200,000 data-parallel iterations), our task-parallel approach, by exploiting additional parallelism, is also significantly faster than the best-available implementations, which exploit only data parallelism.

The remainder of this paper is organized as follows. Section 2 discusses some previous works that considered different programing models for GPUs. Section 3 provides background on GPGPU programming and task parallelism. Section 4 discusses our basic task-queue-based technique for exploiting data parallelism in task-parallel applications. Section 5 discusses the need for locality aware scheduling of subtasks. Section 6 discusses the implementation, Sect. 7 evaluates our system on the four applications mentioned above, and Sect. 8 concludes.

2   Related Work

Due to the increasing prevalence of hardware resources for data parallelism (GPUs, SIMD units, etc.), there has been significant recent interest in techniques for mapping task-parallel computations to data parallel hardware. Gaster and Howes propose a *channels* abstraction for executing Cilk-style task-parallel programs on GPUs, where the GPU hardware manages queues for each type of task, and provides support for dequeueing and enqueuing new tasks [5]. Orr et al. presented an instantiation of the channels model and showed its efficacy on several small Cilk-style programs [12]. Both of these approaches require hardware support, and hence are not suitable to executing task-parallel programs on commodity data-parallel hardware. Moreover, the channels abstraction does not consider locality between tasks; it only concerns itself with grouping together tasks with similar computation.

More recently, Ren et al. described a series of code transformations that transform task-parallel algorithms into *blocked* recursive algorithms: recursive algorithms where each method invocation performs a block of tasks, rather than a single task [13]. These blocks can be executed efficiently in a vectorized manner. While Ren et al.'s general approach—transforming independent, parallel tasks into data-parallel blocks of tasks—is similar to ours, their technique does not apply in our setting for two reasons: (1) they target vector units on CPUs, and hence can support code transformations that require fine-grained interleaving of SIMD and scalar operations; (2) more importantly, the applications they study only manipulate the stack, and hence their technique does not have to account for locality considerations.

In a more general sense, models for executing work-queues on GPUs have been studied extensively in the literature. The *persistent threads* model [7] proposes maintaining a CPU-managed work-queue along with a specially-designed GPU kernel where a limited number of threads each run a simple get-work/execute-work loop until the software-managed queue is empty. This style of programming can be conducive to expressing idioms, such as producer-consumer dependences, that data-parallel programs are ill-suited to capture.

This model has been used to implement several work-queue-style applications [2,10]. For the most part, persistent-thread applications do not consider locality in mapping tasks to threads. Moreover, unlike in a persistent thread model, our approach does not attempt to limit the number of threads executing on the GPU; instead, the entire queue of tasks is sent to the GPU at the same time, to maximize the effectiveness of hardware multithreading.

Chen et al. do consider locality concerns in a persistent-thread-like model [3]. In their programming model, tasks in a task-queue can generate new tasks that may operate on similar data to the parent tasks. They use a compiler-based code transformation to map child tasks to the threads that executed the parent task, to promote reuse. In contrast, our approach considers locality between the tasks that are mapped to the same warp—in other words, locality between tasks that are executed by different threads, rather than consecutively on a single thread—in an attempt to improve memory coalescing and minimize cache pressure. Wu et al. perform affinity scheduling, mapping tasks with overlapping footprints to the same Streaming Multiprocessor (SM) [15]; this notion of locality is far more coarse-grained than the warp-focused affinity scheduling we pursue. Moreover, neither Chen et al. nor Wu et al. focus on the type of task-parallel applications that we tackle.

Goldfarb et al. looked at mapping tree traversal applications to the GPU, as with two of our example benchmarks [6]. They adopt a fully data-parallel approach, meaning that their implementation relies on inputs with a large number of traversals to obtain good performance. Moreover, they do not consider locality between threads, relying on *ad hoc*, programmer-provided scheduling decisions. Liu et al. expanded on this work by developing a hybrid scheduling framework that attempts to reschedule traversals based on similarity [8]. As in Goldfarb et al.'s work, Liu et al. only consider fully data-parallel implementations, and rely on high degrees of data parallelism for their scheduling to be effective. Their implementations, which represent highly optimized GPU implementations of tree traversal applications, form the baseline for our experiments.

3 Background and Motivation

3.1 GPU Architecture and Limitations

A typical GPU consists of multiple streaming multiprocessor units (SMs), each of which features multiple simple cores, a register file, an L1 cache, and a shared memory used by threads within the same thread block to communicate (in NVIDIA GPUs, the shared memory and L1 cache share the same hardware structure, which can be partitioned between the two in different ratios, depending on the workload). There is also a shared L2 cache among all the SMs on the GPU. Finally, there is an off-chip, global memory accessible by all the SMs.

Execution on a GPU consists of a *kernel* that is expressed in terms of a *thread grid*—a set of threads that execute in parallel to complete the kernel[1].

---

[1] For convenience, we use NVIDIA's CUDA terminology to explain the GPU programming model; OpenCL has analogous constructs, but uses different terms.

The thread grid is executed across one or more of the SMs on the GPU. To facilitate this execution, the threads in the grid are partitioned into multiple *thread blocks*. While different thread blocks may execute on different SMs, all the threads in a single block are guaranteed to execute on a single SM. As a result of this thread partitioning, threads in a thread block can communicate through shared memory, but threads in a grid can only communicate through global memory.

Within a thread block, execution proceeds by dividing the block into *warps*: groups of 32 threads that execute *simultaneously* on the SM's 32 cores. These threads execute in a lockstep, SIMT (single instruction multiple thread) manner, for efficiency: all threads must be executing the same instruction for computations to be performed in parallel, and if some threads want to execute different instructions, some of the 32 cores sit idle until the threads in the warp return to executing the same instruction. Paired with this *control divergence* is *memory divergence*: if multiple threads in the warp issue a load, all the threads must wait until all of the loads complete before proceeding. Hence, if some loads miss in the cache, the entire warp can stall for a long time before resuming execution.

As a final complication, GPU cores are extremely simple—in order, no forwarding networks, no branch prediction, etc. Instead, performance is maintained in the face of pipeline stalls and memory divergence through massive multithreading: NVIDIA's latest Kepler GPUs can keep up to 64 warps (2048 threads) in context at the same time, and will context switch between these warps on stalls. Note that this massive multithreading means that a GPU's memory system is much smaller than a CPU's on a per thread basis: a CPU hardware context (core) has access to a 64 KB private L1 cache, and a ~1 MB L2 cache and ~6 MB L3 cache shared among 4–12 cores. In contrast, an SM's 16–64 KB of L1 cache is shared among up to *two thousand* threads, and its ~1.5 MB of L2 cache is shared among all of the SMs in the system. On the flip side, while the amount of memory per thread may be small, the GPU features extremely high throughput to keep the threads fed.

These hardware features conspire in destructive ways when writing programs that do not have very well-structured computation and memory accesses:

- A GPU needs large amounts of parallelism to sustain throughput under memory stalls.
- Memory stalls are more likely due to the SIMT architecture if different threads in the same warp have divergent memory footprints, as each SIMT-coalesced memory access is more likely to result in cache misses.
- These memory stalls require even more parallelism to hide the resulting latency, which places even more pressure on the memory system.

Unsurprisingly, then, while GPU implementations attain extremely high speedups over CPU implementations for data-parallel, regular applications, as programs become less regular and less data-parallel, speedups become harder to attain. This paper describes one approach to achieve good speedup for a class of irregular, task-parallel applications.

```
1 corr(KDNode n, Point p, float r) {
2   if (!canCorrelate(n, p, r)) return;
3   else
4     if (n.isLeaf && dist(n, p) < r)
5       p.count.accum(1);
6     else if (!n.isLeaf)
7       spawn corr(n.left, p, r);
8       spawn corr(n.right, p, r);
9 }
```

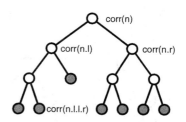

Fig. 1. Example task-parallel algorithm for point correlation

Fig. 2. Computation tree for point-correlation

3.2 Task Parallelism

In this paper, we consider mapping *task-parallel* applications on GPUs. In particular, we consider recursive and task-parallel applications where parallelism arises from executing multiple recursive function invocations simultaneously. Figure 1 shows a task-parallel implementation of a recursive algorithm to compute two-point correlation. The algorithm takes a point p and traverses a kd-tree structure to determine how many points in a metric space are within a specified radius r of that point. Because the kd-tree is a binary tree, each subtree can be searched independently, as indicated by the use of the **spawn** keyword (we borrow the keyword from Cilk [1], perhaps the most well-known task-parallel programming languages). Following the approach of Ren et al. [13], rather than using **sync** and return values to perform the final correlation computation, we instead **accumulate** into a Cilk-style reducer [4]. In Sect. 4, we explain how we use this reduction approach in our implementations.

Two-point correlation has substantial amounts of parallelism, but, nevertheless, is poorly suited to mapping to a GPU: the parallel operations do not arise from a data parallel loop; the parallel operations have very different memory footprints; and the computation itself is highly irregular. While some data-parallelism does arise because this task-parallel computation can be repeated for different points, there may not always be enough data parallelism to provide the parallelism the GPU requires. The best-available GPU implementation of point correlation [8] relies on massive data parallelism to effectively manage the irregularity of the computation.

4 Data Parallel GPU Execution of Task Parallel Code

This section presents our basic technique for extracting data parallelism from task-parallel programs. It shares some basic similarities with the approach of Orr et al. [12] and Ren et al. [13], in that it "expands" out the task parallel work to generate enough tasks that can subsequently be executed in a data parallel manner. Unlike the prior two approaches, though, our approach focuses on cooperation between the CPU and GPU to generate the necessary tasks.

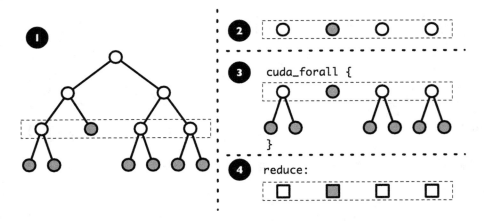

Fig. 3. Steps for executing task parallel code on GPU

4.1 Basic Technique

The key insight underpinning our approach is that the execution of a recursive, task-parallel program with no syncs can be viewed as an execution tree: a program begins at the root of the tree, and at each spawn call generates two leaves: one for the spawn, and one for the continuation. If there is no continuation (i.e., the spawn is the last operation in the function), then only one leaf is generated. Hence, in a code like the point correlation code of Fig. 1, non-base-case executions generate interior nodes of the tree with two leaves each, for each of the spawn calls, and base case invocations of the corr method create leaves of this execution tree. Figure 2 shows an example of the execution tree, with base-case tasks shaded gray. Some of the nodes are labeled with the node argument passed to the task. Note that the nature of the point correlation algorithm means that the execution tree corresponds to the *actual* tree that is being traversed: each method invocation corresponds to operating on a subtree of the overall kd-tree. This connection will become pertinent in Sect. 5.

Because of the nature of task-parallel execution, the nodes in this computation tree can be executed in any order, provided that ancestors always execute before descendants. As nodes are executed, the "frontier" of non-executed nodes represents the set of tasks that are left to be executed (so, for example, in a Cilk-style runtime system, the contents of the threads' deques are this frontier).

Our execution model, then, is straightforward. Figure 3 illustrates the steps.

1. Partially expand the computation tree on the CPU, until a sufficient frontier is generated. (The non-greyed out nodes in the computation tree shown in step 1 of Fig. 3.)
2. Place all the tasks in this frontier into a queue (shown in step 2 of Fig. 3). Note that each of these tasks, by definition, is independent from the others. Moreover, each task can be executed to completion sequentially, executing the entire subtree rooted at that task.

```
 1 corr(KDNode n, Point p, float r) {
 2   if (!canCorrelate(n, p, r)) return;
 3   else
 4     if (n.isLeaf && dist(n, p) < r)
 5       p.count.accum(1);
 6     else if (!n.isLeaf)
 7       if (!thresholdMet)
 8         spawn corr(n.left, p, r);
 9         spawn corr(n.right, p, r);
10       else
11         gpuQ.addTask(n.left, p, r);
12         gpuQ.addTask(n.right, p, r);
13 }
```

Fig. 4. Transformed point correlation algorithm to enable GPU task queue.

3. Execute this task queue in a *data parallel* manner on the GPU, with each task maintaining its own reduction result (shown in step 3 of Fig. 3). Because of the nature of reduction computations [4], each of these tasks can perform its reductions independently.
4. Return the reduction objects (the squares in step 4 of Fig. 3 to the CPU to be combined to produce the final result.

Note that because of the recursive nature of the tasks in the applications we consider, each of the tasks has a fairly similar computational fingerprint. This similarity between tasks helps reduce control divergence. Memory divergence, though, is another issue, as Sect. 5 elaborates.

4.2   Generating GPU Task Queues

The process of enqueuing tasks into the task queue for execution on the GPU is straightforward, and can be accomplished by a basic code transformation. Because spawned tasks are independent of their execution, it is also safe to *not* execute them, and instead defer their execution until a later point in time. Hence, during *sequential* execution of a task-parallel program on the CPU, whenever a threshold is hit, spawned tasks are not executed, but are instead enqueued onto a task queue that will be sent to the GPU. Figure 4 shows a version of our point correlation example that performs this enqueuing.

Note that we do not attempt to perform the CPU work in parallel, though it could reasonably be parallelized; because the work up to the frontier represented by the task queue is small compared to the overall work in the program, executing this work sequentially is a minor overhead, and simplifies implementation.

4.3   Mixing Data Parallelism and Task Parallelism

As mentioned in Sect. 3.2, some applications have a mix of data and task parallelism. In particular, applications such as point correlation often have a data parallel outer loop (in this case, iterating over multiple points), where each iteration of that data parallel loop performs task-parallel work.

Integrating such algorithms into our framework is simple: we merely execute the data-parallel outer loop sequentially, and, upon entering a task parallel iteration, execute it according to the scheme above. Because most of the work is performed by the tasks enqueued into the GPU queue, the data parallel outer loop will "finish," having enqueued most of its computation into the GPU queue. We can then execute the GPU queue and proceed as before. This transformation is safe, since the data-parallel iterations are independent of one another, and each iteration's task-parallel tasks are also independent, hence all the tasks, even if they arise from different iterations, are independent.

Note that in the particular case of point correlation, this execution strategy leads to poor data locality. Suppose we want to process 1000 points. Suppose, further, that the enqueuing threshold for the task parallel computation is two levels deep in the tree (as in Fig. 3). Then each point's execution will lead to the creation of four tasks, touching four different subtrees of the kd-tree, and overall 4000 total tasks will be created, with 1000 tasks touching each subtree. However, if the tasks are placed into the GPU queue in order, then each of a point's tasks will be placed contiguously into the queue. Because these threads are likely to be placed in the same warp during GPU execution, each warp's memory footprint will span the entire tree, leading to very poor locality, and hence poor performance. The next section discusses how to solve this problem.

5   Scheduling for Locality

The execution strategy outlined in the previous section solves the initial problem of executing a task-parallel application on hardware built for data-parallelism. But, as pointed out in Sect. 3.1, while GPUs are very efficient data-parallel execution engines, their efficiency comes with several drawbacks. In particular, the memory resources of the GPU are not well-matched to the massive parallelism that efficient execution requires: the GPU features substantial bandwidth (allowing the threads to be fed), but very small cache resources. As a result, GPUs work well in streaming workloads or workloads with small reuse footprints. But in workloads with large amounts of reuse but also large footprints, the small caches can dramatically reduce performance. Indeed, to avoid the thrashing that can result from too many threads contending for the same small caches, it is often necessary to reduce an SM's warp count from 64 (the maximum supported) to only four or five [14]. Unfortunately, the kinds of irregular, task-parallel workloads we target are precisely workloads that feature substantial parallelism (due to our execution strategy), but potentially-large memory footprints (the trees traversed in point correlation, for example, can feature millions of nodes). Another problem arises in combating memory divergence: while keeping the footprint of a block to a minimum to avoid cache thrashing is important, it is also important to ensure that the threads of a single warp do not encounter widely varying memory latencies: if one thread in a warp encounters a cache miss while the others do not, all the threads pay the penalty of that cache miss.

To address these problems, we propose *locality-aware queue scheduling*. Orr et al. proposed a multi-queue strategy for executing task parallel program where different queues correspond to different types of computations (to reduce control divergence) [12]. Instead, we propose to use multiple queues where different queues correspond to different *locality domains*: an abstract notion of the region of memory a task might access. We create a separate queue for each such locality domain, and tasks expected to access similar regions of memory will be assigned to the same queue. By placing threads from the same locality domain together, we promote threads in the same warp touching similar pieces of memory, both reducing footprints and decreasing memory divergence.

Locality-aware scheduling requires some understanding of the memory access patterns of the tasks that are being scheduled. This is inherently an application-specific property: various features of the application, and the specific task, might be used to map the task to a particular locality domain. To support this type of scheduling, we add an additional parameter to the addTask hook, where the programmer can pass the result of evaluating a simple function to compute the locality domain for the scheduled task.

In many cases, it is straightforward to determine a task's locality domain. For example, in tree-based benchmarks, we originally start with independent tasks each accessing the whole tree i.e. we start with one locality domain. When subdividing these tasks into independent subtasks, each traversal gets divided into multiple traversals each accessing a part of the tree. This suggests a very simple representation of each locality domain: the node the task is invoked on, which is the root of the subtree it will access. Thus, the two addTask calls from Fig. 4 can be replaced with the following:

```
1 gpuQ.getQueue(n.left).addTask(n.left, p, r);
2 gpuQ.getQueue(n.right).addTask(n.right, p, r);
```

Note the effect of this implementation on the mixed data- and task-parallelism scenario from Sect. 4.3. If there are four different subtrees that an enqueued task could access, there will be four separate queues. Each point will enqueue its four tasks onto the four separate queues, and task *from different points that access the same subtree* will be placed next to each other in each of the queues, promoting locality.

6   Implementation

This section describes a few aspects of implementing the scheduling and execution strategy from the previous two sections.

6.1   Determining the Queue Threshold

The pseudocode in Fig. 4 uses an arbitrary threshold for determining when to stop expanding out the computation tree and to instead enqueue tasks into the GPU queue for later execution. In general, the threshold is application-specific, and possibly input-specific. However, we have found that a good rule of thumb is to ensure that the memory footprint of each task is fairly small. Recall that GPUs have limited per-thread memory resources. Hence, if the tasks in the task queue have large footprints, each thread will demand substantial amounts of memory, increasing the per-block memory footprint and lowering performance. Moreover, by keeping tasks relatively small, the likelihood that tasks diverge significantly during execution is reduced, helping further mitigate control divergence. Finally, by keeping individual task footprints small, the total number of tasks increases (because the CPU waits longer before hitting the enqueue threshold), creating enough parallelism to keep the GPU busy. So, for example, in our point correlation example, we might set the threshold at a depth such that the subtree visited by each enqueued task is relatively small.

6.2   Queue Merging

If there are many locality-based queues, the overhead of sending each queue to the GPU separately can be prohibitive. Instead, once the queues are constructed by the CPU expansion of the computation tree are complete, the queues are merged into a single queue and sent to the GPU. Because the threads in the unified queue are still ordered according to their locality-based queues, the schedule of execution will still be consistent with the locality-aware grouping.

6.3   Queue Size Reduction

If there are too many tasks in the queues after expansion, there may be too much parallelism for the GPU, resulting in more scheduling overhead. To avoid this, we implement a queue size reduction optimization. Rather than passing the task queue to the GPU to be executed with a simple do-all loop, where each iteration gets mapped to a separate thread, we can instead rewrite the task queue loop so that each thread processes two (or more) tasks from the queue (essentially, by strip mining the loop that processes the task queue). Because each thread will execute consecutive tasks in the task queue, the locality-aware scheduling policy will promote those two tasks' having overlapping memory footprints, thus not increasing the memory footprint of a given thread, coarsening the computation without increasing cache pressure.

Note that this general strategy: of having a smaller number of threads execute a larger number of tasks by scheduling multiple tasks per thread, is similar to the approach advocated by persistent threads [7]. A key difference is that persistent threads approaches *dynamically* schedule tasks to threads, while we *statically* schedule tasks to threads. While dynamic scheduling can be more flexible, our static scheduling has two advantages: (1) static scheduling means that the multiple tasks scheduled to each thread are guaranteed to come from the same locality domain, improving locality; (2) static scheduling means that we avoid the runtime overhead of managing the task queue.

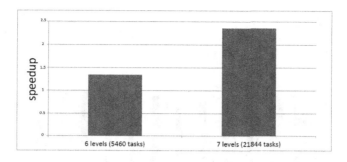

Fig. 5. Speedup of locality-aware FMM over locality-agnostic FMM

7 Evaluation

We evaluate our locality-aware task scheduling approach on three task-parallel applications: fast multipole method (FMM), point correlation (PC), and nearest-neighbor (NN). The CPU on which the experiments are conducted has 2 AMD Opteron 6164 HE processors, each of which has 12 cores running at 1.7 GHz, with 32 GB of system memory. The GPU on which the experiments are run is an nVidia Tesla K20C with 5120 MB of RAM and 2496 CUDA cores. The runtimes of our implementations include the time spent on the CPU to generate tasks and communicate the task queue to the GPU, as well as the time to retrieve the reduction objects from the GPU and complete the reduction. In other words, our implementations' runtimes are directly comparable to GPU-only execution.

7.1 Fast Multipole Method

The fast multipole method is a fast approximation algorithm for the n-body problem. It operates by performing a bottom-up traversal of an quad-tree, at each level of the tree computing for each subtree at that level the forces contributed by the bodies in that subtree on neighboring subtrees. The task parallelism in this program arises because the subtrees can be processed in parallel.

For FMM, we compare a locality-agnostic implementation of our approach to one where subtrees represent locality domains, and hence tasks that operate on the same subtree are grouped together. Figure 5 shows the speedup of the locality-aware approach to the locality-agnostic approach, with two different task granularities: one where tasks originate 6-levels deep in the tree, and one where they originate 7-levels deep. We see that with the coarser-grained tasks, being locality-aware provides a 1.34× speedup. With finer-grained tasks, where grouping together similar tasks results in a smaller footprint that better utilizes the GPU's caches, we can achieve a 2.36× speedup over the locality-agnostic implementation.

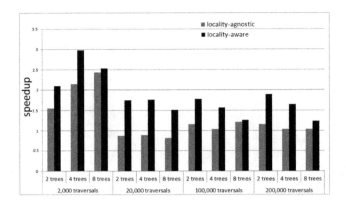

Fig. 6. Speedup of PC over data-parallel GPU baseline

7.2 Point Correlation

Point correlation, our running example, is a mixed data- and task-parallel benchmark: each of a set of independent points traverses a tree (data parallelism), and those points can traverse the tree in parallel by processing independent subtrees simultaneously (task parallelism). Unlike for FMM, where we compare the locality-aware and locality-agnostic implementations of our framework, for PC, we also compare against an optimized GPU baseline [8]. This GPU baseline exploits only data parallelism.

Figure 6 shows the speedup of our locality-agnostic and locality-aware task queue implementations over the data-parallel baseline. We varied both the enqueuing threshold (a given number of trees is the number of tasks per point we generate) and the number of traversals we perform. We see that the locality-aware implementation is consistently faster than the locality-unaware implementation. Indeed, the locality-aware implementation is consistently faster than the baseline data-parallel implementation. Further, we see the effect of the enqueuing threshold on performance: for this particular application, generating four tasks per point provides a good balance between overhead (more tasks means more work generating tasks and performing reductions on the CPU) and locality. Finally, we see that when there are only a small number of traversals, the data-parallel implementation is significantly slower than our mixed implementation, as we are able to generate additional parallelism to keep the GPU busy, achieving a speedup of almost 3× over the optimized baseline.

7.3 Nearest Neighbor

We perform a similar experiment as PC for our nearest-neighbor benchmark, again comparing our locality-agnostic and locality-aware implementations to an optimized, data-parallel-only baseline. Figure 7 shows again that our mixed implementations are consistently faster than the data-parallel-only implementation, and that adding locality awareness consistently adds performance. We

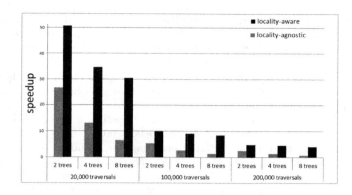

Fig. 7. Speedup of NN over data-parallel GPU baseline

again see the effect of being able to exploit additional parallelism: for 20 K point inputs, our locality-aware task queue implementation is over 50× faster than the baseline!

8   Conclusions

This paper presented an approach to exploiting task-parallelism on GPUs by performing partial execution on the CPU to generate a queue of data-parallel tasks that can be executed on the GPU. We then showed how multiple such task queues can be used to add locality-awareness, with the goal of shrinking the memory footprint of individual warps to reduce cache pressure. Preliminary results are promising, showing not only that our approach to exploiting task-parallelism can result in efficient implementations, but also that locality-awareness can significantly boost performance. Indeed, for an implementation of nearest-neighbor, our approach yields a performance improvement of 50× over an optimized data-parallel implementation. Future work could explore methods of defining locality domains for applications where statically defining the domain is not possible.

Acknowledgments. The authors would like to thank the anonymous referees for their comments and feedback regarding the paper. This work was supported in part by the U.S. Department of Energy's (DOE) Office of Science, Office of Advanced Scientific Computing Research, under DOE Early Career Award DE-SC0010295. This work was also supported in part by NSF awards CCF-1150013 (CAREER) and CCF-1439126.

References

1. Blumofe, R.D., Joerg, C.F., Kuszmaul, B.C., Leiserson, C.E., Randall, K.H., Zhou, Y.: Cilk: an efficient multithreaded runtime system. J. Parallel Distrib. Comput. **37**(1), 55–69 (1996)

2. Capodieci, N., Burgio, P.: Efficient implementation of genetic algorithms on GP-GPU with scheduled persistent CUDA threads. In: 2015 Seventh International Symposium on Parallel Architectures, Algorithms and Programming (PAAP), pp. 6–12. IEEE (2015)

3. Chen, G., Shen, X.: Free launch: optimizing GPU dynamic kernel launches through thread reuse. In: Proceedings of the 48th International Symposium on Microarchitecture, pp. 407–419. ACM (2015)

4. Frigo, M., Halpern, P., Leiserson, C.E., Lewin-Berlin, S.: Reducers and other Cilk++ hyperobjects. In: SPAA 2009, pp. 79–90 (2009)

5. Gaster, B.R., Howes, L.: Can GPGPU programming be liberated from the data-parallel bottleneck? Computer 45(8), 42–52 (2012)

6. Goldfarb, M., Jo, Y., Kulkarni, M.: General transformations for GPU execution of tree traversals. In: Proceedings of the International Conference on High Performance Computing, Networking, Storage and Analysis (Supercomputing), SC 2013 (2013)

7. Gupta, K., Stuart, J.A., Owens, J.D.: A study of persistent threads style GPU programming for GPGPU workloads. In: Innovative Parallel Computing (InPar) 2012, pp. 1–14 (2012)

8. Liu, J., Hegde, N., Kulkarni, M.: Hybrid CPU-GPU scheduling and execution of tree traversals. In: Proceedings of the 21st ACM SIGPLAN Symposium on Principles and Practice of Parallel Programming, PPoPP 2016, pp. 41:1–41:2, New York, NY, USA. ACM (2016)

9. Munshi, A.: OpenCL parallel computing on the GPU and CPU. In: SIGGRAPH

10. Nasre, R., Burtscher, M., Pingali, K.: Data-driven versus topology-driven irregular computations on GPUS. In: IEEE 27th International Symposium on Parallel & Distributed Processing (IPDPS), pp. 463–474. IEEE (2013)

11. NVIDIA. CUDA. http://www.nvidia.com/object/cuda_home_new.html

12. Orr, M.S., Beckmann, B.M., Reinhardt, S.K., Wood, D.A.: Fine-grain task aggregation and coordination on GPUs. In: ISCA 2014, pp. 181–192 (2014)

13. Ren, B., Jo, Y., Krishnamoorthy, S., Agrawal, K., Kulkarni, M.: Efficient execution of recursive programs on commodity vector hardware. In: PLDI, pp. 509–520 (2015)

14. Rogers, T.G., O'Connor, M., Aamodt, T.M.: Cache-conscious wavefront scheduling. In: Proceedings of the 45th Annual IEEE/ACM International Symposium on Microarchitecture, MICRO-45, pp. 72–83, Washington, DC, USA. IEEE Computer Society (2012)

15. Wu, B., Chen, G., Li, D., Shen, X., Vetter, J.: Enabling and exploiting flexible task assignment on GPU through SM-centric program transformations. In: Proceedings of the 29th ACM on International Conference on Supercomputing, pp. 119–130. ACM (2015)

Automatic Copying of Pointer-Based Data Structures

Tong Chen, Zehra Sura$^{(\boxtimes)}$, and Hyojin Sung

IBM T.J. Watson Research Center, New York, USA
{chentong,zsura,hsung}@us.ibm.com

Abstract. In systems with multiple memories, software may need to explicitly copy data from one memory location to another. This copying is required to enable access or to unlock performance, and it is especially important in heterogeneous systems. When the data includes pointers to other data, the copying process has to recursively follow the pointers to perform a deep copy of the entire data structure. It is tedious and error-prone to require users to manually program the deep copy code for each pointer-based data structure used. Instead, a compiler and runtime system can automatically handle deep copies if it can identify pointers in the data, and can determine the size and type of data pointed to by each pointer. This is possible if the language provides reflection capabilities, or uses smart pointers that encapsulate this information, e.g. Fortran pointers that intrinsically include dope vectors to describe the data pointed to. In this paper, we describe our implementation of automatic deep copy in a Fortran compiler targeting a heterogeneous system with GPUs. We measure the runtime overheads of the deep copies, propose techniques to reduce this overhead, and evaluate the efficacy of these techniques.

Keywords: Parallel computing · Heterogeneous systems · Compilers · Memory

1 Introduction

Massive parallelism and heterogeneity are prevalent in current systems designed for compute-intensive applications. These systems typically include multiple distributed memories, and software may need to explicitly copy data from one memory location to another. In some cases, this copying is necessary for certain processors in the system to be able to access the corresponding data. For example, in a system with host processors and GPU accelerators connected via an interconnect (e.g. PCIe), the system-wide memory and the on-chip GPU memory have separate address spaces. Host processors can directly refer to addresses in the system-wide memory, but the GPU processors can only refer to addresses in the on-chip GPU memory. Any program data operated on by the GPU has to be explicitly transferred to/from the system-wide memory. In other cases, all the processors in the system share a global address space, but because of non-uniform memory access times, it may still be worthwhile to copy data between different memory locations to combat performance loss due to NUMA effects.

© Springer International Publishing AG 2017
C. Ding et al. (Eds.): LCPC 2016, LNCS 10136, pp. 265–281, 2017.
DOI: 10.1007/978-3-319-52709-3_20

For application codes that use pointer-based data structures, the data to be copied includes pointers to other data, and the copying process has to recursively follow the pointers to perform a *deep copy* of the entire data structure. Further, pointer address values in the copied data have to be fixed to refer to addresses in the copied version of the data structure. It is tedious and error-prone to require users to manually program the deep copy code for each pointer-based data structure. Instead, a compiler and runtime system can automatically handle deep copies if it can identify pointers in the data, and can determine the size and type of data pointed to by each pointer. This is possible if the language provides reflection capabilities, or uses smart pointers that encapsulate this information, e.g. Fortran pointers that intrinsically include dope vectors to describe the data pointed to.

While our ideas are generally applicable to distributed memory systems, in this paper we focus on a CPU-GPU system with a host IBM POWER8 processor connected to an NVIDIA Kepler GPU via PCIe. Currently, the most common method used to program data transfers in such a system is to use the CUDA API [15] which provides runtime library calls for memory management and data transfers. However, this is a low-level API, and using it to manually program data copies can adversely affect productivity of software development.

An alternative method is to use CUDA Unified Memory [9], which provides a shared address space abstraction across the host processor and the GPU, with the underlying implementation transparently and automatically handling all data copies. Unified Memory is very easy to use from the programmer's perspective, but it can degrade performance for some applications since it is a uniform (one-size-fits-all) solution that works at page-based granularity and cannot be customized per application.

Yet another method for programming data transfers in a CPU-GPU system is to use a directive-based approach, such as OpenACC [17] or OpenMP [3] with accelerator support. These provide high-level annotations that the programmer can insert at appropriate points in the code to identify data that will be accessed on the GPU. The OpenACC/OpenMP implementation then takes care of performing data copies when necessary. This implementation not only performs data transfers, but is also responsible for GPU memory allocation/de-allocation, and for tracking data items that have been previously copied. The directive-based approach has the advantage of allowing application-specific optimization while also alleviating the tedium of programming to a low-level API. However, the OpenACC and OpenMP standards currently do not support deep copy for pointer-based data. Many applications include pointer-based data structures, and to use OpenACC/OpenMP for such applications, programmers must either devolve to using low-level APIs for copying their data, or they must re-structure program data so that deep copy is not needed. The latter may involve major code changes and may not be feasible. While the standards are evolving and trying to address these issues, the deep copy problem is tricky to solve, in part because OpenACC/OpenMP are geared towards high performance computing and are sensitive to runtime overheads introduced due to specification of the standards.

In this work, we explored the design and performance implications of supporting deep copy semantics in a directive-based programming model for Fortran. Our system integrates components at three levels:

1. Language features: In Fortran, implementing some language features (e.g. dynamic array sections) makes it necessary for the executable code to be able to store and access extra information for pointer fields and variables. The format of this information is implementation dependent and is referred to as a dope vector. There is a dope vector associated with each pointer, and the information stored in dope vectors can be accessed by runtime library code. Also, Fortran does not allow indiscriminate pointer casting or pointer arithmetic, which simplifies pointer handling by an automatic system.
2. Compiler analysis: For all types used in an application (intrinsic or user-defined types), information about the size and layout of each type is extracted in the compiler and made available to the runtime system.
3. Runtime system: Runtime library functions implement the code for data transfers, making use of dope vectors and compiler generated information to perform pointer traversals for deep copy.

We inserted OpenMP *map* clauses in Fortran program codes to identify data to be copied to or from the GPU memory. We modified our Fortran OpenMP compiler and runtime implementation to automatically support deep copy for all pointer-based data in the *map* clauses. Since Fortran pointers include dope vectors that describe the data being pointed to, our system has ready access to the information needed to support deep copy.

Contributions of this paper are as follows:

- We describe the design and implementation of our compiler and runtime support for automatically copying pointer-based data structures in Fortran OpenMP codes targeting a CPU-GPU system. Our algorithms include support for recursive data structures and cyclic pointer traversals (Sect. 2).
- We introduce techniques that can be applied to reduce the runtime overhead of deep copy (Sect. 3).
- We collect experimental data to measure the runtime overheads of our deep copy implementation, and evaluate the effectiveness of the techniques proposed to mitigate this overhead (Sect. 4).

2   Design and Implementation

Figure 1 shows a code snippet for declaring a simple pointer-based list data structure, and using OpenMP to copy and process the list on the GPU. Lines 7–9 form an OpenMP *target* region that is to be executed on the GPU. The OpenMP *map* clause on Line 7 is used to identify data to be copied to and from GPU memory. The map clause can be used with multiple options, for example it can specify that data only be mapped to the GPU, or only be mapped from the GPU. The default behaviour for mapping a data item is the following:

– On entry to a target region, if there is no copy of the data item in GPU memory, allocate it and transfer data to GPU memory.
– On exit from a target region, if this is the end of the lifetime of the data item, transfer data from the GPU copy to the host copy, and de-allocate GPU memory. The OpenMP specification includes rules that a runtime implementation has to use to keep track of the lifetimes of mapped data items.

2.1 Compilation

In our system, the compiler performs two functions relevant to data mapping. First, it inserts calls to the OpenMP runtime library to handle data copying for each data item specified in a map clause. These calls, Map_Enter and Map_Exit, are illustrated in Fig. 1 and described in Sects. 2.4 and 2.5. Second, it collects high-level type information and passes it to the runtime. In the example in Fig. 1, information for 3 types is collected: real, integer, and ListElem. The format used for passing type information is described in Sect. 2.2. The compiler can statically determine if a data item requires deep copy (i.e. if it is of pointer type, or if it contains pointer types), and if so, it passes the corresponding runtime type descriptor index as a parameter to the OpenMP library call inserted for the map. The runtime then uses this type descriptor information to recursively traverse the entire data structure and perform deep copy. In our design, the user can control when deep copy is performed by using an extension of OpenMP map-types to override the automatic deep copy behavior in specific map instances.

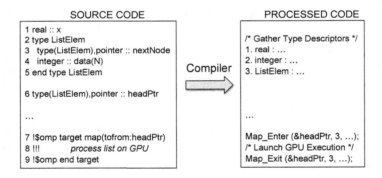

Fig. 1. Example to illustrate compiler actions

Dope Vectors. Information in a pointer variable typically contains only the address of the data pointed to. However, a Fortran pointer variable carries more information, as illustrated in Fig. 2. This information, collectively called the dope vector, is implementation dependent and may include the data address, a flag to indicate if the pointer is associated with valid data, the size of data, and shape of the data for array types. The shape information includes number of dimensions and bounds for each dimension. In our compiler, we use the existing format for dope vectors as-is. Fortran pointers are typed, i.e. a given pointer variable can only be associated with data of a matching type. The size of the dope vector can vary depending on its associated data type, but this size is known statically at compile time. The size of array data and bounds of array dimensions may be dynamically determined and recorded at runtime in the corresponding fields of the dope vector. Our system correctly handles copying of arrays with dynamic lengths. Also, our compiler processes Fortran allocatable arrays and Fortran pointers to arrays in a similar manner, and we treat them uniformly in the copying implementation.

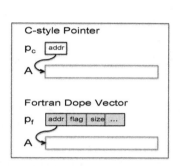

Fig. 2. Dope vector

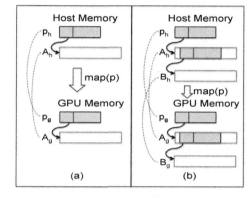

Fig. 3. Mapping fortran pointer-based data

Deep Copy. When copying a Fortran pointer between memories, both the dope vector and the data being pointed to have to be copied. Further, the address in the copied dope vector has to be updated to refer to the copied version of the data, as illustrated in Fig. 3(a). The runtime keeps track of data already copied by recording the corresponding pair of dope vector addresses, and the corresponding pair of data addresses, shown by the dashed lines in the figure.

When performing a deep copy, the data structure has to be traversed by following pointers within the data being copied. For such pointers that are not the top-level pointers, the dope vector is contained within the data already copied over, as illustrated in Fig. 3(b). In this case, only the data being pointed to has to be copied, and the address field in the dope vector has to be updated.

2.2 Runtime Type Descriptors

We introduced *runtime type descriptors* in our compiler and runtime system. To traverse the data structure for deep copy, the runtime has to be able to identify what parts of the data are pointer fields, and the type of data that these pointers refer to. The compiler has access to all type information for variables used in a compilation unit. It can collect the information required for traversals and pass it to the runtime by generating code to initialize runtime type descriptors on program start-up.

Figure 4 illustrates the format of the runtime type descriptor list. The index of an element in the list serves as an identifier for a data type (user-defined or otherwise) in the program code. There is an entry in the list for each type that contains pointer fields or that may be the target type associated with a pointer variable. A list entry is a type descriptor which is an integer value giving the size of the data type in bytes, followed by zero or more integer-triplets. Each triplet denotes a pointer field contained in the corresponding data type, and includes the following information:

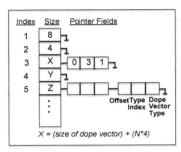

Fig. 4. Runtime type descriptors

1. Offset: length in bytes from the start of the data type to the pointer field.
2. Type ID: the index of the type descriptor list corresponding to the type of data pointed to by this pointer field.
3. Dope vector type: an identifier for the format of the dope vector corresponding to this pointer field. Our compiler uses different dope vector formats for scalar data versus arrays. For array types, each element of the array is traversed for deep copy.

In Fig. 4, index 1 corresponds to real type, index 2 corresponds to integer type, and index 3 corresponds to the ListElem type in the example code snippet of Fig. 1.

2.3   Assumptions

For automatic copying, we assume that the structure of the data is immutable during the time when multiple copies of the data exist. Specifically, this means that pointer fields within the data structure cannot change their value (both on the host, and on the GPU after the initial copy) during the lifetime of the mapped data. As a result, some application codes will not benefit from our automatic deep copy implementation and may need source code modification. However, there exists a large set of applications that will not be limited by this assumption. Note that the restriction applies only to pointers; other data fields may be freely modified.

Non-mutable pointers enable a low-overhead implementation of automatic deep copy. It may be possible to design algorithms that handle mutable data structures and work well in practice, but this is out of the scope of this paper.

2.4   Mapping Data on Target Entry

On entry to an OpenMP *target* region, the compiler generates host code to invoke a runtime library function for handling the data copy for each data item specified in a *map* clause. In our implementation we built upon an open-source OpenMP library[1], and modified it to support deep copy. Figure 5 shows the pseudocode for the runtime implementation. In this code, variable MapCount is used to track the lifetime of mapped data. We maintain MapCount for all data items reachable through deep copy traversals. We introduced variables globalMapID and MapID, which serve as timestamps to identify data items that have already been processed in a specific Map_Enter call. This allows our runtime to correctly handle cyclic pointer traversals in recursive data structures.

Figure 5(a), excluding the bold lines 8–11, 14, 18, and 19, is the existing code without support for deep copy. The Map_Enter function is invoked for each top-level data item to be copied. The runtime code keeps track of data that has been previously copied, maintaining a list of corresponding host and GPU addresses. It allocates GPU memory and transfers data for new copies. It also maintains a counter called MapCount for each host address to keep track of the lifetime of data copies. MapCount represents the number of top-level mapped variables that can reach a given address, either directly or through pointer traversals. It is used to automatically de-allocate GPU memory on exit from a *target* region for copies that can no longer be referenced.

```
1  GetOrCreate (h_addr,…)                       21  Struct DopeVector DV:
2    d_addr = LookupCorrespondence (h_addr)     22    flag IsAssociated
3    If (d_addr==NULL):                         23    address Data
4      IsNew = true                             24    …
5    /* Allocate GPU memory and
6       save addr in d_addr */
7    /* Record correspondence */                25  Map_Enter_DC (h_DV, d_DV, RT_Desc_ID,…)
8    If (MapID[h_addr] == globalMapID):         26    If (not h_DV.IsAssociated):
9      Visited = true                           27      Return
10   Else                                       28    <Visited, IsNew, d_addr> =
11     MapID[h_addr] = globalMapID              29        GetOrCreate (h_DV.Data,…)
12     MapCount[h_addr]++
                                                30    d_DV.Data = d_addr /* copy to GPU memory */

13 Map_Enter (h_addr, RT_Desc_ID,…)             31    If (Visited):
14   globalMapID++                              32      Return
15   <IsNew, d_addr> = GetOrCreate(h_addr,…)
16   If (IsNew):                                33    If (IsNew):
17     /* Copy contents h_addr to d_addr */     34      /* Copy contents h_DV.Data to d_DV.Data */
18   For each ptr field offset DV in h_addr:    35    For each ptr field offset DV in h_DV.Data:
19     Map_Enter_DC (h_addr+DV, d_addr+DV,…)    36      Map_Enter_DC(h_DV.Data+DV, d_DV.Data+DV,…)

                  (a)                                              (b)
```

Fig. 5. Pseudocode for copying data on target entry

---

[1] Intel OpenMP Runtime Library: https://www.openmprtl.org.

The bold sections of Fig. 5(a), together with the code in Fig. 5(b), are our modifications for supporting deep copy. We introduced a variable, globalMapID, that is incremented on each call to Map_Enter and is unique to that instance of the call. We also introduced a MapID variable for each host address mapped, and set it to the globalMapID value whenever a host address is processed as part of a Map_Enter call. Lines 8–11, 14, and 31–32 allow us to correctly handle recursive data structures when performing pointer traversals for deep copy. Lines 18–19 initiate the deep copy traversal by using the runtime type descriptor parameter to identify pointer fields in the data corresponding to the address being mapped. The Map_Enter_DC function is invoked for each of these pointer fields. This function is similar to the top-level Map_Enter function, except that it also checks if the pointer is associated with data (lines 26–27 that handle null pointers), fixes the pointer values in the GPU copy of the data (line 30), and handles recursive traversal (lines 35–36).

Note that the pseudocode in Fig. 5 is simplified for clarity of presentation. The actual implementation is more complex because it includes optimizations as well as functionality to handle various *map* attributes that are part of the OpenMP specification. The deep copy part of the code also handles these attributes, propagating them in the recursive traversal. For aliasing of array sections, we impose the same restrictions as the current OpenMP standard, i.e. the first time an array is copied (mapped) in a *target* region, it must include all subsections of the array that will be subsequently mapped during the lifetime of the initial array copy. This allows us to reuse the existing logic in the runtime library to track corresponding addresses for host and GPU copies and avoid creating multiple copies of the same data.

2.5   Mapping Data on Target Exit

There is a runtime library function Map_Exit analogous to the Map_Enter function described in the previous section. On exit from an OpenMP *target* region, the compiler generates host code to invoke this function for each data item in *map* clauses associated with the *target* region. Map_Exit uses the same globalMapID, MapID, and MapCount variables as Map_Enter, and it similarly traverses pointers for deep copy. The differences between the two functions are that:

- Map_Exit copies data in the reverse direction, from GPU memory to host memory.
- Map_Exit decrements MapCount instead of incrementing it.
- Map_Exit de-allocates GPU memory and deletes the correspondence when the MapCount for an address becomes zero.

3   Optimizations

The ease-of-use and productivity benefits of automatic deep copy have to be balanced with the runtime overhead of traversing data structures and performing multiple transfers corresponding to pointers in the data. In this section, we propose several techniques that can be used to reduce the runtime overhead.

3.1   Transfers to/from GPU Memory

When a user-defined data type contains a mix of pointer and non-pointer data, the pointer data has to be treated differently from the non-pointer data for the purpose of transfers to and from GPU memory. This is because the pointer address values in the GPU copy have to be fixed to point to data in GPU memory (refer to line 30 of the code in Fig. 5). We describe 4 different techniques to perform data transfers of structures with a mix of pointer and non-pointer data. These techniques have different overheads depending on the number and contiguity of pointer fields and the size of data fields in the data type. In Fig. 6, we illustrate the techniques using a simple example. In the figure, p and X represent host values for a pointer field and a data field, while p_g and X_g represent the corresponding GPU values. Dotted lines connect the same memory locations, and numbered circles represent the sequence of operations.

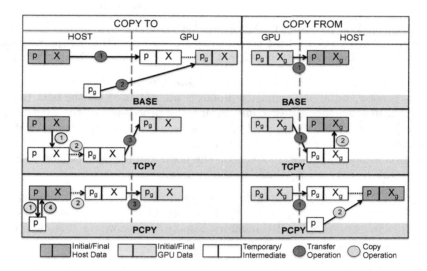

Fig. 6. Techniques to optimize pointer-based data transfers

1. Basic Version (BASE)

Copy to GPU Memory: We first transfer the entire data structure to GPU memory. Then, for each pointer field, we transfer the GPU address value to the corresponding pointer field. Pointer fields are individually transferred only if they are associated.

Copy from GPU Memory: In this case, we cannot transfer the entire data structure to the host, since that will overwrite the original pointer address values on the host. Instead, we individually transfer each contiguous non-pointer data segment in the structure.

2. Basic Version With Self-Managed Memory (BASE+)

This is the same as the BASE version except that it uses self-managed GPU memory in the runtime. The CUDA library function, cudaMalloc, is used to allocate GPU memory. Repeatedly invoking this function during a deep copy can result in high overhead. In our implementation, we use a single call to allocate a large GPU memory space, and then self-manage this space in the runtime library to efficiently perform multiple smaller allocations and deallocations. All following versions (TCPY and PCPY) also use self-managed GPU memory.

3. Version with Temporary Copies (TCPY)

For this version, we first create a temporary copy of the data structure on the host.

Copy to GPU Memory: We overwrite the pointer address fields in the temporary copy with the corresponding GPU address values. Then we do a single transfer of the entire data structure from the temporary copy to GPU memory.

Copy from GPU Memory: We transfer the entire data structure from GPU memory to the temporary host copy. Then we copy only the non-pointer data from the temporary copy to the original data structure on the host.

4. Version with Temporary Pointer Value Copies (PCPY)

For this version, we assume that the pointers are not used on the host (due to accesses in multithreaded host code) during the processing of the map clause. This property can be determined by compiler analysis in some cases, or it can be provided by the user via program annotations.

We first allocate temporary space on the host, and for each pointer field, we copy the value of the host pointer to the temporary space.

Copy to GPU Memory: We update the pointer address values to corresponding GPU address values in-place in the host copy of the data. We then transfer the entire data structure to GPU memory. Finally, we restore the original pointer values in the host copy.

Copy from GPU Memory: We transfer the entire data structure from GPU memory to the host. Then for each pointer field, we copy the host address value of the pointer from temporary space to its original location.

For TCPY and PCPY, the runtime checks if a data item has any associated (non-null) pointers before it creates temporary copies on the host.

Table 1 gives the overheads associated with each technique in terms of number of transfers, size of data transferred, and size of temporary copies on the host. We assume S is the size of the data structure to be copied, DV is the size of a dope vector, and M is the number of pointer fields in the data structure. Note that the number of transfers for the copy-from case in the BASE versions depends on the contiguity of pointer fields in the layout of the data structure.

Table 1. Cost of different data transfer techniques

	Number of transfers	Size of transfers	Size of host copies
BASE copy to	1+M	S+M*DV	0
BASE copy from	varies	S–M*DV	0
TCPY	1	S	S–M*DV
PCPY	1	S	M*DV

3.2 Other Optimizations

In this section, we discuss some other optimizations that can be applied based on information obtained from programmer annotations and/or sophisticated analysis.

Structured Maps. In addition to the assumptions in Sect. 2.3, if it is known that data transfer directives are only associated with structured programming constructs[2], then the runtime overhead can be reduced. In this case, the globalMapID of Sect. 2.4 is used to track the level of the nesting structure by incrementing it on each Map_Enter call and decrementing it on each Map_Exit call. The MapID for an address is set to the current nesting level only when corresponding memory is newly allocated on the GPU in a Map_Enter or Map_Enter_DC call. That corresponding GPU memory is copied back/de-allocated at the end of the structured nesting level (i.e. in the first Map_Exit call that decrements the globalMapID to a value less than the MapID for the address). There is no need to maintain the MapCount for each mapped address. Also, following default OpenMP semantics for data copying (without the *always* modifier on the map clause), data is copied to GPU memory only when it is first allocated and copied back only when it is de-allocated. As a result, there is no need to recursively traverse the data structure multiple times. Only one traversal at the beginning and one at the end of the lifetime of the mapped data is needed. Thus, there is significant potential for improving runtime performance.

User Specified De-allocation. The runtime maintains a MapCount per address so that it can automatically determine the end of the lifetime of a mapped data item, i.e. when the data item should be copied back and de-allocated from the GPU. If the programmer is solely responsible for specifying this, e.g. by using the OpenMP *delete* map-type, then there is no need to maintain MapCounts, or to recursively traverse data structures multiple times. Thus, performance can be improved.

---

[2] This excludes the use of OpenMP directives such as target enter data and target exit data.

Asynchronous Transfers. By default, our implementation uses synchronous data transfer calls. However, NVIDIA GPUs support asynchronous data transfers using the CUDA Streams API. If sufficient bandwidth is available, multiple transfers can be overlapped for better performance. For the techniques described in Sect. 3.1, explicit synchronization is needed in the BASE versions when transferring data to the GPU, between the single transfer of the entire data and the subsequent transfers for fixing individual pointer values. All other transfers corresponding to the same OpenMP *map* clause can proceed in parallel.

Selective Pointer Traversal. Prior work [5] based on OpenACC described ways for the programmer to specify which fields of a data structure to treat as pointers to be traversed in an automatic deep copy implementation. Selective pointer traversal can be applied in combination with any of the optimization techniques discussed in this section.

4   Experiments

In this section, we report the results of experiments performed to measure the overheads of our automatic deep copy implementation. We focused our measurements on the time taken by the runtime library calls invoked for data mapping, and on the time taken by data transfers. We ran our experiments on a system with an IBM POWER8 LE host running Linux Ubuntu 14.04, connected to an NVIDIA Kepler K40 GPU via PCIe, using CUDA version 8.0.

Our compiler system uses the IBM XL Fortran front-end to parse the OpenMP source code. It then translates the output of the front-end to Clang AST format. This Clang AST code is processed by the open-source Clang OpenMP compiler to generate a binary that executes across the host and GPU. We implement our runtime techniques by modifying the open-source runtime library that is included with the Clang OpenMP compiler. For self-managed GPU memory, we use a single call to cudaMalloc to initially allocate 2 GB of GPU memory, and then manage this space in the runtime code.

We use the following benchmark codes for our evaluation:

- **List**: This code constructs and initializes a linked list of length 1024 on the host, and then traverses the list on the GPU. The type of each list element is as shown in Fig. 1. There are 3 versions of the code obtained by varying the size of the list element: 128 bytes, 1 KB, and 1 MB.
- **SplitList**: This code uses a linked list where each list element has 2 data fields that are separated by a pointer field in the middle. As before, there are 3 versions of the code, corresponding to sizes 128 bytes, 1 KB, and 1 MB.
- **Tree**: This is a height-balanced binary tree with 1024 nodes. Each node has a left-child pointer, followed by a data field, followed by a right-child pointer. There are 3 versions of the code, corresponding to node sizes 128 bytes, 1 KB, and 1 MB.

– **UMT**: This is the kernel version of the UMT application [2], which performs three-dimensional, non-linear, radiation transport calculations. It is representative of real application code written using pointer-based data structures, and requires automatic deep copy support for easily porting it to systems with multiple memories. The data structure includes 3-level pointer chains, with multiple pointer fields at levels 2 and 3. We insert OpenMP directives to transfer 2000 nodes in the data structure to GPU memory. Total data size transferred is approximately 2.2 GB.

Results for List, SplitList, and Tree

For benchmarks List, SplitList, and Tree, Fig. 7 shows the time in seconds taken to process data transfers in the runtime. Data is separately presented for transfers to the GPU (Fig. 7(a), (b), and (c)) and transfers from the GPU (Fig. 7(d), (e), and (f)). There are 3 sizes for each benchmark, and 4 versions for each size corresponding to the different techniques described in Sect. 3.1.

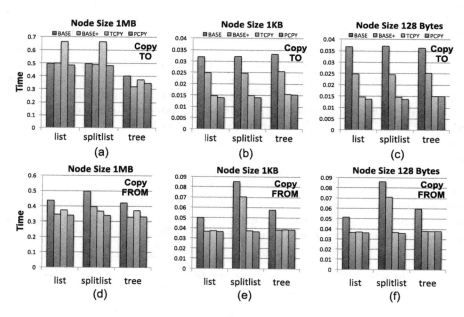

Fig. 7. Time taken for data transfers (seconds)

The data in Fig. 7 is used to compare the relative performance of the different versions. The low performance of the BASE version clearly shows the benefit of using self-managed memory. Overall, the results are as expected: the overhead of the extra host copy in TCPY dominates when data size is 1 MB, and the overhead of extra transfers when copying to the GPU in BASE+ dominates at smaller data sizes. The results for size 128 bytes closely match those for size 1 KB, as latency costs dominate the transfer time for small data sizes. Note that for SplitList, when copying from the GPU, BASE+ always has higher overhead than TCPY and PCPY. This is because SplitList has 2 data fields per node that are separately copied back to the host in BASE+.

In Fig. 7(a), the versions for Tree take noticeably less time than List or SplitList. Tree has 2 pointers per node but the total number of data transfers for fixing pointer values in GPU copies in BASE+ is the same as the number of transfers for List and SplitList. This is because our runtime does not initiate any transfers for fixing pointers that are null, and the pointers in the leaf nodes of Tree are all null. Since the overall number and sizes of transfers initiated for all 3 benchmarks are similar for corresponding versions, the disparate times for Tree are due to differences in data structure traversal and clustering/sequencing of the data transfers. Profiling using nvprof shows that in this case the difference can be attributed to time spent in various CUDA API calls, while the actual transfer times are almost the same. Note that even though Tree BASE+ uses more data transfers than Tree PCPY, it performs better for size 1 MB because PCPY has greater overhead for copying the multiple pointers per node in Tree.

Figure 8 shows the percentage of effectively available bandwidth achieved for each of the testcases in Fig. 7(a), (b), and (c). The effectively available bandwidth is the maximum achievable bandwidth for the pattern of transfers dictated by the data structure traversal (not the maximum bandwidth provided in hardware). We compute the effectively available bandwidth by running a manually coded CUDA version that only does GPU memory allocation/deallocation and the sequence of data transfers corresponding to each optimization version. The CUDA version gives an optimistic upper bound on bandwidth, and it does not include any overheads of our runtime such as data structure traversal, address/offset computation, or checks and updates related to OpenMP implementation. Bandwidth is computed as the ratio of actual data transferred over the wall clock time taken to execute the code that processes transfers. The percent bandwidth achieved compared to the optimistic CUDA version is a measure of the overhead in the OpenMP runtime library code. Note that this overhead depends on data size for some optimization cases.

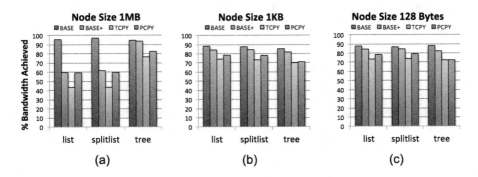

Fig. 8. Percentage bandwidth achieved compared to optimistic CUDA version

In all cases except List and SplitList for 1 MB, we achieve 70% or greater of the optimistic maximum bandwidth. As expected, the absolute values of the bandwidth are proportional to the data size, e.g. bandwidth values for size 1 MB are an order of magnitude larger than the values for size 1 KB. Also, for a given benchmark/size, the optimistic bound computed for BASE is lower than that computed for BASE+, which in turn is lower than that computed for TCPY and PCPY. This explains why the percent bandwidths achieved by BASE and BASE+ are relatively higher even though they spend more time processing data transfers. On average across all cases, 77.5% of the effectively available bandwidth is achieved.

We also implemented a version of our runtime using asynchronous data transfers with two CUDA streams. However, for our testcases, the overheads associated with asynchronous transfers (allocating/copying to pinned host memory, and API calls for synchronization) caused slowdowns in overall performance. Further experiments are needed to determine if these overheads can be overcome.

Results for UMT
We also measured the performance of automatic deep copy for transferring data to the GPU in the UMT benchmark. For each version BASE, BASE+, TCPY, and PCPY, Table 2 shows the time in seconds to process the data transfer, and the bandwidth of the transfer in GB/s. As a reference, the absolute values of the bandwidths achieved by the 1 MB size testcases in Fig. 8(a) ranged from 1.615 GB/s to 3.358 GB/s. The results of our initial experiments indicate that the overhead of automatic deep copy may be tolerable for practical use cases.

Table 2. UMT transfers to GPU memory

	BASE	BASE+	TCPY	PCPY
Time (seconds)	5.4382	3.3708	2.6548	2.3492
Bandwidth (GB/s)	0.4367	0.7045	0.8944	1.0107

5   Related Work

Prior work related to OpenACC [5,17] has addressed the issue of designing automatic deep copy traversals, and it is supported to some extent in the Cray and PGI Fortran compilers. However, overheads associated with deep copy are not well understood. In our work, we described and implemented a specific algorithm for deep copy that also supports cyclic pointer traversals, proposed optimization techniques based on this algorithm, and performed experiments to measure the overheads of different techniques.

The main advantage of our automatic deep copying approach is it enables ease of programming. Software shared memory abstractions (e.g. [4,11,14]) provide another way to make programming easier. CUDA Unified Memory(UM) [9] is a shared memory abstraction available on systems with NVIDIA GPUs. UM is an on-demand solution that works on OS page-size granularity, and can have very high overhead in some cases. In contrast, our approach can incorporate prefetching optimizations, and can be specifically optimized for each application's data structures and access patterns.

The system used in our experiments has a PCIe interconnect between the CPU and GPU. NVLink [7] is a custom high-bandwidth interconnect that can be used with NVIDIA GPUs. We expect that using a system with NVLink will help reduce the overheads associated with automatic deep copies.

Our implementation is based on OpenMP. The directives for data mapping in OpenACC are very similar to those in OpenMP. There are other high-level paradigms for programming heterogeneous systems, such as C++ AMP [8] and Kokkos [6], both of which use the concept of data views. These aim to enable performance portability for data accesses; they do not provide support for automatically traversing recursive pointer-based data structures.

Garbage collection [13] techniques for memory management automatically track the lifetimes of pointer-based data. In our algorithm, we also track the lifetime of data encountered in deep copy traversals, except our case is simpler because we follow OpenMP semantics. Specifically, we only track the number of variables directly specified in map clauses that may reach a given data item through deep copy traversal.

In our work, we rely on Fortran language features to completely automate deep copy traversals. For other languages such as Java/C/C++, there exist libraries and APIs for serialization that can be used to partially automate deep copy traversals.

6   Conclusion

We designed and implemented automatic support for deep copy of pointer-based data structures across multiple memories. We proposed several techniques that can be applied to optimize the overhead of pointer-based data transfers. We obtained experimental data to evaluate the overheads of our implementation in a CPU-GPU system, and to determine the applicability of the different techniques proposed. Overall, our work shows that automatic copying of pointer-based data structures can be implemented using the compiler and runtime with manageable overheads.

Acknowledgement. This work was supported in part by the United States Department of Energy CORAL program (contract B604142).

References

1. MPI: A Message-Passing Interface Standard. Technical report, Knoxville, TN, USA (1994)
2. CORAL Benchmark Codes: Single Node UMT Microkernel (2014). https://asc.llnl.gov/CORAL-benchmarks/#umtmk

3. OpenMP Application Programming Interface, v4.5 (2015). http://openmp.org/wp/openmp-specifications

4. Bershad, B., Zekauskas, M., Sawdon, W.: The midway distributed shared memory system. In: Compcon Digest of Papers (1993)

5. Beyer, J., Oehmke, D., Sandoval, J.: Transferring user-defined types in OpenACC. In: Proceedings of Cray User Group (2014)

6. Edwards, H.C., Trott, C.R., Sunderland, D.: Kokkos. J. Parallel Distrib. Comput. **74**(12), 3202–3216 (2014)

7. Foley, D.: NVLink, Pascal and Stacked Memory: Feeding the Appetite for Big Data. https://devblogs.nvidia.com/parallelforall/nvlink-pascal-stacked-memory-ifeedng-appetite-big-data

8. Gregory, K., Miller, A.: C++ AMP: Accelerated Massive Parallelism with Microsoft® Visual C++®. Microsoft Press, Redmond (2012)

9. Harris, M.: Unified Memory in CUDA 6. https://devblogs.nvidia.com/parallelforall/unified-memory-in-cuda-6

10. HSA Foundation: HSA Runtime Programmer's Reference Manual, version 1.1 (2016)

11. Iftode, L., Singh, J.P., Li, K.: Scope consistency: a bridge between release consistency and entry consistency. Theory Comput. Syst. **31**(4), 451–473 (1998)

12. Jablin, T., Jablin, J., Prabhu, P., Liu, F., August, D.: Dynamically managed data for CPU-GPU architectures. In: International Symposium on Code Generation and Optimization (2012)

13. Jones, R., Hosking, A., Moss, E.: The Garbage Collection Handbook: The Art of Automatic Memory Management. Chapman & Hall/CRC, Boca Raton (2011)

14. Keleher, P., Cox, A.L., Zwaenepoel, W.: Lazy release consistency for software distributed shared memory. In: International Symposium on Computer Architecture (ISCA) (1992)

15. NVIDIA Corporation: NVIDIA CUDA C Programming Guide (2010)

16. NVIDIA Corporation: PGI Accelerator Compilers OpenACC Getting Started Guide (2016)

17. OpenACC-Standard.org. The OpenACC application programming interface, v 2.5 (2015)

18. Tian, C., Feng, M., Gupta, R.: Supporting speculative parallelization in the presence of dynamic data structures. In: Programming Language Design and Implementation (2010)

Automatic Local Memory Management for Multicores Having Global Address Space

Kouhei Yamamoto[1], Tomoya Shirakawa[1], Yoshitake Oki[1], Akimasa Yoshida[1,2], Keiji Kimura[1], and Hironori Kasahara[1(✉)]

[1] Department of Computer Science and Engineering,
Waseda University, Tokyo, Japan
{yamamoto,tshira,okiyoshi}@kasahara.cs.waseda.ac.jp,
akimasay@meiji.ac.jp, kimura@apal.cs.waseda.ac.jp, kasahara@waseda.jp
[2] Graduate School of Advanced Mathematical Sciences,
Meiji University, Tokyo, Japan
http://www.kasahara.cs.waseda.ac.jp

Abstract. Embedded multicore processors for hard real-time applications like automobile engine control require the usage of local memory on each processor core to precisely meet the real-time deadline constraints, since cache memory cannot satisfy the deadline requirements due to cache misses. To utilize local memory, programmers or compilers need to explicitly manage data movement and data replacement for local memory considering the limited size. However, such management is extremely difficult and time consuming for programmers. This paper proposes an automatic local memory management method by compilers through (i) multi-dimensional data decomposition techniques to fit working sets onto limited size local memory (ii) suitable block management structures, called Adjustable Blocks, to create application specific fixed size data transfer blocks (iii) multi-dimensional templates to preserve the original multi-dimensional representations of the decomposed multi-dimensional data that are mapped onto one-dimensional Adjustable Blocks (iv) block replacement policies from liveness analysis of the decomposed data, and (v) code size reduction schemes to generate shorter codes. The proposed local memory management method is implemented on the OSCAR multigrain and multi-platform compiler and evaluated on the Renesas RP2 8 core embedded homogeneous multicore processor equipped with local and shared memory. Evaluations on 5 programs including multimedia and scientific applications show promising results. For instance, speedups on 8 cores compared to single core execution using off-chip shared memory on an AAC encoder program, a MPEG2 encoder program, Tomcatv, and Swim are improved from 7.14 to 20.12, 1.97 to 7.59, 5.73 to 7.38, and 7.40 to 11.30, respectively, when using local memory with the proposed method. These evaluations indicate the usefulness and the validity of the proposed local memory management method on real embedded multicore processors.

Keywords: Parallelizing compiler · Local memory management · Multicore · Global address space · DMA · Data decomposition

© Springer International Publishing AG 2017
C. Ding et al. (Eds.): LCPC 2016, LNCS 10136, pp. 282–296, 2017.
DOI: 10.1007/978-3-319-52709-3_21

1   Introduction

As modern embedded systems demand for more performance with lower power consumption, the architectural design of multicore processor has succeeded in pursuing both requirements. However, in embedded multicores for hard real-time control systems such as automobile engine control units, cache memory cannot be used to meet hard deadline constraints. In these systems, multicore architectures having local memories with addresses mapped to parts of global address space have been generally used. Examples of such embedded multicore processors are Renesas's RP2 [15] and V850E2/MX4 [18].

Local memory is a fast on-chip memory which can be explicitly controlled by software. Typically, local memory is reserved for data that is extensively reused throughout the entire program. A similar class of fast on-chip software controllable memory is scratch-pad memory [1, 11]. Although the functionality of scratch-pad memory is similar to local memory, scratch-pad memory is generally smaller in size and is specialized for data locality on a finer region of the program.

The low latency and software manageable characteristics of local memory offers guaranteed execution timing, which is a crucial property for real-time control embedded domains. Moreover, optimal mapping of data onto local memory through software implementations can achieve data locality and satisfy deadline requirements by removing runtime uncertainties by cache miss hits.

There remains a major obstacle when utilizing software based local memory for embedded systems with multicore processors: the mapping and decomposition of data onto local memory of each processor core. In other words, the use of local memory considering data locality requires comprehensive control of data placement and eviction by the programmer. To overcome this difficulty, a promising approach is to build a compiler algorithm to automatically decompose data and insert data transfer codes. Such compiler based approach will not only prevent error-prone code productions otherwise done by the programmer, but will also allow local memory optimizations to become available for a wide range of applications.

In this paper, a local memory management method with data decomposition for software controlled un-cached local memory on multicore processors is proposed to satisfy deadline constraints and obtain high performance. In particular, the method realizes local memory management techniques that determine data placement and replacement on local memory considering data locality over the whole input C program. The data decomposition process decomposes multi-dimensional arrays for each nested level. Additionally, data transfer costs between multiple processor cores are mitigated through Direct Memory Access (DMA) controllers. To allow automatic parallelization for various applications using local memories, the method is implemented on OSCAR compiler, a C and Fortran source-to-source multi-grain and multi-platform parallelizing compiler [13]. The effectiveness of the proposed method is demonstrated through several benchmark applications written in Parallelizable C [10] that have various data sizes and dimensions.

The rest of the paper is organized as follows. Section 2 introduces related works. Section 3 covers the proposed data decomposition method and local memory management method. Section 4 shows evaluation results of the proposed methods on benchmark applications. Section 5 concludes the paper.

2   Related Works

There have been many researches on local memory management methods.

In static data management, data partitions and allocations remain constant throughout the lifetime of the program. Avissar et al. proposed a compiler strategy that automatically partitions and allocates data onto different memory units [2]. Similar methods were reported by Steinke et al., utilizing a compiler extension technique for embedded systems to analyze the most frequently used data and variable within the application for static mapping onto local memory [3]. Steinke's analysis focuses mainly on reducing energy consumption by utilizing energy efficient local memories over caches. Panda et al. reported a method to partition scalars and array variables and map them onto on-chip scratchpad memory at compile time [1]. Excess variables that could not fit on scratch-pad memory are mapped onto off-chip memory. However, their approach is limited to single thread execution environments. For static allocation of data onto multi-core processor environments, Che et al. presented an integer linear programming formulation and a heuristic technique to model code overlays and communication costs to maximize throughput of stream programs [4]. Their method shows improvement on stream programs for static allocations, but does not mention explicit mapping managements of data onto local memory. Similarly, Issenin et al. proposed a data reuse method for loops on multicore processor environments [8]. Their method focuses on data locality within loops, but does not consider locality between tasks of the entire program.

To achieve flexibility for allocated variables during the entire runtime of the program, several dynamic allocation algorithms for local memory are presented. Udayakumaran et al. proposed a dynamic allocation method that considers runtime behaviors of the program running on a single core processor [5]. Specifically, their method copies frequently accessed data onto scratch-pad memory by compiler codes dynamically and evict unused data to free scratch-pad space. However, the method is relevant only for single thread environments, neglecting communication and synchronization costs that occur for multicore processor environments. For multicore processor systems, Guo et al. proposed a data allocation algorithm for scratchpad memories to reduce memory access cost [6]. They incorporate a data duplication algorithm to extensively copy specific data onto remote processor core's scratch-pad memory to further reduce memory access costs. However, their method does not present explicit management techniques for mapping data onto local memory. Kandemir et al. proposed a data tiling strategy for multicore processor systems [7]. Their method focuses on array-intensive applications, and aims to increase inter-processor data sharing opportunities and minimize off-chip memory requests. Their technique, however, considers data locality within loops and does not extract locality that spreads across the entire program.

As presented in this section, partitioning and allocating data onto software managed memory has been attempted by various researchers. However, the majority of the proposed solutions consider static or dynamic allocations of data that only assume single thread environments. Moreover, previous methods do not target data locality stretched across multiple coarse-grain tasks or local memory management techniques that extensively control the position of the stored data on local memory. Therefore, an integrated analysis of dynamically allocating and evicting data on coarse-grain tasks, including arrays accessed within nested loops, for software managed local memory under a multicore processor environment, to our knowledge, has not been attempted so far.

3   The Proposed Local Memory Management Method

The target architecture of the proposed method consists of multiple processor cores with an on-chip and/or off-chip centralized shared memory, or CSM. An example architecture is the OSCAR multicore architecture shown in Fig. 1 [10]. Each processor core is equipped with local data memory, or LDM, for core private data and a distributed shared memory, or DSM, for data shared among processor cores. In embedded multicores, since the local memories are mapped to global address space, they can be recognized as distributed shared memory. Often, local memory is implemented by a single port memory and distributed shared memory is implemented using two ports memory. Within this memory architecture, the proposed method aims to exploit data locality of core private data on local memory. The main idea of the proposed method is to decompose data so that a working set can fit on LDM and the data on LDM can be reused among different coarse-grain tasks.

An overview of the proposed compiler local memory management method for multicores using adjustable block assignment and replacement technique is summarized below.

1. Chooses block sizes for data transfer between shared memory and LDM specifically for each application.
2. Divides all data in the application into constant size aligned block structures called Adjustable Blocks. In contrast to other block allocation schemes such as buddy memory allocators where block sizes are restricted to multiples of powers of two and the granularity of the block is defined as a single page size, Adjustable Blocks divide data into integer divisible sizes and can further divide blocks into single word sizes for scalar variables.
3. Hierarchically decomposes multi-dimensional arrays by the outer-most loop dimension until the decomposed array fits inside the chosen block size.
4. Maps each decomposed array to assigned blocks on LDM considering locality optimizations.
5. Schedules eviction and reloading of blocks from LDM and shared memory. Blocks with dead variables or blocks with variables that will be reused in the most distant future have high replacement priorities.

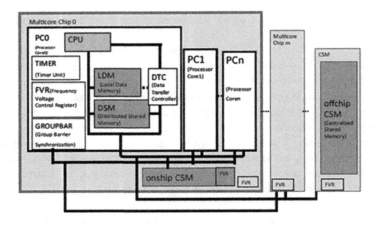

Fig. 1. Overview of the OSCAR multicore architecture

3.1   Coarse-Grain Task Parallelization [13, 14]

The input C program is initially divided into coarse-grain tasks, or tasks with
sufficient amount of work that can be efficiently scheduled to processors by the
compiler. Coarse-grain tasks are also called Macro Tasks (MTs), and are divided
into three categories: Basic Blocks (BBs), Repetition Blocks (RBs) for loops, and
Subroutine Blocks (SBs) for functions. RBs and SBs are hierarchically decomposed into smaller MTs if coarse-grain task parallelism still exists within the
task, as shown in RB number 7 in Fig. 2. After all MTs for the input program
are generated, they are analyzed to produce a Macro Flow Graph (MFG). MFGs
depict the control flow and the data dependencies of the entire input program
as a graph structure. Further, Macro Task Graphs (MTGs) are generated by
analyzing the earliest executable condition [13] of every MT and analyzing the
control dependencies and data dependencies among MTs on the MFG. MTGs
illustrate parallelism among MTs and are utilized as the baseline structure for
the proposed data localization method to extract data locality from the entire
input program. An example MFG and MTG is illustrated in Figs. 2 and 3.

The scheduling of MTs to processor cores can be done either statically at
compile time or dynamically at run time. The decision of static or dynamic
scheduling of MTs depends on the topology and the branch structure of the
MTG of the input program.

3.2   Data Decomposition Method

By analyzing the MTG of the input program, the data decomposition phase
decomposes RBs connected by data dependence edges on the MTG so that data
transfers among the data dependent RBs can be made through LDMs.

The data decomposition process begins by creating groups of loops, or Target
Loop Groups (TLGs), from the MTG that access the same arrays. The loops

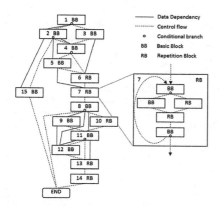

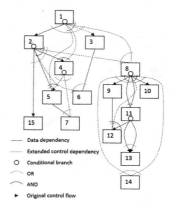

Fig. 2. Macro flow graph (MFG)   **Fig. 3.** Macro task graph (MTG)

within these groups are then analyzed for dependencies through the Inter-Loop Dependency (ILD) analysis phase [14]. Once this dependency analysis completes, the number of required decompositions, namely the number of small loops each loop should be decomposed into, is decided from the available LDM size and the array sizes accessed by the decomposed loops.

3.2.1 Target Loop Group (TLG) Creation and Inter-Loop Dependency (ILD) Analysis

Loops that access the same array are gathered into group of loops called TLGs. The loop with the largest estimated time within a TLG is chosen as the baseline loop for that specific TLG. This baseline loop is used as a criterion for the data dependency check on the ILD analysis phase. Figure 4 depicts an example where the baseline loop is chosen as RB3, which is data dependent on indices i and i−1 of RB2 and i−1, i, and i+1 of RB1. The ILD analysis phase resolves data dependencies between loops within the generated TLGs and detects relevant iterations of those loops that have dependence with the iterations of the baseline loop. Moreover, the ILD analysis phase detects Commonly Accessed Regions (CAR), or array regions accessed by multiple processors, and Localizable Regions (LR), or array regions accessed by a single processor, of each TLG. Data reuse

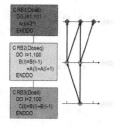

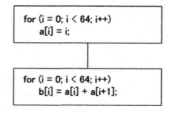

Fig. 4. Example of ILD analysis   **Fig. 5.** A simple TLG with two loops

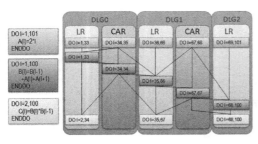

Fig. 6. Example of localizable regions (LR) and commonly acccessed regions (CAR)

can be performed on arrays accessed by LRs that stretch across multiple loops within a TLG, since LRs encompass loop regions that can be safely kept in LDMs of each processor. An example diagram of IR and CAR is shown in Fig. 6. Figure 5 shows an example of a TLG. In this example, the second loop is chosen as the baseline loop since its estimated cost is larger than the first loop. For the indices of array a, iteration i of the baseline loop has dependencies on iteration i of the first loop and iteration i+1 of the current loop.

3.2.2 Decomposition Count

The working set size of data shared across multiple decomposed small loops after decomposition must be strictly less than the available LDM size of the target processor core. To mitigate the algorithmic complexity for parameter calculations, the presented method chooses decomposition counts, namely the number of small data portions each data should be decomposed into, that allows all decomposed arrays within a TLG to simultaneously exist on LDM. By simplifying the decomposition decision algorithm, the method guarantees mapping of arbitrary sized arrays onto LDM with low overhead.

3.2.3 Extending the Data Decomposition Method to Multi-dimensional Loops

Previous data decomposition schemes that exploit data locality mostly focus on dividing the outer-most loop of a nested loop. Hence, these methods can not treat cases where decomposition of the outer loop fails to generate array sizes smaller than the available LDM size. In contrast, the data localization method presented in this paper is safely applicable to loops with arbitrary dimensions.

Figure 7 depicts an example of decomposing only the outer-most loop of a nested loop. In this example, dividing the outer-most loop still leaves behind a 64 iteration inner loop, which accesses an array shared between two loops. Previous data decomposition methods will fail to place the array onto LDM if this target array size is larger than the available LDM size. Figure 8 illustrates an example of decomposing both the outer and the inner loop of the original loop

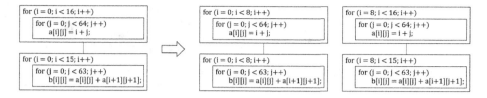

Fig. 7. Decomposition of only the outer loop

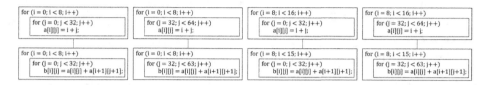

Fig. 8. Decomposition of outer and inner loops

code of Fig. 7. By calculating the necessary decomposition count from the total array size and the LDM size, the decomposition process not only terminates on the outer-most loop, but continues inwardly onto inner loops and decides the decomposition count for each nest level. By hierarchically dividing each nest level, data size of the accessed array can be significantly reduced, ultimately allowing programs with large data size to adjustably fit on LDM.

3.3   Scheduling of Decomposed Loops

Decomposed loops with common iteration ranges are placed and executed on the same processor core to achieve data locality. Decomposed loops with accessing the same iteration ranges are grouped together into Data Localizable Groups (DLGs) [14]. An example of DLG is shown in Fig. 6. Once DLGs are generated, the decomposed small loops within each DLG are statically scheduled to the same processor core.

3.4   Local Memory Management

The challenge of mapping and evicting decomposed data for LDM still remains. To address this problem, the LDM memory management phase of the method utilizes scheduling results of DLGs to make appropriate mapping decisions on LDM and insertion choices of data transfer codes for every decomposed data.

After mapping decisions are determined from the DLG scheduling phase, the method adopts Adjustable Blocks and Template Arrays for the actual mapping of the decomposed data onto LDM [9]. Adjustable Blocks are hierarchical structures of constant size blocks and are used to flexibly choose appropriate memory block sizes for each application program. Template Arrays are mapping structures that maps multi-dimensional arrays to specific one-dimensional blocks of LDM, and are also used to maintain code readability of the indices of the arrays.

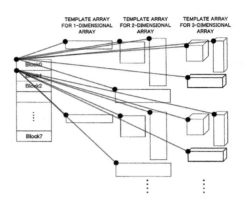

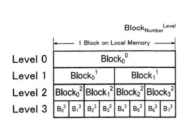

Fig. 9. Hierarchical structure of adjustable blocks

Fig. 10. Overview of template arrays

3.4.1 Adjustable Blocks

The decomposition count of data varies with the characteristic and the complexity of the application, which require the LDM management method to handle arrays with arbitrary sizes. However, simply adopting memory blocks with varying sizes is insufficient, since the data placement and eviction process induces memory fragmentation. To avoid such inefficiency, the proposed method maps data onto LDM using hierarchically aligned constant size blocks called Adjustable Blocks [9]. The basic structure of Adjustable Block is depicted in Fig. 9. Adjustable Blocks allow flexible selection of block sizes depending on the data size present in the input program, and can be further divided into smaller blocks with integer divisible sizes of the parent block, unlike buddy memory allocators where block sizes are limited to multiples of powers of two. The constant size blocks and the hierarchical structure of Adjustable Blocks allow efficient mapping of blocks with varying size and dimension onto LDM as well as avoiding performance critical fragmentations of LDM. For the current implementation of the method, the block sizes of Adjustable Blocks are reduced by powers of 2 for each level down the hierarchy.

When the Adjustable Block size for each application program is decided, the LDM address space is decomposed into a set of blocks. During parallel execution, the decomposed data are loaded to a block and evicted from the block managed by the compiler.

3.4.2 Template Arrays

LDM can be represented as a one dimensional array. Therefore, when a multidimensional array is allocated onto LDM, the index calculation of the array becomes complex. To overcome this complexity, the method introduces an array mapping technique called Template Arrays [9]. Figure 10 displays an overview of Template Arrays. The basic idea of Template Arrays is that each block on LDM corresponds to multiple empty arrays with varying dimensions. These arrays have an additional dimension augmented to its structure to store the corresponding block number. By maintaining block numbers for every array on each block, the method manages to systematically decide which region and block of LDM memory is appropriate for the target decomposed array. Moreover, by choosing a block that has the same dimension with the target array, the mapping provides better readability for the array indices.

3.4.3 Block Eviction Policy

To adjustably utilize LDM during the runtime of the program, the proposed method appropriately evicts memory blocks guaranteed to be unused or to be reused latest in the future from LDM to off-chip shared memory to create new spaces for incoming variables, unlike Least Recently Used (LRU) policies where variables with the longest unused period are evicted. The live and dead information of each variable is analyzed by the OSCAR compiler. In order to minimize data transfer latencies and fully utilize data locality, data with high probability of being accessed again continues to reside on LDM. In particular, the method adopts the following block eviction priority policy to maintain data locality, listed from most to least significance:

1. Dead variables (variables that will not be accessed further in the program)
2. Variables that are accessed only by other processor cores
3. Variables that will be later accessed by the current processor core
4. Variables that will immediately be accessed by the current processor core

3.5   Data Transfer Between Off-Chip Memory

Data transfer codes between LDM and off-chip shared memory is inserted according to the scheduling results of the DLGs as presented in Sect. 3.3. The method assumes DMA controllers as the underlying data transfer hardware to allow fast and asynchronous burst transfers between processor cores. The current implementation of the method explicitly inserts data transfer codes before MTs that load data and after MTs that store data. Overlapping of data transfers and task executions is not achieved due to a hardware bug in the RP2 multicore processor used in this evaluation. Still, this MT-granularity data transfer policy minimizes synchronization overheads and maintains data coherence with other processing cores that work on the same array.

3.6   Code Compaction Method

3.6.1 Overview of the Code Compaction Method

The LDM management approach presented by previous researches produces duplicated code for each decomposed loop. This straightforward scheme generates multiple copies of the loop body with different lower and upper bounds,

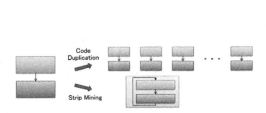

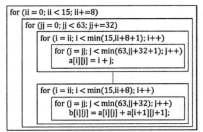

for (ii = 0; ii < 15; ii+=8)
  for (jj = 0; jj < 63; jj+=32)
    for (i = ii; i < min(15,ii+8+1); i++)
      for (j = jj; j < min(63,jj+32+1); j++)
        a[i][j] = i + j;

    for (i = ii; i < min(15,ii+8); i++)
      for (j = jj; j < min(63,jj+32); j++)
        b[i][j] = a[i][j] + a[i+1][j+1];

Fig. 11. Overview of the strip mining technique for nested loops

Fig. 12. Code compaction applied to the nested loop on Fig. 7

effectively creating unique loop codes for each decomposition count. To prevent such code bloat, the proposed method adopts code compaction techniques based on strip mining [12]. Figure 11 depicts the strip mining scheme incorporated to the method. By applying mid-grain parallelization to the outer-most blocking loop, proper mapping onto processor cores and execution order can be guaranteed without applying scheduling.

3.6.2 Code Compaction Method for Multi-dimensional Loops

To utilize code compaction techniques for multi-dimensional loops, iteration ranges among multiple loops within TLGs must first be aligned by loop peeling [16,17]. After peeling the excessive iteration ranges for every loop, the target loops are fused as a single MT. Figure 12 shows an example with multi-dimensional loops, illustrating the code compaction method applied to the original loop code on Fig. 7. Since the first and the second loops within the TLG on Fig. 7 has different iteration ranges, the iteration of the first loop with indices $i = 15$ and $j = 63$ will be peeled to match up with the smaller iteration ranges of the second loop. Following this loop peeling, the method then performs loop decomposition. If the decomposition count is 2, each loop nest will be divided into 2 pieces, consequently performing strip mining with block sizes of 8 as the outer loop and 32 as the inner loop.

4   Evaluations

To show the effectiveness of the method, this section presents evaluation results on several benchmark applications. The method was implemented on the OSCAR automatic parallelization compiler and tested on Renesas's RP2 SH4A processor based 8 core homogeneous multicore processor [15]. The RP2 multicore processor is based on the OSCAR multicore architecture shown in the previous section. Each processor core of RP2 is based on SH4A with 600 MHz, and has dedicated LDM to freely load and evict data during program execution. To share data among processor cores, each core has access to a processor wide

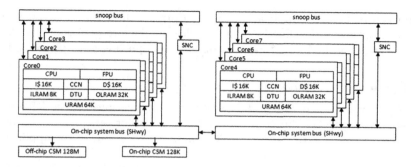

Fig. 13. Architecture of the RP2 multicore processor

distributed shared memory. An overview of the RP2 architecture is depicted in Fig. 13. RP2 is equipped with LDM (OLRAM) with a 1 clock cycle latency, distributed shared memory (URAM) on each processor core with a 2 clock cycle latency, and a 128 MB DDR2 CSM with a 55 clock cycle latency. Data cache, or D\$, is not used for the evaluation. Every processor core is connected with SHwy, which is Renesas's standard bus.

4.1   Tested Applications

To evaluate the performance of the proposed data localization method, 5 sequential programs written in Parallelizable C [10], such as the example code in Fig. 7 used for the explanation of the proposed method, an AAC encoder, a MPEG2 encoder, SPEC95 Tomcatv, and SPEC95 Swim were used. Tomcatv and Swim are chosen from the SPEC95 benchmark suite since both applications in this version have data size small enough to fit into the limited off-chip CSM size of RP2. The method applied one-dimensional decomposition to AACenc and Mpeg2enc, and two-dimensional decomposition to the sample program, Tomcatv, and Swim. These applications were compiled by the OSCAR source-to-source automatic parallelization compiler for multiple platforms with the proposed method integrated as part of OSCAR's analysis phase, followed by a backend compilation process by a native compiler for each target multicore processor to generate machine codes. The 4 programs, except the example program of Fig. 7, are explained below.

- AACenc is an AAC encoder application provided by Renesas Technology. For evaluation, a 30 s audio file was used as input to generate an audio file with a bit rate of 128 Kbps.
- Mpeg2enc is a MPEG2 encoder application which is part of the MediaBench benchmark suite. For evaluation, a 30 frame video with a resolution of 352 by 256 pixels was used as input.
- Tomcatv is a loop-intensive benchmark application from the SPEC CPU95 benchmark suite. Before performing the LDM management method, loop fusion and variable renaming were applied.

– Swim is a benchmark application that performs 2 dimensional array computations from the SPEC CPU95 benchmark suite. Before performing the LDM
management method, loop distribution and loop peeling were performed.

4.2   Evaluation Results

Figure 14 shows the experimental results of the applications on the RP2 8 core
processor. Since, to our knowledge, there are no other open-source compilers
that explicitly manage LDM, the results compare executions of the applications
that utilize the proposed LDM management method and off-chip CSM.

In the sample program of Fig. 7, the parallelized program by the OSCAR
compiler using off-chip CSM, or DDR2 memory, achieved speedups of 3.85 for 4
cores and 6.49 for 8 cores. On the other hand, the proposed LDM management
method obtained better speedups, such as 2.64 for single core, 12.61 for 4 cores,
and 20.64 for 8 cores, compared to single core executions using off-chip CSM.

For AACenc, the speedups using the off-chip CSM was 3.58 for 4 cores
and 7.14 for 8 cores compared with single core environment. By contrast, the
speedups for AACenc using the proposed LDM management method were 2.06
for 1 core, 8.94 for 4 cores, and 20.12 for 8 cores. For Mpeg2enc, the speedups
obtained using the off-chip memory were 2.00 on 4 cores and 1.97 on 8 cores
against sequential execution. The proposed method outperformed off-chip memory solutions by obtaining speedups of 2.33 for single core, 6.81 for 4 cores, and
7.59 for 8 cores. In Tomcatv, speedups achieved by utilizing the CSM were 3.18
for 4 cores and 5.73 for 8 cores. Compared to the CSM environment, the proposed method obtained higher speedups of 1.88 for 1 core, 5.07 for 4 cores, and
7.38 for 8 cores. For Swim, speedups using the off-chip CSM were 3.76 for 4 cores
and 7.40 for 8 cores against 1 core execution. In contrast to those results, the
proposed method showed speedups of 1.33 for 1 core, 5.50 for 4 cores, and 11.30
for 8 cores. The evaluations show that the proposed LDM management method
achieves scalable speedups for embedded and scientific applications.

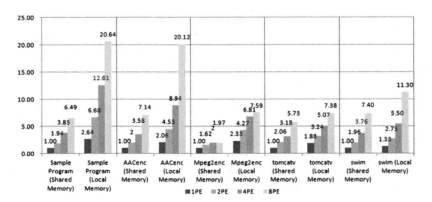

Fig. 14. Speedups of the proposed method (Local Memory) compared to executions
utilizing shared memory (Shared Memory) on benchmarks applications using RP2

5 Conclusions

This paper has proposed automatic local memory management method with data assignment to adjustable blocks chosen for each application utilizing data assignment units between off-chip shared memory and local memory. The method also incorporates multi-dimensional templates that allow programmers to understand the parallelized program using local memory management. Utilizing local memory is necessary to satisfy deadline requirements for applications of embedded systems, such as automobile engine control programs, with multicore processors. This software managed local memory control approach successfully decomposes large size data into smaller chunks so that the working set fits on local memory, while avoiding fragmentation and maintaining readability of code using Adjustable Blocks and Template Arrays. Data transfer between local memory and off-chip memory is managed through insertion of data transfer codes between coarse-grain tasks. Additionally, the proposed method allows reuse of data on local memory over different loops. The proposed method further integrates code compaction technique to mitigate code bloat, allowing the technique to successfully decompose multi-dimensional arrays. The method was implemented on the OSCAR source-to-source parallelization compiler to automatically generate data locality optimized code. Evaluations were performed on the RP2 8 core multicore processor equipped with off-chip shared memory and local memory. For the sample program in Fig. 7, the proposed local memory management method achieved a speedup of 20.64 times for 8 cores against sequential execution using off-chip shared memory of RP2. Similarly, on 8 cores using local memory, AACenc, Mpeg2enc, Tomcatv, and Swim obtained speedups of 20.12, 7.59, 7.38, and 11.30, respectively, against 1 core execution using the off-chip shared memory. These results reveal that the proposed automatic local memory management method is effective for reducing execution times for embedded applications with deadline constraints.

Acknowledgments. This work was partly supported by JSPS KAKENHI Grant Number JP15K00085.

References

1. Panda, P.R., et al.: Efficient utilization of scratch-pad memory in embedded processor applications. In: Proceedings of European conference on Design and Test (1997)
2. Avissar, O., et al.: An optimal memory allocation scheme for scratch-pad-based embedded systems. ACM Trans. Embed. Comput. Syst. **1**(1), 6–26 (2002)
3. Steinke, S., et al.: Assigning program and data objects to scratchpad for energy reduction. In: Proceedings of Design, Automation and Test in Europe Conference and Exhibition (2002)
4. Che, W., et al.: Compilation of stream programs for multicore processors that incorporate scratchpad memories. In: Proceedings of Design, Automation and Test in Europe Conference and Exhibition (2010)
5. Udayakumaran, S., et al.: Dynamic allocation for scratch-pad memory using compile-time decisions. ACM Trans. Embed. Comput. Syst. **5**(2), 472–511 (2006)

6. Guo, Y., et al.: Data placement and duplication for embedded multicore systems with scratch pad memory. IEEE Trans. Comput. Aided Des. Integr. Circuits Syst. **32**(6), 809–817 (2013)
7. Kandemir, M., et al.: Exploiting shared scratch pad memory space in embedded multiprocessor systems. In: Proceedings of Design Automation Conference (2002)
8. Issenin, I., et al.: Multiprocessor system-on-chip data reuse analysis for exploring customized memory hierarchies. In: Proceedings of Design Automation Conference (2006)
9. Kasahara, H., et al.: U.S. Patent No. 8,438,359, U.S. Patent and Trademark Office, Washington, DC (2013)
10. Kimura, K., Mase, M., Mikami, H., Miyamoto, T., Shirako, J., Kasahara, H.: OSCAR API for real-time low-power multicores and its performance on multicores and smp servers. In: Gao, G.R., Pollock, L.L., Cavazos, J., Li, X. (eds.) LCPC 2009. LNCS, vol. 5898, pp. 188–202. Springer, Heidelberg (2010). doi:10.1007/978-3-642-13374-9_13
11. Banakar, R., et al.: Scratchpad memory: design alternative for cache on-chip memory in embedded systems. In: Proceedings of International Symposium on Hardware/Software Codesign (2002)
12. Wolfe, M.: More iteration space tiling. In: Proceedings of ACM/IEEE Conference on Supercomputing (1989)
13. Kasahara, H., Honda, H., Mogi, A., Ogura, A., Fujiwara, K., Narita, S.: A multigrain parallelizing compilation scheme for OSCAR (optimally scheduled advanced multiprocessor). In: Banerjee, U., Gelernter, D., Nicolau, A., Padua, D. (eds.) LCPC 1991. LNCS, vol. 589, pp. 283–297. Springer, Heidelberg (1992). doi:10.1007/BFb0038671
14. Yoshida, A., et al.: Data-localization for Fortran macro-dataflow computation using partial static task assignment. In: Proceedings of International Conference on Supercomputing (1996)
15. Ito, M., et al.: An 8640 MIPS SoC with independent poweroff control of 8 CPU and 8 RAMs by an automatic parallelizing compiler. In: Proceedings of IEEE International Solid State Circuits Conference (2008)
16. Kennedy, K., et al.: Optimizing Compilers for Modern Architectures: A Dependence-Based Approach. Morgan Kaufmann Publishers Inc., San Francisco (2001)
17. Padua, D., et al.: Advanced compiler optimizations for supercomputers. Commun. ACM **29**, 1184–1201 (1986)
18. https://www.renesas.com/en-in/products/microcontrollers-microprocessors/v850/v850e2mx/v850e2mx4.html

Run-time and Performance Analysis

Mapping Medley: Adaptive Parallelism Mapping with Varying Optimization Goals

Murali Krishna Emani[(✉)]

Lawrence Livermore National Laboratory, Livermore, USA
emani1@llnl.gov

Abstract. In modern day computing, the performance of parallel programs is bound by the dynamic execution context that includes inherent program behavior, resource requirements, co-scheduled programs sharing the system resources, hardware failures and input data. Besides this dynamic context, the optimization goals are increasingly becoming multi-objective and dynamic such as minimizing execution time while maximizing energy efficiency. Efficiently mapping the parallel threads on to the hardware cores is crucial to achieve these goals. This paper proposes a novel approach to judiciously map parallel programs to hardware in dynamic contexts and goals. It uses a simple, yet novel technique by collecting a set of mapping policies to determine best number of threads that are optimal for specific contexts. It then binds threads to cores for increased affinity. Besides, this approach also determines the optimal DVFS levels for these cores to achieve higher energy efficiency. On extensive evaluation with state-of-art techniques, this scheme outperforms them in the range 1.08x up to 1.21x and 1.39x over OpenMP default.

1   Introduction

Modern day parallel computing landscape is rapidly evolving in all aspects: right from applications composed of diverse workloads, middle-ware up to the hardware. The diversity and dynamic nature of all elements in this vertical stack is becoming more obvious than ever before. Given a parallel application is unlikely to run on the same platform and the same environment for its lifetime, we need a way to future-proof application development cost. The mainstream applications have no longer have the privilege of having exclusive access to hardware resources; but have to share dynamically with co-executing applications. Similarly, there is no longer a single optimization goal for the parallel applications. Earlier either it used to be either of latency or throughput or energy efficiency. However this is no longer the case. Multi-objective optimization is growing as the ultimate desired goal for parallel applications and systems, such as high

This work was performed under the auspices of the U.S. Department of Energy by Lawrence Livermore National Laboratory under Contract DE-AC52-07NA27344. LLNL-CONF-696003.

© Springer International Publishing AG 2017
C. Ding et al. (Eds.): LCPC 2016, LNCS 10136, pp. 299–313, 2017.
DOI: 10.1007/978-3-319-52709-3_22

throughput with minimum energy expenditure. Consider the case of software applications on a mobile device or embedded system. In a scenario when it is connected to external power source, the goal may be more on maximizing application performance. But when the power source is disconnected, it no longer has access to external power supply and has to rely only on its battery. In this scenario, the goal of maximizing energy efficiency may become as important as the application performance.

Thus the program performance is bound by the dynamic *execution context* which we define as composed of factors such as inherent program behavior, resource requirements, co-scheduled programs sharing the system resources, hardware failures, ever-changing software versions, and input data. Oversubscription with more software threads than the hardware threads may lead to program slow-down due to delays in threads gaining access to hardware. Under-subscription may result in poor resource utilization. Hence a judicious parallelism mapping is crucial to improve program performance. Thread to core affinity also impacts program performance. Frequent migration of threads and the data in respective caches drastically degrades the performance. It is also thus important to minimize thread placements across cores. Tuning CPU core frequencies is one approach to control the power consumption in the system. The frequencies can be lowered in many ways to improve power efficiency. Hence reducing power and the execution time may lead to high energy efficiency. Most of the existing approaches rely on a single mapping policy which remains the same irrespective of the current system characteristics. There is no ability to determine if this mapping is indeed optimal if the execution context changes. Any monitoring mechanisms if present, are reactive in that they observe the program execution with a configuration for few cycles. Based on the observed behaviour, the program mapping is varied. It is highly unlikely that the mapping determined by these approaches will be optimal for evolving workloads and hardware. Such policies cannot be easily advanced as they need radical changes in the policy, which are expensive to be performed at runtime.

Our Idea: In this paper we focus on determining the best thread numbers for every parallel section of a parallel program and binding them to hardware cores. This is a key decision on maximizing parallelism with available resources. To optimize for the energy efficiency, we also determine the optimal frequency level for each core utilizing Dynamic Voltage Frequency Scaling (DVFS) mechanism. In the program execution context, we primarily focus on contention due to co-executing workloads, hardware failures and changes in the external power supply. We take inspiration from early work [8] which shows that a mixture of specialized models often outperforms a single policy. It maintains a collection of mixture of models which can be added to and updated as time goes on, selecting the model that is best suited to the current context. It avoids over-complex heuristics and over-fitting training data by allowing different models to be selected based on their worth. The work closest to our approach is the Ensemble mapping [5]. It uses predictive modeling that considers different mapping policies called *experts* at runtime and selects the one that is determined to be the optimal one at every parallel loop. As the program execution context changes, different mapping policies will be dynamically selected at runtime. We extend and improve over the ensemble technique to optimize for both execution time and power and also consider the case of varying external power supply. We also optimize all executing programs in the system unlike just the target program in the ensemble method.

Our technique **Mapping Medley** uses a collection of exclusive mapping policies where each policy takes as input the execution context i.e. current co-executing workload, hardware and power supply and then determines the best threads numbers and optimum frequency levels for all cores. At runtime the question of which mapping policy to select is crucial for achieving the optimization goals. The standard method would be to run each policy for few runs or cycles and observe the program behaviour, identify and select the best mapping policy. Policy evaluation in such manner would be prohibitively expensive in terms of the overhead incurred at runtime. We avoid this overhead by instantly selecting the best expert based on the context. Our idea is to optimize program performance and energy by determining best thread numbers, pinning them to cores and determine optimal frequencies for the cores. Predictive modeling is the core strategy to our approach.

This paper makes the following contributions:

- First to optimize multi-objective goals in varying execution contexts.
- Propose techniques to optimize execution time and energy efficiency simultaneously.
- Outperforms existing state-of-art approaches on extensive evaluation.

2   Related Work and Motivation

Related Work: The works closest to ours are Ensemble mapping [5] and Feedback-driven technique [6]. The ensemble mapping approach employs 'Mixture of Experts' concept [8] from machine learning domain. Here multiple specialized mapping policies called *experts* are employed which are offline trained machine learning models. These individual experts determine thread numbers and future system state. An online expert selector chooses the best expert based on what expert predicted the most accurate system state. This technique aims only at thread number prediction but does not mention about their placement and run all cores at maximum frequencies. The feedback driven policy [6] uses control theory-based techniques to tune different knobs based on feedback from the system. It first changes the power control knob to get the power consumption below a capped value and then tunes a performance knob to extract maximum performance possible. It relies on an incremental approach; tune for one goal first and later tune for another goal. Though this approach may eventually find the optimal configurations, it may take a while to reach which is not desirable at runtime. Our work directly tackles both execution time and energy efficiency at once, thus ensuring quick arrival to an optimal configuration. The approach presented in [14] uses analytic model to determine best number of threads at runtime. It includes an observe-and-change policy where every parallel loop is run with random thread numbers for few cycles. Then based on the observed performance, it builds an online regression model to determine the optimal thread number. DVFS techniques are employed in solutions proposed in [11] which change the processor frequencies, according to the code characteristics and runtime information. A machine learning mapping policy is proposed in [15]. The policy employs no way to adjust the policy based on the execution context changes and no method to measure its efficiency online. Another ensemble search approach proposed in [2] involves running multiple configurations at the same time on partitioned system space. Once a best configuration is found, it replaces the previous best configuration. Multiple policy evaluation at the same time limits the physical resource availability for the target program. This problem worsens when the hardware is dynamic with changing number of processors. Energy efficient parallelism is well studied in embedded systems community dealing with computing devices with limited power sources in [3]. Adagio [13] is a runtime system that makes DVFS practical for complex high performance computing applications. Implications of thread level parallelism on performance and power are discussed in [9].

Motivation Example: In this section, we provide an example to motivate the goal. The experimental set up is a co-execution of parallel programs with varying thread numbers and a sudden change in the power supply at runtime. On a two 4-core Intel Xeon machine laptop with 16 GB RAM running Ubuntu 3.7 kernel, we ran a target program *pagerank* from Green-Marl benchmark [7]. There is a co-executing workload program *cg* with 4 threads till time t = 25 s and later another workload *is* with 2 threads both from NAS benchmark suite [1]. The number of processors remains constant throughout. We then simulated a change in power supply to the system. Till 30 s, external power supply was connected to this system after which it was disconnected leaving the system to run on its battery power till the end of program execution. In this set up we evaluated the target program performance and plotted the number of threads determined by the OpenMP default scheme, analytic, feedback and ensemble techniques as described in Sect. 4. The obtained speedups over default are 1x, 1.21x, 1.32x and 1.34x. We also then tried running the target exhaustively with all thread numbers to identify the maximum possible performance (1.6x) and plotted the optimal threads numbers. The thread numbers are plotted in the second graph in Fig. 1. We also measured the energy consumption and plotted the energy efficiency normalized over the default scheme. We observe that the evaluated techniques fall short of the optimal thread numbers needed for best performance. They become more unstable after time t = 30 s and for poor performance and energy efficiency.

The figure demonstrates that there still is a large room for improvement in execution time in terms of better thread numbers and energy efficiency. We try to tackle this issue of how to quickly and efficiently obtain the best thread numbers for maximizing speedup and optimal core frequencies for higher energy efficiency. We discuss our idea in the next section.

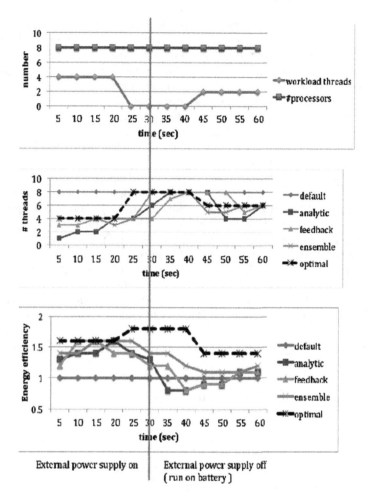

Fig. 1. Graph showing how #threads and energy efficiencies of different approaches vary with a change in the power supply. The top graph shows the number of processors and co-executing workload threads. The second graph shows the #threads determined by default, analytic, feedback, ensemble and optimal values. The bottom graph shows energy efficiency values normalized to the default policy. At time $t = 30$ s, external power supply is removed to run rest of the program execution on battery source. It can be observed that all policies become unstable and move away from the optimal, with a change in power supply and remain far from the optimal value.

3   Mapping Medley

3.1   Optimal Thread Number

The primary goal of this work is to achieve maximum speedup with minimum energy expenditure. This goal can be achieved by tuning multiple configurable parameters or *knobs*. In this work we limit the tunable parameters to (i) *thread number*, (ii) *thread placement* and (iii) *DVFS level of cores*. on which the threads are placed. We try to optimize (a) *Execution time:* We try to achieve best execution time by (a) determining the best number of threads for the target program that minimizes the execution time and (b) setting up threads-to-core affinity that minimizes data movement across cores. (b) *Energy efficiency:* Once the optimal number of threads are determined and pinned to respective cores, we then maximize energy efficiency. This can be achieved in multiple ways; here we utilize the most widely used technique: changing the frequency levels of the cores where the threads are mapped.

We built our approach over the mapping technique in [5]. This ensemble technique is composed of multiple specialized mapping policies called experts. Each expert is an offline trained linear regression model trained in a specific setting. It has two predictors that predict (i) best thread number and (ii) expected system state. The online expert selector evaluates the most appropriate thread-predictor based on the current system state and determines thread numbers of that predictor to be ideal at that point of time. Each expert is tuned on program scalability and different hardware. The inputs to the thread predictor are a set of features that capture both code and system characteristics obtained from the compiler and the kernel respectively. The set of features are listed in Table 1.

Table 1. List of features and weights used in thread predictor obtained from [5]

Feature	E^1	E^2	E^3	E^4
Memory-accesses	1.05	−0.84	0.14	0.05
Instructions	−1.52	1.12	0.95	0.03
Branches	0.87	0.84	−0.87	−0.57
Software-threads	−0.62	0.05	−0.48	0.004
Processors	0.98	0.98	0.99	0.92
Task queue size	0.003	0.02	−0.15	0.22
CPU load-1	0.002	0.03	0.473	0.01
CPU load-2	−0.013	0.227	−1.07	−0.62
Cached memory	−0.07	0.002	0.007	0.03
Pages free list rate	0.004	−0.08	0.01	−0.14
Error	−1.21	−6.8	−3.03	−2.5

We differ from [5] in the expert selection mechanism. They use a second machine learning model *environment predictor* that predicts what the system should be if the thread number was indeed optimal. This may cause additional overhead and may not accurately capture the system state specially when the power supply source varies. We use the four thread predictors or experts as in [5]. Here each model determines a thread number based on the current parallel section characteristics and execution context that include any co-executing workloads and hardware changes. Our approach now deploys a simple yet smart technique where it switches between the largest thread number with external power supply on and the least thread number when the external power supply is off. The reason is that large number of threads increase the power consumption though reduce the execution time. Note that if the power sources from a battery, the optimization goal now prioritizes energy efficiency to execution time.

3.2   Thread Placement

Once the best number of threads are determined, we pin them to the cores to minimize frequent thread migration. It is widely acknowledged that the placement of parallel threads across cores can greatly affect the program performance. Migrating a thread from one core to another also involves either moving the data it requires from caches of current core to the caches of the core to which it is migrated to. Else this thread has to remotely access its data from the caches of core it was previously running on. Both mechanisms are highly expensive in terms of the overhead and drastically degrade performance. Ideally threads finish their computation faster when the data they require is within caches of local cores. In this approach, once the thread number is determined, these threads are pinned to the hardware cores to enhance affinity. This reduces the chances of potential problems with thread migration as discussed above. If the thread number of a current parallel section is lesser or equal to thread number of previous parallel section, we do not change the affined cores. Only when the number of threads are larger, we include more affined cores. The threads are affined using *sched_setaffinity* system call.

3.3   DVFS Level

Dynamic Voltage and Frequency Scaling (DVFS) is one of the methods to alter the processor frequencies to reduce power consumption of the cores. Each processor can be assigned with a set of frequencies that varies with the processor family and type. In our experiments the list of available frequencies is: (2.3, 1.8, 1.6, 1.4, 1.2, 1.0, 0.8) GHz. The frequency levels of each core can be tuned on-the-fly, however, in this work we change the frequency levels of only the cores to which threads are pinned to a single value. It may be noted that an optimal DVFS level for cores is determined at every parallel section.

3.4   Components

The two components core to our approach are (i) thread predictor and (2) frequency predictor. The thread predictor chooses best expert with its thread number and pins them to equal number of cores. The frequency predictor determines the best DVFS level and sets corresponding frequencies to these cores. The idea of our approach is shown in Fig. 2. We use *likwid* [10] to set CPU core frequencies and measure the power consumption obtained from from the MSR registers using likwid-powermeter.

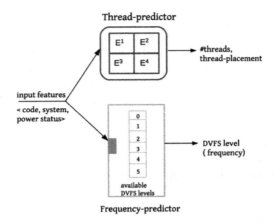

Fig. 2. Mapping Medley approach. The input feature vector is passed to two components (i) thread-predictor that determines the best number of threads and pins them to equal number of cores (ii) frequency-predictor that determines the optimal DVFS level and sets its corresponding frequency level to cores.

Thread-Predictor: Each expert policy takes code and system features as inputs to determine a thread number each. Our thread predictor chooses the best expert and its thread number based on the power supply status. It switches between the largest thread number with external power supply on and the least thread number when the external power supply is off. Let E^1, E^2, E^3, E^4 be the four thread mapping policies or experts. Let c be the set of code features, s the set of system features and p indicates the status of power supply, 0 for *full* (has external power supply) or 1 for *discharging* (runs on battery power). Let $t(E^i)$ be the thread numbers of ith expert. Then the policy of this thread predictor 'g' is to determine the optimal thread number t (1–8) in this work as shown in Eq. 1.

$$g(c, s, p) = \begin{cases} t | max(t(E^1), .., t(E^4)), & \text{if } p = 0 \\ t | min(t(E^1), .., t(E^4)), & \text{if } p = 1 \end{cases} \tag{1}$$

Thread Placement: The number of threads are then pinned to cores using 1:1 thread-to-core mapping. For example, if this model outputs 5 threads, then these threads are affined to 5 cores. The affinity holds till the parallel section execution is finished. Let P_{max} be the maximum number of available processors and c_j be the jth core. The set of cores to pin these threads is $(c_i, ...c_t)$ for any $i, t < P_{max}$ and $i < t$ chosen from the set of free cores.

Frequency-Predictor: Let l denote a DVFS level. The frequency predictor model uses the policy 'f' that takes the combined code, system and power supply status as input feature vector and outputs the optimal DVFS level (0–6 in this work) as shown in Eq. 2. The corresponding frequency is then set to the cores using: *likwid-setFrequencies -c set-of-cores-to-pin -f predicted-frequency.*

$$f(c, s, p) \rightarrow l \tag{2}$$

Machine Learning: Both thread predictor and frequency predictor are offline trained machine learning models. We use linear regression model for the thread-predictor and a support vector machine (SVM) for the frequency predictor. The weights for four experts used by our thread predictor are listed in Table 1. These weights when multiplied with values of the extracted features, yield a thread number. Our thread predictor determines thread numbers that differ from [5] as they take the power supply information as one of the input features. SVM is a supervised classifier that assigns a class (DVFS level from 0–6) for every given input. We evaluated the frequency predictor using a regression model, but surprisingly it yielded poorer prediction accuracy of 78% compared to 89% of SVM. Hence we chose SVM to build the frequency predictor model.

Training Data and Features: The training data is generated using the replicated set up as in [5]. On two different hardware platforms, training programs are run with co-executing workloads, while collecting all possible features. Two classes of program scalability on two platforms provides the training data for the four experts. Thread numbers are varied for each training run to determine the configuration that yields least execution time. In another set of training runs, the frequency levels are varied to determine the best DVFS level that has the least energy consumption. These supervised models are cross-validated to avoid overfitting the data. They are trained on a set of training programs and evaluated on new unseen test programs. The set of features are obtained after collecting all possible features and then eliminating those which do not provide any meaningful hints using entropy estimation.

Portability: It is always ideal to enable portability of the generated models to avoid extensive retraining on every platform of interest. The thread predictor captures basic system information as processors and memory in its feature set. The frequency predictor gets the number of processors from thread predictor and available set of frequencies from the kernel. It then determines the best frequency level. Moreover, on a new platform with different hardware, the corresponding set of available frequencies are known to choose the best one.

4 Experimental Setup

4.1 Platform

The hardware and software platform setup used in the evaluation experiments is listed in Table 2. Note, we have not evaluated this work on hardware that supports the Intel Turbo Boost Technology in this work and would consider that as a planned future work. All the programs start execution at the same time and continue till the other finishes. Each experiment was repeated 10 times and the geometric mean value of execution time is reported. The energy efficiency is computed by the product of measured power and the execution time. The power consumed is obtained from likwid-powermeter [10] that reads power consumption values from the model specific registers (MSR). Note that the measured speedups and energy efficiencies are averaged for all co-executing programs.

4.2 Applications

We use a variety of parallel programs from benchmark suites of different computational behaviours each with largest input data set. These include all OpenMP-based C programs from NAS [1], Parsec [12] and *pagerank* from Green-Marl project [7] benchmark suites. To ensure fair comparison, we replicate a similar experimental set up and workload applications from [5].

Table 2. Experimental setup

Hardware	Laptop with two 4-core Intel Core i3-2350M, @ 2.30 GHz 16 GB RAM, 3 MB shared LLC
OS	64-bit Ubuntu, 3.7.10 kernel
Compiler	*gcc* 4.6 -O3 optimization

Table 3. Programs that constitute two types of workloads.

Workload type	Programs
Light	(i) ep, bodytrack
	(ii) is, ft
Heavy	(i) pagerank, blackscholes, bt, sp
	(ii) lu, freqmine, bt, freqmine

4.3 Competitive Policies

We evaluated our approach against the following state-of-art mapping policies. The experimental setup along with same set of workload programs are replicated to ensure fair comparison with the evaluated policies.

Default: OpenMP default policy [4] assigns a thread number equal to the current number of available processors.

Analytic: In [14] an analytical model determines the degree of parallelism at runtime based on observed speedups at fixed time-intervals and estimated using regression techniques.

Feedback: The feedback driven policy [6] uses techniques to adjust programs performance and power by tuning different knobs based on feedback based on control theory principles. It first changes the power control knob to get the power consumption below a capped values and then changes to performance knob to extract maximum performance possible.

Ensemble: The Ensemble technique [5] uses a mixture of offline trained machine learning models that predict the best number of threads in dynamic program environments. The experts are highly specialized based on the executing environment and the online expert selector switches between experts choosing the optimal one as and when required.

4.4   Experimental Scenarios

The dynamic execution context is composed of co-executing workloads and hardware in terms of number of processors and power supply.

(i) Workloads: The external workload consists of multiple parallel programs selected from the above benchmarks. We vary the number of workload programs chosen from above programs classified as '*light*' and '*heavy*'. For each workload type, we consider different sets of programs as shown in Table 3. All results are averaged over these different benchmark sets. The same external workload is reproduced for all evaluated policies in all cases. This ensures a fair comparison across different mapping policies.

(ii) Hardware: To reflect any change in hardware, we vary the number of available processors during program execution. Changes in the number of processors can be due to several factors including hardware failures, assigning more/less cores for other high/low priority jobs, turning them off for saving power. The number of available processors is varied in two different frequencies: *low* and *high* where it is changed at every 40 s and 10 s in low frequency and high frequency settings respectively. We modify the processor count by switching '*online*' values (1 = enable, 0 = disable) for each CPU in */proc* file-system. Disabling a CPU is logically shutting it down on-the-fly. Hence no threads are scheduled on the disabled cores.

(iii) Power supply: In all experiments, we reflect a change in the power by starting each run with power supply on and later disconnecting it during program execution. The status of power source can be observed from observing the battery status value obtained from the kernel */sys/class/power_supply/BAT0/status*. If the status values reads *full*, it implies that the system has external power supply, else if it reads *discharging*, it means that power supply is no longer available and the system has to utilize its battery power.

5   Evaluation

Here we show the summary of performance results of speedup and energy efficiency of all policies, averaged across all the experimental settings on the evaluated scenarios. In all cases, the baseline is OpenMP 3.0 default policy and the

average values (geomean) are geometric means to avoid outliers. The measured
speedups are for both target program and any co-executing workloads and the
energy efficiency is across all cores.

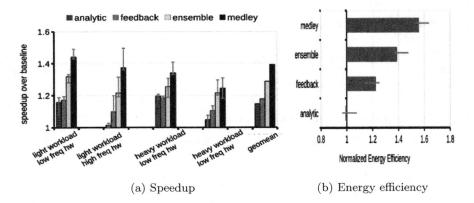

(a) Speedup   (b) Energy efficiency

Fig. 3. (a) Performance of program speedup all evaluated approaches averaged across
all programs and experimental settings. Our approach outperforms all by greatly
improving speedup by 1.39x over baseline. (b) Performance of energy efficiency of
all evaluated approaches. The medley approach outperforms all by significantly by
achieving 1.44x efficiency.

Speedup: Fig. 3(a) shows the summary of evaluation results for speedups across
all benchmark programs and all experimental scenarios. The x-axis shows each
scenario for workload type and frequency of hardware changes and the geomean.
The analytic, feedback, ensemble improve program speedup by 1.15x, 1.18x,
1.28x over the baseline. Our medley mapping outperforms all these competitive
techniques by recording 1.39x improvement over baseline. It has better speedup
of 21.28% over analytic, 18.19% over feedback and 8.14% over ensemble techniques. The primary reason for these speedups is the optimal determination of
thread numbers along with minimizing frequent thread placements across cores
reducing latencies in data accesses.

OpenMP default policy assigns same number of threads as the number of
available processors. Due to increased resource contention caused by the dynamic
execution context and reduction in power source, it is unable to modify thread
numbers accordingly. The analytic technique sustains workload changes but does
not adjust to varying number of processors. It also suffers from frequent thread
movements across cores. The feedback policy relies on the signal it receives from
the system and changes configurations based on the observed system changes. It
is a reactive policy and tunes the available knobs for execution time and power in
exclusion. The ensemble approach is quick to react to execution context changes
and selects thread numbers owing to the presence of expert mapping policies. It
however does not pin down threads to cores which may lead to frequent changes

in threads to cores placements. Our medley approach utilizes the same number of threads as the ensemble, but also pins threads to hardware cores to reduce any chance of thread migration to minimal. Therefore it further improves the program execution time.

Energy Efficiency: Overall energy efficiency results. The values reported are normalized to the OpenMP default baseline. The value more than 1 implies that the policy achieved better efficient mapping over the baseline, else a poor mapping in terms of energy consumption.

Figure 3(b) shows the energy efficiency values averaged across all evaluated scenarios. It can be observed that our medley approach always achieves better efficiency by lowering the power consumption and the execution time. It improves over 1.44x over the baseline outperforming the compared approaches. The ensemble technique also improves energy efficiency in a range of 1.12x to 1.55x. The feedback mechanism performs poorer due to the frequent change in the number of processors where it rapidly changes its configuration leading to fluctuations in thread numbers and DVFS levels. The analytic approach improves energy in only two scenarios with light workloads, however, with heavy workloads it significantly drops down below the default baseline. This is due to the increased execution time due to the enormous time taken to reach the optimal thread number.

6 Analysis

6.1 Thread Number Variation with Change in Power

In this section we analyze the thread number counts averaged across all parallel sections for all evaluated benchmarks, determined by all evaluated approaches in two phases: before and after the change in the power supply. This is to understand how the thread numbers are affected by the changes in optimization goals and external parameters. It can be observed from Fig. 4 that with external power supply on, all policies determine larger thread numbers most of the time. But when the power supply is removed, the system relies on battery power. Now all policies try to determine smaller thread numbers to minimize the energy expenditure.

6.2 DVFS Level Variation with Change in Power

Figure 5 shows how frequently a DVFS level is determined by our approach before (top) and after (below) the power supply change. The values are normalized to 100%. It can be observed that with external power supply on, our policy determines larger frequency levels for all cores to improve the execution time of all running programs. After the power supply is removed, the goal to minimize energy expenditure is prioritized and lower frequency levels are determined.

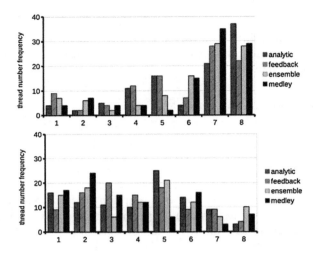

Fig. 4. Distribution of thread numbers by all evaluated policies before (top) and after (below) the power supply change. With external power supply on, all policies determine large thread numbers most of the time and vice-versa.

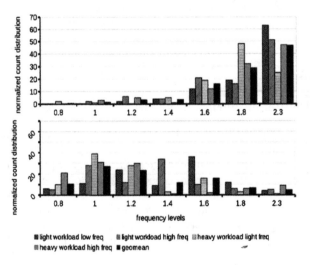

Fig. 5. Distribution of DVFS levels by our approach before (top) and after (below) the power supply change. With external power supply on, our policy determines larger frequency levels. After the power supply is removed, lower frequency levels are determined.

7   Conclusion and Future Work

We presented a novel parallelism mapping technique that optimizes execution time and energy efficiency in dynamic execution contexts. The work is more relevant in modern day hardware devices where multiple workloads co-execute with changes in hardware and the source of power supply. Our technique determines best number of threads at runtime and pins them to underlying hardware cores and sets optimal core frequencies. As part of future work, we would like to evaluate on embedded platforms and mobile devices running parallel workloads. We also would explore changing DVFS levels per-core instead of all cores.

References

1. NAS 2.3. http://phase.hpcc.jp/Omni/benchmarks/NPB/index.html
2. Ansel, J., Pacula, M., Wong, Y.L., Chan, C., Olszewski, M., O'Reilly, U.-M., Amarasinghe, S.: Siblingrivalry: online autotuning through local competitions. In: Proceedings of the 2012 International Conference on Compilers, Architectures and Synthesis for Embedded Systems, CASES 2012 (2012)
3. Cloutier, M.F., Paradis, C., Weaver, V.M.: Design and analysis of a 32-bit embedded high-performance cluster optimized for energy and performance. In: Proceedings of the 1st International Workshop on Hardware-Software Co-Design for High Performance Computing, Co-HPC 2014 (2014)
4. Dagum, L., Menon, R.: OpenMP: an industry-standard API for shared-memory programming. IEEE Comput. Sci. Eng. **5**(1), 46–55 (1998)
5. Emani, M.K., O'Boyle, M.F.P.: Celebrating diversity: a mixture of experts approach for runtime mapping in dynamic environments. In: Proceedings of the 36th ACM SIGPLAN Conference on Programming Language Design and Implementation, Portland, OR, USA, 15–17 June 2015
6. Filieri, A., Hoffmann, H., Maggio, M.: Automated multi-objective control for self-adaptive software design. In: Proceedings of the 10th Joint Meeting on Foundations of Software Engineering, ESEC/FSE (2015)
7. Green-Marl. https://github.com/stanford-ppl/Green-Marl
8. Jacobs, R.A., Jordan, M.I., Nowlan, S.J., Hinton, G.E.: Adaptive mixtures of local experts. Neural Comput. **3**(1), 79–87 (1991)
9. Li, J., Martinez, J.F.: Power-performance implications of thread-level paral- lelism on chip multiprocessors. In: IEEE International Symposium on Performance Analysis of Systems and Software, ISPASS 2005, pp. 124–134. IEEE (2005)
10. "likwid," https://github.com/RRZE-HPC/likwid
11. Merkel, A., Bellosa, F.: Memory-aware scheduling for energy efficiency on multicore processors. In: Proceedings of the Conference on Power Aware Computing and Systems, HotPower 2008 (2008)
12. "Parsec 2.1," http://parsec.cs.princeton.edu/
13. Rountree, B., Lownenthal, D.K., de Supinski, B.R., Schulz, M., Freeh, V.W., Bletsch, T.: Adagio: making DVS practical for complex HPC applications. In: Proceedings of the 23rd International Conference on Supercomputing, ICS 2009, pp. 460–469. ACM, New York (2009). http://doi.acm.org/10.1145/1542275.1542340
14. Sridharan, S., Gupta, G., Sohi, G.S.: Adaptive, efficient, parallel execution of parallel programs. In: Proceedings of the 35th ACM SIGPLAN Conference on Programming Language Design and Implementation, PLDI 2014 (2014)
15. Wang, Z., O'Boyle, M.F.P., Emani, M.K.: Smart, adaptive mapping of parallelism in the presence of external workload. In: Proceedings of the IEEE/ACM International Symposium on Code Generation and Optimization (CGO), CGO 2013 (2013)

The Contention Avoiding Concurrent Priority Queue

Konstantinos Sagonas$^{(\boxtimes)}$ and Kjell Winblad$^{(\boxtimes)}$

Department of Information Technology, Uppsala University,
Uppsala, Sweden
{Konstantinos.Sagonas,Kjell.Winblad}@it.uu.se

Abstract. Efficient and scalable concurrent priority queues are crucial for the performance of many multicore applications, e.g. for task scheduling and the parallelization of various algorithms. Linearizable concurrent priority queues with traditional semantics suffer from an inherent sequential bottleneck in the head of the queue. This bottleneck is the motivation for some recently proposed priority queues with more relaxed semantics. We present the contention avoiding concurrent priority queue (CA-PQ), a data structure that functions as a linearizable concurrent priority with traditional semantics under low contention, but activates contention avoiding techniques that give it more relaxed semantics when high contention is detected. CA-PQ avoids contention in the head of the queue by removing items in bulk from the global data structure, which also allows it to often serve DELMIN operations without accessing memory that is modified by several threads. We show that CA-PQ scales well. Its cache friendly design achieves performance that is twice as fast compared to that of state-of-the-art concurrent priority queues on several instances of a parallel shortest path benchmark.

1 Introduction

The need for scalable and efficient data structures has increased with the number of cores per processor chip which has steadily increased for the last decade. Concurrent priority queues in particular are important for a wide range of parallel applications such as task scheduling [20], branch-and-bound algorithms [10], and parallel versions of Dijkstra's shortest path algorithm [18]. Typically, the interface of concurrent priority queues consists of an INSERT operation that inserts a key-value pair (called item from here on) to the priority queue, and a DELMIN operation that removes and returns the item with the smallest key from the priority queue. Strict (linearizable) priority queues require that the DELMIN operation always returns an item that had the smallest key of all items in the priority queue at some point during the operation's execution, while relaxed priority queues can return an item that was not the one with the minimum key.

Research supported in part by the Linnaeus centre of excellence UPMARC (www.upmarc.se).

© Springer International Publishing AG 2017
C. Ding et al. (Eds.): LCPC 2016, LNCS 10136, pp. 314–330, 2017.
DOI: 10.1007/978-3-319-52709-3_23

Until quite recently, most research on concurrent priority queues has focused on strict priority queues, e.g. [2,7,12,16–18,21]. Still, even in the 1990's, there have been a few papers on parallel priority queues that consider more relaxed semantics [8,15].

Inspired by the realization that the DELMIN operation induces an inherent sequential bottleneck in the head of strict priority queues, some recent papers have proposed relaxed priority queues for modern multicore machines [1,13, 19,20]. Even though all these proposals are successful in reducing the sequential bottleneck in the head of the priority queue, they all have a performance problem in that all DELMIN calls access memory that is frequently written to by multiple threads. This is especially expensive on NUMA machines, as it causes data to be transferred between processor chips which in turn may cause long stalls in the processor pipeline and contention in the memory system.

In this paper, we describe a new concurrent priority called the *contention avoiding concurrent priority queue* or CA-PQ for brevity. CA-PQ does not have the performance problem mentioned above. Furthermore, CA-PQ differs from recent proposals in that it works as a strict priority queue when contention is low. Its semantics is relaxed only when operations frequently observe contention. Previously proposed relaxed priority queues have relaxed semantics even when this is not motivated by high contention. This is a problem because unnecessary use of relaxed semantics causes items with high priority to be ignored by DELMIN, which can cause unnecessary computations and performance degradation in some applications. Finally, in contrast to related work, CA-PQ has two contention avoidance mechanisms that are activated separately: one to avoid contention in DELMIN operations and one to avoid contention in INSERT operations.

Using a parallel program that computes the single source shortest paths on a graph, a benchmark which is representative for many best-first search algorithms that use priority queues, we compare CA-PQ's performance with that of other state-of-the-art concurrent priority queues. As we will see, CA-PQ's cache friendly design lets it outperform all other data structures with a significant margin in many scenarios. Furthermore, CA-PQ's adaptivity to contention helps it perform well across a multitude of scenarios without any need to manually tune its parameters.

We start by giving a high-level overview of CA-PQ (Sect. 2). We then describe its operations in detail (Sect. 3) and the guarantees that they provide (Sect. 4). Details of our implementation of the global CA-PQ component appear in Sect. 5. We then contrast CA-PQ with related work (Sect. 6), experimentally evaluate CA-PQ variants with other state-of-the-art data structures (Sect. 7) and conclude (Sect. 8).

2   A Brief Overview of the Contention Avoiding Priority Queue

As illustrated in Fig. 1, the CA-PQ has a global component and thread local components. When a CA-PQ is uncontended it functions as a strict concurrent

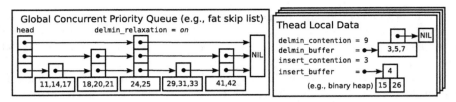

Fig. 1. The structure of a CA-PQ.

priority queue. This means that the DELMIN operation removes the smallest item from the global priority queue and the INSERT operation inserts an item into the global priority queue.

Accesses to the global priority queue detect whether there is contention during these accesses. The counters delmin_contention and insert_contention are modified based on detected contention so that the frequency of contention during recent calls can be estimated. If DELMIN operations are frequently contended, contention avoidance for DELMIN operations is activated. If a thread's delmin_buffer and insert_buffer are empty and DELMIN contention avoidance is turned on, then the DELMIN operation will grab up to k smallest items from the head of the global priority queue and place them in the thread's delmin_buffer. Grabbing a number of items from the head of the global priority queue can be done efficiently if the queue is implemented with a "fat" skip list that can store multiple items per node; see Fig. 1. Thus, activating contention avoidance for DELMIN operations reduces the contention on the head of the global priority queue by reducing the number of accesses by up to $k - 1$ per k DELMIN operations.

Contention avoidance for INSERT operations is activated for a particular thread when contention during INSERT operations is frequent for that thread. The INSERT contention avoidance reduces the number of inserts to the global priority queue by buffering items from a bounded number of consecutive INSERT operations in the insert_buffer. When at least one of the delmin_buffer and insert_buffer is non-empty, the DELMIN operation takes the smallest item from these buffers and returns it.

3   Implementation

We will now give a detailed description of CA-PQ's implementation. First we will describe the implementation of the two operations, INSERT and DELMIN. We will then describe the general requirements for the global priority queue component.

3.1   Operations

The Insert Operation. Pseudocode for this operation can be seen in Algorithm 1. Items are inserted in the global priority queue (line 3) when contention is low or when the number of items in the thread-local insert_buffer equals its capacity. By initially setting the buffer's capacity to zero and setting it to a

non-zero value when INSERT operations frequently observe contention, these two
tests are folded into one; cf. line 2.

Algorithm 1. The INSERT operation

```
1  Function INSERT (pq, item)
2      if pq.local.insert_buffer.size == pq.local.insert_buffer.capacity then
3          contended = GINSERT(pq.global_pq, item);
4          if contended then pq.local.insert_contention += INS_CONT ;
5          else pq.local.insert_contention -= INS_UNCONT ;
6      else
7          INSERTBUFFERINSERT(pq.local.insert_buffer, item);
8      end
```

The INSERT operation on the global priority queue, called GINSERT, returns
true if it observed contention during the operation and false otherwise. To estimate the contention level for INSERT operations in the priority queue, the
thread local counter insert_contention is incremented by INS_CONT if contention was detected and is decremented by INS_UNCONT if no contention
was detected (lines 4–5). In our implementation, INS_CONT is equal to two and
INS_UNCONT is equal to one. As we will soon see, these values ensure that
adaptation to contention in INSERT operations will eventually happen if more
than one out of two INSERT operations are contended for a sufficiently long
period of time. Finally, if the thread local insert_buffer has a size that is less than
its capacity, the item is inserted into the insert_buffer (line 7).

The DELMIN Operation. Pseudocode for this operation is displayed in Algorithm 2. If at least one of the thread local buffers is non-empty, the operation
removes the smallest item from these buffers (lines 4 and 7). If an item is removed
from the insert_buffer, the buffer's capacity is also decreased by one (line 6). This
is done to ensure that DELMIN will fetch the minimum item from the global
priority queue at least once in a given number of DELMIN operations performed
by a particular thread.

If both buffers are empty, the GDELMIN operation is called on the global priority queue (line 9). This operation also returns an indication whether contention
was detected during the operation in addition to the removed minimum item (if
contention avoidance is turned off) or a buffer with the removed minimum items
(if contention avoidance is turned on). (If the global priority queue is empty a
special empty_pq item is returned.) After the call to GDELMIN, we record the
contention by adjusting the delmin_contention variable (lines 10–11) in a similar
way as was done for the insert_contention variable in the INSERT operation. In
our implementation, the constants DELMIN_CONT and DELMIN_UNCONT
are set to 250 and 1 respectively. These values ensure that adaptation to contention in DELMIN operations will happen if more than one out of 250 DELMIN
operations are contended during a long period of time.

We then proceed to check if delmin_contention has reached one of the
thresholds for turning on or off contention avoidance on the global priority queue (lines 12–17). The thresholds called DELMIN_RELAX_LIMIT and
DELMIN_UNRELAX_LIMIT in the pseudocode are in our implementation set
to 1000 and −1000 respectively. Calling TURNONDELMINRELAXATION on the

---

Algorithm 2. The DELMIN operation

```
 1  Function DELMIN (pq, item)
 2      switch SELECTBUFFERWITHSMALLESTKEY (pq.local.delmin_buffer, pq.local.insert_buffer) do
 3          case pq.local.delmin_buffer do
 4              return DELMINBUFFERDELMIN(pq.local.delmin_buffer);
 5          case pq.local.insert_buffer do
 6              pq.local.insert_buffer.capacity -= 1;
 7              return INSERTBUFFERDELMIN(pq.local.insert_buffer);
 8          otherwise do
 9              contended, ret_val = GDELMIN(pq.global_pq);
10              if contended then  pq.local.delmin_contention += DELMIN_CONT ;
11              else pq.local.delmin_contention -= DELMIN_UNCONT ;
12              if pq.local.delmin_contention > DELMIN_RELAX_LIMIT then
13                  TURNONDELMINRELAXATION( pq.global_pq);
14                  pq.local.delmin_contention = 0;
15              else if pq.local.delmin_contention < DELMIN_UNRELAX_LIMIT then
16                  TURNOFFDELMINRELAXATION( pq.global_pq);
17                  pq.local.delmin_contention = 0;
18              end
19              if pq.local.insert_contention > INS_RELAX_LIMIT then
20                  pq.local.insert_buffer.max_size = MAX_INSERT_BUFF_SIZE;
21                  pq.local.insert_contention = 0;
22              else if pq.local.insert_contention < INS_UNRELAX_LIMIT then
23                  if pq.local.insert_buffer.max_size > 0 then
24                      pq.local.insert_buffer.max_size -=1;
25                  pq.local.insert_contention = 0;
26              end
27              pq.local.insert_buffer.capacity = pq.local.insert_buffer.max_size;
28              if ret_val is a buffer then
29                  pq.local.delmin_buffer = ret_val;
30                  return DELMINBUFFERDELMIN(pq.local.delmin_buffer);
31              else return ret_val ;
32          end
33      end
```

---

global priority queue will cause subsequent GDELMIN calls to delete up to k smallest items from the global priority queue and return these items in a buffer. Doing the reverse call, TURNOFFDELMINRELAXATION will cause subsequent GDELMIN calls to only remove and return the smallest item.

We then go on to check if one of the thresholds for changing the contention avoidance for INSERT operations has been reached (lines 19–25). In our implementation, the constants INS_RELAX_LIMIT and INS_UNRELAX_LIMIT are set to 100 and −100 respectively. Adapting to high contention for INSERT operations is done by setting the max_size value of the insert buffer to the constant MAX_INSERT_BUFF_SIZE (500 in our implementation) on line 20. When INSERT operations experience low contention we decrease max_size of the insert_buffer by one (line 24). We set the capacity of the insert_buffer to the max_size value of the insert_buffer on line 27.

Note that adaptation to contention in INSERT operations is done by only doing thread-local modification while adaptation to contention in DELMIN operations is done by changing the state of the global component. One could also implement DELMIN contention avoidance by only changing a thread local flag if the global priority queue exposes separate operations for deleting a single item and a buffer of items. We expect this alternative design choice to work equally well.

At the end of DELMIN's code, we check if the value returned by GDELMIN is a buffer of items or a single item (line 28). If the value is a buffer, we set it to be the thread local delmin_buffer and return an item from that buffer. Otherwise, if it is a single item, we simply return that item (line 31).

3.2 Global Concurrent Priority Queue Component

The requirements for the global priority queue are as follows. First, it should support linearizable INSERT and DELMIN operations. Second, it should also support a linearizable bulk DELMIN operation that returns up to the k smallest items from the priority queue in a buffer. Furthermore, all these operations need to be able to detect contention so as the contention avoidance mechanisms are activated. With these properties fulfilled, it is easy to see that the interface used for the global priority queue in Algorithms 1 and 2 can be implemented. The ability to turn off and on DELMIN relaxation can be implemented by associating a flag with the global priority queue. The GDELMIN operation simply needs to check this flag and use the bulk DELMIN functionality to return a buffer of items if the flag is on, or use the single-item DELMIN functionality to return a single item otherwise.

For the DELMIN contention avoidance to work as intended, it is crucial that the bulk DELMIN operations can remove and return the k smallest items much faster than doing k single-item DELMIN operations. To make this possible, our implementation of the global concurrent priority queue makes use of a skip list data structure with fat nodes; see Fig. 1. As every skip list node in our implementation can store up to k items, the bulk DELMIN operation can remove and return up to k smallest items with as little work as the single-item DELMIN operation needs to do in the worst case. A k value that is equal to or greater than the number of threads should be enough to eliminate most of the contention in DELMIN. Our implementation uses 80 as the value of k.

4   Properties

We will now state the guarantees provided by the CA-PQ. As some applications might not need the contention avoidance for both INSERT and DELMIN, we will first state and prove the guarantees of the CA-PQ variants derived by turning these features off.

First note that turning off the contention avoidance for both INSERT and DELMIN results in a strict priority queue. We call the data structure that results from turning off contention avoidance for INSERT operations CA-DM. To state the guarantee provided by CA-DM we first have to define a particular time period.

Definition 1 (*Time period* TP(k, D_n)). *Let an integer $k \geq 1$, $D_1, \ldots, D_n$ be the sequence of DELMIN calls performed by a thread T on a priority queue Q, and let $j = max(1, n - k + 1)$. Then $TP(k, D_n)$ is the time period that starts at the time D_j is issued and ends when the call D_n returns.*

We can now state and prove the guarantee that the CA-DM priority queue provides.

Theorem 1 *(CA-DM* DELMIN *Guarantee). The item returned by a* DELMIN *call D on a CA-DM priority queue Q is guaranteed to be among the $k \cdot P$ smallest items that have been inserted into the priority queue at some point in time t during the time period $TP(k, D)$, where P is the number of threads that are accessing Q and k is the maximum size of the buffer returned by the global priority queue that is used by Q.*

Proof: Let t be the linearization point of the latest GDELMIN call G (Algorithm 2, line 9) performed by the issuer of D before D's return. Note that t must then be in the time period $TP(k, D)$ as the number of items in the delmin_buffer decreases by one in every DELMIN call that does not get its item directly from the global priority queue. All items in the buffer returned by the call G are among the $k \cdot P$ smallest items in Q at the time of G's linearization point. To see this, note that no items in the global priority queue were smaller than the at most k items returned by G at G's linearization point and no more than $(P - 1) \cdot k$ items can be buffered in the delmin_buffers of other threads.   □

We call the priority queue derived from CA-PQ by turning off contention avoidance for DELMIN CA-IN. The guarantee provided by CA-IN is arguably even weaker than that provided by CA-DM.

Theorem 2 *(CA-IN* DELMIN *Guarantee). At least one in every $m + 1$* DELMIN *operations performed by a thread is guaranteed to be among the $m \cdot (P - 1) + 1$ smallest items in the CA-IN priority queue Q at some point in time during the operation's execution, where m is equal to MAX_INSERT_BUFF_SIZE and P is the number of threads that are accessing Q.*

Proof: At least one call D in every $m + 1$ DELMIN calls returns an item I from a GDELMIN call G since the capacity of the insert_buffer is decreased when items are removed from it (Algorithm 2, line 6). This item I must be among the $m \cdot (P - 1) + 1$ smallest items in the priority queue at the linearization point of G since there can be at most $m \cdot (P - 1)$ smaller items in the insert_buffers of other threads.   □

The guarantee provided by a CA-PQ that has both contention avoidance for DELMIN and INSERT operations turned on is very similar to that of CA-IN.

Theorem 3 *(CA-PQ* DELMIN *Guarantee). At least one in every $m + 1$* DELMIN *operations performed by a thread is guaranteed to be among the $m \cdot (P - 1) + 1$ smallest items in the CA-PQ priority queue Q at some point in time during the operation's execution, where m is equal to $k + MAX\_INSERT\_BUFF\_SIZE$, k is the maximum size of the buffer returned by GDELMIN, and P is the number of threads that are accessing Q.*

Proof: The proof is very similar to the proof of Theorem 2. The difference is that there is now also the delmin_buffer so that m becomes slightly larger.   □

All priority queue variants mentioned above also support the property specified in the theorem below which is important for the termination of many parallel algorithms that employ concurrent priority queues.

Theorem 4 (DELMIN *Deletes All*). *Let S be the set of all threads that have issued operations on a priority queue Q and t be a specific point in time after which no* INSERT *operations are issued. If all threads in S issue a* DELMIN *operation after time t and all get the special item* empty_pq *as results, then all items that have been inserted into Q have been deleted and returned by* DELMIN *operations.*

Proof: An item that is inserted into Q and has not yet been deleted is stored in the global priority queue or in one of the thread-local buffers of threads in S. It is easy to see that all these locations must be empty if all threads in S issue DELMIN operations after t and get the empty_pq symbol as return value.   □

5   Our Implementation of the Global Priority Queue Component

Our global concurrent priority queue is constructed from a contention adapting search tree (CATree) [14] using a skip list with fat nodes as backing data structure. We refer to the original CATree paper for a complete description of the CATree data structure and will here just briefly describe how we extended it to support the DELMIN operations. Fig. 2 shows the structure of a CATree. The routing nodes are used to find the location of a specific item in the data structure. The actual items stored in the data structure are located in the sequential data structure instances in the last layer. These sequential data structures are protected by locks in the base nodes where they are rooted. Base nodes can be split and joined with each other based on how much contention is detected in the base node locks. As the smallest items in a CATree are always located in the leftmost part of the tree when depicted as in Fig. 2, the DELMIN operation first finds and locks the leftmost base node in

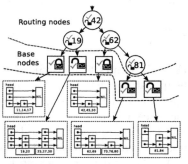

Fig. 2. The CATree data structure.

the CATree. When the leftmost base node is empty it is joined together with its neighbor using the CATree algorithm for low contention adaptation until the leftmost base node is non-empty[1]. As depicted in Fig. 1, we reuse the fat skip list nodes as delmin_buffer and use a binary heap as insert_buffer.

---

[1] The only difference between the low-contention join function described in the CATree paper [14] and the one used to create a non-empty leftmost base node is that the latter uses a forcing LOCK call instead of a TRYLOCK call to lock the neighbor. (This cannot cause a deadlock since no other code issues forcing lock calls in the other direction).

Traditional locks are well known to give poor performance when they are contended [3,6,9]. Therefore, to improve the performance when base node locks in the CATree are contended we use a locking technique that we call delegation locking but that is also called combining in other places [3,6]. More specifically we use a delegation locking technique, called queue delegation locking [9], when locking base nodes. Delegation locking lets the current lock owner thread help other threads perform their critical sections that are waiting to acquire the lock. By doing so the throughput of critical sections executed on a particular lock can be substantially increased because the current lock owner can keep the data protected by the lock in its private processor cache while helping critical sections from other threads. Queue delegation locking has the additional benefit compared to other locking algorithms that critical sections for which the issuing threads do not need any return value (such as the INSERT operation) can be delegated to the lock owner without any need to wait for the actual execution of the critical section. Linearizability is still provided as the order of the delegated operation is maintained by a queue. Contention in the operations is detected by checking whether another thread is holding the base node lock that the operation needs to acquire.

Memory Management. The only nodes of the data structure that need delayed memory reclamation in our CA-PQ implementation are the routing nodes and base nodes in the CATree component. These nodes can be read by multiple threads concurrently so it is unsafe to reclaim these nodes before it is certain that no threads can hold references to them. To reclaim these nodes we use Keir Fraser's epoch based reclamation [4].

6   Related Work

Early attempts to construct concurrent priority queues, e.g. [7], were based on heap data structures. More recent concurrent priority queues have often been based on concurrent skip lists as empirical evidence suggests that this design is more scalable than the heap based design [16]. Both the priority queue by Shavit and Lotan [16] and the one by Sundell and Tsigas [17] handle DELMIN by first doing a logical deletion of the node to be deleted by marking it before it is physically removed from the skip list. The skip list based priority queue by Lindén and Jonsson [12] (called **Lindén** from here on) also uses logical deletion before physical removal but achieves better performance and less memory contention by physically removing a prefix of logically deleted nodes in one go, in contrast to previous algorithms that physically remove one node at a time. Calciu *et al.* have explored the idea of using combining and delegation to speedup the DELMIN operation. Their data structure [2] uses a sequential skip list managed by a server thread for small keys and a concurrent skip list for larger keys to exploit the parallelism of INSERT operations. In a very recent work, Zhang and Dechev have proposed a concurrent priority based on multi-dimensional linked lists [21]. We consider all the above works on concurrent priority queues orthogonal to the main contribution of this paper which is a priority queue with more relaxed semantics.

Concurrent priority queues with relaxed semantics have also been proposed. The **MultiQueue** data structure by Rihani *et al.* [13] is created from $C \cdot P$ sequential priority queues protected by locks, where C is a constant and P is the number of threads using the priority queue. An INSERT operation in a MultiQueue selects one of the sequential queues at random and inserts in that queue. MultiQueue's DELMIN operation checks the minimum item in two of the sequential priority queues selected at random (without acquiring locks) and does the actual DELMIN in the one of these priority queues with the smallest key if that priority queue is successfully locked with a try-lock call. The process is retried if the try-lock call fails. The MultiQueue does not provide any guarantee, but an experimental evaluation suggests that DELMIN often returns an item with one of the smallest keys in the priority queue [13].

Alistarh *et al.* have created the **SprayList** which is a relaxed priority queue based on the skip list data structure [1]. SprayList relaxes the result of the DELMIN operation by "spraying" into a random position close to the head of the skip list. The SprayList guarantees that the item returned by DELMIN is among the $\mathcal{O}(P \log^3 P)$ smallest items with high probability, where P is the number of threads.

For scheduling purposes in a task-based parallel programming framework, Wimmer *et al.* have created relaxed priority queues that have different trade-offs between quality of the items returned by DELMIN and scalability [20]. Of these, the queue that seems to perform best is called Hybrid k. A later publication, also by Wimmer *et al.*, introduced the k-**LSM** priority queue [19]. k-LSM provides the structural guarantee that no more than $k \cdot P$ items might be skipped by DELMIN, where k is a configurable parameter and P is the number of threads. We will here focus on the k-LSM priority queue rather than Hybrid k because the implementation of the latter is optimized for a particular task-based parallel programming framework, making it difficult to compare with, and experiments by Wimmer *et al.* suggest that k-LSM performs slightly better than Hybrid k [19]. The k-LSM data structure is based on so called log-structured merge-trees (LSM) and consists of a thread local LSM component and a shared relaxed LSM component. INSERT inserts the item to the thread local LSM component. If this results in a block larger than a certain size, that block is merged into the shared LSM. DELMIN compares one of the k smallest items in the shared LSM with the smallest item from the local LSM and tries to remove the smallest of those items.

All the above relaxed priority queues (MultiQueue, SprayList, Hybrid k and k-LSM) utilize relaxations to avoid contention in DELMIN operations. However, in contrast to CA-PQ, they all access non-thread-local memory in every DELMIN operation. As this shared memory is written to by many threads frequently, many of these accesses induce cache misses. This can be expensive as it causes the core executing the thread to wait for data to be transferred from remote locations and causes contention in the memory system. On big multi-cores, especially on NUMA machines with several processor chips, getting data from remote locations can be several orders of magnitude more expensive than getting data from the same processor's cache. There are two reasons why CA-PQ can avoid the frequent remote memory accesses in DELMIN. Firstly, its DELMIN fetches a block containing several items from the global priority queue, i.e., it gets several items for a single cache miss (because several items can be stored on the same cache line). Secondly, the guarantees provided by CA-PQ are more permissive than those provided by SprayList, Hybrid k and k-LSM, which makes it possible to allow CA-PQ's DELMIN to often be performed without checking if other threads have changed the data structure.

Another major difference between CA-PQ and other relaxed priority queues is that CA-PQ only activates relaxations when this is motivated by detected high contention. As we will see in the next section, this makes it possible for CA-PQ to achieve high performance in a wide range of scenarios.

7   Experimental Evaluation

We evaluate the scalability and performance of CA-PQ and the variants CA-IN (INSERT contention avoidance turned off), CA-DM (DELMIN contention avoidance turned off) and CATree (the global priority queue component of our algorithm) in a parallel single-source shortest-path (SSSP) benchmark. The benchmark uses a parallel version of Dijkstra's algorithm using a concurrent priority queue; see Tamir *et al.* [18]. We note that we avoid the node locks used in this parallelization by updating the node weights in *compare-and-swap* loops. CA-PQ does not have a DECREASEKEY operation that changes the key of an item in the priority queue — such is also the case for the other concurrent priority queues that we compare against. Changing the weight of a key in the priority queue is therefore implemented by an INSERT operation and the other reference to the node that might exist in the queue is lazily removed when it is deleted by a DELMIN operation. As noted by Tamir *et al.* [18], this lazy removal scheme can induce some overhead over having a concurrent priority queue with a DECREASEKEY operation. To get a hint of how big this overhead might be, we include the sequential version of Dijkstra's algorithm that uses DECREASEKEY with a Fibonacci Heap [5] as priority queue as a base line. The overhead of not having DECREASEKEY operation seems to be quite low in many cases as the sequential Dijkstra has similar performance as the parallel SSSP algorithm using CA-PQ when using just one thread.

Data Sets. We include results from running the SSSP benchmark on the California road network (called RoadNet from now on) and a social media network obtained from LiveJournal (called LiveJournal from now on) [11]. RoadNet is a relatively sparse network containing 1.95 million nodes connected to the source involving 5.5 million edges. LiveJournal is a more dense network containing 4.4 million nodes connected to the source and 68 million edges. As we do not have any natural weights for these networks we used two versions of these networks. A weight of one on all edges is used in the unweighted version. In the weighted version, a random weight from the range $[0, 1000]$ is assigned to each of the edges.

Data Structures and Parameters. We compare our priority queues to Lindén [12], MultiQueue [13], SprayList [1] and k-LSM [19]. Section 6 contains a description of these data structures. All implementations are those provided by their inventors except the MultiQueue which is implemented by the authors of k-LSM. We use the default parameters for SprayList as configured by its authors because the SprayList was evaluated in a very similar benchmark to ours [1]. To find a good value for the C parameter used by the MultiQueue, we ran the benchmarks with C equal to 2, 4, 8, 16, 32 and 64. We found that the values 8 and 16 gave the best performance and the difference between these two parameters was very small in all cases. We therefore use MultiQueue with $C = 16$. Similarly, to find a good value for the k parameter used by k-LSM we ran the experiments with k equal to 2^n for all integer values of n from 8 to 17. From this, we found that $k = 2^{10} = 1024$ gave the best performance on RoadNet and that $k = 2^{16} = 65\,536$ generally gave the best performance on LiveJournal. We therefore show k-LSM with both $k = 1024$ (klsm1024) and $k = 65\,536$ (klsm65536).

Methodology. We show results from a machine with four Intel(R) Xeon(R) E5-4650 CPUs (2.70 GHz, turbo boost turned off), eight cores each (i.e. the machine has a total of 32 physical cores, each with hyperthreading, which makes a total of 64 logical cores). The machine has 128 GB of RAM and is running Linux 3.16.0-4-amd64. We compiled the benchmark which is written in C and C++ with GCC version 5.3.0 and used the optimization flag -O3. We have verified our results by running the experiments on a machine with four AMD Opteron 6276 (2.3 GHz, in total 64 cores)[2]. Threads are pinned to logical cores so that the first 16 threads in the graphs run on the first processor chip, the next 16 on the second, and so on. We ran each measurement three times and show the average and error bars for the minimum and maximum in the graphs. As a sanity check we compared the calculated distances against the actual distances after each run.

Results. The results from the SSSP benchmark are displayed in Fig. 3. The graphs show throughput $N \div T$ on the y-axis, where N is the number of nodes in the graph and T is the execution time of the benchmark in μs. We show throughput rather than time because this makes the scalability behavior easier to see. (The poor performance of some data structures would otherwise make the results unreadable.) The dashed black line shows the performance of the sequential Dijkstra's algorithm with a Fibonacci heap. The red line with legend Lock shows the performance of a binary heap protected by a lock.

RoadNet. Let us first look at the results for the RoadNet graphs shown in Fig. 3a and b. With RoadNet, none of the data structures manages to provide much increase in performance when more than one processor chip is utilized (after 16 threads). However, in the scenario with edge weight range $[0, 1000]$, CA-PQ archives a speedup of 11 compared to its single thread performance

---

[2] Results from the AMD machine and from additional scenarios as well as the benchmark code are available at http://www.it.uu.se/research/group/languages/software/ca_pq.

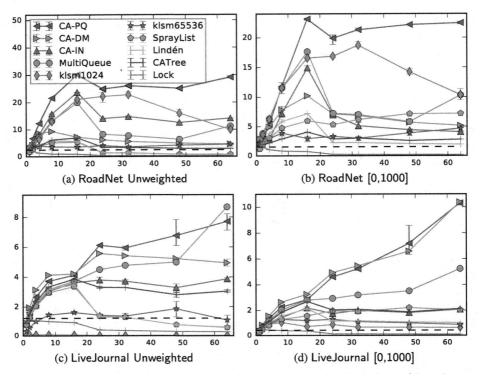

Fig. 3. Graphs showing results from the SSSP experiment. Throughput (# nodes in graph ÷ execution time (μs)) on the y-axis and number of threads on the x-axis. The black dashed line is the performance of sequential Dijkstra's algorithm with a Fibonacci Heap.

when running on 16 threads (remember that these 16 threads run on 8 cores with hyperthreading). It is clear from the worse performance of CA-DM (INSERT contention avoidance turned off) and CA-IN (DELMIN contention avoidance turned off) that both contention avoidance mechanisms are beneficial to achieving this performance in the relatively sparse RoadNet graph that gives high contention both in INSERT and DELMIN operations. The data structure that achieves the second best performance after CA-PQ in these scenarios is klsm1024. It is interesting to note that klsm1024 also buffers inserted items in a thread local storage.

To investigate the reason for the performance further, we show number of L2 cache misses (measured with hardware counters) divided by the number of nodes in the graph in Table 1. As the L2 cache is private to a core on this processor, more L2 cache misses is an indication of worse memory locality and more accesses to memory modified by several thread. Unsurprisingly, CA-PQ has the least amount of L2 cache misses in the RoadNet scenarios due to its cache friendly design.

In the sequential version of Dijkstra's algorithm each node is processed exactly once. In the parallel version, this is not always the case as the node with the smallest distance estimate is not always processed first. We can therefore

Table 1. Waste and cache misses (64 threads). The column *time* shows execution time in seconds, *waste* shows the number of nodes unnecessarily processed and the column $miss shows number of L2 cache misses divided by number of nodes in the graph.

Graph	RoadNet						LiveJournal					
Weights	1			[0,1000]			1			[0,1000]		
	Time	Waste	$miss	Time	Waste	$miss	Time	Waste	$miss	Time	Waste	$miss
CA-PQ	0.07	$1730k$	7.8	0.09	$1927k$	12.2	0.63	$924k$	30.1	0.47	$353k$	95.4
CA-RM	0.43	$7k$	14.8	0.38	$11k$	34.6	0.98	8	32.2	0.47	$2k$	94.1
CA-IN	0.14	$2264k$	8.2	0.48	$2030k$	27.3	1.25	$1768k$	37.0	2.34	$714k$	110.5
MultiQ.	0.18	$8k$	32.2	0.19	$58k$	36.1	0.56	39	63.4	0.93	$2k$	112.2
kl.1024	0.20	$2498k$	12.4	0.19	$2222k$	15.8	161.39	174	33980.3	7.63	$3k$	2538.5
kl.65536	0.44	$28411k$	82.5	0.42	$26115k$	105.6	4.76	$688k$	601.7	5.48	$1857k$	1192.7
Spray	2.51	$134k$	461.0	0.27	$230k$	88.3	8.33	41	314.9	2.39	$7k$	755.5
CATree	0.68	9	20.9	0.71	36	40.2	1.59	1	40.8	2.27	5	107.5
Lindén	3.39	206	108.4	1.01	252	114.6	7.96	21	142.6	4.64	0	353.1
Lock	7.06	210	39.7	11.02	490	59.0	17.01	54	62.4	49.73	86	163.4

use the number of nodes processed by the parallel algorithm as a measurement of how precise the DELMIN operation is (how far from the actual minimum the returned items are). In the column "waste" of Table 1 we show the number of nodes processed minus the number of nodes in the graph. We see that the strict priority queues CATree, Lindén and Lock all do a small amount of wasted work in both the unweighted and the weighted scenarios. CA-PQ, CA-IN and the k-LSMs all waste quite a lot of work considering that RoadNet only has 1.95 million nodes. However, as the contention on the priority queue is high in this scenario it can be less wasteful for the priority queue to be less precise in order to reduce the contention inside the priority queue. As CA-PQ only activates the relaxed semantics when high contention is detected, one can see it as opportunistic in the sense that it lowers precision and risks more wasted work in the application only when time and resources would be wasted anyway due to contention.

The MultiQueue achieves very good precision according to the waste estimate but as each operation accesses at least one of the shared priority queues, it suffers from bad memory locality; see Table 1. Since communication between processor chips is more expensive than communication within the chip, the bad memory locality of MultiQueue becomes apparent first when more than one NUMA node is utilized; see Fig. 3a.

LiveJournal. We now go on to discuss the results from the graph LiveJournal that can be seen in Fig. 3c and d. As the LiveJournal graph is relatively dense there will be many priority queue items with the same distance (key) while running the parallel SSSP. This is especially true in the unweighted case (Fig. 3c). This can lead to a lot of contention in INSERT operations as the skip list based data structures (CA-*, SprayList, Lindén and CATree) all try to insert an item with the same distance in the same location. The MultiQueue however is excellent in avoiding contention and achieves the best performance in the unweighted LiveJournal (Fig. 3c). However, MultiQueue is tightly followed by CA-PQ as CA-PQ is also good at avoiding contention with its contention avoidance mechanisms and has good memory locality; see Table 1.

In the weighted LiveJournal scenario (Fig. 3d), where the contention in INSERT operations is not as high as in the unweighted case, CA-PQ and CA-DM are by far outperforming the other data structures. Some hints about the reason for this is given in Table 1: one can see that CA-PQ and CA-DM induces less L2 cache misses than the other data structures. However, we want to stress that the number of L2 cache misses is a course-grained measurement of memory locality. The cost of cache misses can differ depending on whether it is a read miss or write miss and whether the miss causes communication outside the chip or not.

From Table 1, we see that CA-DM generally does relatively little wasted work while CA-PQ is more wasteful which is natural as CA-PQ provides weaker guarantees than those provided by CA-DM. This also explains why CA-DM performs better than CA-PQ by a very small amount for most thread counts in the weighted LiveJournal scenario.

A Note on Denser Graphs. We have also run experiments on randomly generated graphs that are more dense than the graphs used in the experiments we just presented. (Refer to http://www.it.uu.se/research/group/languages/software/ca_pq for the results of these experiments.) Dense graphs tend to give an access pattern on the concurrent priority queue with many more INSERT operations than DELMIN in the beginning of the run and then many more DELMIN than INSERT in the end of the run. CA-PQ is efficient in these kinds of scenarios because of its cache friendly DELMIN operation. For example, CA-PQ's execution time on a graph with 100 edges per node and edge weights from the range [0, 1000] is only about one third of the execution time of the second best data structure in this scenario (SprayList). The access pattern produced by denser graphs also explains why k-LSM performs badly with the LiveJournal graphs. When DELMIN operations are frequent and INSERT's are less frequent, most DELMIN calls will take items from the shared LSM, which induces contention and cache misses.

Usefulness of Adaptivity. To investigate the usefulness of adaptively turning on the contention avoidance techniques we have run experiments where contention avoidance for both INSERT and DELMIN are always turned on (not shown in graphs to not clutter them). We found the performance of this non-adaptive approach to be similar to CA-PQ in scenarios where INSERT contention is high, but significantly worse in scenarios with low INSERT contention (e.g. LiveJournal weight range [0, 1000]). Thus, CA-PQ's ability to adaptively turn off and on the contention avoidance techniques is beneficial because it helps it perform well in a multitude of scenarios without any need to change parameters.

The Global Component. Finally, we comment on the performance of the strict priority queue that we developed as the global component of CA-PQ which is called CATree in Fig. 3 and Table 1. CATree beats the state-of-the-art lock-free linearizable priority queue by Lindén by a substantial amount in several of the scenarios and especially when more than one NUMA node is used. We attribute this good performance to the good memory locality provided by delegation locking and the fact that we use fat skip list nodes which increase locality and reduce the number of memory allocations.

A Note on Thread Preemption. In our benchmark setup, thread preemption is uncommon since we use one hardware thread per worker thread. In setups where threads often get preempted or stalled for some reason, CA-PQ's buffering of items can be problematic, as small items can be stuck for a long period of time in the buffers of these threads. It remains as future work to investigate solutions for this problem, perhaps using a stealing technique similar to the one proposed by Wimmer et al. [19].

8   Concluding Remarks

We have introduced the CA-PQ concurrent priority queue that activates relaxed semantics only when resources would otherwise be wasted on contention related overheads and on waiting. CA-PQ has a cache friendly design and avoids accesses to memory that is written to by many threads when its contention avoidance mechanisms are activated, which contributes to its performance advantage compared to related relaxed data structures.

It would be interesting to investigate other strategies for adapting the relaxation. For example, one can experiment with a more fine grained adjustment of the relaxation than what is done in CA-PQ or consider relaxation based on feedback about wasted work from the application. However, the investigation of such strategies is left for future work.

References

1. Alistarh, D., Kopinsky, J., Li, J., Shavit, N.: The spraylist: a scalable relaxed priority queue. In: Proceedings of 20th ACM SIGPLAN Symposium on Principles and Practice of Parallel Programming, PPoPP 2015, pp. 11–20. ACM, New York (2015)
2. Calciu, I., Mendes, H., Herlihy, M.: The adaptive priority queue with elimination and combining. In: Kuhn, F. (ed.) DISC 2014. LNCS, vol. 8784, pp. 406–420. Springer, Heidelberg (2014). doi:10.1007/978-3-662-45174-8_28
3. Fatourou, P., Kallimanis, N.D.: Revisiting the combining synchronization technique. In: Proceedings of 17th ACM SIGPLAN Symposium on Principles and Practice of Parallel Programming, PPoPP 2012, pp. 257–266. ACM, New York (2012)
4. Fraser, K.: Practical lock-freedom. Ph.D. thesis, University of Cambridge Computer Laboratory (2004)
5. Fredman, M.L., Tarjan, R.E.: Fibonacci heaps and their uses in improved network optimization algorithms. J. ACM **34**(3), 596–615 (1987)

6. Hendler, D., Incze, I., Shavit, N., Tzafrir, M.: Flat combining and the synchronization-parallelism tradeoff. In: Proceedings of 22nd Annual ACM Symposium on Parallelism in Algorithms and Architectures, SPAA 2010, pp. 355–364. ACM, New York (2010)
7. Hunt, G.C., Michael, M.M., Parthasarathy, S., Scott, M.L.: An efficient algorithm for concurrent priority queue heaps. Inf. Process. Lett. **60**(3), 151–157 (1996)
8. Karp, R.M., Zhang, Y.: Randomized parallel algorithms for backtrack search and branch-and-bound computation. J. ACM **40**(3), 765–789 (1993)
9. Klaftenegger, D., Sagonas, K., Winblad, K.: Delegation locking libraries for improved performance of multithreaded programs. In: Silva, F., Dutra, I., Santos Costa, V. (eds.) Euro-Par 2014. LNCS, vol. 8632, pp. 572–583. Springer, Heidelberg (2014). doi:10.1007/978-3-319-09873-9_48
10. Kumar, V., Ramesh, K., Rao, V.N.: Parallel best-first search of state-space graphs: a summary of results. In: AAAI, vol. 88, pp. 122–127 (1988)
11. Leskovec, J., Krevl, A.: SNAP Datasets: Stanford Large Network Dataset Collection, June 2016. http://snap.stanford.edu/data
12. Lindén, J., Jonsson, B.: A skiplist-based concurrent priority queue with minimal memory contention. In: Baldoni, R., Nisse, N., Steen, M. (eds.) OPODIS 2013. LNCS, vol. 8304, pp. 206–220. Springer, Heidelberg (2013). doi:10.1007/978-3-319-03850-6_15
13. Rihani, H., Sanders, P., Dementiev, R.: Brief announcement: multiqueues: simple relaxed concurrent priority queues. In: Proceedings of 27th ACM Symposium on Parallelism in Algorithms and Architectures, SPAA 2015, pp. 80–82. ACM, New York (2015)
14. Sagonas, K., Winblad, K.: Contention adapting search trees. In: 14th International Symposium on Parallel and Distributed Computing, ISPDC, pp. 215–224. IEEE (2015)
15. Sanders, P.: Randomized priority queues for fast parallel access. J. Parallel Distrib. Comput. **49**(1), 86–97 (1998)
16. Shavit, N., Lotan, I.: Skiplist-based concurrent priority queues. In: Proceedings of 14th International Parallel and Distributed Processing Symposium, pp. 263–268 (2000)
17. Sundell, H., Tsigas, P.: Fast and lock-free concurrent priority queues for multithread systems. In: 2003 Proceedings of 17th International Symposium Parallel and Distributed Processing Symposium, p. 84, April 2003
18. Tamir, O., Morrison, A., Rinetzky, N.: A heap-based concurrent priority queue with mutable priorities for faster parallel algorithms. In: Proceedings of Principles of Distributed Systems: 19th International Conference, OPODIS 2015 (2015)
19. Wimmer, M., Gruber, J., Träff, J.L., Tsigas, P.: The lock-free k-LSM relaxed priority queue. In: Proceedings of 20th ACM SIGPLAN Symposium on Principles and Practice of Parallel Programming, PPoPP 2015, pp. 277–278. ACM, New York (2015)
20. Wimmer, M., Versaci, F., Träff, J.L., Cederman, D., Tsigas, P.: Data structures for task-based priority scheduling. In: Proceedings of 19th ACM SIGPLAN Symposium on Principles and Practice of Parallel Programming, pp. 379–380. ACM, New York (2014)
21. Zhang, D., Dechev, D.: A lock-free priority queue design based on multidimensional linked lists. IEEE Trans. Parallel Distrib. Syst. **27**(3), 613–626 (2016)

Evaluating Performance of Task and Data Coarsening in Concurrent Collections

Chenyang Liu$^{(\boxtimes)}$ and Milind Kulkarni

Purdue University, West Lafayette, IN 47907, USA
{Liu441,Milind}@purdue.edu

Abstract. Programmers are faced with many challenges for obtaining performance on machines with increasingly capable, yet increasingly complex hardware. A trend towards task-parallel and asynchronous many-task programming models aim to alleviate the burden of parallel programming on a vast array of current and future platforms. One such model, Concurrent Collections (CnC), provides a programming paradigm that emphasizes the separation of the concerns–domain experts concentrate on their algorithms and correctness, whereas performance experts handle mapping and tuning to a target platform. Deep understanding of parallel constructs and behavior is not necessary to write parallel applications that will run on various multi-threaded and multi-core platforms when using the CnC model. However, performance can vary greatly depending on the granularity of tasks and data declared by the programmer. These program-specific decisions are not part of the CnC tuning capabilities and must be tuned in the program. We analyze the performance behavior based on tuning various elements in each collection for the LULESH application using CnC. We demonstrate the effects of different techniques to modify task and data granularity in CnC collections. Our fully tiled CnC implementation outperforms the OpenMP counterpart by 3× for 48 processors. Finally, we propose guidelines to emulate the techniques used to obtain high performance while improving programmability.

Keywords: Concurrent collections · LULESH · Coarsening · Parallel programming

1 Introduction

Developing scientific applications for high performance computing is no easy task. Knowledge of the scientific domain is necessary in order to understand the underlying methods and equations required to solve the problem. Correctly mapping and distributing that algorithm onto modern parallel architectures is another task in itself. Modern clusters are increasingly sophisticated, with various forms of heterogeneous and homogeneous parallelism while sporting complex memory hierarchies. A recent emergence of high-level programming models aim to alleviate the burden of parallel programming on a vast array of future

© Springer International Publishing AG 2017
C. Ding et al. (Eds.): LCPC 2016, LNCS 10136, pp. 331–345, 2017.
DOI: 10.1007/978-3-319-52709-3_24

platforms. These frameworks, based on the asynchronous many-task model, split programs into smaller units of computation and associated dependencies, relying on runtime schedulers to correctly synchronize task execution. The programming model we explore is Concurrent Collections (CnC), which is a data-driven task-parallel programming model designed to change the way we approach parallel programming.

The key motivation for developing in CnC is its *separation of concerns* philosophy. The concerns of the domain expert, whose knowledge is used to correctly develop the method and algorithm, is separated from that of the performance expert, whose strengths are in hardware and software optimization. Programs using CnC are expressed as a partially-ordered set of computations with explicitly defined dependencies and seamlessly exploit parallelism by following the constraints of data dependencies using a data driven approach. The CnC scheduler synchronizes data and maps computational tasks to the target hardware at runtime. However, dynamic runtime mapping does not always yield high performance for the following reasons. Excessive fine-grain-parallelism will overburden the scheduler, while sub-optimal data movement leads to poor memory performance. In this paper, we analyze and quantify the effects of high level changes to the granularity of collection items in CnC programs. We use step fusion and tag tiling to coarsening task parallelism, while data is tiled to match the larger computation blocks. We perform these optimizations on the Livermore Unstructured Lagrange Explicit Shock Hydro (LULESH) mini-app, a hydrodynamics code created in the DARPA UHPC program [1,2].

We present the LULESH application, starting from a minimally constrained implementation, and analyze opportunities to reduce the fine-grained parallelism through step fusion and tag tiling. Previous work has shown that these high level techniques improves performance, but does not outperform simple interfaces such as OpenMP [3]. However, with homogeneous tiling of the coarsened execution along with data items, our optimized LULESH implementation outperforms the LULESH 2.0.3 with OpenMP directives by 3× on 48 cores for a 60^3 sized problem. Finally, we present a recommended method for writing CnC programs using automation tools for setting up CnC directives for increased programming productivity.

2   Concurrent Collections Model

In this section, we provide some background on the Concurrent Collections (CnC) programming model. We discuss the methodology for writing programs using CnC and explain how it achieves its philosophy of separation of concerns, making it a compelling model to use for programming applications such as LULESH. A more in-depth description of CnC can be found in previous works [4,5].

Unlike traditional programming approaches, the CnC programming paradigm avoids expressing control flow or parallelism in its program structure. CnC replaces the need for threads and locks or parallel regions, instead satisfying dependence constraints using a data-driven execution model to exploit parallelism. This model is an attractive solution for a domain scientists, whose concern is focused on algorithmic correctness and stability. In contrast, CnC employs various tuners for performance experts to best map certain aspects of an application to target platforms. These tuners are often used for machine-specific optimizations such as memory locality, thread affinity, and resource mapping for distributed applications [6]. CnC is also compatible with a number of programming languages including C/C++, Python, Scala, and Haskell, and also supports various back-end runtime frameworks such as Intel's Thread Building Blocks (TBB) library, Open Community Runtime (OCR), and CnC-HC for GPUs [7–9]. In our research, we use the C++ interface along with the Intel runtime and TBB based work-stealing scheduler for its robustness and tendency to outperform the other schedulers.

There are three basic building blocks that constitute a CnC program. These are referred to as the *collections*, whose purposes are to establish the computation *steps* being performed, *tag* and prescribe those step with unique identifiers, and express which *data* are consumed and produced by computation steps. Figure 1 depicts the three collections and their relationships along with a high level overview of the data-driven execution in CnC.

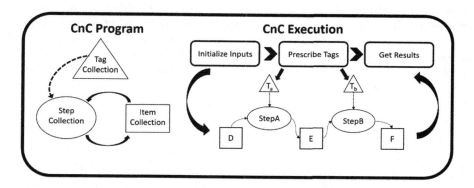

Fig. 1. CnC program and execution

The three types of nodes in Fig. 1 correspond to the computation steps (ovals), data items (rectangles), and control tags (triangles) in CnC. The step collection contains stateless computation steps of a program which are dynamically instantiated when control tags such as T_a *prescribe* those steps. This collection of tags usually contains temporal/spacial data to assist with control flow and proper execution for dynamic steps. Finally, the set of producer/consumer dependencies comprises the (data) item collection. Data items follow dynamic single-assignment, meaning they are immutable, but elements in the data (item) collection may have multiple dynamic instantiations using unique handles, similar to hashing key/value pairs.

The step collection contains a program's computational steps, similar to that in traditional functions. However, these steps do not modify global data, and input/output dependencies are handled by CnC constructs. Steps routines must use *get* constructs to access/consume data (item collection) inputs and *put* constructs to write/produce updated values. Valid steps must perform all *get* operations at the start of each step and *put* operations may only occur after all *gets* finish. Additionally, each step may only have a single associated tag, but a single tag may prescribe multiple steps. Steps will execute when a tag has prescribed it, and all data dependencies are ready from previous steps or the environment.

While step collections specify the computation on data, control tags dictate which steps are dynamically created during runtime. Tags can prescribe steps at any time in the program, whether it be dynamically during runtime or during program initialization. However, once a step is prescribed, the CnC runtime will ensure that step executes before program completion. In Fig. 1, *StepA* begins execution only once tag T_a prescribes it and D is supplied by the environment. Similarly, *StepB* will not begin executing until tag T_b prescribes it and *StepA* finishes producing the data for E. The CnC program terminates once the last prescribed step is finished executing.

Conceptually, the CnC model is ideal for programmability on parallel platforms; however, shifting too much burden from the programmers to the runtime may become prohibitive for performance. After investigation, we find that expressing algorithms as steps that correspond to equations of a method does not translate into an efficient CnC program, unless task and data granularity are considered. Tuners are not sufficient because they mainly focus on machine-specific optimizations, whereas opportunities to reduce the runtime overheads rely on coarsening the task and data granularity, which depend on program structure.

3   LULESH Overview

In this section, we describe the LULESH 2.0 application and the details of the algorithm written in CnC. LULESH is a fully-featured hydrodynamics mini-app developed by Lawrence Livermore National Laboratory that simulates the effect of a blast wave in a physical domain by explicit time-stepping [1]. LULESH is a complex algorithm which performs both computation and communication based work, and optimizations in its code should apply similarly to other applications which exhibit stencil-like and/or time-stepping behavior.

The LULESH 2.0 specification is physics code that operates on an unstructured hexahedral mesh with two centerings. The element centerings (center of the hexahedral) handles data for thermodynamic and physical properties whereas the nodal centerings (the corners of each hexahedra) track spatial and kinetic values such as the position and velocity. The application begins by initializing a 3-dimensional hexahedral mesh and initializing components for each centering. The time-stepping begins as a force is then applied at the origin, updating the kinetic values for all the nodal centerings. Once nodal computation completes, a series of element-centered computations occurs, updating the thermodynamic variables for all elements. More in-depth papers describing the LULESH algorithm can be found in previous work by Karlin et al. [1,2].

One key observation is that a great deal of computation is performed each iteration for both centerings. Furthermore, several computations are 3-dimensional stencil calculations that require neighboring communication, which due to the dual-centered scheme, creates unique challenges for optimization. Additionally, there are producer/consumer relationships that span across cycles of time-stepping, making data synchronization a likely bottleneck. These unique characteristics present more opportunities for optimization unlike those in traditional *(AxPy)* matrix computation.

3.1   The LULESH Domain Specification

Following the CnC philosophy of separation of concerns, we map the LULESH algorithm as a high level graph, with computation steps and producer/consumer dependencies labeled. This *domain specification* of LULESH represents how a domain scientist might describe the algorithm, as seen in Fig. 2. Each node in the graph represents a vital computational required by the algorithm, and the edges clearly depict from which steps that data is being produced and consumed for. We list and give a brief description of each computational step.

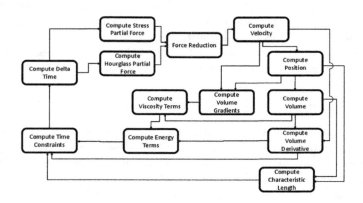

Fig. 2. High-level LULESH algorithm

- **Compute Delta Time:** Prior to every iteration, this checks all element data from the previous iteration to determine the next time step value. Has a separate tag space.
- **Compute Stress/Hourglass Partial Force**: Forces are calculated for each element using data from the previous iteration's elements.
- **Force Reduction**: Partial forces for every node are summed up from 8 neighboring elements.

- **Compute Velocity/Position**: Kinetic values are computed for each node using previous nodal forces/positions/velocities.
- **Compute Volume/Derivative/Gradient/Characteristic**: Physical properties are computed for each element using kinetic values.
- **Compute Viscosity Terms**: Previous values and gradient data from 6 element neighbors is used to calculate element viscosity terms.
- **Compute Energy Terms/Time Constraints**: Thermodynamics/Physics terms are calculated for each element using previous element data.

Using the *domain specification*, a direct translation is made to the *CnC specification*, which is a textual representation describing the step, tag, and data collections. The *CnC specification* defines and declares most of the high level information inside the CnC *context* required in the program. Whereas step computation and data are the norm in traditional programming, tags are conceptually different. In the context, tags are declared along with which steps they prescribe. The number of prescribed steps and unique tag identifiers are not required for declaration; this occurs during runtime. In the following sections, we discuss our approach for optimizing this minimally constrained LULESH implementation.

Our baseline uses a CnC specification identical to that in Fig. 2. Three sets of tags are used: per iteration, per node centering, and per element centering. Every step computation performs its required computation according to the hydrodynamics method, but the concerns for task granularity are neglected. In the following sections, we describe the coarsening techniques for each collection and its performance impact, with the task coarsening based on previous work [10]. However, that work was incomplete due to the lack of cohesive tiling with the data item collection members, which we include.

3.2   Step Fusion

Step fusion is an effective way to serialize multiple steps in a CnC program without altering the underlying computation. The decomposed LULESH algorithm has steps that operate on node and element centerings. Steps that share the same tag and operate on the same data can be legally fused, creating a new legal algorithm, as seen in Fig. 3. However, this fusion is only legal when dependencies from previous steps are guaranteed to be ready under serial execution, or if the resulting fused step would require interleaving with another step (or itself) and become a coroutine. Therefore, computation requiring updated neighbor data such as ghost exchanges cannot be fused because the data will likely come from a step prescribed from a separate tag. When steps are fused, data dependencies that exist between original steps are serialized in the fused step. The set of producer/consumer data dependencies from each step are joined and become the new set of producer/consumer dependencies for the fused step.

Step fusion is applied to the CnC-LULESH program to reduce the number of step collection items from 13 down to 5. Figure 3 highlights the step computations that get fused in the updated algorithm. The leftmost node, *Compute Delta*

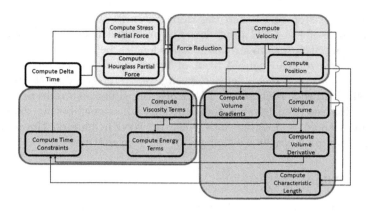

Fig. 3. Fused LULESH algorithm (Color figure online)

Time requires its own space of tags per iteration due to the delta time calculation, but the other steps are either in the nodal iteration space (red) or element iteration space (blue/green), and can be properly fused. We fuse the force computations (green) which require element-wise computations for all elements, as well as the spatial/kinetic steps which operate on nodes (red). Fusing the force computation reduces parallelism, but it is helpful in our case where abundant parallelism exists. Also, the bottom 6 element computations (blue) can only be fused into 2 routines, due to ghost exchanges at the viscosity step, requiring data dependencies computed from the prior gradient step from multiple neighboring elements, thus preventing legal fusion.

3.3 Tag Tiling

Tag tiling is an optimization used to reduce number of step prescriptions during execution. While a naive implementation would prescribe every step in the domain specification for each node and element, such a brute-force distribution would not scale to larger problem sizes. Tag tiling replaces multiple dynamic step instances by coalescing those tags into fewer larger step computations that span multiple tags. Similarly to step fusion, tag tiling serializes the computation in the new step. The new tiled computation will likely require large temporary working sets, as well as code modifications to reorder computation and optimize for potential locality.

In the LULESH code, we successfully tile all steps corresponding to the nodal and element-wise tags. Each tile contains a 3-dimensional spatial region that consists of the nodes or elements. Other tile shapes were considered, but we use hexahedral blocks to minimize the number of ghost regions when performing stencil updates. Implementing tag tiling involved minor changes to the steps themselves, as loops were introduced to handle additional work, step prescriptions were reduced, and indices remapped for correctness.

The effects of step fusion and tag tiling extend beyond just coarsening the task parallelism of the CnC program. The modified collections result in different behavior. Step fusion serializes dependencies between steps, eliminating synchronization overhead caused from obligatory *put* and *get* calls. For steps with common consumer dependencies, fusing those steps reduces the total memory bandwidth during runtime. In LULESH, tag tiling also reduces total data communication required by step computations when neighboring data is local to a tile, and there is possible data reuse between neighbors. However, these optimizations require moderate changes to the step routines.

3.4 Data Tiling

Following task coarsening through tag tiling and step fusion, we can perform data tiling optimizations to coarsen data in the item collection. Although the total number of algorithmic steps is reduced along with the number of tags prescribing those steps, the data elements are singleton values dynamically assigned by the CnC runtime, requiring a multitude of *gets* for each element or node dependency in the tiled step. Although straightforward, revamping the data layout of a program is a time consuming task, and potentially prohibitive depending on the specific application. For LULESH, we modify kernel routines and place calls inside CnC steps which provide flexible parameters and future modifications.

Modifications to core computations aim to take advantage of data locality and reduce communication using larger block sizes. We create tiled objects and use pointers to reduce unnecessary data movement. However, the data is treated as immutable, using *get/put* clauses to ensure proper synchronization and execution. During the node-to-element force computation, we overlap node tiles at element interfaces, propagating communications across tiles in a wave front manner, removing the need for two-way communication to update both tiles. Spatial stencil computation is also optimized and packed to match tile-size, requiring additional code changes. Despite underlying code changes, performance benefits from data tiling cannot be overlooked, especially in LULESH where numerous data items are used at every node/element and sometimes persist for multiple iterations.

We note that without first performing tag tiling, and ideally step fusion, data-tiling is not a viable optimization. Without coarsened tasks, blocked data is not useful under the strict dynamic-single-assignment properties of CnC item collections. In our experiments, we compare this final full-tiled implementation of LULESH to our other progressions as well as OpenMP implementations distributed by LLNL.

4 Results

In this section, we evaluate the performance of our multiple configurations of the CnC LULESH application for a problem size of 60^3. These include the domain expert baseline, a fused-only, a tiled-only, a fused & tiled, and a fully-tiled implementation. Additionally, we benchmark the LLNL LULESH 2.0.3 implementation with OpenMP directives as a comparison representing a more traditional parallel programming model. We measure their execution times running on our shared-memory system running on up to 48 processors. The following implementations are tested:

Baseline - Our baseline expresses the LULESH application at its most decomposed level, with minimal dependence constraints. There are 13 steps, 35 data items, and 3 tags which prescribe steps for every iteration, node, and element in the mesh, requiring dynamic step instances for each, but allow any order of scheduling. The item collections also correspond to individual nodes and elements in the mesh. It follows CnCs principles of expressing a program as partially ordered computations and its dependencies, but excessive fine-grained parallelism plagues performance.

Fused Only - Using step fusion, we reduce the step collection size from 13 to 5. This minimizes the number of prescribed dynamic steps as well as several consumer/producer data dependencies, reducing the item collection size by 5. However, communication and scheduling overheads prevent scaling.

Tiled Only - Tiling coarsens the tag space by prescribing blocks of work corresponding to a 3-dimensional spatial block instead of individual element, improving scalability and performance by reducing scheduling overhead and improving data locality. A tilesize of 10–15 is typically used for a problem size of 60 when running on 48 processors. The CnC specification is identical to the baseline.

Tiled and Fused - Both step fusion and tag tiling are applied at a high level. In step routines, we attempt to exploit locality for data that is shared between common neighbors, as well as reuse common data inputs from fused steps. These transformations require some coding changes and extra bookkeeping for extra variables and computation re-ordering to preserve step-like properties required by every CnC step. The corresponding CnC specification contains 5 steps, 27 data items, and 3 tags which prescribe steps for every tiled block. However, the data items still pertain to individual elements and nodes.

Data Tiled - The data tiled code incorporates the optimizations from step fusion and tag tiling, as well as tailoring each task with its working data set. A single *get* and *put* reads or writes a block of variables for each tiled computation step, albeit most steps still require multiple *gets* due to needing multiple data sets from different sources. The underlying computations are rewritten to accommodate the updated data structures. There are still 5 steps, 27 data items, and 3 tags, but data items are of a *tiled* construct.

4.1   Evaluation

Experiments were run on mesh sizes up to size 60^3 for 30 iterations, ten times per configuration, with minimum and maximum results excluded to reduce variance. The hardware is a shared memory, AMD Opteron 6176 SE system configured with four 12-core processors (48 cores total) per socket, each processor running at 2.3 GHz, with 512 KB per-core level 2 cache, and 12 MB level 3 cache. Table 1 shows the timing results per-iteration for a mesh of dimension 60^3 for each configuration.

Table 1. LULESH iteration runtimes (sec): 60^3 sized mesh

	Number of cores						
	1	2	4	8	16	32	48
Baseline	148.40	141.68	135.18	154.89	160.27	154.70	158.47
Fused only	101.36	95.281	72.273	58.508	60.269	59.995	64.056
Tiled only	19.147	18.919	10.539	5.7492	3.4986	2.4606	2.2643
Tiled and fused	11.767	11.725	6.5347	3.9041	2.3639	1.6201	1.3920
Data tiled	0.2268	0.2339	0.1242	0.0644	0.0360	0.0255	0.0277
OpenMp	0.6882	0.3784	0.2167	0.1219	0.0852	0.0814	0.0833

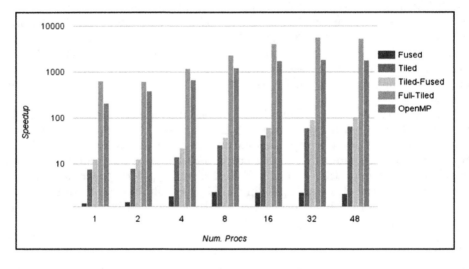

Fig. 4. Performance speedup

Figure 4 shows the performance speedups against the sequential baseline for our 4 benchmarks of LULESH in CnC and the provided OpenMP code from LLNL. For our CnC baseline, 60^3 dynamic step instances are created for each minimally-constrained step, performing and scaling extremely poorly. Applying step fusion reduces the number of steps by more than half, and results in a 1.6–2.5× speedup, with some improvement in parallel execution. Fusion by itself does not impact when compared to tiling, which coarsens the computation to a much greater extent. Looking at the tiled only implementation, we see speedups of 60× compared to sequential baseline when running on 48 threads.

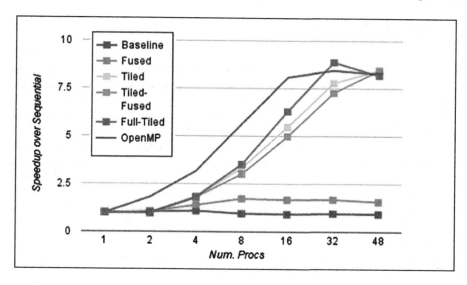

Fig. 5. Scalability results

This improvement is a result of coarser grained steps, reducing the synchronization required by the scheduler to instantiate the schedule so many step instances. In our next code iteration, we combine both step fusion and tag tiling technique, yielding greater performance, but it still does not surpass the performance from OpenMP. Finally, our fully tiled LULESH code with step and data tiling gives an additional order of magnitude of performance improvement over purely task coarsening implementations (note logarithmic axis). Tiling the data collections to correspond to the step collections When compared to similar processor configurations in OpenMP, our CnC code outperforms it by 3× for 32 and 48 processor. We reason that the OpenMP implementation has a number of inefficiencies, such as requiring barriers before each ghost exchange, as well as extra data movement to temporary buffers when updating data for reduction operators using multiple threads. Because CnC utilizes an asynchronous task-parallel model, it is more efficient than synchronous models such as OpenMP. However, both programs perform the exact same computation—the difference being the scheduling of work and movement of data.

In Fig. 5 we observe almost no scaling from the non-tiled implementations, whereas the tiled codes exhibit weak scaling, starting at 4 processors. However, CnC dedicates one processor exclusively for scheduling purposes, whereas OpenMP does not since parallelism must be explicitly expressed by the programmer. As a result, OpenMP offers an advantage when a few processors are used, but our fully-tiled code scales more strongly. Scaling beyond 32 processors should be possible, but we reason our machine configuration skews results at 48 cores. In the next section, we discuss the lessons learned and recommend an approach for achieving high performance while maintaining programmability.

5   Lessons Learned

In our study, we focus on the LULESH application, starting from the domain expert's minimally constrained algorithm, and applied high level fusion and tiling transformations on the program by altering the step, data, and tag collections while preserving program semantics. However, the applicability of these coarsening techniques are not limited to LULESH. Multiple factors contribute to performance improvement over the baseline LULESH code. From the perspective of code modifications, step fusion requires the fewest modifications, while data tiling requires an overhaul of underlying data structures and computation code. Both step fusion and tag tiling give substantial speedup, with tag tiling provides the most benefit, but it was a prerequisite for implementing data tiling in our application. Once the cohesive tiling implementation was produced, the performance of LULESH using CnC begins to shine and greatly outperforms the OpenMP implementation.

In hindsight, the most efficient method would have been to decompose the algorithm, compose the computation steps for generalized tiled data, and then map those computations to a high level *domain specification* that can be mapped to a valid *CnC specification*. Such a process would generate similar results to our final implementation while providing flexibility to apply step fusion and tag tiling for various tile sizes. We recommend using the *CnC translator* to generate source code containing the *CnC context* and additional scaffolding step code from the high level specification. This translator was recently developed by the CnC Habenero research group to assist their work on declarative tuning [6]. However, it is not a tuning mechanism, but an automation tool provided for programming portability. Following their syntax to describe the *CnC specification*, which include all tags collections, item collections, steps, and their dependencies, source files will be generated that for the context as well as skeleton code for each step with predetermined *get* and *put* constructs. The programmer's primary responsibility is to initialize their problem, set up their work routines, and insert the proper computation for each step. In our final tiled LULESH implementation, the CnC code and work routines were decoupled in such a way. Using this translator along with modular kernel routines, while keeping granularity in mind, should improve productivity while preserving performance for future CnC applications.

6   Related Work

Parallelizing applications requires programmers to be keenly aware of a range of system level as well as algorithmic details in order to achieve performance speedup. Managing this level of detail remains a difficult task, even for the most experienced programmers. In addition, determining the best trade-off between programming portability and performance is an active research area. Concurrent Collections is just one approach that uses a model that takes advantage of asynchrony and task-based parallelism to efficiently program parallel applications.

Task Parallel Models. Researchers have begun to shift toward task-parallel and asynchronous many-task models to provide performance portability for high performance scientific applications. In recent years, programming models such as CnC, Charm++, Legion, OpenMP 4.0 have began a trend toward programmability with task-parallel support, but none have matured into a one-size-fits all solution [3, 11, 12]. Legion avoids employing data-drive execution and instead focuses on controlling execution via mapping interfaces, opposite to the CnC approach. Charm++ offers similar constructs to CnC, but uses a message passing interface for driving execution and offers fewer high level abstractions. OpenMP has long been a recognized for its superior ease of parallel programmability, but has only recently supported task-based parallelism. In our work, we show our CnC tuned version of LULESH greatly outperforms older models such as OpenMP, but we surmise performance would at least rival those of newer task-based models.

Tiling. Although tiling is a well-known technique, there are few practical ways to obtain automatically tiled code. Researchers have long tried to obtain coarse grained task parallelism since the early versions of OpenMP [13]. Other approaches have employed polyhedral frameworks such as PLuTo to generate tile loop iterations for matrix based computations, as seen in Kong et al. [14, 15]. However, their approach creates coarsened computation for affine loops contained matrix computations, unlike LULESH, which requires irregular control flow using data dependencies from various computation methods. Another similar work that has connections to both CnC and polyhedral compilation frameworks is Data Flow Graph Representation (DFGR), an intermediate graph representation for macro-dataflow programs [16]. In their work, Sbirlea et al. utilizes the CnC specification to produce tiled code, but those tiles leverage OpenMP directives to achieve parallelism.

7 Conclusion

In this paper, we discuss and evaluate the performance impact of coarsening the step, tag, and data collections of the LULESH written in CnC. Although Concurrent Collections offers intuitive parallel programming constructs, achieving good performance requires program tuning that does not directly follow the separation of concerns philosophy. In our work, we demonstrate the effects of task and step coarsening to improve the performance and scalability of the LULESH application. We begin with a decomposed LULESH algorithm consisting of minimally constrained computational steps. Step fusion and tag tiling optimizations improve performance by coarsening the task-granularity of the program, and creates the opportunity to additionally tile the data collection to reduce data synchronization overheads. This fully tiled CnC LULESH code outperforms OpenMP parallel implementations by 3× for up to 48 processors and exhibits scalable performance. In our discussion, we present the CnC translator as a means of generating CnC code to handle control flow and data synchronization between steps. In the future, we hope to extend the functionality of the translator tool as well as provide better abstractions for handling task and data coarsening in CnC.

CnC goes beyond just scientific applications. The CnC philosophy to approach algorithms using collections is aimed to abstract layers of complexity of hardware mapping and work scheduling at the thread level. Dedicated tuners exist for that purpose of optimizing platform-specific hardware, but our contribution is to identify the ideal CnC code to run on those machines. Naive programmers will be quick to discredit the merits of CnC when they believe the ease of programmability comes at the price of poor performance when their application is minimally constrained. Instead, using the available CnC translator and an approach that takes task granularity in mind, one can achieve both programmability and performance in CnC.

Acknowledgments. This research is supported by the Department of Energy under contract DE-FC02-12ER26104. We would also like to thank Ellen Porter, Kath Knobe, Nick Vrvilo, and Zoran Budimlic for their comments and feedback during discussions regarding CnC.

References

1. Karlin, I., Bhatele, A., Chamberlain, B.L., Cohen, J., Devito, Z., Gokhale, M., Haque, R., Hornung, R., Keasler, J., Laney, D., et al.: Lulesh programming model and performance ports overview. Technical report, Lawrence Livermore National Laboratory (LLNL), Livermore, CA (2012)
2. Karlin, I., Keasler, J., Neely, R.: Lulesh 2.0 updates and changes. Livermore, CA, August 2013
3. OpenMP C and C++ Application Program Interface (2002)
4. Budimlić, Z., Burke, M., Cavé, V., Knobe, K., Lowney, G., Newton, R., Palsberg, J., Peixotto, D., Sarkar, V., Schlimbach, F., et al.: Concurrent collections. Sci. Program. **18**(3–4), 203–217 (2010)
5. Burke, M.G., Knobe, K., Newton, R., Sarkar, V.: Concurrent collections programming model. In: Padua, D. (ed.) Encyclopedia of Parallel Computing, pp. 364–371. Springer, Heidelberg (2011). doi:10.1007/978-0-387-09766-4_238
6. Chatterjee, S., Vrvilo, N., Budimlić, Z., Knobe, K., Sarkar, V.: Declarative tuning for locality in parallel programs. In: Proceedings of the 45th International Conference on Parallel Processing, ICPP 2016, August 2016, to appear
7. Sbîrlea, A., Zou, Y., Budimlíc, Z., Cong, J., Sarkar, V.: Mapping a data-flow programming model onto heterogeneous platforms. In: ACM SIGPLAN Notices, vol. 47, pp. 61–70. ACM (2012)
8. Habanero-Rice: Concurrent collections on OCR (2015)
9. Frank Schlimbach, I.C.: Intel concurrent collections for C++ for Windows and Linux (2015)
10. Liu, C., Kulkarni, M.: Optimizing the LULESH stencil code using concurrent collections. In: Proceedings of the 5th International Workshop on Domain-Specific Languages and High-Level Frameworks for High Performance Computing, p. 5. ACM (2015)

11. Bauer, M., Treichler, S., Slaughter, E., Aiken, A.: Legion: expressing locality and independence with logical regions. In: Proceedings of the International Conference on High Performance Computing, Networking, Storage and Analysis, p. 66. IEEE Computer Society Press (2012)

12. Kale, L.V., Krishnan, S.: CHARM++: a portable concurrent object oriented system based on C++, vol. 28. ACM (1993)

13. Kasahara, H., Obata, M., Ishizaka, K.: Automatic coarse grain task parallel processing on SMP using OpenMP. In: Midkiff, S.P., Moreira, J.E., Gupta, M., Chatterjee, S., Ferrante, J., Prins, J., Pugh, W., Tseng, C.-W. (eds.) LCPC 2000. LNCS, vol. 2017, pp. 189–207. Springer, Heidelberg (2001). doi:10.1007/3-540-45574-4_13

14. Bondhugula, U., Hartono, A., Ramanujam, J., Sadayappan, P.: Pluto: a practical and fully automatic polyhedral program optimization system. In: Proceedings of the ACM SIGPLAN 2008 Conference on Programming Language Design and Implementation (PLDI 2008), Tucson, AZ. Citeseer, June 2008

15. Kong, M., Pop, A., Pouchet, L.N., Govindarajan, R., Cohen, A., Sadayappan, P.: Compiler/runtime framework for dynamic dataflow parallelization of tiled programs. ACM Trans. Archit. Code Optim. 11(4), 61:1–61:30 (2015)

16. Sbirlea, A., Pouchet, L.N., Sarkar, V.: DFGR an intermediate graph representation for macro-dataflow programs. In: 2014 Fourth Workshop on Data-Flow Execution Models for Extreme Scale Computing (DFM), pp. 38–45. IEEE (2014)

Author Index

Printed in the United States
By Bookmasters